Human Resources at the Cabinet's Table

A Guidebook for HR Transformation In Higher Education

Beth Heuer
Timothy Danielson
Donna Robole

UNIFIED FOCUS • TRUST

LEADERSHIP •

STRATEGY

PARTNERSHIP

CULTURE

Human Resources at the Cabinet's Table

"Institutions of higher education are complex organizations that have historically been slow to change. However, external challenges—reduced resources, changing student and workforce demographics, increased demand for accountability, greater competition—contribute to the need for colleges and universities to undertake significant changes and reforms. Addressing these complex challenges effectively calls for the engagement of all faculty and staff. The HR function is uniquely positioned to engage with faculty and staff in multiple arenas as a partner and relationship builder.

Human Resources at the Cabinet's Table provides a compelling blueprint for refocusing HR from a primarily administrative to a strategic function. Today, we need HR leaders who can engage and energize the academic community, resulting in a strategic move from "vision" to "action." Aligning HR strategy and initiatives to those of the institution, and being a strategic partner are behaviors leaders expect of their leadership teams every day. HR can and must contribute to institutional performance. This book is valuable for HR leaders and chancellors/presidents who want their HR function to contribute strategically to the vision and mission of the institution."

-Dean Van Galen, Chancellor
University of Wisconsin River Falls

"*Human Resources at the Cabinet's Table* is an essential guide for any HR professional or leader wanting to raise the bar and develop a transformative service model for HR in a higher education environment. For that matter, it is an essential read for CEOs, CFOs or other administrative leaders in higher education searching for ways to more effectively utilize HR to recruit, retain, develop and promote top talent in today's complex, competitive higher education market. There is nothing glib about this volume. It carefully and expertly walks readers through every phase necessary for developing an HR department to become the transformative, strategic partner the organization deserves, from preparing HR staff for new expectations to fully equipping them to confidently sit at the cabinet's table."

-Daniel B. Griffith, J.D., SPHR, Manager of Training and Organization Development
Human Resources Administration, IUPUI, Indianapolis

"*Human Resources at the Cabinet's Table* is long overdue. This excellent compilation of thoughts and strategies for leading transformative change in the Human Resources practice within higher education is sure to become the cornerstone reference for Higher Ed HR leaders across the country. This is the perfect mix of theoretical discussion and practical thought-provoking strategies that we can all use to better serve our colleges, universities, and most importantly our students. As we all know, the best and most effective way to impact our institutions is to positively affect our people. HR can be key to working closely with presidents, provosts, vice presidents, faculty and staff to further the success of our institutions. This book provides the road map and tools for HR to be significant contributors to our institutions' success over the long-term. I look forward to referencing this material for years to come."

-David Trainor, Associate Vice President, Human Resources Services
Iowa State University, Iowa

"Very engaging! *Human Resources at the Cabinet's Table* does a wonderful job capturing relevant topics surrounding the human resources function and providing practical guidance on how to move the conversations surrounding these functions to the strategic level of the organization. The applications used in the book are on-target and relatable for every human resources professional in higher education. In our opinion, this book is a must-read for every higher education HR practitioner!"

-The Office of Human Resources Staff, Leslie Fern, Employee Relations Specialist
Bowling Green State University, Ohio

"*Human Resources at the Cabinet's Table* is a poignant, concise, and thorough analysis of human resources in higher education. The authors' use of case studies taken from university life assists readers in developing plans to transform the human resources function from a transactional service area to that of a true partner. The book is a must-read for human resources professionals aspiring to lead their teams by getting involved and providing input into cabinet level decisions. It is also a must-read for existing top executives contemplating the inclusion of human resources input into decisions affecting the operations of their institution."

-Craig Ahrndt, Assistant to the Vice President for Human Resources
Oakton Community College, Illinois

Human Resources at the Cabinet's Table takes the HR transformation process where it needs to go with logical, step-by-step instructions. The clear, intuitive directions for implementing change first within human resources will help departments recognize not only why change fails but give them practical advice for initiating change and succeeding."

-Deborah E. Fillmore, PHR, Employee Relations Manager
Tulsa Community College, Oklahoma

For all human resources professionals in higher education,
who work diligently within a culture that may or may not be ready for change.
May this book provide a distinctive path toward a successful HR function paradigm shift,
creating strategic outcomes for your institution.

Contents

Unit One

A Vision: the Human Resources Function at the Strategic Level

Unit Two

Build the Foundation

Unit Three

Become Catalysts for Change

Unit Four
Set the Stage

Unit Five
Become a Strategic Partner

Acknowledgments

We thank the following HR professionals within higher education for their assistance in reviewing the manuscript and their invaluable recommendations for improvement.

Nancy Aebersold, Executive Director, National Higher Education Recruitment Consortium, www.nationalherc.org

Craig Ahrndt, Assistant to the Vice President for Human Resources, Oakton Community College, Illinois

Rob Aspy, EEO Specialist, Indiana University, Bloomington

Linda Berauer, Director, Michigan Higher Education Recruitment Consortium, www.michiganherc.org

Phyllis Brust, Director, Greater Chicago Midwest Higher Education Recruitment Consortium, www.gcmherc.org

Theresa Feldmeier, Director of Human Resources, Capital University, Columbus.

Leslie Fern, Employee Relations/Employment Specialist, Bowling Green State University, Ohio

Jan Graunke, Director of Human Resources, Silver Lake College, Manitowoc, Wisconsin

Daniel Griffith, Manager Training and Organizational Development, IUPUI HR Administration, Indianapolis, Indiana

Joseph Harbouk, Vice Chancellor for Administration and Finance, University of Wisconsin River Falls

E. Alan Hartman, Professor of Management and Human Resources, Former Dean College of Business and Interim Provost, University of Wisconsin Oshkosh

Barbara Rau, Professor of Human Resources, University of Wisconsin Oshkosh

Karl Sparks, Former Director of Human Resources, University of Wisconsin Milwaukee

We thank **Susan Hegedus** for her timeless effort in editing the book, which has contributed toward its improved organization and readability.

We thank **Lynn Stuart**, whose design "magic" resulted in an improved professional work. Her design and graphics directly enhance the reader's understanding and provide a clear focal point for discussions.

Any error within the book is the responsibility of the publisher.

The Authors

Beth Heuer is the Emeritus Director of HR at the University of Wisconsin Oshkosh. She received a Bachelor of Business Administration and Master of Business Administration, both from the University of Wisconsin Oshkosh. Heuer has been instrumental in moving three departments to the strategic level of the institution within higher education. Her publications include textbooks for two academic courses developed and initially taught by her—Career Exploration and Student Development Series—and resource books for several mentoring programs. Her current interests include organizational change within higher education, and personal development and change. Heuer received the University of Wisconsin Oshkosh Outstanding Service Award and the University of Wisconsin System Regents Excellence Award. She serves as a HR consultant within higher education, a facilitator of change, and author.

Timothy Danielson is the Director of HR at the University of Wisconsin Oshkosh. He received a Bachelor of Science and Master of Public Administration, both from the University of Wisconsin Oshkosh. Danielson's experience includes managing large-scale change efforts, building strong teams, organizational development and consulting. He received the UW Oshkosh Outstanding Service Award in 2005.

Donna Robole is the Director of HR at the University of Wisconsin River Falls. She received a Bachelor of Science in Business Administration from the University of Wisconsin Platteville, a Master of Business Administration from the University of Wisconsin River Falls, and a certification as a Senior Professional in Human Resources Management (SPHR). Robole has more than 20 years of HR experience within higher education and state government. She is a member of the National Higher Education Recruitment Consortium Board, the Upper Midwest Higher Education Recruitment Consortium Board and the Society for Human Resources Management..

The authors appreciate hearing from readers and welcome comments,
questions, suggestions or accounts of experiences that bear on the ideas in the book.
Readers can contact the authors at the following website: www.HR-higher-ed.com

Foreword

Richard H. Wells, Chancellor
University of Wisconsin Oshkosh

"Our higher educational institutions and leaders have been slow in responding strategically to external challenges, especially those that have altered the fundamental financial structures within which we operate. We spend enormous amounts of time "budgeting" in the short-term and little or no time on developing long-term strategies that provide for improved and sustainable strategic financial planning models. We have become obsessed with our plans to prioritize how we spend our ever-shrinking funding base.

Similarly, we address our most central and crucial resource—the time and talent of our faculty and staff—in a short-term perspective. Relatively speaking, we give only lip service to strategic human resources planning, instead of making meaningful progress in helping the HR function contribute to the performance of the institution. What is the result? Strategic organization and development of our human talent and time are either absent or misaligned with other key operational plans. The higher educational institution's values, mission, vision and strategic goals are just words to most faculty and staff. A mostly transactional HR function discounts the value of human talent to accomplish strategic outcomes.

More than any other function within the institution, human resources engages with each faculty and staff in unique ways. Moving HR to a primarily transformational function is necessary if we are to focus strategically on performance, outcomes and competitive advantage. Having the HR function at the executive table as a leader of change and a partner with the cabinet and other stakeholders supports our strategic vision and provides a competitive advantage for our institution. As leaders, we need a strategic HR function that is integrated, aligned, innovative, and business-focused.

Packed with effective frameworks, tools, and approaches of immense practical value, *Human Resources at the Cabinet's Table* delineates the map to transform the HR function from primarily transactional to transformational and strategic. Using real-life case studies and an ongoing theme of leadership of change, the book methodically outlines successful transition and change, along with the forces that drive it.

With a transformative HR at the strategic level of the university, faculty and staff are engaged strategically with the institution, HR staff members possess the necessary skills and competencies to contribute strategically, and a HR strategic plan aligns with the strategic goals of the institution. The work of the HR function contributes towards the strategic success, performance, and distinctiveness of the institution.

This book, rich in valuable insight, challenges the boundaries of HR in higher education in bringing this timely topic to the academic agenda. *Human Resources at the Cabinet's Table* demonstrates the need for and outcomes of HR's leadership in providing critical linkages to institutional effectiveness while enhancing deliverables to its key internal stakeholders."

–Richard H. Wells, Chancellor
University of Wisconsin Oshkosh
Oshkosh, Wisconsin
2012

Preface

Where This Book Comes From

We wrote this book to serve as a guide to refocus and expand the HR function within higher education in two significant ways. First, it is targeted to address the needs of those in the HR function within the higher education community. We provide a detailed organizational development process to accomplish an HR paradigm shift. We acknowledge that many references and guides exist for the HR community in the private sector, yet few of these resources are designed for those conducting an HR paradigm shift in the university setting.

Second, we believe that many of us in the university setting lag behind our private sector counterparts in the overall transition to strategic HR. Simply put, we have continued to spend more time on HR transactions than on HR transformation. We convey the value and urgency of bringing HR to the executive table, showing how our actions, policies, and reinforcements can align with and support the overall strategic purpose and vision of our college or university. The result is an HR function contributing a "distinctive advantage" for the institution.

We know personally that change often occurs slowly in higher education. Therefore, the first unit provides a context for understanding the current crisis facing higher education, why the HR function must be at the strategic level of the university, what it looks like for the HR function to be transformational and the process for HR paradigm change. We want to inspire and motivate change. These statements generate multiple questions addressed in **Unit One**:

1. What are the current challenges within higher education?
2. How can a strategic HR function partner with the cabinet to address these challenges successfully?
3. What does a strategic HR function look like?
4. What is an HR paradigm shift?
5. How will the HR paradigm shift occur?

Unit Two summarizes the process for preparing the HR department for change. It is critical that all HR staff members understand the new HR paradigm, are ready for organizational change and are motivated to be part of it. The work in this unit contains a step-by-step process and materials for developing HR staff into a cohesive team, motivated to work in transformational ways.

Unit Three provides the framework for the HR staff to become catalysts for change, first by reengineering the HR department internal functions. HR staff will participate in developing more efficient internal processes, which continue to expand their skills, provide increased stakeholder value, and free up time for them to become involved in further change initiatives.

Unit Four delineates the structure for creating more efficient and effective external HR processes for improved stakeholder service and relationship-building.

Unit Five concludes with the development and implementation process for the HR strategic plan.

Throughout the book, we thread three themes: leadership of change, appreciative inquiry, and reframing to resolve issues. These tools contribute toward a deeper and broader perspective through each stage of the transformation process, challenge your thinking, and provide for effective decision-making.

Who Should Read This Book

We target three groups within the institution who, because of their distinct roles in the HR paradigm shift, must read this book. First is that of the **HR leadership**, to include the HR director, the director's supervisor, the assistant/associate provost, and others within the HR function with managerial or supervisory responsibilities. Their roles include the following: leading change, knowing the institution's political, symbolic, structural and human resource environments, developing a vision of the HR paradigm shift, communicating with stakeholders throughout the institution, supporting the HR paradigm shift, and engaging stakeholders in the HR paradigm shift.

The second group contains all **HR staff**, to include HR managers, assistants, program managers, data administrators, receptionists, benefit specialists and payroll specialists. Their roles in the HR paradigm shift include the following: operationally accomplishing the HR paradigm shift, recognizing their engagement is key to an effective change process, understanding the reasons for and methods to accomplish an HR paradigm shift, and gaining new skills to work differently.

The members of the **cabinet** comprise the third group, to include the president or chancellor. Their roles in the HR paradigm shift include the following: supporting the HR paradigm shift, communicating support of the organizational change to stakeholders, engaging the HR function in strategic and visionary work, and understanding how a transformative HR function at the strategic level of the institution can contribute toward distinctiveness.

How To Use This Book

This book provides an extensive menu of ideas, techniques, and examples relevant to an HR paradigm shift within the higher education setting. Depending on your potential role in the transformation as outlined above, you can choose what is right for you. If you are a member of the **HR leadership** group, we recommend you read and know the book from cover to cover. A first review can quickly determine chapters to concentrate on that are relevant to your position. If you serve as the leader of the change initiative, all the chapters are relevant. If you are an **HR staff** member, read and study the book from cover to cover. If you are a member of the **cabinet**, review the book in light of your roles, concentrating on strategic and visionary chapters.

This book is like a mosaic: each chapter has a unique significance, and together the chapters contribute something new to the overall picture. We advise beginning your review with chapter 1, and then applying the practices and principles in each chapter in the order provided. Even if you believe some processes and outcomes are already part of your HR structure and culture, it is extremely important that you do not either "skip" any part of the process, or implement it only superficially. Doing so will generate issues in the long-term and impact the strength of the HR transformation.

Case studies are provided to explain processes and tools, provide in-depth study of the chapters, and challenge you to utilize the models. We recommend that the HR professional leading the paradigm shift and the HR staff collectively work through each of the chapter case studies to "polish" skills and improve understanding of a particular topic.

Beginning with chapter 4, a chart of key indicators follows each chapter summary. This chart lists the projected outcome, the change needed, key indicators that signify accomplishment of the change, and potential barriers to the change. Utilize this chart as a checklist to ascertain that the needed outcomes have been accomplished, and to learn of potential barriers to change to address. Key indicators of success can serve as material for success stories, a communication plan, or to develop metrics for measuring success.

A website accompanies this book at www.HR-higher-ed.com. This website contains templates for forms, samples, assessments, and other materials discussed in the book. You are encouraged to utilize the templates as-is or to revise them to suit your purposes. You also will find recommended answers to case study discussion questions. As a method to communicate with your peers also working to transform their HR function, the website contains a blog. Please utilize it to ask questions, share information, converse with your peers, and provide suggestions to us for the next edition of the book. We wish you good fortune on your journey!

Beth Heuer
Tim Danielson
Donna Robole

Wisconsin
February 2012
www.HR-higher-ed.com

Unit One

A Vision: The Human Resources Function
at the Strategic Level

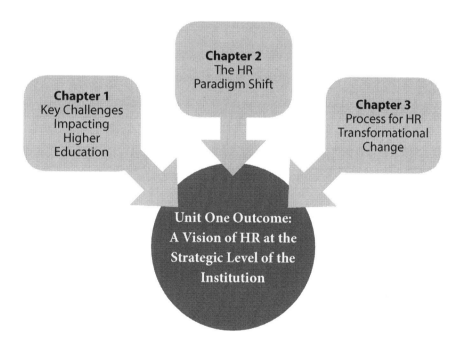

Chapter 2
The HR
Paradigm Shift

Chapter 1
Key Challenges
Impacting
Higher
Education

Chapter 3
Process for HR
Transformational
Change

Unit One Outcome:
A Vision of HR at the
Strategic Level of the
Institution

Unit One Model to describe the vision of the HR function at the strategic level of the institution

Within recent years, priority has been placed upon the strategic aspects of the human resources (HR) function, emphasizing how HR strategies, policies and procedures align to organizational strategy and objectives. The HR function in the private sector has led the way in this endeavor, while that in higher education has lagged behind, still focusing predominantly upon transactional and administrative HR tasks.

The current challenges in higher education create a pressing need for higher education HR departments to strategically align their policies, procedures, and other work efforts to their institution's vision and mission, thereby enhancing value for all stakeholders. HR work must be redefined to become integrated, aligned, innovative and business-focused. According to a College and University Professional Association for Human Resources 2009 Benchmarking and Workforce Planning Survey, only 14% of the 214 HR departments responding said that they currently were responsible for or involved in their institution's strategic planning. Conversely, 63% of the 214 respondents said that they were trying to increase their involvement in strategic planning (Survey: HR Departments Working to Expand Level of Responsibility in Key Areas, 2009).

Unit One's outcome is a vision of HR at the strategic level of the institution. It focuses on defining the HR paradigm shift, how it will benefit the institution, why it is needed now, and outlines the process to move to the new paradigm.

Key Challenges
Impacting Higher Education

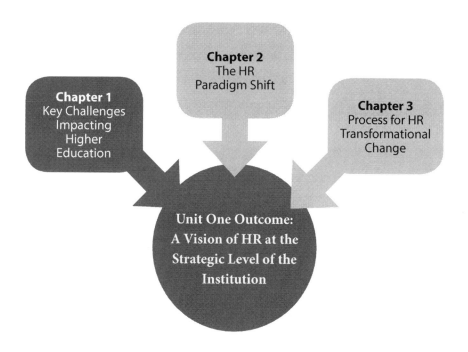

Chapter 1 Key challenges impacting higher education

What Are the Current Challenges within Higher Education?

Five major interrelated challenges in the higher education environment, identified in Figure 1.1, contribute toward the need for not only incremental, but also major structural changes and reforms.

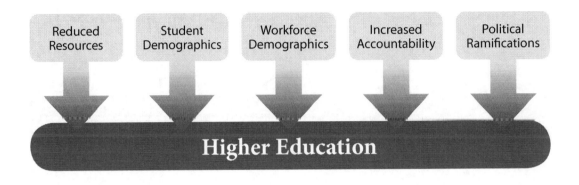

Figure 1.1 Major challenges impacting higher education

Reduced Resources

Survey of College and University Presidents

The economic and financial crisis, which began in 2008, has negatively impacted state and federal budgets, causing increased dependence on state or federal funding by higher educational institutions. With 956 of 2,900 invited campus chief executives responding, a report from the 2011 *Inside Higher Ed* survey of college and university presidents indicates that the two major challenges facing public institutions over the next few years are budget shortfalls (62%) and changes in state support (42.6%). For private non-profit colleges and universities, rising tuition/affordability (42.2%) and increased competition for students (35.3%) comprise the top challenges (Green, with Lederman and Jaschik, 2011). (Those invited to participate in the survey were chosen from two- and four-year colleges and universities that enroll 500 or more students, as found in the U.S. Department of Education 2007 IPEDS data files.)

The majority of the campus leaders responding indicated they addressed the budget crisis by cutting administrative costs, hiring more part-time faculty members, raising tuition and/or student fees, pruning selected academic programs, and providing more financial aid to offset their higher tuitions (Green, with Lederman and Jaschik, 2011).

On the other hand, the survey report reveals that a quarter of institutions have created new self-sustaining programs such as alliances with other colleges or corporate partners and niche-oriented degree and non-degree academic programs. Others have started or grown online education programs, invested in technology, expanded research capabilities, engaged in licensing and sponsorship agreements, and pursued auxiliary enterprises, e.g., managing real estate and running conference centers (Green, with Lederman and Jaschik, 2011).

Other Budget Reductions

Our observations in working within academic institutions indicate that other budget reductions due to the economic crisis include reduced resources for employees, to include travel time to conferences for professional development, to present and learn best practices, and to present faculty research. Salaries have been reduced. Many position openings are not being filled, causing faculty to teach more classes and class sizes to be increased. Many positions within the administrative and support staff are being combined or not filled on a permanent basis, causing more work to be given to current employees. Employees are pressured to do more with less.

Comments on the Results of the Survey of College and University Presidents

Many feel the current financial climate represents a permanent shift in higher education financing, for which new and innovative models must be developed. William Durden, president of Dickinson College, a private liberal arts college, notes in reviewing survey results that nearly half of private college presidents participating said they had allowed their institution's discount rate, the percentage that students receive off their total tuition price, to be used as one strategy to deal with the current economic environment. Other reviewers of survey results felt that many college leaders may be underestimating the extent to which the current economic climate represents a permanent shift in higher education financing, and that higher education leaders are failing to respond strategically (Lederman, 2011).

Says Nancy Zimpher, chancellor of the State University of New York System, of the survey results, "The issues of how we are going to really reinvent ourselves for what looks like a long haul of self-sufficiency just did not get reflected.... Most of the strategies going forward were largely negative, about cutting. There aren't growth ideas, change ideas, ideas reaching outside our boundaries" (Lederman 2011, p 2).

An independent college president, S. Georgia Nugent of Kenyon College, is troubled that the survey reveals how much public college presidents are inclined to adopt the "high tuition, high aid" business model that has gotten private colleges into difficult positions. Says Nugent, "So many of us in the private sector think our model is broken, that this decades-long reliance on high tuition/high aid is not working. Now (public institutions) are jumping off the cliff like we have" (Lederman, 2011, p 2).

According to Cary Nelson in the January-February 2011 issue of *Academe Online*, "The era of the state funding budget cycle for higher education has, for all practical purposes, come to an end. Public funding is being replaced by incremental cost shifting from states to students, with tuition revenue and student debt replacing tax dollars.... Only a complete restructuring of the financial model and a redefinition of the social purpose of public higher education will suffice" (Nelson, 2011, p 1).

It is clear that leadership in all sectors of higher education will face self-sufficiency challenges for some time, and that this challenge integrates with the other four challenges—student demographics, workforce demographics, increased accountability and political ramifications.

Student Demographics

Demographics

According to the Association of American Colleges and Universities Board of Directors' Statement, January 6, 2006, the demographics of college attendance are changing in the following ways (Academic Freedom and Educational Responsibility, 2006):

- a larger percentage of students lack recommended college preparatory curricula
- a higher proportion of high school graduates attend college
- a greater number of non-traditional students, as three out of four students are classified as "non-traditional"
- a greater cultural diversity with higher minority participation, as one-third of college students are of racial or ethnic diversity

Remediation

Responses to the report, *Presidential Perspectives: The 2011 Inside Higher Ed Survey of College and University Presidents*, indicate that 27% of two-year college leaders listed student remediation as one of the top two issues facing their institutions over the next three years (Green, with Lederman and Jaschik, 2011). This is critical because it is very unlikely that additional state money will be forthcoming. In response to the survey report, Glenn DuBois, chancellor of the Virginia Community College System, says, "half of the Virginia System's students are now entering needing developmental courses to prepare them for college-level work.... We are in a position where we have to rethink just about everything we do" (Lederman, 2011, p 2).

Enrollment Patterns

Increased part-time attendance indicates that one-half of all college students are part-time. In addition, 60% of students attend multiple institutions to receive their degree, with some taking courses at more than one institution simultaneously. The explosion in the offering of online courses and degrees has contributed toward this pattern (Eckel and King, 2004).

Tuition and Financial Aid

Despite the increase in the price of attending college, the American student population continues to grow rapidly in both size and diversity. Twenty percent of students are now from families with incomes at or below the federal poverty level. Because a primary source of additional revenue to colleges and universities is student fees and tuition, these have risen at twice the rate of inflation over the last 20 years, exceeding increases in both family income and financial aid resources. Consequently, 80% of students now work during the academic year (Eckel and King, 2004).

Competition for Students

An exponential growth of online courses and degrees increases the competition for students who are working either full- or part-time. Private universities expand beyond their initial geographical customer base. An increased growth in the number of for-profit universities leads to competition for public funds. Faculty members spend more time developing and learning to teach online courses. (Academic Freedom and Educational Responsibility, 2006) In addition, faculty must become involved in marketing to new students, retaining current students and maintaining relationships with alumni.

In many ways, universities feel they are working harder to stay in the same place.

Workforce Demographics

Current Demographics

Many employees in higher education have retired over the last five years, with more considering retirement in the next five to ten years. Higher education faculty definitely are aging, with full-time faculty averaging 50 years of age and about a third of them 55 years or older. Research indicates most faculty members retire around age 65, and that many faculty members are interested in a phased retirement in which they continue to work part-time over a period of several years. Currently, full-time faculty members are approximately 38% women and 14% racial/ethnic minorities (American Association of State Colleges and Universities, April 2006).

More than a third of presidents who responded to the *Inside Higher Ed* survey indicate there is a growing distance between faculty members and institution presidents. Many relate that they haven't seen faculty leaders as key partners in the current economic downturn. They also indicate they are interested in changing employment policies valued highly by faculty members: mandate faculty retirements, change tenure policies, increase teaching loads (Green, with Lederman and Jaschik, 2011).

New Faculty

Our observations from working within higher education indicate most new faculty members tend to spend more time on teaching in order to develop their distinctive and effective teaching styles. Research is a key component to faculty renewal and receiving tenure in seven years. New or non-tenured faculty members must spend a great deal of time to determine their research topics, publications to approach, and alternate types of research to consider.

In addition, new faculty must spend time learning the political structures of their department, college and university. With obtaining a Ph.D. and a new faculty position in academia, many faculty are beginning families. Therefore, work-life balance becomes more important to them at a time when it is difficult to achieve that balance.

Job Satisfaction

Tomorrow's faculty will be increasingly female, will be more diverse racially and ethnically, and will bring different expectations to their careers. This is especially important knowing the results from 9,512 respondents to a survey of over 16,000 untenured assistant professors at research universities conducted by the Collaborative on Academic Careers in Higher Education (COACHE). The report, *The Experience of Tenure-Track Faculty at Research Universities: Analysis of COACHE Survey Results by Academic Area and Gender*, which categorized data in 12 academic areas for 83 survey dimensions, reveals recurring themes relating to faculty job satisfaction.

In many disciplines, male faculty rated survey items significantly higher ($p<0.01$) than female faculty. The following are particularly noteworthy examples where male faculty in the Social Sciences rated survey items significantly higher than female faculty (The Collaborative on Academic Careers in Higher Education, 2010).

1. **Agreement that**: tenure decisions are based on performance; on the whole, the institution is collegial; the institution makes raising children and tenure-track compatible; there are consistent messages about tenure from tenured colleagues; and colleagues are respectful of faculty efforts to balance work/home responsibilities.
2. **Clarity of**: the tenure process and the tenure criteria.
3. **Satisfaction with**: the number of hours worked as a faculty member; influence over one's research focus; degree of influence over which courses are taught; fairness of immediate supervisor's evaluations; the department as a place to work; the amount of time to conduct research; the ability to balance one's professional and personal time; and the amount of access to teaching and research assistants.
4. **Reasonableness of**: expectations for performance as a teacher and as a scholar.

In general, male faculty are more satisfied with many dimensions of their work than female faculty. In addition to its faculty satisfaction survey, COACHE has studied the conditions that make working in higher education more appealing for young faculty, especially women and minorities. A recent study, based on qualitative data from 16 interviews with faculty and administrators (born 1964-1980, known as Generation X) at three COACHE institutions in the mid-Atlantic region, found that junior faculty tend to especially value the following aspects of the workplace (Helms, 2010):

- teaching that includes less formal interactions with students as well as use of technology
- interdisciplinary research
- quality over quantity in their work
- efficiency in how they do their work
- mentoring others and being mentored

- a sense of community (which many find lacking)
- more clarity about the tenure and renewal processes
- collegiality and non-competitiveness with colleagues
- work-life balance

To attract and retain the next generation of faculty, institutions need to commit to making the academic workplace attractive by providing systems and colleagues to support great work.

Increased Accountability

Regulatory Issues

In 2006, then Secretary of Education Margaret Spellings commissioned a study of higher education in the United States. The subsequent report states, "There is inadequate transparency and accountability for measuring institutional performance, which is more and more necessary to maintaining public trust in higher education.... Accreditation reviews are typically kept private, and those that are made public still focus on process reviews more than bottom-line results for learning or costs. The growing public demand for increased accountability, quality and transparency coupled with the changing structure and globalization of higher education requires a transformation of accreditation." The report recommends, "To meet the challenges of the 21st century, higher education must change from a system primarily based on reputation to one based on performance." (The Commission Appointed by Secretary of Education Margaret Spellings, 2006, p 14-15, 21).

Consequently, accrediting bodies within higher education—for both the over-all institution and the departments within the institution—are requiring more accountability. Many higher education departments and colleges, such as social work, journalism and business, are accredited by outside agencies. These agencies demand more stringent assessment measures to retain accreditation, meaning more time spent compiling data and generating reports by faculty and staff. In addition, taxpayers, policy makers, and students and their families are placing pressure on institutions to document student learning and increase transparency.

In response to these increased pressures to define, measure and report on the outcomes of higher education, numerous national and international projects were initiated. To help members of the higher education community keep track of these new developments, the ACE Center for Policy Analysis has an online resource that profiles nine major accountability and learning outcome initiatives. Each initiative includes a description of project goals, a work plan, accomplishments, upcoming activities, and a web address for further information. The length of this list itself demonstrates the critical nature of this challenge (American Council on Education Center for Policy Analysis).

1. Assessment of Higher Education Learning Outcomes
2. Council for Higher Education Accreditation Initiative
3. National Institute for Learning Outcomes Assessment

4. New Leadership Alliance for Student Learning and Accountability

5. Pathways Construction Project (Higher Learning Commission)

6. Tuning USA

7. University and College Accountability Network

8. Rising to the Challenge

9. Voluntary System of Accountability

Changing Mission of Higher Education

Most people expect college to be a challenging, life-enhancing experience, with highly developed and useful outcomes resulting from study and earning a degree. Many expect direct involvement with communities outside of higher education. Each group tends to have a different view of what that implies, as outlined below (Academic Freedom and Educational Responsibility, 2006).

- Many **students** expect job-related courses that prepare them to enter or change their chosen careers, and then advance within them.
- **Employers** focus on the specific abilities and skill sets they need in their employees. Inconsistent results lead employers to question the effectiveness of higher education.
- **Policy makers** expect colleges and universities to produce enough highly skilled graduates to satisfy workforce needs and to attract business and industry to local regions to broaden the local tax base.
- Many who want to apply a **corporate management model** to higher education argue that colleges and universities should treat their students as consumers whose preferences direct services offered, rather than as individuals with minds that need nurturing and development.
- The **general public** recognizes differences among higher education institutions and expects quality and empowering education from all of them. No matter where they graduate from, students are expected to be better at thinking and at knowledge-based work after graduation. The general public also expects that attendance will pay off in a successful career and place in society. On the other hand, the general public knows comparatively little about the structure, mission and governance of higher education.

Characteristics that contribute toward the uniqueness of higher education institutions are changing. In some states, two-year community colleges seek to offer four-year degrees to meet the growing demand for higher education. In response to the changing mission of higher education and the blurring of institution types, higher education administrators see little option but to respond to the marketplace to obtain the necessary resources to offer high quality and diverse academic programs. Many believe that the marketplace has overtaken state government as the dominant external force shaping higher education, even for public colleges and universities (Eckel and King, 2004).

The result is that activities and research in certain fields become higher priorities for institutions because they offer stronger market value than other programs. Institutions seek contracts and partnership agreements that have large financial payouts. They build conference centers and add new units that focus on generating external grants and bringing new technologies to market. In essence, the ability to compete for students, resources, faculty and reputation becomes a driving strategic priority (Eckel and King, 2004).

The mission of higher education has included a widespread belief in the power of education to create social and economic mobility and in the morality and social value of making higher education available to everyone. This tension between the competitive and ambitious nature of institutions and the interests of government in promoting important public goals will continue to cause challenges for institutions of higher education (Eckel and King, 2004).

Political Ramifications

Governments impact the work of higher education institutions with new rules, laws, regulations and budgets. One example is a requirement to conduct criminal background checks for all new employees, without giving additional resources to complete this responsibility. Another example is recent legislative activity in some states seeking to reduce statutory protected collective bargaining rights.

Whereas the primary results of education and most academic research are long term, decisions in the political arena have shifted from a long-term to a short-term focus, resulting from a need to balance the budget for the next year or two, and from programs competing with education for state funds. This situation will persist as states continue to struggle because of expansion in various programs such as Medicaid, corrections, and state aid to K-12 schools. Most states also will need to replenish retiree pension and health care trust funds and finance maintenance, technology and infrastructure investments that were deferred during the 2008 economic crisis (Lyall, 2011).

The current Obama administration has pledged to preserve Pell Grants and other federal financial aid programs. However, it is obvious that all federal programs are "on the table" as 2012 federal budget deficit negotiations ensue.

In her June 2011 article published by the Center for Studies in Higher Education at the University of California, Berkeley, Katharine Lyall, former President of the University of Wisconsin System, contends that there is a current crisis in higher education. Says Lyall, "unsustainability of the current business models… derives from fundamental long-term changes in states' economic bases, in the growth of competing programs and in the political processes, which inhibit state legislatures from getting their budgets in order. Underlying all this is a clear shift from viewing the benefits of higher education as a social, collective good to regarding it primarily as a private, individual benefit" (Lyall, 2011, p 1).

Although Lyall's article speaks mainly of public institutions, it is clear from the results of the 2011 *Inside Higher Ed* survey that private institutions are dealing with similar issues. Lyall indicates that early approaches to resolving the crisis have centered on incremental changes such as the following (Lyall, 2011):

- Accelerating study to reduce costs
- Policies to reduce time-to-degree
- Use of instructional technology to reach more and/or cut costs
- Change enrollment mix to generate more revenue
- Substitute more ad hoc faculty and/or modify tenure and evaluation policies

However, Lyall contends that more radical "structural changes" that alter the fundamental political, legal and financial relationships between a state and its higher education institutions must be considered (Lyall, 2011).

Summary

The five major interrelated challenges in the higher education environment include reduced resources, student demographics, workforce demographics, increased accountability, and political ramifications. These major challenges contribute toward the need for not only incremental, but also major structural changes and reforms within higher education.

Potential structural changes, as well as increasing numbers of incremental changes needed to sustain higher education, will touch the lives of all faculty, staff and administrators at all institutions. A fully engaged workforce, with a high level of skills in change management, organizational communication, and strategic focus, is critical to addressing this crisis successfully.

A transformative HR function, serving as a strategic partner with the cabinet, can play a vital role in supporting institutions as they face these realities and challenges.

The Human Resources Paradigm Shift

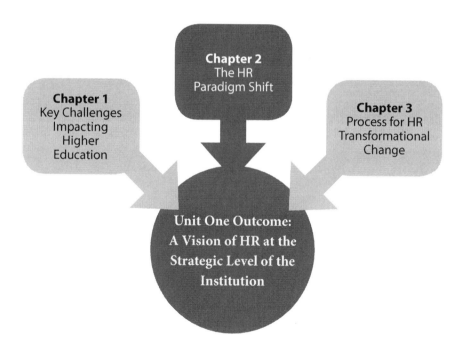

Chapter 2 The HR paradigm shift

How Can a Strategic HR Function Partner with the Cabinet to Address the Crisis in Higher Education?

No other department or unit of the institution understands the organization as completely, or has the opportunity to engage with faculty and staff in multiple arenas as a partner and relationship-builder, as the HR function. It is the "business" of the HR function to create an organization that constantly builds its capacity through building the capacity of the people employed. This ensures the institution can attract, hire, retain and develop those faculty and staff needed to accomplish the mission and vision in times of competitive change. In addition, a transformative HR function serves as a tool to align each department and unit with the institution's strategy, creating a distinctive advantage. Consequently, the HR function is an intimate part of the work lives of employees as it carries out the following roles:

1. An employee advocate role results in increased employee commitment and engagement;
2. As HR specialists, HR professionals connect with all employees throughout the entire employment processes, e.g., hiring, onboarding, promotion, training and development, tenure and renewal, performance management, etc.;
3. The organizational design specialist role results in the creation of a renewed and stronger organization; and
4. As a strategic partner and leader, HR strategy aligns with institution strategy, resulting in HR recognized by all stakeholders as adding value to the institution. Outcomes include an HR strategic plan with a staffing plan, an institution-wide recruitment and leadership brand, and performance measures at department and unit levels that align with those of the institution.

These multiple roles offer the opportunity for a transformational HR function to create tremendous value for the institution by delivering strategic results in efficient and effective ways. To accomplish this most effectively, the HR function must either be physically present at the cabinet's table, or seen and perceived by all stakeholders as valued and supported by the cabinet. In addition, HR work must be seen as strategic and transformational.

Due to the challenges facing higher education institutions, the HR function is being asked to play a vital role in supporting institutions as they face these realities. According to Allison Vaillancourt, vice president for HR at the University of Arizona, and Andy Brantley, president and CEO of the College and University Professional Association for Human Resources, "From offering advice about how to frame institutional change messages to providing support to down-sized employees, HR organizations are playing a vital role in supporting institutions as they adjust to new resource realities.... There is no doubt that providing value in the 'new normal' requires a more complex set of HR deliverables" (Vaillancourt and Brantley, 2009, p 23).

Although benefits of a transformative HR function at the strategic level of the institution are identified easily, summarizing actual examples allows for greater understanding. Following are seven examples:

Example 1: University of Tennessee: HR at the Strategic Level

In January 2009, the University of Tennessee then-president wanted HR to be a fully engaged strategic partner, one that could efficiently and effectively develop and nurture the workforce and work culture necessary for the continued success of the university. A directive was given to Linda Hendricks, the chief HR officer, to evaluate the structure of the HR function across the entire system to determine how best to transform from a mostly HR transactional entity to a more strategic one. Says Hendricks, "For years, HR had been a transactional, functional unit—busying itself with policies and procedures and processing manual transactions—instead of trying to align itself with the university's priorities and goals." This redesign, implemented in January 2010, has increased HR's effectiveness, streamlined service delivery and reduced costs. In addition, it has "allowed HR to focus on the more strategic issues at hand. We have been able to turn our attention to issues such as succession planning, capturing data and analyzing workforce trending, developing a recruitment brand, and implementing an HR technology plan," says Hendricks (Kline, 2009, p 16).

> No other department or unit of the institution understands the organization as completely, or has the opportunity to engage with faculty and staff in multiple arenas as a partner and relationship-builder, as the HR function.

Example 2: University of Michigan: Joint Education Program

From 2005 through 2008, 1,465 grievances were filed by members of the American Federation of State, County and Municipal Employees local union against the University of Michigan. In addition, employee surveys showed represented staff felt the least satisfied, least engaged and least empowered of all employee groups. HR and union leaders agreed to work together toward a shared vision: building a positive relationship and working collaboratively. As a result, a year-long Joint Education Program was developed that included training for all supervisors and union stewards. The initial goals incorporated improving local problem solving, building relationships and developing capacity for continuous improvement, with a short-term target of reducing grievances. As a result, in just three years, grievances fell by 76%, resulting in $300,000 in productivity savings across University of Michigan departments. Long-term goals are being achieved through investing time in communication, meetings and training sessions by all participants. More than 80% of all supervisors across the institution have participated in training and relationship-building programs (Lilly, Owens and Parsons, 2010-2011).

Example 3: Pace University: Business Process Change

When Stephen J. Friedman assumed the president position in 2007 at Pace University in New York City, he declared that a rapid, internal turnaround was needed to assure the university's reputation for academic excellence and capacity to thrive in the highly competitive New York marketplace. Process change became the vehicle for university-wide culture change. Over the next two years, more than 50 process change leaders participated in the process change management workshops. Christian N. Madu, Ph.D., research professor of management science in the Lubin School of Business, says, "Every employee has the opportunity to contribute to and many have already seen the impact of their efforts for positive change. The focus on technological tools and change management have become a reflection of the new Pace culture—individuals are working harder, working more closely, breaking down silos and really starting to work as a team." The HR function plays a key role in Pace's process change initiatives, with responsibilities for managing the overall "process" of process change, soliciting and presenting process change project ideas, workshop facilitation, resource support and overall project monitoring and reporting. In addition, HR offers training for process leaders in project management, presentation skills and meeting management. Involving key stakeholders in process change has been critical to its success, as it contributes to greater understanding and commitment to the change initiative (Lazer and Robilotta, 2010-2011).

Example 4: Towson University: Building Bridges Program

Through a needs assessment of Towson University support staff and management, training and develop-ment manager Kristi Yowell identified a confirmed need for development programs. The initial Building Bridges program fostered collaboration and idea sharing among employees at Towson University, Univer-sity of Baltimore, Goucher College, Loyola University Maryland, College of Notre Dame of Maryland, and the Maryland Institute College of Art. The group attended six sessions—one at each participating school—during the seven-month program. Session topics included managing priorities, enhancing individual effec-tiveness, customer service and conflict resolution. Since then, similar programs have been developed for management. Says Yowell, "Collaborative programs like this one enable employees of smaller institutions to have access to meaningful professional development and networking opportunities, and allow participating institutions to minimize costs while maximizing return. It is really a win-win for everyone!" (Building Bridges Across Maryland, 2009, p 27).

Example 5: University of San Diego: First-Year Employee Experience Program

In early 2008, data showed that half of all new employees who left the University of San Diego did so within one to three years, and 16% left in the first year. Karen Kitchen Briggs, director of employment and training, wanted new employees to be immediately submerged in the campus culture and engaged on a strategic level. The First-Year Employee Experience program, an adaptation of the university's first-year experience program for students, subsequently was implemented for all new hires except faculty. Program components include pre-arrival resources and preparation, orientation, the new employee learning path, and an ambas-sador program. Preliminary data show that since the program's inception, the number of employees leaving the university within the first year of employment has dropped 6% for a 94% retention rate. In addition, results of a survey of new employees participating in the new program indicate a larger percentage feel more welcome in the first few months of work, better understand the university's mission and values, and plan to stay employed by the university. "Leadership at the University of San Diego genuinely values each employee for his or her unique contributions to our students, campus and community," says Kitchen Briggs (The First-Year Employee Experience: A Unique Onboarding Program, 2009, p 7).

Example 6: Seton Hall University: HR Strategic Plan

During difficult economic times, the HR professionals at Seton Hall University in New Jersey felt called upon to aid institutional leadership in resolving financial crises through data-driven decision-making. The HR function was extremely transactional until 2008, when multiple new HR technologies were implemented. They were determined to reinvent the HR function for the sole purpose of enhancing HR's contribution to the university. They understood that no transformation effort would work unless key stakeholders are engaged, fiduciary responsibilities are adhered to and technology implementations are aligned. They began by developing an HR strategic plan to support institutional goals, and then tweaked their model to achieve optimum delivery of services through the utilization of the technology. Says Susan McGarry Basso, associate vice president for HR, "Using a sophisticated web portal has revolutionized the way services are offered to our faculty and employees. Accessible data capture and retrieval has freed the HR department from administrivia and has allowed us to concentrate more on strategy.… As HR professionals, our agile response and willingness to reinvent and transform could mean the difference between failure and success" (McGarry, Basso, 2009, p 20).

Example 7: University of Missouri System: University Performance Measures

In late 2007, Gary Forsee became the new president of the University of Missouri System with four campuses. Shortly thereafter, he compiled 80 accountability measures that encompassed the five facets of the system's mission: (1) teaching and learning; (2) research; (3) service and engagement; (4) economic development; and (5) developing and managing human, financial and physical resources. Says Forsee, "Our accountability measures are derived from the strategy, vision and core values of the system as a whole, but are also designed to provide each of our four campuses with the flexibility to customize and tailor their metrics to fit their specific missions and goals.… Every single staff member, faculty member and administrator in the UM System has a role to play in helping to meet these goals." The 25 measures under the fifth category include those related to attracting, developing and retaining talented faculty and staff, sustainability and flexibility in resource management and stewardship. The strategic HR function then can develop metrics for each deliverable that tie back to one or more of these university-wide performance measures (80 Ways to Measure Success, 2010).

These are a few of the examples of what it looks like to have a transformative HR function at the strategic level of the institution. Each example possesses the following commonalities:

1. Stakeholders feel they are being provided value through the work of a transformative HR function;
2. The HR function is aligned with the strategic goals of the institution;
3. HR staff members possess the necessary skills and competencies for transformational work;
4. The HR function is connected and engaged with all segments of the institution; and
5. The work of the HR function contributes toward the strategic success of the institution. In addition, a transformational HR frames this function as a source of competitive advantage and creates distinctiveness for the institution.

What Is an HR Paradigm Shift?

The HR paradigm shift involves moving the HR function to focus primarily on delivering transformative or strategic work instead of transactional work. Transactional work is reengineered to provide more time for the HR staff to work in transformative ways. In many cases, HR staff members must learn entirely new skills that include expertise in change management, process reengineering, teamwork, conflict resolution, strategic management, re-structuring and group facilitation.

There are several potential challenges in shifting HR department focus in a time of declining resources within higher education. One includes reallocating resources to ensure that current program offerings continue to align with the institution's vision and mission. Another is needing to say "farewell" to current staff who are unable or unwilling to develop the expertise needed for an HR paradigm shift.

What Is Transactional vs Transformative HR Work?

Transactional work in an HR department encompasses administrative functions that are required legally or are necessary to the operations of the university, e.g., payroll, fringe benefits, leave accounting, recruitments, complaints, grievances, FMLA, ADA accommodations, etc. Although improvements can be made to these processes that create increased effectiveness and efficiency for HR staff and employees, they still are considered transactional functions. Although creating efficiencies for transactional work does create a great deal of stakeholder value for the HR department, it still is considered transactional work because the focus is on what the department does.

As noted in Table 2.1, transactional work is primarily reactive, in that the HR department must react to a specific event, e.g., a new employee was just hired, a new recruitment has been announced, a grievance has been brought forward, an employee has questions on rights under FMLA, etc. In addition, the HR staff work with employees to accomplish the purpose of the event.

Table 2.1 Transactional versus transformative work

FROM: HR Transactional Work	TO: HR Transformative/Strategic Work
Creates efficiency through standardization, automation and consolidation	Aligns vision, mission and goals of HR with strategy of the organization
Mostly reactive	Proactive
Focus is on what we do	Focus is on what we deliver
Work with employees	Create relationships/collaborate
Implement best HR practices	Deliver value-added HR practices
Build HR functions for efficiency	Build HR functions for stakeholder value

Transformative work in a HR department consists of aligning goals of the HR department with the strategic goals of the organization. As indicated in Table 2.1, the work is primarily proactive—based on creating relationships and collaboration, focused on the work or value "delivered" to stakeholders and aligned with the strategy of the organization.

An example of transformative work is the development and implementation of the University of Wisconsin Oshkosh *ACES Mentoring Network*. Members of the HR department first noticed the need for a mentoring program as part of new employee onboarding, and then developed a draft program plan. In working with the provost and vice chancellor and a team of support, administrative and ad hoc teaching staff throughout the university, the *ACES Mentoring Network* was implemented to include all new staff. Subsequently, a process for current staff to be matched with a mentor for professional development purposes was added to the program. A year later, academic deans requested the HR department to provide resources for the new faculty mentoring program.

What Does a Strategic HR Function Look Like?

In graphic form, what does a higher education institution with its HR function transformational and at the strategic level look like? What are the outcomes to its stakeholders and to the institution as a whole?

The model in Figure 2.1 graphically portrays the new partnership relationship between stakeholders and the human resources function, and outlines the strategic outcomes for the university.

Figure 2.1 Model of HR at the strategic level of the university

University Stakeholder Perspective

Let us first look at stakeholder perspectives as the HR function works through the HR paradigm shift. Stakeholders include the chancellor or president's cabinet, which normally comprises people in those positions reporting directly to the chancellor or president. Note that within the inner ring in Figure 2.1, each word denotes the partnership that results between the human resources function and stakeholders. This partnership is described as follows:

Valued: The first difference noticed by stakeholders, after the initial changes to the HR function, is HR staff members offering deliverables that have increased value. These initial changes include the HR department developing core values and a core competency framework, a new vision and mission statement that focuses on providing value to stakeholders, and an increased knowledge of the HR paradigm shift. As a result, the HR staff asks more questions regarding needs and expectations of stakeholders, and how those can be satisfied.

Innovative: As the transformation progresses, stakeholders notice that common transactional functions are done more quickly, with increased focus on valued outcomes. The HR staff reaches out to them with improved methods. Examples include the hiring and training process for limited term employees, and assisting in the evaluation of skills of candidates for permanent faculty and staff positions.

Trust: Because of regular updates by the HR director on the progress of the HR transformation, and "in the trenches" stories from their constituents emphasizing the change in HR, stakeholders have increased trust in the process. They see their expectations of the transformation fulfilled.

Influence and Advocate: Stakeholders are invited to participate on teams to reengineer HR processes that definitely impact and involve the entire university. A common example is the recruitment and hiring processes for professional and administrative staff. Stakeholders note that the HR staff members appear to have higher levels of skills in facilitating discussions and managing conflict. They have an organization-wide perspective, spend time developing relationships of trust, and understand the inner workings of the university. Stakeholders discover they can influence organizational change and institution policies and procedures, contacting HR to partner in resolving major issues.

Unified Focus: Although the HR function may be considered credible, ethical, approachable and knowledgeable, the level of these perspectives increases as relationships are strengthened and built, and the HR staff are considered as adding increased value through innovation and broader thinking. All HR functions and practices are integrated with a unified strategic focus in that the same voice and vision is being projected throughout the university.

Synergy: Note in Figure 2.1 that arrows move from the inner ring—stakeholder perspective—to the HR function in the center, demonstrating the new partnership with the HR function. With stakeholder perspectives of the HR function changing in a positive way due to the HR paradigm shift and the delivery of valued outcomes, HR staff members are motivated to continue with their transformation. As stakeholder engagement deepens, a definite synergy develops within the institution. As equal partners, together the HR function and stakeholders implement short- and long-term strategy.

Strategic Leadership: As the transformation accelerates, stakeholders at all levels of the organization participate in the process of developing and implementing the HR strategic plan. They serve in a capacity of their choice: membership on the advisory team; interviewed to assess organizational readiness or components of the plan; membership of a transition monitoring team, a goal implementation team or an evaluation team.

Strategic Institution Outcome

The following words in the outer ring of Figure 2.1 signify the strategic outcomes to the institution resulting from the HR paradigm shift and the new partnership between the HR function and stakeholders:

Integrated Strategy: With the implementation of the HR strategic plan aligned with the institution's strategic plan, the cabinet has increased trust in the HR function. Cabinet members, as well as all stakeholders, observe that operational outcomes are beginning to take place that strengthen and influence the identity, culture, and image of the university. The *Recruitment Brand* and the *Leadership Brand* are the first, being the outcome of work—facilitated by the HR department—by broad teams of people across the university.

Engagement: Over the next few years, data show the institution's *Recruitment and Leadership Brands* are successful by attracting, hiring and retaining people with skills and experiences identified as being needed within the institution. The *Leadership Brand* demonstrates leadership basic principles, aligns all leaders to embody these basics, trains and develops others as leaders, and embeds leaders throughout the organization that embody this brand. The institution is immersed in leadership development and other types of training, causing employees to feel valued and deeply connected.

Because of the emphasis on metrics and accountability in the HR strategic plan, improvements are made to the plan as data indicate those are necessary. The campus-wide evaluation team is trained in metrics and evaluation procedures, and is engaged and committed to its work. On at least an annual basis, the HR strategic plan's goals are updated by the Advisory Team, using a SWOT analysis.

Culture Change: A result of the HR strategic plan is the development—by a campus-wide team facilitated by the HR function—of alternative methods to resolve conflict more effectively. Policies are changed, and all employees are trained in conflict resolution. Conflict is not perceived as totally negative, with the need to be erased from the institution, but considered to be instrumental in creating a better place for people to work effectively and be successful. People are taught to address conflict in positive ways.

Distinctiveness: Through an HR paradigm shift, the "capabilities" of the institution are created, developed or enhanced. Examples of capabilities are the talent of faculty and staff, ability to address conflict, decision-making, efficiency and effectiveness, innovation, leadership, collaborating and partnering toward common goals, strategic integration, and accountability. These capabilities contribute toward defining the culture that shapes the institution and its stakeholders—what the institution is known for—its "brand."

Transformative: A transformative HR department's ability to define, create, manage and change cultures is considered a unique source of strategic competence by all stakeholders, causing the HR leader to participate in cabinet meetings, including workshops and retreats. How does this HR paradigm shift cause the HR department to be considered a unique source of competence by all stakeholders?" As outlined in the book, *HR Transformation: Building HR from the Outside In*, by Dave Ulrich, et. al. (2009), the "outcomes" from the HR transformation must be "valued" by stakeholders and meet their expectations. Therefore, knowing these "expectations" through the initial data gathering, discussed in chapter 4 and elsewhere in this book, is crucial to the HR transformation.

To summarize, the model of the HR function at the cabinet's table, depicted in Figure 2.1, illustrates that the strategic partnership between a transformative HR function and the institution's stakeholders provides a source of competitive advantage and creates distinctiveness for the institution. Outlined in the next chapter is the process for getting there.

> … the strategic partnership between a transformative HR function and the institution's stakeholders provides a source of competitive advantage and creates distinctiveness for the institution.

Summary

The HR paradigm shift demands that the competencies of HR professionals include expertise in change management, work redesign, process reengineering, employee engagement, information acquisition and dissemination, organizational communication, and planning and analysis. This means a paradigm shift to a transformational focus.

Utilizing techniques from the private sector and shaping them to work within the distinctiveness of higher education will enable a paradigm shift for the HR function to become transformational. As a strategic partner, HR can serve as a tool to provide structure for discussions of change, to provide leadership in developing plans to address the challenges, and to serve as a conduit to bring together others throughout the university to prepare for and implement change.

Process for Human Resources Transformational Change

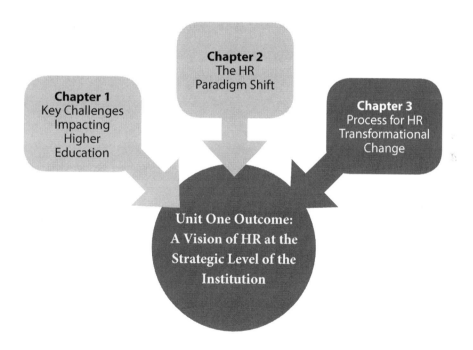

Chapter 3 Process for HR transformational change

How Will the HR Paradigm Shift Be Implemented? From "Vision" to "Action"

Figure 3.1 describes the four-phase process for moving the HR function to the strategic level of the university. This model applies to both transformational change and "quantum leap" change.

Phase 1 Build the Foundation prepares the HR professionals for transformational change. This includes transitioning the HR staff to the new HR paradigm, discussing conflict and methods of resolution, assessing skills and developing plans to increase the skill level of employees, developing the HR staff into a cohesive team motivated to work in different ways, and discovering stakeholder value and obtaining their support.

Figure 3.1 Model for HR transformation within higher education

Phase 2 Become Catalysts for Change develops the more efficient and effective internal and external HR processes. This phase includes the HR staff learning and utilizing reengineering processes while working as equal members of a team. In addition, the HR staff determine the department's vision and mission, evaluate its structure, and establish an HR recruitment brand.

Phase 3 Set the Stage creates more efficient and effective external HR processes for improved stakeholder value and relationship-building. This includes partnering with stakeholders to evaluate all HR processes impacting external HR department stakeholders to determine those providing a quick win. Included are the steps to measure progress of the HR paradigm shift, a process to enable transformative work, and steps to engage the university in the new HR transformational paradigm.

Phase 4 Become a Strategic Partner develops and aligns the HR strategic plan to the organization's strategic plan. This includes the assessment of organizational readiness, the components of the plan, development of an organization-wide advisory team, and development, implementation and evaluation of the plan.

Barriers Faced in Moving to the New HR Paradigm

Although it is exciting to consider the outcomes to the university with the HR function at the strategic level, we need to identify critical barriers that may impede our progress. Table 3.1 lists these barriers and

Table 3.1: Barriers to the HR paradigm shift

Barrier	Discussed in Chapter
1. Little or support from cabinet and/or supervisor	7
2. Little or no support from key constituents	7
3. HR employees do not possess knowledge of the needed HR paradigm shift	4
4. HR employees do not possess transformative skills	5
5. HR employees do not want to change	4,5,8,14
6. Little knowledge on how to lead the change and transition processes	8,13,16
7. Functional silos exist within the HR department	11,12
8. Needed resources, including "time," are not available	4,7
9. Staff issues: turnover, inherited staff, quality of work	4,5,6,13,14
10. Conflict and other dysfunctions exist within the HR department	6
11. Inadequate structure of the HR department	12
12. Systems within the HR department not aligned with goals, e.g., performance evaluations, reward/recognition, etc.	9,12
13. Not having updated HR department vision, mission, core values, goals	9
14. Not having an HR recruitment brand	10
15. Inefficient or ineffective HR processes	11,14,15
16. Not having an HR strategic plan aligned with the university strategic plan	17,18,19

includes the relevant chapters of the book that provide resources for confronting and eliminating them. Consider using Table 3.1 as a "checklist" to identify barriers that currently provide challenges to your HR paradigm shift. Knowing these barriers allows you to move to those chapters. For example, if HR staff plan to retire or leave, using chapter 10 to develop an HR recruitment brand becomes a priority. If you have little or no support from key constituents or the cabinet, using chapter 7 to determine stakeholder value and obtain support is a priority. If a major barrier is the level of skills, knowledge and engagement of HR staff members, your priority becomes chapters 4, 5, 8, 13 and 14.

Especially crucial to an HR paradigm shift is the support given by the cabinet members and supervisor. As HR professionals, we enter higher education because we enjoy working with people and want to contribute toward the growth and strength of the institution. In college we learned expectations for how the HR role can contribute toward shaping the future of the organization and its culture. However, we may not feel valued by administrators and key constituents. Although the HR function is intimately involved at all levels of the university, because it does not sit at the cabinet's table or is not perceived as transformational, it is not viewed as strategic. This is primarily a systemic issue—difficult for HR directors and vice presidents of HR to change.

Which comes first, HR's presence at the cabinet's table or HR viewed as transformational? It depends. Some HR directors are invited to the cabinet's table when a new president or chancellor arrives in the position. Others are invited to the table as a result of an HR paradigm shift and changed perceptions. Some are not physically at the cabinet's table on a regular basis but viewed by the cabinet as strategic partners. Regardless of whether or not the HR function is physically at the cabinet's table, the process outlined in the following chapters will change the perception of the HR function throughout the institution. The vision of the HR function at the strategic level of the organization can be yours.

Unit One Summary

Transactional work in a HR department encompasses administrative functions that are required legally or are necessary to the operations of the university, e.g., payroll, fringe benefits, leave accounting, recruitments, complaints, grievances, FMLA, ADA accommodations, etc. Transformative work consists of aligning goals of the HR department with the strategic goals of the organization. The work is primarily proactive—based on creating relationships and collaboration, focused on the work or value "delivered" to stakeholders and aligned with the strategy of the organization. The HR paradigm shift encompasses moving the HR function to focus primarily on transformative work.

The role of a transformative HR function is to create an organization that constantly builds its capacity by building the capacity of the people employed by the institution. This provides a crucial benefit in that it ensures the institution can attract, hire, retain and develop those faculty and staff needed to accomplish the mission and vision in times of competitive change. Moving to a transformative HR paradigm will ensure the creation of HR strategy that sets an agenda for how HR will help the institution address the challenges of reduced resources, changing demographics of students and the workforce, and increased accountability, and emerge successful.

The four-phase process for moving the HR function to the strategic level of the institution includes building the foundation for change, developing the HR staff to become catalysts for change, setting the stage for change outside of the HR function, and becoming a strategic partner through developing and implementing an HR strategic plan aligned with that of the institution.

We hope you are inspired to move forward with transformational change in the HR function at your institution. The materials in Unit One serve as resources in several chapters.

Unit Two

Build the Foundation

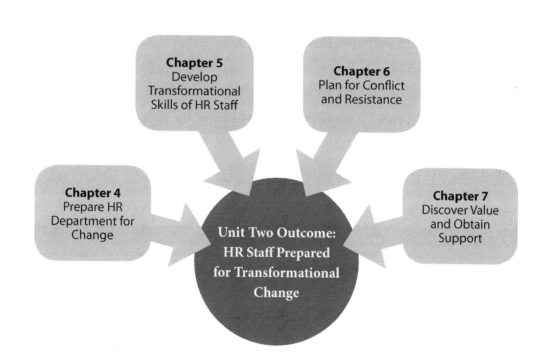

Unit Two Model for preparing the HR department for transformational change

We have discovered in our experiences of moving departments to the strategic level of the university that we must begin with strengthening the HR function, as a whole and individually, in order to build the foundation for preparing the department for change. This is consistent with what Dave Ulrich, et. al. (2009) communicate in their book, *HR Transformation: Building HR from the Outside In*. HR transformation requires change in strategy around the HR department and its practices and people.

It is critical that all those individuals within the HR function understand the new HR paradigm, are ready for organizational change and are motivated to be part of it. This unit contains a step-by-step process and materials for developing HR staff into a cohesive team, motivated to work in transformational ways.

Unit Two contains the following topics in this process:

1. Preparing for change by understanding the new HR paradigm and roles of HR staff within it.
2. Developing transformational skills of the HR staff.
3. Planning for conflict and resistance among the HR staff.
4. Discovering stakeholder value and obtaining support for the paradigm shift.

Unit Two provides an extensive menu of ideas, techniques, and examples that are relevant to the practice of HR within the higher education setting. You can choose what is right for you, depending on where your HR function currently is in the transformation continuum. Even if you believe some processes and outcomes are already part of your HR structure and culture, it is extremely important that you do not "skip" any part of the process, or implement it only superficially. Doing so will generate issues in the long term and impact the strength of the HR transformation. Utilizing the case studies in each chapter can serve as additional learning or refreshing of the topic for the HR staff.

Introduction to Book's Themes

Throughout this book, we use the three themes of Leadership of Change, Appreciative Inquiry, and Reframing in two ways: (1) to indicate how a theme is important in accomplishing the outcome of a chapter; (2) to indicate alternate methods of resolution for consideration. Following is an introduction to each theme to give a general idea of the topic.

Leadership of Change

Our responsibility as a leader of change is to adapt the HR department to significantly changing circumstances. We help define what the future should look like for our HR department, align the HR staff with that vision, and inspire them to accomplish it. Change is definitely a process that can involve obstacles and errors in decision-making. This theme outlines successful change and the forces that drive it, utilizing the eight-stage process of creating major change described by John P. Kotter in his book, *Leading Change* (Kotter, 1996).

Appreciative Inquiry

Appreciative inquiry is an affirmative approach to change that completely lets go of problem-based management. Evolving in the 1980s as a positive philosophy to guide change in organizations, it is based on the assumption that inquiry into and dialogue about strengths, successes, hopes, and dreams is itself a transformational process. It involves the practice of asking unconditionally positive questions that strengthen a department or organization's capacity to anticipate and heighten positive potential.

The process of appreciative inquiry involves carefully crafted questions to create a joyfully focused state of mind as the person considers and answers them. Research indicates the following basic assumptions about appreciative inquiry (Orem, Binkert and Clancy, 2007):

- What people focus on becomes their reality.
- The act of asking questions of a group or individual influences the group or individual in some way.
- People are more confident in their journey to the future, which is not known, when they carry forward the best parts of the past, which is known.
- The language people use creates their reality.

We encourage you to keep an open mind as you read the positive outcomes of using appreciative inquiry, and consider utilizing it within your department as part of managing change.

Reframing

In their popular book, *Reframing Organizations*, Lee Bolman and Terrence Deal (2003) outline an approach for looking at situations from more than one angle. Essentially, they view an organization—or a department in our case—as possessing four frames: structural, human resources, political and symbolic. Reframing a situation in each of these four ways provides for a comprehensive picture of an issue and describes alternatives that might work best to resolve it effectively. Following is a brief discussion of each frame, which is expanded in subsequent chapters.

1. The **structural frame** focuses on how the department is organized; its rules, roles, goals and policies that shape and channel its decisions and activities. It aligns internal department processes with its external environment. Two design issues are at the heart of organizational structure: how to allocate work and how to coordinate roles after leaders define responsibilities.

2. The **human resources frame** focuses on the needs and skills of individuals; emphasizing an understanding of people, with their strengths, weaknesses, emotions, desires and fears. This

frame views people as an investment: we want to hire the right people, keep them, invest in them, empower them and promote diversity.

3. The **political frame** focuses on conflict and arenas. It sees the department as a competitive arena characterized by scarce resources, competing interests, and struggles for power and advantage. Sources of power are position, information, control of rewards, alliance and networks, access and control of agendas, control of meaning and symbols, and personal power to include charisma, energy and stamina.

4. The **symbolic frame** focuses on loss of meaning and the importance of creating new symbols and common ground. It puts ritual, ceremony, play and culture at the heart of department life. Most important in a workplace is not what happens, but what it "means." Events can have multiple meanings because people interpret experiences differently, based on their background. During change and transition, people create symbols to resolve confusion, increase predictability, and find direction.

Leaders who understand the power of symbols are much better equipped to understand and influence their department or organization. Examples of leading symbolically include: leading by example; using symbols to capture attention, e.g., doing something visible and dramatic to signal that change is coming; communicating a vision that addresses both the challenges of the present and the hopes and values of the department members; telling stories that are embedded with this vision, stories about "us" and about "our" past, present and future; respecting and using department history; creating rituals that signify change.

Chapter 4

Prepare the Human Resources Department for Change

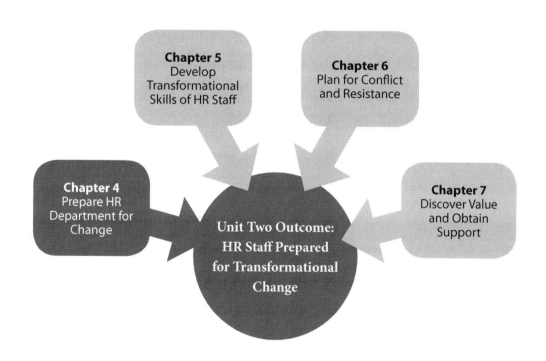

Unit Two Model for preparing the HR department for transformational change

Higher education often is criticized for not changing fast enough. Due to the external and internal forces driving change discussed in Unit One, higher education institutions are ripe for change. As an HR leader within higher education, you probably are experiencing retirements and new people coming onboard. Many are from the private sector, have experiences within a different workplace and are knowledgeable about transition and change.

This provides a unique opportunity to build the HR staff, both new and current individuals, into a strong, unified and focused team. In most cases, current staff members are knowledgeable about the organization, its work practices and policies; new staff members bring knowledge of transition and change, and are motivated to learn and work together.

The process described in this chapter may seem simple, but each step revitalizes staff, helps them to think differently, and births the seeds of innovation and teamwork.

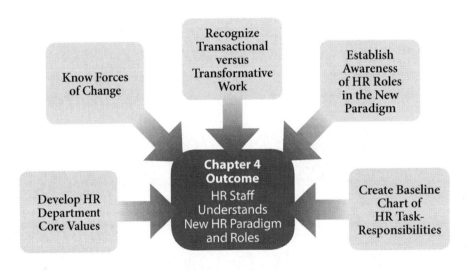

Figure 4.1 Model to begin transitioning staff to new paradigm

Core Values and Why They Are Important

Culture is the environment that surrounds employees in the workplace, and contributes toward shaping the enjoyment of work, relationships, and how work is done. Culture is used to describe the behaviors among people who work together and interact with others outside the department or organization. Culture can be "seen" within a workplace by observing language, symbols, rituals, workplace setting to include objects and artifacts, decision-making, interactions among people, emotions, daily work processes and stories told by employees.

As described in Figure 4.2, the composition of culture is similar to that of an onion: we need to peel away layers of culture to get to its core. At the core, we find that a department's or an organization's culture essentially consists of employees' collective core values that result from each individual's life experiences, behaviors, beliefs, strengths, weaknesses and education.

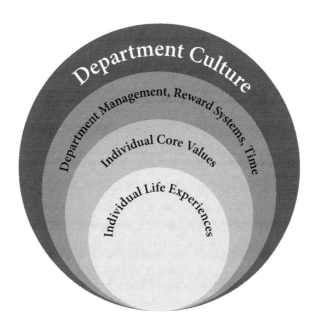

Figure 4.2 Relationship of core values to culture

A department's or an organization's core values can be described as principles, standards, or qualities considered worthwhile or desirable as part of working together with others internal or external to the department. These core values are learned quickly by new employees, are strengthened over time, and are solidified by the appropriate reward system and behaviors of management.

Without managers working proactively with employees to develop common core values as part of a framework that includes mission and vision, a department's or an organization's culture evolves on its own and is dominated by individual core values of influential employees. It is very difficult in this type of environment for a department to reach its full potential in developing employees and contributing toward the goals of the organization.

Especially within higher education, with the tenure of faculty members and the tendency toward valuing seniority within the administrative and support staff, employees who may not be a good fit with a new transformational culture may find it difficult to leave. This contributes toward conflict and dysfunction within departments, which impacts the long-term success of the department and the university.

> Without managers working proactively with employees to develop common core values as part of a framework that includes mission and vision, a department's or an organization's culture evolves on its own and is dominated by individual core values of influential employees.

Therefore, it is paramount to work with our HR staff to develop common core values, and to develop a process for addressing situations where these values are not utilized in the workplace. In chapter 14, we discuss methods to help an employee "exit" gracefully if he or she is not a good fit for the department.

Developing core values—how to work together—for the HR department, gets HR staff talking about what is important to them in working with others, begins breaking down the functional silos within the HR department, and develops five to seven common core values that can be used to manage and improve team functioning. We want the environment in the HR department to motivate, excite and retain employees who are a good fit with the collective culture.

The process of developing department core values has the following positive outcomes and expectations:

1. indicates to the HR staff that a new paradigm is beginning in the department
2. demonstrates that the core values of each individual are important to the department
3. symbolizes the importance of how individuals work together
4. helps shape behaviors so that HR staff work together internally and externally in ways that engender trust and promote learning and communication
5. reinforces the need for teamwork, respect, and cooperation
6. aligns the HR department's core values with those of the institution

Before we outline two examples to facilitate the process of developing core values for the HR department, we discuss consensus decision-making. Found throughout this book are situations where we need a decision-making model to use when working together. We recommend using a consensus-building model that promotes participation by all involved, encourages brainstorming, and provides for the best decision. From our experiences, the strengths of consensus-building as a decision-making model are the following:

1. Individuals are afforded equal input into the decision-making process.
2. Each individual visually indicates his/her level of support for the recommendation. If there are reservations, he/she is required to participate in strengthening the recommendation.
3. Better decisions are made and supported by the entire team or group.

4. Individuals have greater buy-in for decisions made. There are fewer, or no complaints outside of the meeting because all individuals participated in the process.

The *Fist-to-Five* model, described in Exhibit 4.1, is one method for building consensus (Fletcher, 2002).

Exhibit 4.1 The *Fist-to-Five* consensus-building model

At the point where a decision is being recommended—in the core value example it would be when recommending the high priority core values for the department— state the recommendation or proposal, and ask individuals to demonstrate their support of that recommendation by raising one hand, with the fingers shown on that hand indicating the strength of their support.

Five fingers indicate total support for the recommendation, with the person agreeing to serve as a "leader" in implementing the specific decision.

Four fingers indicate that although the person has minor reservations about the recommendation, he/she thinks it is a good decision and will support it.

Three fingers indicate the person is not in total agreement with the decision, but feels comfortable to let the decision be made without further discussion and will support it.

Two fingers indicate the person is not comfortable with the proposal and wants to discuss one or more minor issues in hopes of improving it.

One finger indicates the person has very strong reservations about the recommendation and needs to discuss certain issues or suggest changes to the proposal.

No fingers raised—thus the "fist"—indicates the person cannot support the recommendation at all, and needs to discuss specific issues and make changes to it.

When all individuals in the group raise all five fingers, or a combination of four and five fingers, the recommendation is supported totally and the decision has been made. For any other situation, individuals need to indicate suggestions for changing the recommendation in order for them to support it, or indicate their issues with the recommendation so further discussion can ensue.

Modifications can be made to the *Fist-to-Five* model to accommodate potential cultural and physical attributes that cause hesitation to participate. For example, the hand "gestures" can be replaced by a once-around to all members to get general feelings on the proposal, or through a signal such as a "thumbs up/middle/down." Those without a "thumbs up" for the proposal must provide details why they cannot totally support the proposal, or suggest modifications.

Example 1: Develop Core Values

Indicate to your staff during a staff meeting that you will have one-on-one meetings with each, and then will facilitate a staff meeting discussion about core values—their meaning and importance, and how they are seen in the workplace. The outcome of the process will be the development of core values for the department. Ask each staff member to reflect on the following three questions prior to your meeting:

1. Talk about a time in your life when you felt truly energized and alive at work. Describe it in rich detail, so that I can experience it just as you did.

2. Think of the person with whom you have most enjoyed working in the past, such as a favorite colleague who also might have been a friend. How did the person treat you that impacted you in such a positive way?

3. Step into the shoes of all the people who most respect and value you, both in the workplace and at home. Through their eyes, tell me your four or five most important personal core values.

Give them four or five days to reflect on these questions before you meet with them individually. In reviewing their responses, feel free to ask them follow-up questions to clarify their answers, and to offer your own core values after they describe their own.

After each meeting, list the core values described, noting those that were discussed by more than one staff member. At the next group staff meeting, list all the core values on a flip chart. Then lead a discussion to define each core value. Normally, four to six high priority core values stand out very clearly, with all or a majority of the staff stating those values as being important to them. Integrity, treating each other with respect, trust, open and honest communication, and building relationships are examples of values that we find are consistently given. Facilitate the discussion to choose four to six high priority core values.

Next, ask the staff to describe further what each of those core values means and how it can be seen in the workplace. For example, integrity can be described further as follows: being accountable, demonstrating trust (voice plus touch equals trust—what we say is the same as what we do), respecting each other, being honest, challenging each other, adhering to ethics, addressing issues that arise in working together, valuing each other, and having patience.

Then, compare these HR department core values to the core values of the organization. Are they aligned? They do not have to be identical to those of the organization, but should reflect similar ideals. Finally, use the *Fist-to-Five* consensus-building model to make a group decision. At the end of the meeting, ask a volunteer to record the core values. Table 4.1 is an example of the core values one HR department developed utilizing the process in this example.

Your department core values should be visible in multiple ways, e.g., placed on the department website, on the staff meeting agenda template, and in a prominent place in the department office. This symbolizes

Table 4.1 Example of HR department core values

Core Value	Definition
Integrity	• be accountable, trustworthy, honest, ethical and patient
	• respect each other
	• challenge each other
	• address issues when they arise
	• treat others as we want to be treated
	• value others
Open Communication	• keep an open mind to change
	• continue to learn
	• use active listening/questioning techniques, e.g., how?, why?
	• be patient
Relationship Building	• take time/effort to build relationships with each other
	• appreciate the effort of others (internal and external to HR)
	• respect diversity
	• utilize teamwork in HR collaborative efforts
	• gain a reputation for extraordinary service
	• be committed to the department's goals
	• reflect or mirror change
	• know the difference between efficiency and effectiveness
	• be patient
Professionalism in Work Environment	• respect diversity
	• enjoy each other, having fun/using humor in the workplace
	• be compassionate
	• be organized
	• know the difference between efficiency and effectiveness
	• be patient

to the HR staff and those external to the department the importance of these department core values. Keeping them continually visible also contributes toward their becoming a priority for all HR staff.

The last step in this process is to discuss with the HR staff how these core values will be used. For example, they can be part of the performance evaluation process; each staff member, including you, can reinforce them during day-to-day activities in the office, etc. If staff members are not comfortable dealing with a conflictive situation, they can come to you for help.

Example 2: Develop Core Values

This Example is similar to Example 1, except the discussion of high priority core values is facilitated in a staff meeting with all staff members. All other steps are the same.

Although it may be a simple process to develop the core values for the department, this will contribute toward building a strong foundation for successful change. Without a commitment to department values, there is no framework for how individuals will behave toward one another. Without this framework, the department culture will evolve on its own, and will be dysfunctional at times. Cliques will form, where some are "in" and some are "out." Trust becomes a value that applies only within the cliques. No one will trust management.

Case Study 4.1: Utilizing Core Values in the Workplace

As the new head of the HR Department, Demond just finished facilitating the process of developing department core values with the staff. He felt good about this, as he learned that for years, the department operated in a "silo mentality," with people working separately and not helping each other. Those responsible for payroll did not talk with those who managed recruitments; those responsible for benefits did not know what work the managers did and did not care. No one backed up others when the workload was heavy. All expected the receptionist to consider their project to be the most urgent and to help to complete it. During the process of developing core values, the HR staff members were very participative; they were excited about working together and being asked for their opinions. They took this project very seriously.

About one month later, a staff member came into Demond's office, closed the door, and told him that someone, who had been in the office for more than 20 years, just treated the receptionist very disrespectfully, and she was trying to keep back her tears. Demond thanked the staff member, walked out into the office, and asked the receptionist to come into his office for a few minutes. He then asked her if someone had treated her disrespectfully. Immediately, she began crying and explained the situation. She was young, a temporary employee, and did not want Demond to do anything about this situation. She was afraid the staff person involved would hold this against her, and did not want to rock the boat.

Demond explained that it was important to address this situation, because treating each other with respect comprised their department core values of integrity and building relationships. He told her he would talk with the other staff member to get perspective on the situation, and then ask her to come into that person's office so both of them, in his presence, could listen to each other and provide closure.

Demond walked into the office of the second staff member, closed the door, and said there was a situation that he needed to discuss. He indicated that the reception-

ist was very upset about a situation that had occurred between them, and that he wanted to hear both perspectives. After listening, Demond gave a brief synopsis of the receptionist's perspective. He talked about the department core values of integrity and building relationships; how important treating others with respect was integral to them. The second staff member indicated remorse for any confusion caused, and felt there had been miscommunication between them.

Demond brought the receptionist into the second staff member's office, and asked each to share his/her perspective with the other listening. He asked questions of both, and without prompting, the staff member apologized to the receptionist for the situation. The receptionist also apologized, and they ended up laughing over several parts of the miscommunication. They agreed to work harder on the value of open communication, to listen more carefully to each other, and to develop trust between them. Demond shook hands with each, and thanked them for their openness to learning from this experience.

Case Study Questions:

1. What worked well with how Demond dealt with this situation?
2. What could Demond have done to improve how he dealt with this situation?
3. In looking back on the process of how the HR core values were developed, could Demond have done anything differently to avoid this situation?
4. In some respects, the incident could be thought of as an "initiation ritual," a clash between a new employee and an established veteran, and a long-standing component of the department culture. In fact, after this situation occurred, others told Demond of similar incidents in the past by this person and others that had contributed toward an environment of distrust. Discuss how Demond dealt with this situation could be considered a "symbol" to the HR staff, and what that means for the future. Knowing this, what are Demond's next steps?

To review discussion of recommendations for Case Study 4.1 go to **www.HR-higher-ed.com**

Forces of Change—New HR Paradigm

The information in chapters 1-2 of this book serves as a reference to understand the need for change, and to recognize drivers of the HR paradigm shift in the external and internal environments.

> **ASSIGNMENT** *After all HR staff review chapters 1-2 individually, discuss them together in a staff meeting. Perhaps your university has additional internal or external factors driving the need for change. It is important these are discussed before moving further.*

Transactional Work versus Transformative Work

Transactional work in a HR department encompasses administrative functions that are legally required or are necessary to the operations of the university, e.g., payroll, fringe benefits, leave accounting, recruitments, complaints, grievances, FMLA, ADA accommodations, etc. Although improvements can be made to these processes that create increased effectiveness and efficiency for HR staff and employees, they are considered transactional functions. Examples of these follow:

- using document imaging to reduce paper and increase the efficiency at which the transactional functions are completed
- placing W-2, earnings and other statements in a portal for employees to access instead of sending paper copies each payroll period
- purchasing an electronic program for recruitments that eliminates paper and improves access for the search committee
- emailing contracts and required employee documents to new employees instead of sending hard copies through the mail

It is important to note that technology enables employees to manage much of their own administrative work as part of self-service. Although creating efficiencies for transactional work does create a great deal of value for the HR department, these still are considered transactional work due to their focus being on what the department does.

As noted in Table 4.2, transactional work is primarily reactive, in that the HR department must react to a specific event, e.g., a new employee was hired, a new recruitment has been announced, a grievance has been brought forward, an employee has questions on rights under FMLA, etc. In addition, the HR staff work with employees to accomplish the purposes of the events.

Table 4.2 Transactional versus transformative work

FROM: HR Transactional Work	TO: HR Transformative/Strategic Work
Creates efficiency through standardization automation and consolidation	Aligns vision, mission and goals of HR with strategy of the organization
Mostly reactive	Proactive
Focus is on what we do	Focus is on what we "deliver"
Work with employees	Create relationships/collaborate
Implement best HR practices	Deliver value-added HR practices
Build HR functions for efficiency	Build HR functions for stakeholder value

Transformative work in an HR department consists of aligning goals of the HR department with the strategic goals of the organization. As indicated in Table 4.2, the work is primarily proactive—based on creating relationships and collaboration, and focused on the work or value "delivered" to stakeholders. To help understand the differences between transformative and transactional work, see the following two examples.

Example 1: Transactional versus Transformative Work

Within transactional work, it is common that an HR staff member is approached to assist in hiring a temporary employee. In many cases, the supervisor has a person in mind, and after receiving the position description, the HR staff member completes the necessary hiring, payroll and fringe benefit work. If the supervisor does not have a person in mind, perhaps the HR staff member shares a pool of potential employees, with resumes, with the supervisor. If, after several weeks, the supervisor is not pleased with the person's work, the supervisor can tell the HR staff member the person was fired, and the termination paperwork is completed.

Within transformative work, the HR department has developed a recruitment brand in collaboration with supervisors, aligned with the goals of the university. Because the recruitment brand includes temporary employees, the HR staff member, in partnership with the supervisor, works through the process as specified in the brand. In this case, HR has a strong pool of potential employees, and with the supervisor, develops an evaluation tool and interviewing process to choose the best employee for the position. Because the HR staff member has developed a partnership with the university's technology-training department, that department participates in evaluating the technology and self-management skills of applicants.

After an employee is hired, the IT department develops individualized training to strengthen needed

> Transformative work in an HR department … is primarily proactive—based on creating relationships and collaboration, and focused on the work or value "delivered" to stakeholders.

technology skills of the employee. Because of the relationship developed with the supervisor, when there are issues with the new employee, the supervisor approaches HR for advice. An employee is rarely terminated because of weak skills or poor performance. Often the temporary employee is hired to fill the permanent position, or a different permanent position, in the organization.

Example 2: Transactional versus Transformative Work

A common complaint by supervisors to HR is that when performance issues arise with a permanent employee, there is not much HR can do to help. For example, a permanent employee who has been in the position for one year is causing problems within the department. He/she does not work well with those in other departments, and often disrupts the work place while in conflict with other employees. In a discussion with the supervisor, HR determines that the employee is accomplishing his/her work responsibilities, but is very conflictive and disruptive. In addition, he/she is a union employee and no longer on probation. The supervisor shares that these actions were the same during the probationary period, but because the job was getting done, did not address the situation. At this point, the supervisor does not want to take the time to document the situation and work with the employee to change his/her behaviors. The supervisor does not feel it will help.

Within a transformative HR department, it is very likely that the recruitment brand includes core competencies, which indicate "how" an employee accomplishes his/her major responsibilities, and this supervisor was part of the process in developing the employee core competencies. Because these core competencies serve as a continuing thread throughout the entire employment process, beginning with the recruitment and continuing with evaluating candidates, checking references, interviewing, hiring, evaluating, promoting, developing, and terminating an employee, they can serve as an integral component to deal proactively and timely with this situation. In many cases, an employee would not have been hired, as the supervisor is trained to utilize the core competencies during each phase of the hiring process. The process for developing core competencies is discussed in detail in chapter 5.

In summary, both transactional and transformative work is being done in HR; employees must value both. It is important that we are able to distinguish between these types of work and be able to perform transactional work efficiently. If not, our department is not credible when we transition into transformative work. We will talk more about credibility when discussing the various roles of HR staff members.

Potential Outcomes (or Capabilities) for an Organization When The HR Function Transforms Strategically

Chapter 2 details what the university will look like—in both operational and broad perspectives—with the HR function at the "strategic level" of the organization. In summary, HR at the strategic level signifies that the department's focus aligns with the strategy of the institution in day-to-day activities and long-term goals. HR staff members develop measureable deliverables that provide value to stakeholders and include defining, creating or enhancing the following capabilities of the institution:

1. ability to attract, motivate and retain competent and engaged employees
2. ability to generate quick change within the organization
3. positive image of the organization by stakeholders
4. accountability
5. collaboration between departments and units
6. innovation that fosters growth within the organization
7. generation of leaders throughout the organization
8. integration of HR functions
9. ability to anticipate and manage risk

> **ASSIGNMENT** *During a special meeting of the HR staff, discuss each of these outcomes in relation to your specific HR function and institution of higher education. Which of the capabilities are current strengths? Which are weaknesses?*

Creating Value

The value of a particular service is defined by the receivers of HR work—employees, supervisors, applicants for positions and administrators. The HR function is successful if and when its stakeholders perceive that it produces "value." Delivering what matters most to stakeholders focuses on the outcomes of HR rather than on the activities of HR.

Components that create value include the following:

1. The HR function recognizes external forces that impact the organization, modifies HR practices and aligns resources.
2. The HR function provides value to internal and external stakeholders.
3. The HR function develops, implements and manages processes and practices that add value.
4. The HR function aligns strategically with that of the organization.
5. The HR function develops HR staff members to be successful in new roles.

Creating value is probably an entirely new topic for many HR staff members. A book that can serve as a resource is *The HR Value Proposition* by Dave Ulrich and Wayne Brockbank (2005). One model that works very well to transition people to the idea of "value creation" is for all HR staff to read the applicable chapters, and then as the HR leader, meet with them individually each month for an hour to discuss a chapter and apply it to current department culture. Each month during a staff or special meeting, a chapter topic comprises an agenda item. It may take several months to work through the applicable chapters, but this process generates fantastic discussion and serves as a foundation for future change.

Creating stakeholder value for the HR function is addressed more thoroughly in chapter 7 and throughout this book.

Roles for HR Staff in the New Paradigm

In the past, the primary role of the HR function was viewed as the systematizing and policing of policies, rules and procedures, and the coordination of paperwork flow required by these policies. Therefore, the HR professional could be viewed as providing a roadblock by much of the rest of the university. Although a need for adherence to federal and state laws will continue to be part of the transactional nature of HR work, much of the HR role needs to transform to parallel the needs of the changing university—becoming more adaptable, resilient, quick to change direction, and customer-centered.

In the new HR transformational paradigm, the roles of HR professionals in higher education consist of the five indicated in the outside ring of Figure 4.3. It is very possible that one staff member will have responsibility for more than one of these roles. In addition, an individual may move from one role to another multiple times during a single day, and serve in the Leader role along with one of the other five roles simultaneously.

Figure 4.3 Roles of HR staff members in the new paradigm

Consider a university employee who just learns that she was not given the opportunity to purchase life insurance for her husband when they married several years ago. She contacts an HR benefits person to complain about the situation. The HR benefits person has two options at this point.

The first option is to state the policy to the employee, which includes a 30-day open period to add benefits after a marriage. Because it is now several years past that period she apologizes that nothing can be done. In this option, the HR staff member serves in the role of an Human Resources Specialist, one of the HR roles identified in Figure 4.3. This role is essentially transactional, with the HR staff member being reactive, relaying policy and focusing on work traditionally done in the department.

The second option includes researching the employee's benefit file to obtain any information that she was offered benefits when she married. Finding none, the HR benefits person offers the employee the opportunity to add life insurance for her husband. Choosing this option places the HR benefits staff member in multiple roles: (1) a Human Resource Specialist; (2) an Employee Advocate; and (3) a Leader. Although this option continues to be transactional, it is accomplished in a way that builds tremendous value for the employee toward the HR function. This example portrays the multiple roles that each HR staff member can play on a daily basis.

A second example includes an HR staff member serving in the role of a Human Resources Partner, who after receiving hiring paperwork from the academic department for a new faculty member, completes the contract and other employment paperwork and emails them to the faculty member for signatures. This is transactional work as it is reactive, focuses on what HR does, and uses policies and procedures designed for efficiency and effectiveness.

However, in this case, the HR staff person serves as a Human Resources Partner to the College of Liberal Studies. In meeting with the dean's administrative assistant, the HR staff person learns that the college has no salary structure in place for hiring ad hoc instructional staff. He/she suggests working with the administrative assistant to research other "best practices," and together to develop the best salary structure for the college as an outcome. This situation includes transformative work because it is proactive, focuses on what is "delivered," is valued by the constituent, and involves creating relationships and collaborating. The HR staff person serves as a HR Partner and a Leader.

In whatever role each HR professional has at a given time, the Leader role can be parallel and come into play. In other words, how each HR staff member serves in a role in the outer ring of Figure 4.3 indicates whether he or she is also a Leader in that situation.

Table 4.3 details each of the roles in which an HR staff member participates, with the expected outcomes and activities of each role.

ASSIGNMENT *Discuss these roles with the HR staff as part of a staff meeting. Ask for additional examples of HR staff serving in multiple roles.*

Table 4.3 Description of HR roles in the new paradigm

Role	Outcome of Activities	Activities
Strategic Partner • transformative work	Align HR and organizational strategy	• culture and change management • partner with administrators, supervisors, faculty and staff to develop and implement an HR strategic plan that is aligned and integrated with the organization's strategic plan
Organizational Design Specialist • transformative work	Create a renewed and stronger organization	• identify, frame and solve problems • build relationships of trust • assist in restructuring departments/units • implement new programs, projects, procedures • improve core processes
Human Resources Partner • combination of transformative and transactional work	Design and deliver efficient and effective HR processes	• staffing/competencies • training/development/talent management • appraising/evaluating • rewards/recognition • merit • promoting • career progression, development plans
Human Resources Specialist • transactional work	Ensure legal obligations are met	• payroll • benefits • salary equity • contracts • renewal and tenure • labor relations and grievances • alternative methods for conflict resolution • AA/EEO • retirements • complaints • organization, system and state policies • other legal issues
Employee Advocate • transactional work	Increase employee commitment and engagement	• assist employees to develop competence, generate commitment, and discover contribution • day-to-day operational problems, concerns and needs of employees • systematic discussion of employee concerns; listen to employees, assimilate and share different points of view • balance demands made of employees with the resources provided to them by the organization • work/life balance programs, wellness programs, EAP
Leader • transformative work	All stakeholders recognize HR as adding value to the organization	• set clear goals; set a vision • communicate inside and out • engage others • define results in terms of value-added for stakeholders • act with integrity, authenticity; be present • ensure HR professional development • shape the programs that implement administrators' agenda • assist in creating a consistent organizational culture and identity

Case Study 4.2: Overcoming Fear of the New Paradigm

Henry has been the HR director at his institution for two years. During these two years, he has worked hard to develop relationships with key administrators on campus, including vice presidents, deans, directors and other administrators. These administrators see Henry as a valuable resource. They contact Henry frequently and request to meet with him to discuss HR goals for their division, college or unit. These include reorganization plans, staffing plans and compensation goals. Having these relationships and being utilized as a strategic partner has made Henry, and thus HR, a valued commodity. Although Henry really enjoys this work, it leaves him fatigued and looking for an outlet, someone on his staff, who can assume some of this work.

Julie, an HR manager in Henry's office, has been with the office for nine years. During that time, she has become very skilled at recruiting federal Fair Labor Standards Act (FLSA) non-exempt support staff, the major component of her job. In fact, Julie has become so adept at this, completing recruitments has become routine and boring.

Two months ago, Henry held a performance review meeting with Julie. Henry indicated he is pleased with Julie's performance, especially her ability to complete recruitments. Near the end of the review meeting, Henry asked Julie if she is happy in her job. She responded, "Honestly, no, I'm bored. I need more challenge. I know recruiting qualified people to the university is important, but I have been doing it for so long, I feel like I could complete the process blindfolded. I need a chance to find another way to make a contribution and to be seen as more than a good recruiter. I would love to spend more time working with upper level administrators and not just first-line supervisors." Henry assured Julie that he would look for such opportunities to see her grow and make a stronger contribution to the institution.

Yesterday, the dean of a college at Henry's institution called him and requested to meet to discuss potentially reorganizing the support staff in her college. The college has five support staff providing support to the dean, faculty, adjuncts and administrative staff. The dean believes they may be able to utilize the support staff in a better fashion to provide greater efficiency and effectiveness. From the HR side, the discussion with the dean will require knowledge of the classification system for support staff, a basic knowledge of the organizational structure of the college, great listening skills and the ability to think creatively.

Shortly after talking to the dean, Henry walked into Julie's office and brought up their conversation during the performance review meeting, reminding Julie of her desire to seek more challenge and contribute in new ways. Henry discussed with Julie his conversation with the dean. He talked about how this would enable the dean to see Julie as more than just someone who could complete recruitments, and as someone who could strategically plan with them. This would be the first step toward establishing

Julie as being able to think strategically and being viewed as a partner who could add value beyond transactional work

Julie responded, "I do not know anything about organizational structure. I know about recruitments. What if she starts asking me questions I cannot answer? What if the conversation veers into administrative staff, which I know little about? What if I do not have answers for her, and I am unable to help her? How will that make me look?"

Case Study Questions:

1. *What is the major reason Julie has expressed fear of the situation?*
2. *How could Henry have dealt differently with the performance review meeting with Julie to begin preparing her for the current situation?*
3. *What skills has Julie used in working with first-line supervisors that can be transitioned to the new HR paradigm of transformative work?*
4. *How should Henry deal with Julie's fear of the situation?*
5. *How can Henry tie "transactional vs. transformational" work into the conversation?*

To review discussion of recommendations for Case Study 4.2 go to **www.HR-higher-ed.com**

Baseline Chart of HR Task-Responsibilities

In managing priorities and workloads, all staff members need to know what tasks each is responsible for, including back-up or team responsibilities. However, often we enter a new department as the director and find that work functions are within separate silos, with little communication or back-up between them. Following are the weaknesses of this model:

1. Staff do not know or value the work done by those in different functional responsibilities.
2. Weak customer service provided when one individual is gone from the office.
3. Weak customer service provided when work cycles cause one individual to be extremely busy.
4. The opportunity for some individuals to feel the work they do is priority, or more important than the work of others.
5. Poor or little communication among functions within the office.

A method we have used many times is to develop a task-responsibility chart. A sample chart is included in Table 4.4. The first column lists all tasks-responsibilities in the department. The second column indicates the name(s) of the person(s) with primary responsibility for this task. The third column indicates the name(s) of the person(s) with back-up responsibilities for this task.

Table 4.4 Sample HR department task-responsibility chart

Task-Responsibility	Name of Primary or Lead Person(s)	Name of Back-up Person(s) or Team Members
1 Permanent recruitments		
2 Other recruitments		
3 New hires, appointments, contract letters		
4 Payroll and leave accounting		
5 Benefits and retirements		
6 FMLA		
7 Performance evaluation		
8 Employee relations		
9 Promotions and renewals of appointment		
10 Terminations of appointment		
11 Grievances and complaints		

To download the complete template to customize for your department go to **www.HR-higher-ed.com**

This table serves multiple purposes: (1) to develop a baseline for current responsibilities; (2) to determine the percentages of transactional and transformational work done in the HR department; (3) to transition staff to different responsibilities; and (4) to transition to a team environment. In fact, it can be used every six months to a year as part of a department in transition. Most staff, especially those new to a department, benefit from this process, as it develops a structure for them to understand all department staff responsibilities. In addition, it naturally leads to the discussion of "teams" that may follow later.

The table is completed best during a staff meeting, with all staff present and participating. As the facilitator, simply work through each of the tasks-responsibilities, asking who currently is responsible, and who, if anyone, is the back-up. Discuss the definition of "primary or lead" and "back-up" in advance. You may find that "back-up" means responsibility for the task when the primary or lead person is absent from the office.

After the table is completed, facilitate a discussion with the HR staff to identify those responsibilities on the chart that are transformational, and their approximate percentage of the total responsibilities in the HR department. This discussion may assist people to emotionally "see" or "feel" the urgency for change.

In Unit Three, we utilize this baseline chart as part of improving internal HR department processes and structure. For now, after the staff has completed the chart in its current form, ask a volunteer to develop an excel spreadsheet and forward it via email to all staff to use as a reference.

Summary

Culture is the environment that surrounds employees in the workplace, and contributes toward shaping the enjoyment of work, relationships, and how work is done. Culture is used to describe the behaviors among people who work together and interact with others outside the department or organization.

A department's or an organization's core values can be described as principles, standards, or qualities considered worthwhile or desirable as part of working together with others, internal or external to the department. These core values are learned quickly by new employees, are strengthened over time, and solidified by the appropriate reward system and behaviors of management.

Transactional work in a HR department encompasses administrative functions that are legally required or are necessary to the operations of the university, e.g., payroll, fringe benefits, leave accounting, recruitments, complaints, grievances, FMLA, ADA accommodations, etc. Although improvements can be made to these processes that create increased effectiveness and efficiency for HR staff and employees, they are considered transactional functions.

Transformative work in a HR department consists of aligning goals of the HR department with the strategic goals of the organization. As indicated in Table 4.2, the work is primarily proactive—based on creating relationships and collaboration, and focused on the work or value "delivered" to stakeholders.

In the new HR transformational paradigm, the roles of HR professionals in higher education consist of the following: Strategic Partner, Organizational Design Specialist, Human Resources Partner, Human Resources Specialist, Employee Advocate and Leader. These roles are interrelated and often are completed simultaneously.

Major Themes

Leadership of Change

Kotter (1996) indicates the first step in the process of creating major change is to establish a sense of urgency. This confronts the potential issue of complacency among the HR staff by identifying and discussing the external and internal environment realities, crises, potential crises, and major opportunities.

What causes complacency? There are multiple reasons including the following: low overall performance standards; a lack of performance feedback; the absence of a major crisis; too many resources; human nature, with its capacity for denial; and a kill-the-messenger-of-bad-news culture.

In this chapter, we began to set the stage for a sense of urgency around the HR function. Later chapters talk more about complacency and how to establish a sense of urgency.

Appreciative Inquiry

Notice that the three questions to help determine department core values earlier in this chapter are based on appreciative inquiry. We are not asking the HR staff to discuss the problems they have in working together, but to look back at a time when they felt fully alive and motivated in the workplace, and to indicate what that looked like. In essence, the process described serves to bring about shared meaning, innovation and collaboration across multi-functional stakeholder interests—to begin pulling together a group of people into a highly integrated team. This process encourages individuals to cooperate and learn to respect each other through their differences and uniqueness.

Reframing

Using the **structural frame**, in this chapter we began the process of utilizing a clearly defined approach to develop an appropriate relationship between the HR department's structure and its environment. Without a workable structure, people become unsure about what they are supposed to be doing. The result is confusion, frustration and conflict. In moving the department to a new paradigm, we want individuals to be clear about their responsibilities and their contributions. In developing the right structure, that people understand and accept, the department can achieve its goals, and individuals can see their new roles within this structure.

Within the **structural frame**, our communication with the HR staff focuses on organization of the department, how the staff work together, the roles of the staff members, and the goals and policies that shape decisions and activities. Together, we developed a current task-responsibility chart to enable all staff to understand the responsibilities of everyone in the department. We utilize the structural frame to understand the need for change.

We also focused on the **human resources frame**, with its emphasis on understanding people. We empowered staff by having them participate in developing the department core values. They were able to influence their immediate work environment and the factors that impact them. We invested in them by discussing the new HR paradigm and the roles of HR staff within that environment.

We touched slightly on the **political frame** in this chapter. Developing the department core values begins to place all HR staff on equal footing.

Regarding the **symbolic frame**, the development of new core values becomes a symbol of work being done differently. The core values are visible and dramatic, and signal that change is coming. They have the attention of the HR staff.

Evaluation of "Your" HR Department's Chapter 4 Outcome

Outcome Desired: HR staff prepared for transformational change

Change: An urgency is developed among the HR staff for the HR function to move from transactional to transformational

Key Indicators of Success: (check if *"yes"*)

- ☐ HR staff understand the need for change
- ☐ HR staff ask hard questions, taking the time to understand the meaning of the change
- ☐ HR staff "see" and "feel" the need for change
- ☐ HR staff support the need for change on a day-to-day basis
- ☐ HR staff understand transactional versus transformational work
- ☐ HR staff actions reflect HR department core values
- ☐ HR staff discuss potential changes among themselves
- ☐ HR staff develop enhanced long-term perspective

Potential Barriers to Change: (check if *"needs attention"*)

- ☐ One or more HR staff are not included in a "key indicator of success" above
- ☐ One or more HR staff do not see or feel the rationale for change is compelling
- ☐ The rationale for change does not include both internal and external data
- ☐ Overall performance standards in the HR department are not adequate
- ☐ The HR department organizational culture avoids confrontation
- ☐ The organizational or department structure supports narrow functional goals

Develop Transformational Skills of Human Resources Staff

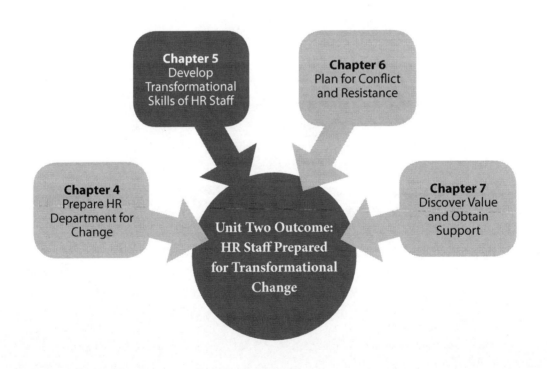

Chapter 5 Develop transformational skills of HR staff

We now must confront what sometimes is difficult, the current skill level of HR staff compared to that required in the new paradigm. This is the topic of chapter 5, where the components of the human resources frame must be utilized. The outcome of chapter 5 is to raise the skill level of the HR staff through developing an integrated competency-based HR system, a process to assess employee skills, and individual development plans.

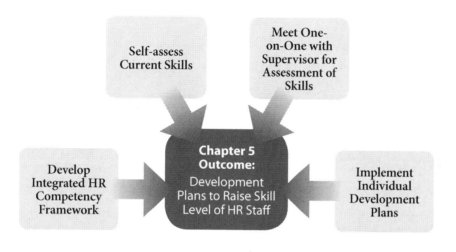

Figure 5.1 Model to raise the skill level of HR staff

Develop An Integrated Competency-Based HR System

The HR Strategic Framework outlined in Figure 5.2 demonstrates that our work in transforming the HR department needs to begin with the core values, because a department's employee core competencies reflect the core values of the department. Therefore, the HR department core values were developed in the previous chapter.

As HR professionals, we cannot count the number of times a supervisor approached us with employee performance issues based on the employees performing their job responsibilities in a way that created conflict or contributed toward a dysfunctional workplace. Most position descriptions contain only the key job responsibilities, along with the skills and experiences necessary to accomplish those responsibilities. Because these employees were accomplishing their job responsibilities according to their position description, how could the supervisor deal with the conflict that

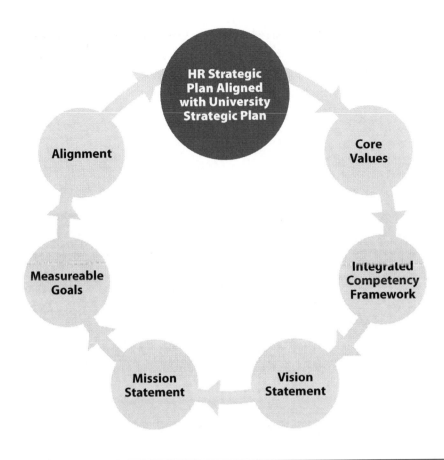

Figure 5.2 HR strategic framework

resulted? An integrated competency-based HR system provides a comprehensive model for resolving this issue and motivating employees to focus strategically.

Employee core competencies, the main component of an integrated competency-based system, are described as clusters of universally expected, observable behaviors, necessary for successful performance in the position and in the organization. They define the skills, knowledge, learning and behaviors critical to achieving the department's vision and mission, and ultimately the strategic plan. An outcome is that the integrated system can distinguish performance in a particular work context.

> Employee core competencies… define the skills, knowledge, learning and behaviors critical to achieving the department's vision and mission, and ultimately the strategic plan.

An example core competency, "Collaboration and Partnership," is described in Exhibit 5.1. First, we define it according to our needs; in this case, the definition is: "Effectively develop relationships and collaborate with all stakeholders; value teamwork and apply a variety of strategies to meet the needs of a diverse constituency." The definition should be short and understandable by all employees.

Exhibit 5.1 Example of an employee core competency

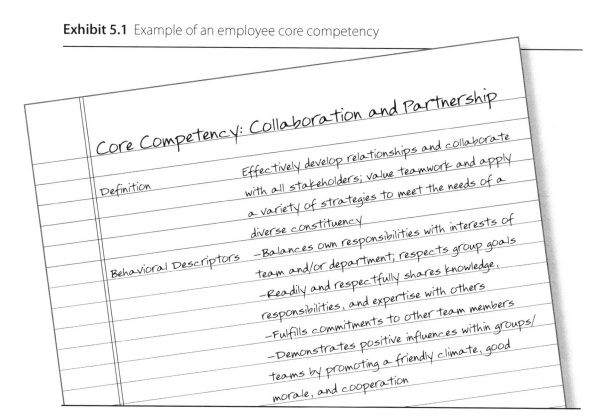

Next, we develop "behavioral descriptors" for each competency. Behavioral descriptors are the smallest units of on-the-job behavior that are measurable, can be observed in the day-to-day work of an individual employee, are objective, and are subject to change or improvement over time. Effective behavioral descriptors describe the behavior so that it is understandable, observable, and at the right level. In the example, the behavioral descriptors are:

- balances own responsibilities with interests of team and/or department; respects group goals
- readily and respectfully shares knowledge, responsibilities, and expertise with others
- fulfills commitments to other team members
- demonstrates positive influences within groups/teams by promoting a friendly climate, good morale, and cooperation.

Note that all these behavioral descriptors can be observed in the day-to-day work of an individual. This is the most important component of a behavioral descriptor. In addition, observe that each begins with an action verb.

Benefits of an Integrated Competency Framework

When a supervisor approaches an HR staff member for help with an employee who is creating conflict within the workplace, having an integrated competency framework serves as a tool to remedy the situation. The core competencies in the position description serve as a source for the supervisor to work with the employee on a plan to improve the core competency in question. A particularly difficult employee may decide to leave or transfer outside the university.

In many cases, having the core competencies in the position description eliminates this type of situation. In other words, utilizing core competencies to evaluate candidate materials, check references, and prepare interview questions causes different outcomes in determining final candidates for the position. A person's lack of, or weakness in, these core competencies quite possibly means he/she is not hired.

The benefits of an integrated competency framework for the HR department as well as the institution—where employee core competencies are integrated with all segments of the total employment process—include improved and integrated processes for the following:

- recruitment and retention of talent
- assessment and selection
- performance communication and support
- leadership development
- succession planning
- career development
- total compensation

Supervisors utilize core competencies throughout the total employment process to:

- develop the position description for a position
- detail qualifications for advertising
- evaluate potential candidates for a position using behavioral-based questions
- discuss with references using behavioral-based questions
- explain "how" major responsibilities of a position should be done
- address how a professional can best add value for a constituent
- discuss the position description with a new employee, and develop a training plan
- evaluate the performance of employees
- explain what "mastery performance" in a position looks like
- discuss ideas for employee development, including developing goals
- carry out processes such as professional development, career planning, performance coaching, evaluation and promotion

When utilizing an integrated competency-based framework, supervisors incur the following benefits:

- improved communication with each staff member regarding expectations, especially the performance evaluation and goal development process
- improved and integrated processes for recruitment and retention of talent
- a process for leadership and career development
- increased retention of talented employees
- increased accountability of staff
- improved skills and knowledge of staff in working with stakeholders

In addition, employees benefit from:

- clarity about knowledge, skill, and ability expectations
- improved supervisor and employee communication
- more consistent behavioral performance feedback (based on articulated competencies)
- improved recognition for skill growth as well as achievement
- clearer paths for career development
- supervisors' increased ability to demystify HR processes

Steps to Develop and Implement an Integrated Competency Framework

Step 1: Discuss competency framework with HR staff
Step 2: Determine HR employee core competencies
Step 3: Define HR core competencies
Step 4: Develop behavioral descriptors
Step 5: Utilize integrative competency framework

Step 1: Discuss competency framework with HR staff. Although the entire process of developing HR employee core competencies will take approximately eight to ten hours, begin with a four-hour meeting of the entire HR staff. You can meet for two-hour sessions, although it is preferable for the first meeting to be four hours so the staff can be immersed in the topic.

> **ASSIGNMENT:** *Prior to discussion of the competency framework, download the list of Potential Core Competencies found on the website. We recommend adding to this list by utilizing Google or another search engine, and entering "employee core competencies" to find numerous other examples of core competencies for the HR staff to consider.*

To download the list of Potential Core Competencies go to
www.HR-higher-ed.com

Step 2: Determine HR employee core competencies. After a discussion of core competencies, how they are used in the total employment process, their benefits, and an example of a core competency with its definition and behavioral descriptors, ask each person to choose four competencies he/she feels are most critical for working in HR. These may be competencies from the samples, or those they determine on their own. Give them about 15 minutes.

Next, ask each person to name one competency that he/she feels is the most important—write this on the flip chart. If a person's highest priority competency has been listed by someone else, ask for their second, and so on. Continue until all competencies are listed.

It is possible that some of the competencies can be combined; facilitate this discussion. When it appears that the group may have reached consensus on the core competencies, use the *Fist-to-Five* consensus-building tool to agree.

If there are more than seven competencies and the group feels they cannot be combined, we recommend a multi-vote process to reduce the number. It becomes increasingly complex to keep track of more than seven core competencies after they are integrated into the HR framework.

Here is how the multi-vote process works:

1. Number the competencies on a flip chart.
2. Ask group members to choose one more than half of the competencies listed, e.g., if there are ten competencies listed, they will choose their top six. Indicate their choices using hash marks on the flip chart.
3. One of the group members tallies the votes.
4. The seven competencies with the highest number of votes become the core competencies for the HR department.

If a two-hour time frame was used to discuss and then develop the HR employee core competencies, that time frame probably has been reached. Divide the group into teams of two, and assign them to meet to develop the first draft of definitions for their team's competencies. Allow each two-person team to choose those competencies they want to define, with each team having the same number of competencies to work with. Schedule a second two-hour meeting.

Step 3: Define HR core competencies. If the first meeting is a four-hour meeting, divide the HR staff into groups of two, dividing the core competencies among them so that all groups have the same number, if possible. The groups may want to choose those competencies they want to work on.

Their first task is to develop simple and clear definitions for each competency. They can utilize a definition from one of the sample competencies, revise or add to it, or develop a new definition. Give them approximately a half hour.

After all groups have finished their competency definitions, ask them to write the definitions on the flip chart. Then facilitate a discussion among the entire HR staff to improve the definitions. Sometimes at this point it becomes apparent that one or more competencies can be combined. Feel free to do that if the group agrees, using the *Fist-to-Five* consensus-building tool.

Step 4: Develop behavioral descriptors. The next step is for the teams to begin the process of developing the behavioral descriptors. Undoubtedly, this step will be more difficult than the others. We recommend that the first meeting is four hours, so this process can be initiated while the entire group is together.

It is important to emphasize that effective behavioral descriptors ***must*** be:

- understandable by every staff member
- objective
- measureable
- observable as people go about their day-to-day work

In addition, use action verbs to begin each behavioral indicator; eliminate "is able to," "understands." Refer to Exhibits 5.1 and 5.2 for examples of effective behavioral descriptors.

Exhibit 5.2 Example of a "customer orientation" core competency

Core Competency: Customer Orientation

Definition — Emphatically seek understanding of what stakeholders require and expect

Behavioral Descriptors
— Use available resources, policies and opportunities in their best interest without compromising institutional values
— Give customers full attention, ask appropriate clarifying questions when necessary, and understand and respond quickly to needs of internal and external customers
— Address customers' concerns with courtesy and respect even when upset; demonstrate sincere ... to build a "win–win" relationship

To review further examples of core competencies with definitions and behavioral descriptors go to **www.HR-higher-ed.com**

Case Study 5.1: Developing Core Competencies, Definitions, Behavioral Descriptors:

Discuss the sample HR core competencies found in Case Study 5.1 on the website. These core competencies, with their definitions and behavioral descriptors, comprise the first draft outcome of an actual HR staff going through this process. They can be used to determine if the HR staff agree first, if the definitions are understandable, and second, if the behavioral descriptors are understandable, objective, measureable and observable. Case Study 5.1 can provide a good learning outcome before the HR staff write behavioral descriptors for their own core competencies.

To download Case Study 5.1 draft core competencies to review
plus recommended changes go to **www.HR-higher-ed.com**

Case Study Questions:

1. Can any core competencies be combined? If so, which ones, and why?
2. Can any of the core competency definitions be improved? If so, which ones, and how can they be improved?
3. Are any behavioral descriptors NOT understandable, measureable and observable as HR staff accomplish their daily responsibilities? If so, which ones, and how can they be improved?

After completion of the case study, allow a half hour for the teams to begin developing the behavioral descriptors for their competencies. Then have them write what they have developed on the flip chart under each competency and its definition. Involve the entire HR staff in discussing whether the behavioral descriptors are understandable, objective, measureable and observable. Remember to use action verbs to begin each behavioral indicator; eliminate "is able to," "understands."

At the end of the meeting, charge the teams with meeting before the next session to finish writing the behavioral descriptors for their core competencies. Ask them to bring the behavioral descriptors to the next session to obtain feedback from the rest of the HR staff.

Now is the time to discuss and improve the behavioral descriptors until you feel they are complete. Use the *Fist-to-Five* consensus-building tool to agree. Finally, ask a volunteer to write the core competencies, their descriptions and behavioral descriptors, and email them to everyone in the department.

Step 5: **Utilize integrative competency framework.** Now that the HR core competencies have been developed, how are they utilized within the HR department?

First, add them to the performance evaluation form that is used for the HR staff. Refer to the website to download several examples of performance evaluation forms. We recommend the HR staff be involved in revising the performance evaluation form to include the core competencies.

> *To download Performance Evaluation Forms with core competencies go to* **www.HR-higher-ed.com**

Second, include the core competencies in updated position descriptions for all HR staff. The next recruitment will include utilizing these core competencies in assessing and selecting the best candidate for the position, including questioning references. A great book for developing behavior-based questions for candidate interviews and reference checks is *High-Impact Interview Questions: 701 Behavior-Based Questions*, by Victoria A. Hoevemeyer, 2006. In fact, many HR departments purchase this book for supervisors to use when interviewing candidates.

Third, use the core competencies when working with individual HR staff members to develop goals for growth and development during the next evaluation period. For example, if an HR staff member is weak in an HR department core competency of "Collaboration and Partnering," the supervisor will work with this person to develop a goal to improve this competency.

At this point, referring to the HR department's strategic framework outlined in Figure 5.2, the core values and an integrated HR competency-based system have been developed. Eventually, the process of core competencies should be taken to the next level. In many cases, it is beneficial to develop core competencies in a step-by-step approach. Because the concept will be new to many HR staff who have been in the HR department for a long time, this approach offers a better transition to the new approach and indicates your willingness to understand that change can be difficult.

> *To download the Phase-in Process for Implementing HR core competencies go to* **www.HR-higher-ed.com**

Case Study 5.2: Developing HR Department Core Competencies

James' most recent career move involved accepting an HR director position with a university that had not changed in many years. His supervisor made it clear when James was hired that he wanted systemic change within the HR department. The president just finished the first phase of taking the university through discussions of strategic direction, with a new model now in place.

Because James has had several career moves in the last 20 years, he knew he should spend the first few months getting to know the staff and the culture in the HR department. In addition, he planned to spend this time developing relationships with key administrators and others within the organization, and to understand the history of the organization and the current changes.

James quickly realized there were silos within the HR department, developed over many years. Some people felt their responsibilities were more important than those of others, and often treated others with disrespect—even in front of other HR staff or a customer. Although individuals told James they were "back-up" to another person's responsibilities and he read this in their position descriptions, when staff were gone from the office, he saw their desks piled up with work. As he developed relationships with others outside the department, James heard complaints about work not getting done in a timely manner.

James recently attended a conference where another university presented the topic of employee core competencies, their benefits, value, and process for implementation. He retrieved materials from that presentation and prepared a plan of action. This project was the first change effort in his position, and he wanted it to be succeed. At the next HR staff meeting, James presented the topic of a core competency framework and described its components and benefits. He stated that at a special meeting next week, he planned to facilitate the process to develop core competencies for the department.

James was surprised at the reaction of the staff. Several employees were familiar with the topic, having previously been in a workplace that utilized core competencies. They were excited and motivated by the topic. On the other hand, James could see non-verbal cues from other employees that either they did not understand the benefits of a core competency framework, or did not like the idea. In fact, he heard one whisper to another, "Remember that the old HR director tried this once?", and then rolled his eyes. Others looked down at the meeting agenda, appearing to be in deep thought.

The day of the special meeting arrived, and James noted that several staff had either taken vacation or were ill. He told himself, "I should have checked the vacation calendar and announced that no one was approved for vacation today."

The meeting was a disaster. At first, newer employees shared their positive experiences with core competencies. Then a veteran employee followed with a smart remark,

"We tried this before, but in this organization that kind of 'fruh-fruh' stuff just does not work." Someone laughed out loud when James spoke about a particular benefit of the framework. Soon James was the only person talking. He decided that he needed to pull back and make a fresh start. So he said, *"It is too bad that we chose to have this meeting on a day when everyone couldn't participate. We will adjourn, and I'll let you know our next step."*

James was extremely stressed after this meeting. There were critical systemic issues in the department. He knew his boss wanted change, and thought he knew how to begin the process. Although he was embarrassed with the outcome of the meeting, his major emotion was anger with those who placed barriers in the way of positive change.

Case Study Questions:

1. *What worked well about how James dealt with this situation?*
3. *What could James have done to improve how he dealt with this situation?*
4. *What could James have done differently to avoid this situation?*
5. *What should be his next steps?*

HR Staff Self-Assess Current Skills

The first step toward improving the skill level of the HR staff is to have them self-assess their current skills using a tool similar to that in Exhibit 5.3. This tool includes criteria from discussions of the changing HR paradigm, new HR staff roles, and the new employee core competencies. In addition, the questions target their knowledge of the organization, knowledge of HR practices, management of change/processes, personal credibility/engagement, and employee core competencies. For these categories, they indicate to what extent they need to improve.

If a person feels his/her knowledge of the organization is strong, he/she may check box number 1, indicating a low need for improvement. On the other hand, if a person is new to the organization, he/she may check box number 4 or 5, indicating a weakness in this skill and a need to improve.

> The first step toward improving the skill level of the HR staff is to have them self-assess their current skills…

The "Skill Category" section of the tool is followed with open-ended discussion questions. This tool is provided as a template on the website so you can make changes by inserting your employee core competencies, and other changes to customize the tool.

In presenting this tool and process to the HR staff, give them a week to complete the self-evaluation before the individual meetings. Ask each person to schedule two 90 minute meetings with you, one week apart. You may not need that much time, but it is better always to finish the discussion sooner than to run out of time. The purpose of this process is threefold:

1. Identify skills each individual needs to improve, resulting in a future individual development plan.
2. Begin a discussion around the topic of "adding value" to stakeholders.
3. Identify the work each person finds enjoyable, motivating and energizing. This information will be helpful in any plan to realign responsibilities within the HR department.

Exhibit 5.3 HR staff self-evaluation tool

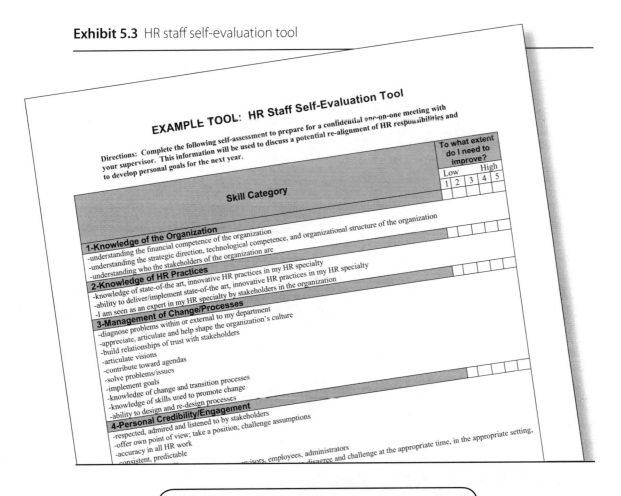

EXAMPLE TOOL: HR Staff Self-Evaluation Tool

Directions: Complete the following self-assessment to prepare for a confidential one-on-one meeting with your supervisor. This information will be used to discuss a potential re-alignment of HR responsibilities and to develop personal goals for the next year.

Skill Category	To what extent do I need to improve? Low 1 2 3 4 5 High
1-Knowledge of the Organization -understanding the financial competence of the organization -understanding the strategic direction, technological competence, and organizational structure of the organization -understanding who the stakeholders of the organization are	
2-Knowledge of HR Practices -knowledge of state-of-the art, innovative HR practices in my HR specialty -ability to deliver/implement state-of-the art, innovative HR practices in my HR specialty -I am seen as an expert in my HR specialty by stakeholders in the organization	
3-Management of Change/Processes -diagnose problems within or external to my department -appreciate, articulate and help shape the organization's culture -build relationships of trust with stakeholders -articulate visions -contribute toward agendas -solve problems/issues -implement goals -knowledge of change and transition processes -knowledge of skills used to promote change -ability to design and re-design processes	
4-Personal Credibility/Engagement -respected, admired and listened to by stakeholders -offer own point of view; take a position; challenge assumptions -accuracy in all HR work consistent, predictable	

...visors, employees, administrators ...disagree and challenge at the appropriate time, in the appropriate setting,

To download a template of this Staff Self-Evaluation Tool to customize go to **www.HR-higher-ed.com**

HR Staff Meet One-On-One with Supervisor for Discussion of Skills

Prior to the first meeting with each staff member, your work is to complete a Self-Evaluation of Skills tool for them. As you begin the meeting, ask each person if he/she has questions or concerns about the process. Each person is integral to the department, and does not need to worry about losing his/her job or being given responsibilities he/she does not like. The goal is to have each person leave the meeting motivated and excited about the process.

Ask them to discuss their answers to each section, beginning with the skill category and ending with the open-ended questions. Add your perspective on each; ask additional probing questions, ask for examples, or dwell more on one question if needed. Your goal is to keep them talking about themselves, their strengths and weaknesses, and the type of work they enjoy.

The next step is to prioritize those skills needing improvement and determine the top three skills to include on the Individual Development Plan. If a fourth skill will not take much effort and time to develop, it should be the employee's choice whether to include it. Keep in mind that it is very important to "get some early wins" to keep people motivated.

Give them a copy of the Individual Development Plan template as shown in Exhibit 5.4. Discuss each section of the form and ask them to complete as much as they can, prior to your second meeting, in the sections on skills and core competencies that need to be developed. This will give them a framework for participating fully in the discussion. A goal to include in the department goal section of the Individual Development Plan can be, "Align the HR staff's skills and knowledge with those needed in the new HR paradigm."

End the meeting by thanking them for taking this process seriously, and being honest about their strengths, weaknesses and interest in HR work. Tell them you look forward to meeting again in a week to discuss the development plan. Ask them again if they have any further questions or concerns. Retain a copy of their self-assessment of skills document.

To prepare for the second meeting with each HR staff to complete the Individual Development Plan, review the skills to be improved that were prioritized in the last meeting.

STEPS TO IMPLEMENT HR STAFF DEVELOPMENT PLANS

> **Step 1:** **Determine primary learning style and "type" of skills to be developed**
> **Step 2:** **Develop an action plan for each skill**
> **Step 3:** **Determine "indicators of success" and resources/support needed**
> **Step 4:** **Determine completion dates**
> **Step 5:** **Discuss your expectations**

Step 1: **Determine primary learning style and "type" of skills to be developed.** Each individual has a primary learning style, which is one of the following:

- visual: learn by seeing and doing
- auditory : learn by hearing and listening
- kinesthetic: learn by touching and doing

In determining how to develop each skill included in the action plan, it is preferable to choose methods that match the person's preferred learning style, e.g., kinesthetic learners should use a more hands on approach so they can learn by doing things.

For each skill to be developed, determine its "type":

- knowledge gap: requires some form of education or training, e.g., read, discuss and presenting summaries of books, classroom training, take a short course, e-learning, formal education, work-shops or conferences
- skill or experience gap: requires some form of exposure to situations, e.g., work experience, on-the-job learning, involvement in job design changes, represent the department on a team or commit-tee, take on a challenging task or special project, work in a cross-functional team, work simulations, job rotation, cross training
- leadership gap: requires some form of real experience to exercise and demonstrate leadership, e.g., read and self-reflection, personal development, coach, mentor, observe someone having these skills

Exhibit 5.4 Individual development plan template

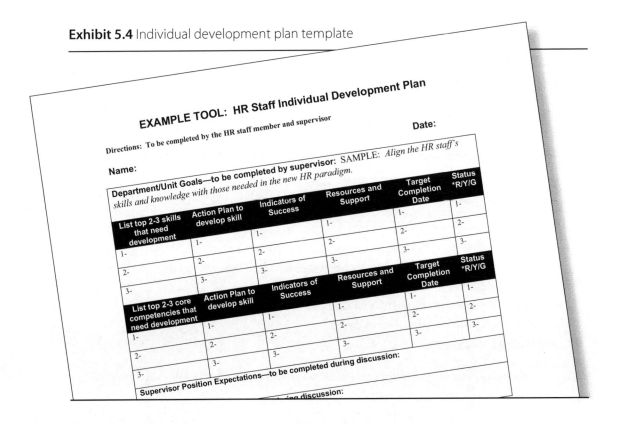

To download a template of this Individual Development Plan to customize go to **www.HR-higher-ed.com**

Step 2: Develop an action plan for each skill. When preparing an action plan to develop each skill, note from Table 5.1 that future chapters of this book offer opportunities for further training and experiences for the HR staff to develop needed skills. Include any of these situations in the action plan. It is important to ask, "What activities would help you develop this skill?"

Table 5.1 Experiential opportunities for HR staff to develop skills

Chapter or Unit	Topic	Potential Experiences to Develop Skills
Chapter 6	Address conflict	Address and resolve situations that involve not adhering to department core values or competencies
Chapter 7	Discover stakeholder value	Participate in conversations with campus stakeholders to determine what they value about the HR function
Chapter 8	Change and transition processes	Present book summary to other HR staff; participate in preparing transition plan; improve skills in managing change and transition processes; improve credibility and core competencies
Chapter 9	Determine HR department vision and mission statements	Serve as a team leader, facilitator, recorder; improve knowledge of the organization; improve core competencies
Chapter 10	Develop HR department recruitment brand	Serve as a team leader, facilitator, recorder; improve knowledge of the organization; improve core competencies
Unit Three	Develop teams within the HR department	Serve as team leader, facilitator, recorder; develop relationships among team members; coordinate projects; improve engagement; improve core competencies
Units Three & Four	Improve internal and external HR processes	Serve as a team leader, facilitator, recorder; improve innovation and creative skills; develop relationships among team members; coordinate projects; give presentations to groups; improve knowledge of HR practices; improve credibility and core competencies
Unit Five	Develop HR strategic plan	Serve as a team leader, facilitator, recorder; accumulate data; improve innovation and creative skills; develop relationships among team members, coordinate projects; give presentations to groups; improve credibility and core competencies

Step 3: Determine "indicators of success" and resources/support needed. Determine the "Indicators of Success"—how you and the HR staff member will know the particular skill has been developed. Determine resources needed by the HR staff member to develop the skill, and any support needed from you or others. It is important to ask, "In what ways can I help and support you to develop your skills?" Use these activities outlined in step 2 above to begin your conversation.

Step 4: Determine completion dates. Determine a completion date for developing each skill, keeping in mind that it is important to "get some early wins" to generate the employee's motivation. The "Status" column on the form is used to keep track of project completion. It is very possible that steps to achieve a goal will not begin immediately.

Step 5: Discuss your expectations. Discuss your expectations with staff members for their position over the next year. An expectation that works well is, "Identify one current responsibility of your position, and develop a plan to transform how it is accomplished in a more transformative manner." You can serve as a coach to work through the steps of developing and implementing this plan as they develop their other skills. Case Study 5.3 gives an example of this process.

To support the completion of the Individual Development Plan, we recommend you meet with each person once per month to monitor progress, and determine necessary changes. This will provide timely behavioral feedback on performance and the opportunity to discuss ways to improve and develop further.

Create confidence by telling staff you are always available to talk with them. Give them the encouragement and support to feel confident in their ability to be successful. When problems arise, help them to focus on what went right and what can be learned from what went wrong. Sometimes people must take smaller steps to ensure a successful outcome.

Case Study 5.3: Example of an Individual Development Plan

Janice is an HR assistant in the HR department at National College, and within the last six months has taken on the responsibility of hiring limited term employees (LTEs) for the university. There are approximately 150 LTEs, and Janice has a small pool of people interested in future open positions. At this point, Janice completed the skills self-assessment tool and is meeting with her supervisor to discuss an individual development plan.

Step 1: Determine primary learning style and "type" of skills to be developed. *Janice prefers to learn by doing, and feels that her weakness in the HR department core competency of "service orientation" reflects an experience gap that requires her to meet with stakeholders to determine what they value about her responsibilities.*

Step 2: Develop an action plan for each skill. *With her supervisor, Janice developed the following action plan goal to improve this core competency: Interview 3-4* supervisors of LTEs to determine: (1) what currently is valued by the interviewee; (2) whether any of Janice's work responsibilities can be done differently so that the HR department is valued by the interviewee.

Step 3: *Determine "indicators of success" and resources/support needed.* Indicators of success and resources needed: Indicators of success include: (1) an increase in stakeholder value for the HR function; (2) improved quality of LTE hires; (3) an increased number of LTEs hired into permanent positions; and (4) increased transformative work. Janice's supervisor agreed to serve as a coach and to provide reference materials on developing appreciative inquiry questions.

Steps 4-5: *Determine completion dates, and discuss your expectations.* Janice estimated the project can be completed in approximately two months. Her supervisor expects that the project will result in increased transformative work within Janice's responsibilities.

Implementation of Action Plan:

In reflecting on the stakeholders or customers that she interacts with frequently, Janice chose to interview two supervisors who currently have LTEs working in their department, and another two supervisors who just hired several LTEs. Janice chose the following questions:

1. What is an example of a positive past experience you have had with hiring LTEs? What contributed toward that positive experience?
2. What are the qualities of an LTE that contribute toward their being successful in your department?
3. In considering your responsibilities that interact with my position in the HR department, what are the common challenges you face?
4. In what way can I help you address these challenges?

Janice conducted the interviews, taking notes of the key points. From her readings, she learned that the most important quality of an appreciative interview is the spirit of inquiry—the willingness to listen and learn from the interviews. Therefore, she practiced attentive listening and empathy, resulting in people proactively sharing their ideas and thoughts with her. Following is a summary of what Janice learned from her interviews:

1. The interviewees valued working with people whom: they trusted to do what they said they would do, were willing to try innovative and new approaches to solving problems, were action-oriented, and were honest and straight-forward, even when delivering bad news.
2. The supervisors felt their major challenge in hiring an LTE was to find someone with the necessary skills who could start immediately. Many appli-

cants indicated they knew of the computer skills needed, but after they were hired, their skills were weak. Could Janice help them?

Janice shared with each interviewee that she would bring the information to the HR department, talk with other HR staff, and get back to them within a month with ideas to address the person's challenges. She understood this follow-up is extremely important to the continuing respectful and trusting relationship with each person.

After discussing the results of her interviews with the HR director and others in the HR department, Janice met with training staff in the IT department. One of their services included training sessions to employees on Microsoft products and other campus technology, e.g., email, PeopleSoft, etc. Janice shared the challenge the supervisors faced when hiring LTEs, and asked if the trainers could help. Through additional discussions to learn more about the challenges and needs of the supervisors, Janice and the IT training staff prepared a plan to design testing for LTE applicants that evaluated their current technology skills needed by supervisors.

This plan included feedback from the training staff in additional areas they observed when working with the LTE applicant, e.g., interpersonal skills, spelling, promptness, neatness, time management, etc., that were important in hiring LTEs. The training staff also offered to prepare individual training to improve needed skills for those LTEs hired.

Janice brought the plan to the supervisors, who were ecstatic about the support received from both the HR and IT departments. After a successful pilot program, the plan was implemented on the entire campus for LTEs, and eventually expanded to hiring all permanent support staff. The pilot program was completed within the two month target date, and extending it to the entire campus, with subsequent evaluation of the indicators for success, took approximately six months. Accomplishing the key indicators for success contributed toward moving the pilot program to the entire campus.

Beginning with a few interviews using appreciative inquiry questions, the resulting collaborative partnership between the HR and IT departments and supervisors hiring LTE and support staff brought a new definition of "creating value."

We can evaluate this project to determine if it, indeed, contributed toward "transformational" work by using the data shown in Table 5.2. Although the HR department in this case did not yet have a strategic plan, the remaining criteria for this innovative project—proactive, focus on what is "delivered," create relationships, deliver value-added HR practices, build HR functions for stakeholder value—meet the definition of transformative work.

Finally, supervisors indicate a substantial increase in the quality of LTE hires, substantiated by increased LTEs hired for permanent support staff positions. All four indicators of project success were accomplished.

Table 5.2 Transactional versus transformative work

FROM: HR Transactional Work	TO: HR Transformative/Strategic Work
Creates efficiency through standardization, automation and consolidation	Aligns vision, mission and goals of HR with strategy of the organization
Mostly reactive	Proactive
Focus is on what we do	Focus is on what we "deliver"
Work with employees	Create relationships/collaborate
Implement best HR practices	Deliver value-added HR practices
Build HR functions for efficiency	Build HR functions for stakeholder value

Summary

Employee core competencies, the main component of an integrated competency-based system, are described as clusters of universally expected, observable behaviors, necessary for successful performance in the position and in the organization. They define the skills, knowledge, learning and behaviors critical to achieving the department's vision and mission, and ultimately the strategic plan. An outcome is that the integrated system can distinguish performance in a particular work context.

The benefits of an integrated competency framework for the HR department as well as the institution—where employee core competencies are integrated with all segments of the total employment process—include improved and integrated processes for the following: recruitment and retention of talent, assessment and selection, performance communication and support, leadership development, succession planning, career development and total compensation.

The process to develop and implement an integrated HR competency framework within the HR department comprises the following five steps: present competency framework to HR staff, determine HR employee core competencies, define HR core competencies, develop behavioral descriptors and utilize integrative competency framework.

The first step toward improving the skill level of the HR staff is to have them self-assess their current skills prior to a discussion with the supervisor. The purpose of this process is threefold:

1. Identify skills each individual needs to improve; resulting in a future individual development plan comprised of goals, indicators of success, action plans, and resources needed.
2. Begin a discussion around the topic of "adding value" to stakeholders.
3. Identify the work each person finds enjoyable, motivating and energizing. This information will be helpful in any plan to realign responsibilities within the HR department.

Major Themes

Reframing:

In this chapter, we focused on the human resources frame, with its emphasis on understanding people. We empowered staff by having them participate in developing the department core competencies. They were able to influence their immediate work environment and the factors that impact them. We invested in them by spending time discussing their skills, and helping them determine those that need to be developed through the Individual Development Plan.

Leadership of Change:

This was a major thread in this chapter, showing a process for the HR director to empower HR staff members to shape their environment, develop plans to improve their skills, and cultivate relationships with stakeholders to create value through innovation and collaboration.

Appreciative Inquiry:

Note that many of the items in the skills self-assessment document and Case Study 5.3 stakeholder interviews are based on appreciative inquiry.

Evaluation of "Your" HR Department's Chapter 5 Outcome

Outcome Desired: HR staff improves level of transformational skills

Change: The development plan process continues to build the HR staff into a team for achieving transformational change

Key Indicators of Success: (check if *"yes"*)

☐ Each HR staff member participates openly and positively in building his/her individual development plan

☐ The development plans include goals, time lines and action plans

☐ Periodic one-on-one meetings occur between the HR director and individual staff to evaluate progress of their development plans

☐ The development plans include a clear method for measuring success of the goals

☐ All HR staff are committed to accomplishing their development plans

☐ Open and honest communication occurs between the HR director and all HR staff

Potential Barriers to Change: (check if *"needs attention"*)

☐ Maintaining the commitment of the HR staff to accomplish development plan goals

☐ HR staff who carry out the development plan only superficially

☐ HR staff who use excuses for not completing development plan goals

☐ HR staff who do not want to change

☐ HR staff who are unable to improve necessary skills

Plan for Conflict and Resistance

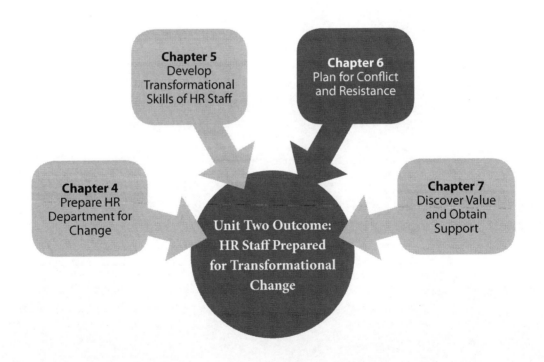

Chapter 6 Plan for conflict and resistance

A typical signal that conflict may erupt is the initiation of any significant change, especially for individuals who are involved in the transition process. A change involves a new way of doing things, whereas the transition is the process of getting from the old way to the new way. For example, a new HR system is a change—from the old one to the new one; the transition is the process of moving from the old to the new system. Transition always involves at least three stages: (1) letting go of the old way of doing things; (2) being in a period where we do not know what the change is going to be like; (3) accepting the change. We discuss change and transition in chapter 8.

Typically, change is not welcomed by individuals who have become accustomed over many years to doing their jobs in the same way. Change creates stress for many people, which often is interpreted as resistance. William Bridges, in his book *Managing Transitions* (2003), says that most resistance to change is not due to the change itself, but to the transition or process of moving to change.

Major change generates at least four categories of issues:

1. Change can impact the ability of individuals to feel effective, valued and in control. Providing support, a chance to participate in the process, and training reduces resistance to change.
2. Change can disrupt the existing pattern of roles and relationships, contributing to further uncertainty. Restructuring to support the new direction reduces confusion and gives people a sense of control.
3. Change can create conflict between those who feel they are "winning" and those who feel they are "losing." Developing a plan to deal with the conflict when it arises, or even better, to diffuse it before it happens, is optimal.
4. Change can create a loss of meaning for those involved. Developing transition rituals and other symbols helps people to let go of the past and embrace new ways of doing things.

A major part of your position responsibilities as a leader includes dealing with conflict. If the EEO, sexual harassment and discrimination functions are part of your responsibilities, addressing conflict is probably a part of your day-to-day activities. Chapter 6 focuses on conflict within the HR department.

> A major part of your position responsibilities as a leader includes dealing with conflict.

Because moving the HR function to the strategic level of the organization involves multiple changes, including changed roles of HR staff and changed processes, it is normal to anticipate conflict among the HR staff. The important point is to anticipate and plan for it. First, we discuss conflict with the HR staff, and then develop plans to deal with it.

The outcome of chapter 6 is to plan for conflict and resistance by preparing the HR staff for any conflict that may arise due to the HR paradigm change. As shown in Figure 6.1, there are four main topics to discuss in addressing conflict and resistance.

Figure 6.1 Model to plan for conflict and resistance

Define Conflict

Although there are many definitions of conflict, Sandra Cheldelin and Ann Lucas in their book, *Academic Administrator's Guild to Conflict Resolution* (2004), describe it best, using the following characteristics:

1. Expressed disagreement occurs between at least two people.
2. The parties differ around goals, methods, values, or all three.
3. The interaction between the parties involves behaviors designed to defeat, reduce or suppress each other.
4. Each party acts to gain an advantage over the other in an effort to "win."

Causes of Conflict

Causes of conflict include: differing viewpoints, personality, structure of the department or organization, poorly defined responsibilities, inequality in treating people, competition over scarce resources, clashes of values, human drives for success, recognition, power, attacks on personal characteristics and the initiation of significant change.

Conflict need not be destructive; it can be constructive when it produces change, leads to unity of purpose, and promotes collaboration. Addressing conflict in creative ways can enhance problem solving, clarify decision making, and strengthen the HR staff as a team. Conflict can improve team members' understanding of each other, increase their skills in working together in extremely productive ways, and generate synergy and engagement.

Constructive conflicts encourage open discussion and allow full exploration of each person's needs, concerns, values, and interests, which are the essential ingredients of authentic communication. In addition, conflict can be constructive by providing individuals an opportunity to release pent-up emotions (Cheldelin and Lucas, 2004). Many people are not taught how to deal with conflict, and may either avoid it, or simply give in to allow others to get their way, or use aggressive tactics to meet their own needs. None of these methods are optimal, and all will lead to further conflict.

As we see in the case studies in this chapter, conflict can be very destructive, causing individuals to form alliances, take things personally, disrupt the workplace, impact service to stakeholders and potentially lead to complaints or grievances.

> Constructive conflicts encourage open discussion and allow full exploration of each person's needs, concerns, values, and interests, which are the essential ingredients of authentic communication.

Understand Types of Conflict

Interpersonal Conflict

Individuals working under increased levels of stress are susceptible to conflict—both intrapersonal and interpersonal—especially during times of change and transition. Because the HR function serves the entire university in multiple ways, role ambiguity, role conflict, or role overload can become causes of stress and conflict. These three types of precursors to stress and conflict often are interrelated.

For example, an HR staff member who needs to take on additional work due to preparing for workplace change (role overload), also has increased responsibility with elderly parents needing health care, and does not want to work any overtime (role conflict). If this person is involved at work in transitioning to a new HR system and does not understand how his/her responsibilities will change, we can add role ambiguity to the mix.

A person normally can manage stress for a short time. However, in the long term, his/her stress will manifest as a health-related issue, or result in conflict with one or more people in the department or organization. People who believe they have the understanding and support from their supervisor can handle high levels of stress more effectively than those who do not have this support. As a supervisor, be aware of and watch for signs of stress in employees. Provide the help and support they need before their health or morale deteriorates, or interpersonal or group conflict develops.

Negative Thinking

Have you ever presented an idea to an individual or during a team meeting, only to have someone tell you what is wrong with the concept, why it will never work, or that it was tried in the past and did not work? We all know individuals who react in this way, and they rarely give additional details—they just place barriers in the way of discussing the idea further. Frequently called "negative thinking," this is a learned concept, and therefore can be "unlearned."

As a supervisor or team member, do not let the discussion stop. You need to listen to this person, and ask more questions to get past the negativity. The idea, the situation, or the timing often is not the same as it was in the past. Spending a few moments listening to the individual, asking him/her what was good about the idea, what was different about the past, or how he/she prefers to solve the issue, often can engage him/her in problem solving and moving past the negativity. For many people, just being heard and feeling their thinking and point of view are valued, are effective methods to moving past the negative thinking.

If this does not work, we do not want negative thinkers to hinder the work of others on the team or in the department. There are a number of methods to deal with this situation, as part of developing the environment for teams to work together productively. Although we will discuss developing effective meeting guidelines in Unit Three, Exhibit 6.1 offers several tools.

Exhibit 6.1 Meeting tools to address negative thinking

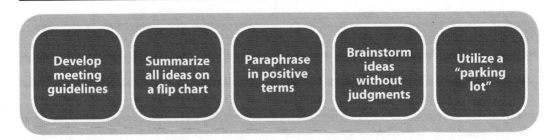

Tool 1 Develop meeting guidelines: As part of meeting guidelines, include one that members must discuss the positive aspects of all new ideas before discussing any negative ones.

Tool 2 Summarize all ideas on a flip chart: Summarize all ideas—both positive and negative—on a flip chart so all members feel they have been heard.

Tool 3 Paraphrase in positive terms: Many times when an individual uses negative thinking, he/she eventually feels alienated from the group. Other group members do not know how to deal with this behavior and become quiet or rally around a person who confronts the behavior. If the negative thinker becomes alienated, the team loses this person's input. Remember, often disagreement and constructive conflict can challenge the status quo and provide for better outcomes. Paraphrase in positive terms what the person said. Look him/her in the eye and smile.

Tool 4 Brainstorm ideas without judgments: Brainstorming is a process where ideas first are collected, with no positive or negative judgments made until later. As part of the meeting agenda, outline the process so all team members understand. If the process is not followed, anyone in the meeting can bring the team back to the agreed-upon process.

Tool 5 Utilize a "parking lot": Utilize a "parking lot" as part of a meeting agenda. This is a flip chart to record ideas or topics that are voiced by a meeting participant but are not included in the agenda. When a topic is brought up and not germane to the immediate agenda, it is placed in the parking lot for future discussion.

Patterns of Conflict

There are times when we can observe a chronic conflict pattern that has existed over time. This involves a repetitive, predictable pattern of behavior among individuals or groups that causes a conflict situation. This pattern normally consists of the following steps:

1. An "action" that begins the conflict. This could be a non-verbal expression, a tone of voice, a word or phrase—any behavior that starts the "explosion."
2. A "reaction" that moves the conflict along a predicable path. It indicates that the second person fell into the expected pattern of behavior. It could be another non-verbal expression, a sarcastic tone of voice, etc.
3. An expected "cycle" of actions and reactions.
4. A "high point" when the conflict reaches a climax.
5. A "conclusion" when one of the parties ends the current conflict… until the next time.

The best method to deal with a conflict pattern is to interrupt it. Although it can be interrupted at any point, it is most effective at step #2, the point of the first "reaction." Then the "cycle" never begins. The "interrupt" can be any behavior that the other party does not expect; the more unexpected or surprising, the better.

Case Study 6.1

Paula, Steve, Aaron and David are members of an on-going team with the goal of improving and simplifying several institutional HR policies. Aaron noticed after several meetings that he and David developed a negative pattern of behavior that stalled the efforts of the team and frustrated him a great deal. When he suggested changes to a policy, David took a deep breath, rolled his eyes, and then went off on long tangents, giving reason after reason why that change would not work.

Aaron would sit for a while, become frustrated and angry, then interrupt and give reasons why it will work. Then they argued back and forth until either Paula or Steve interrupted to move on to the next agenda item. The team went around in circles, not making any headway.

Aaron realized that they had not given much structure to their team or meetings. He brainstormed ways he could interrupt the pattern. At the next meeting, as Aaron predicted, shortly into the meeting, David took a deep breath, rolled his eyes, and began to disagree with Aaron's idea.

Suddenly, Aaron took a large brown paper bag out of his briefcase, unfolded it, and put it over his head. The effect was immediate: David was astounded, and stared at the bag on David's head, confused about what to do next. Paula and Steve began to laugh, and then David joins them, all pointing at the bag on Aaron's head.

Sheepishly, Aaron removed the bag and said, "You know, there are times I want to put that bag over my head so that I cannot hear—for the hundredth time—the same reasons we shouldn't make a change. I have not been a good team member because I haven't expressed how I've been feeling. I recommend that the four of us start over by brainstorming guidelines for our meetings that will allow us to be more productive." With that, they brainstormed guidelines, and included several from Exhibit 6.1. One was having a sense of humor, and after that, David always brought the brown bag to meetings.

Case Study Questions:

1. *What are additional methods for dealing with negative patterns of behavior?*
2. *What specific meeting guidelines can help to break negative patterns of behavior?*
3. *How can team members break negative patterns of behavior and still allow all team members to participate in discussions?*

Although this example may be extreme, it has been used successfully to interrupt a conflict pattern, with the outcome of increased respect among team members. However, if team members have not formed an authentic relationship, this action may cause additional conflict. In many cases, the tendency for this type of "pattern" to exist can be diminished by including a meeting guideline for dealing with conflict. Perhaps a "time out" hand signal utilized as a method to stop the conversation enables a team member to express his or her feelings, resulting in disruption of the conflict pattern and positive relationship-building.

Develop Effective Skills: Leadership of Change

One responsibility of a supervisor is to raise the skills of people that report to him/her. Although a supervisor is always available to an employee to discuss and give recommendations regarding conflict situations, all employees should have the skills to deal with many conflict situations on their own. This, of course, means that all are given the "authority" to confront and resolve conflict situations.

Individual skills needed for effective conflict and resolve resolution include:
- self-management skills, such as the ability to keep disruptive emotions and impulses in check
- communication skills, such as active listening
- not making assumptions
- affirming each other
- not using criticism
- influencing skills, such as negotiation and problem-solving

In addition, having a personal support network helps an individual deal with workplace stress. Most of these skills are considered to be part of a person's emotional intelligence, the ability to manage feelings so that they are expressed appropriately and effectively, enabling people to work together efficiently toward common goals.

According to the research done by Daniel Goleman and others, a person's IQ is fixed genetically and changes very little after the teen years. However, a person's emotional intelligence is learned, and it continues to develop as one moves through life and learns from experiences. Studies show that people improve in these abilities as they grow more proficient at dealing with their own emotions and impulses, motivating themselves, and sharpening their empathy and social skills (Goleman, 1998).

For many organizations, when recruiting for entry-level positions, specific technical skills are now less important than the underlying strength of a person's self-awareness, self-regulation, motivation, empathy, and social skills.

Methods for Improving Conflict Resolution Skills

Although there are many options for improving conflict resolution skills of the HR staff, following are two we recommend:

Conflict resolution simulation
Involving the HR staff in a conflict resolution simulation is an excellent method to improve their skills in confronting and resolving conflict—in a safe environment. Although it is easy to understand that conflict can be productive and lead to creative solutions and a greater understanding of others, it normally is difficult for most people to deal with confrontations, to remain objective, and to understand

the other person's point of view. "Practicing" conflict through simulations can help people get past the emotion to concentrate on the issue that is creating the conflict and on its resolution.

> *To download the Conflict Resolution Simulation Outline go to* **www.HR-higher-ed.com**

Assess emotional intelligence skills

Another method for strengthening people's conflict resolution skills is first to assess their emotional intelligence skills, and then to develop a plan to improve specific skills shown to be weak. *The Handbook of Emotionally Intelligent Leadership* by Daniel A. Feldman, Ph.D., is a great resource. In addition to describing emotional intelligence skills, it includes an online self-assessment that provides a report that can be used for skill development. A person can retake the self-assessment periodically to check for improvement.

Transform Conflict or a Major Issue into a Problem to Be Resolved

An onion is the perfect metaphor for conflict. An onion has many layers, as can conflict. There is not always one cause of conflict, as indicated in the discussion on intrapersonal conflict. Two or more factors can contribute to a multi-dimensional conflict situation that must be addressed in several ways.

Conflict not addressed soon after it happens becomes deeper ingrained, and is more painful when it is exposed, similar to an onion that causes our eyes to water when we slice into the inner core. Conflict that is older than six months can be extremely difficult to resolve, often taking as long to resolve as how old it is. Some long-standing conflict cannot be resolved until one or more persons leave the department or team.

Case Study 6.2: To be referred to throughout this section

> *Thomas was hired as the director of HR six months ago. He knew his predecessor had been in the position for many years, and was told by his supervisor when he accepted the job that he was expected to make many changes in the department. Most of the HR staff were in functional silos and did not work well together, and the department was not widely valued in the organization. The role of the HR staff was primarily transactional. Most were not comfortable with making decisions, preferring to carry out their responsibilities by using existing policies and procedures.*

The last six months were not easy. As Thomas met with HR staff to discuss their responsibilities and how their role needed to change, he met with resistance from many. He continually heard, "We have never had to do things that way. You do not understand how this organization works. You're not supporting us to administration like our last director did." He realized that, essentially, there were systemic problems in the department, with a two-tier system, where some did not value the work of others, kept them out of the communication loop, and at times treated them disrespectfully. The previous director gave many opportunities for promotion to some staff, but not to others. Customer service, both inside and outside the HR department, was not a priority.

Several months after Thomas became the director, two staff members retired and a third transferred to another department within the organization. All three were among the group that fought any change in the office, and Thomas looked forward to filling the positions with individuals who understood the new HR paradigm. On the other hand, all three left within a few weeks, and other staff needed to take on their recruitment, payroll and benefits work. Thomas had to do some of this work himself, knowing the staff were stretched thin.

Conflict among groups of the staff always was under the surface of their day-to-day interactions. Groups had formed to align around specific "positions" soon after Thomas became director, and he knew that although three people left the office, several of those who remained often talked with those who left. He made a structural change in that all staff now reported to him, but that did not eliminate the factions within the office. One staff member openly resisted Thomas' efforts to do her work differently; two others silently did the same.

In the last two weeks, Thomas hired two new individuals, with the third recruitment in the final candidate interviewing stage. He was excited about building a new team within the office, one that worked together effectively and understood the expectations of the new paradigm. At 7pm on Thursday, one of the staff left the office, after talking with Thomas about several conflict situations that occurred the past few days. It appeared that the two new staff already felt "in the middle" of group conflict.

Thomas' supervisor and other administrators expected quick change in the department, but Thomas felt he needed to focus first on building an effective HR team.

Throughout the remainder of this chapter, we use the following model (depicted below with Stage 1 highlighted) to transform conflict or a major issue into a problem to be resolved. In addition, this model forms the basis for addressing several case studies.

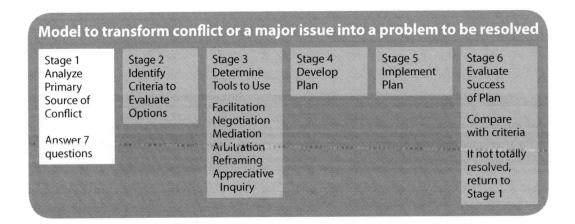

Model to transform conflict or a major issue into a problem to be resolved

Stage 1 Analyze Primary Source of Conflict	Stage 2 Identify Criteria to Evaluate Options	Stage 3 Determine Tools to Use	Stage 4 Develop Plan	Stage 5 Implement Plan	Stage 6 Evaluate Success of Plan
Answer 7 questions		Facilitation Negotiation Mediation Arbitration Reframing Appreciative Inquiry			Compare with criteria If not totally resolved, return to Stage 1

Stage 1: Analyze Primary Source of Conflict

Throughout Case Study 6.2, conflict is apparent between groups and between individuals, resulting in multiple conflict situations. There is conflict between the new director and several individuals, who feel they are right and do not want to change, and who have aligned themselves together as a group against the director. Those in this group have treated others in the department in disrespectful ways, as they were given the power to do that by the previous director. Conflict in the department has been verbal and non-verbal, consistently present in the work environment.

Several causes of conflict in our case study include systemic issues within the HR department. Systemic issues can arise within the workplace when inequitable structures and procedures have been in place for a long time. People working within an inequitable structure become used to having power and authority over others, or feel helpless to create change. Creation of a two-tier system becomes a "living" system, part of the workplace culture, and therefore difficult to change.

In Case Study 6.2, most of the causes of conflict are present—some have been present for a long time. The previous director allowed some within the department to treat others disrespectfully, structured the department so that some reported to others, gave some the opportunity for promotion and not others, and valued the work of some above others. Because of the imbalance of power in the department,

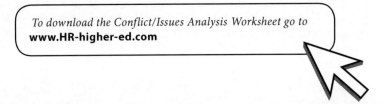

To download the Conflict/Issues Analysis Worksheet go to
www.HR-higher-ed.com

the conflict was always under the surface, without the opportunity to deal with it. This conflict caused factions within the office—groups that aligned together and against other groups. This systemic situation resulted in escalating conflict with the hiring of a new director and the HR paradigm shift.

Questions to consider when analyzing a conflict situation (Cheldelin and Lucas, 2004) are summarized in Figure 6.3 and explained below. We use Case Study 6.2 to work through these questions in order to analyze the conflict situation.

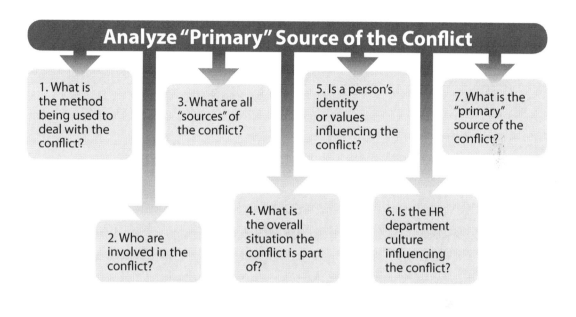

Figure 6.3 Questions used in analyzing a conflict situation

Question 1: **What is the method being used to deal with the conflict?** Considering the persons involved in the conflict, determine the method they are using to deal with the situation, e.g., avoidance, accommodation (giving in to what the other person wants), aggression (forcing the issue to get what a person wants), compromise (some give and take by all parties), collaboration (find ways to resolve a situation so that both parties rights' and needs are addressed). How is this being represented in the conflict?

Answer: Considering our case study, one of the people who retired is using aggression. The other two (one retired, one left the department) avoid the conflict, but are aligned with the first person. Others in the department who feel they have no power avoid the conflict. The new director uses aggressive strategies.

To review more information on the five "Methods for Resolving Conflict" go to **www.HR-higher-ed.com**

Question 2: **Who are involved in the conflict?** Determine the placement of the conflict interaction: between two people in the department, between one person in the department and the other external, between more than one person in the department/group.

Answer: The conflict in the case study is multi-level: between the director and one staff person; between the director and that staff person and two others who are silent, but verbal behind the director's back. In addition, systemic conflict pits groups in the office against each other.

Question 3: **What are all "sources" of the conflict?** Determine all sources of the conflict: personality conflicts, differing viewpoints, relationships, needs, interests, positions, values, perceived injustice, imbalance of power, etc. (Refer to Exhibit 6.2 for the difference between "interest" and "position.") In their book, *Getting to Yes*, Fisher and Ury (1983) present four principles of negotiation that effectively resolve almost any type of dispute: (1) separate people from the problem; (2) focus on interests rather than positions; (3) generate a variety of options before settling on an agreement; and (4) insist that the agreement be based on objective criteria.

Answer: With the new director comes an imbalance of power that creates conflict between him and others who once had that power. Because not all staff have their needs met in the workplace, this is another source. The imbalance of power negatively influences the building of effective relationships among the staff.

Question 4: **What is the overall situation the conflict is part of?** Determine the overall situation in which the conflict exists.

Answer: The context of the situation includes the retirement of an HR director who has been in the position for many years, working with most of the HR staff for that entire time. The hiring of a new HR director includes expectations from his supervisor and other administrators to create change in the HR function.

Question 5: **Is a person's identity or values influencing the conflict?** Determine if an individual's identity is influencing the conflict, e.g., more authority, more experience, more knowledge of the organization, more education, etc.

Exhibit 6.2 Interest versus position

A **position** is what an individual "wants," e.g., to complete a project prior to the deadline date.

An **interest** is "why" the individual wants it, e.g., to take a vacation without having to worry about the project.

If one or both of these is determined to be the source of a conflict, a method to resolve the conflict is to focus on interests instead of on positions. For example, there may be other ways for the person to take a vacation and not have to worry about the project than to complete the project prior to the deadline. Perhaps others on the team can take on the responsibilities of the individual while he/she is on vacation. Brainstorming among the team members may create other alternatives that satisfy the interests of all team members.

Answer: This is the case with the vocal person who retired, as well as several others in the department. They feel the new HR director and the institution in general discount their valuable experience and knowledge. Their changing workplace causes feelings of anger, personal attack, frustration and bewilderment.

Question 6: **Is the HR department culture influencing the conflict?** Determine if the culture of the HR department—customs, belief systems, policies, traditions, and structure—is a part of the conflict.

Answer: There definitely are systemic issues that led to the seriousness of this conflict.

Question 7: **What is the "primary" source of the conflict?** Determine the primary source of the conflict.

Answer: In our case study, the primary source of the conflict is the culture of the HR department—there are negative systemic issues that were in play for a long time.

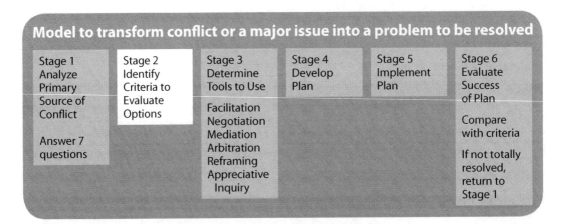

Stage 2: Identify Criteria to Evaluate Options

Back to Case Study 6.2

Considering the aspects of the conflict, Thomas felt the following criteria must be satisfied in developing an action plan:

1. contribute toward the HR staff feeling they are being listened to and valued
2. provide an arena for the HR staff, including him, to honestly and in a forthright manner discuss issues and develop shared agreements
3. rebuild trust among the HR staff, including Thomas
4. develop at least one ritual that indicates transition, captures the attention of the HR staff, and frames this experience

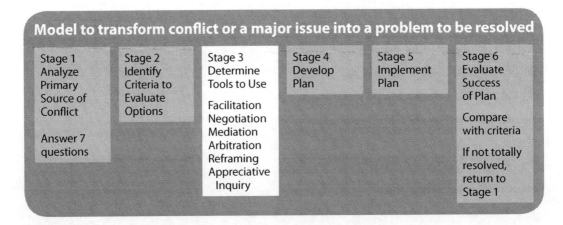

Stage 3: Determine Tools to Use

It is important to repeat that often there are multiple sources of conflict. In analyzing the conflict situation of Case Study 6.2, in stage 1 we determine the "primary" source of the conflict, which is the negative culture of the HR department. This primary source gives us a starting point for conflict intervention. The following six tools serve as potential methods to positively and proactively resolve conflict.

Conflict Resolution Tool #1: Facilitation

Although facilitation often is used to resolve conflicts between two people, it is particularly helpful where there are more than two people involved in the dispute. An individual, who is considered external to the conflict and neutral by all parties (this could be the supervisor), works through a process to help reach an agreement to resolve the conflict. In facilitation, the emphasis is on the "process" used for negotiating the outcome. The typical steps the facilitator utilizes are the following:

1. The facilitator meets separately with all parties before a group meeting to obtain their perspective and cause(s) of the issue(s), and agreement on the goal or outcome of the group meeting.

2. The group meeting begins with the facilitator highlighting the HR values they all agreed to utilize in working together in the workplace. These should be visible on a flip chart or elsewhere in the room. The facilitator reviews the expected outcome for the meeting, and states ground rules, e.g., only one person speaks at a time, no interrupting, etc. Finally, the facilitator reflects on the current situation by presenting a general context of the situation, including a description of the problem(s), cause(s) and potential barriers.

3. The facilitator helps the group to develop possible solutions to the problem. Before brainstorming potential solutions, it is helpful to determine the criteria by which the group will evaluate them, e.g., does the alternative address a barrier to resolving the issue. During the brainstorming phase, the alternative solutions first are listed on a flip chart, without any evaluation of them. Then the benefits and weaknesses of each alternative are evaluated and compared to the criteria.

4. Through consensus-building, the facilitator helps the group choose effective alternatives to resolve the issues. The *Fist-to-Five* model identified in chapter 4 is one option. Another is the model developed by Roger Fisher and William Ury (1983). It is important for the facilitator to engage all participants and ensure each is committed to the resolution, or voices concerns to improve the resolution. The meeting concludes with the group developing an action plan to put the agreement into place. The agreement should include an evaluation plan.

5. Before adjourning the meeting, the facilitator thanks the group for working together collaboratively and honestly, and concludes with a process for group members to affirm each other, described in Exhibit 6.3.

Exhibit 6.3 Process to affirm each other

> *Each person is affirmed by others present in the meeting. Each says something he/she likes or respects about the other person, or something he/she saw the person do or say that expressed the department core values. The affirming process can impact interpersonal relationships in a positive way. In addition, when there was disagreement or conflict within the meeting, the process can take all the "heat" out of the room and allow people to return to the values that bring them together.*

Facilitation Option for "Viewpoint" Conflict

Individuals often can be correct in their viewpoint, but wrong in their interpretation of the situation. A supervisor or project leader can utilize the facilitation tool to help each person clarify the situation. The people switch roles and points of view. Each assumes the viewpoint of the other and makes that argument. The objective is not to get them to change their viewpoints, but to develop insight and understanding about the other's viewpoint. Give them time to prepare their argument.

Then ask them to work together on a process that will satisfy both viewpoints. Separately, each could write a procedure that satisfied their concerns, and then they could work together to integrate them.

The most important outcome of this process is that the individuals are brought together, face-to-face, to discuss the differences before the conflict worsens.

Conflict Resolution Tool #2: Negotiation

Negotiation focuses on the relationship between the process used and the expected outcome of the process. Negotiation is a process whereby a resolution is determined through give and take by the parties, who come to a mutual agreement. Essentially the resolution becomes a "compromise," where each person is willing to give up something in order to gain something else. Therefore, consideration of each party's needs and wants is part of the negotiation. An example of using this tool is in Case Study 6.3 at the end of this chapter.

Conflict Resolution Tool #3: Mediation

Mediation utilizes an acceptable neutral third party who has limited, but no authoritative, decision-making ability. Within higher education, very often the HR function itself serves as the neutral third party who mediates the conflict between parties outside of the HR department. It is often a good tool for addressing personality conflicts.

Mediation can resolve complex conflict that has been long-standing and found on various levels. The process normally follows these steps:

1. The mediator talks with all parties in advance to get their perspective, to explain the mediation process, and to ascertain the willingness of each to honestly desire to resolve the conflict.
2. During the meeting, the mediator welcomes the parties, outlines the process, and states the ground rules. The first party describes the situation from his/her perspective, during which time the second party cannot speak, but only listen and take notes. The mediator may ask clarifying questions. Then the mediator paraphrases what the first party explained. This process repeats for the second party.
3. The mediator tries to find common goals between the parties and to determine which issues will contribute toward resolution of the conflict. Normally, a serious conflict has emotional overtones for those involved, with one or more of the following issues at the source of the conflict: communication, relationship, trust, respect.
4. Using the information learned, the mediator asks the parties questions that explore potential solutions. This can lead to a final written agreement, which diffuses the conflict and provides a new basis for the relationship of the parties. Included in the agreement is a section on what will happen if either party does not live up to the agreement.
5. The session ends with the parties affirming each other.

Conflict Resolution Tool #4: Arbitration

Arbitration involves an impartial third party who hears the evidence and then makes either a binding or a nonbinding decision based on agreed-upon conditions. This is a more formal process than facilitation, mediation or negotiation, and is normally not used in higher education other than in dealing with union contracts.

Conflict Resolution Tool #5: Reframing

Back to Case Study 6.2

Utilizing Case Study 6.2, Table 6.1 outlines the questioning process for reframing conflict (Bolman and Deal, 2003): (a) From this perspective/frame, what is going on? (b) What alternative options for conflict resolution does this viewpoint suggest?

From this analysis, Thomas can use any or all of the options in the four frames above. However, an immediate need is to bring the HR staff together around a common interest or ground. Because Thomas just hired two new staff, with a third recruitment in process, he needs to begin laying the foundation for a team spirit.

A multi-phase approach to show the HR staff they are valued and cause them to come together in a common interest may be the best way to approach this complex issue. Bringing in an aspect of the symbolic frame to show their history is respected gives the HR staff a basis for new meaning and purpose.

Thomas decided to incorporate the reframing tool into his resolution process, discussed in detail in stage 4.

Table 6.1 Questioning process for reframing conflict in Case Study 6.2

Frame	What is Going On?	What are the Options?
Structural	Rules and roles are changing, resulting in confusion and conflict	Communicate and define new HR paradigm; renegotiate new roles of HR staff
HR	Anxiety and uncertainty among the HR staff; some do not feel valued	Show HR staff they are valued: listen to their concerns; invest in them with training to develop new awareness and skills; involve them in transition
Political	Competing interests and struggles for power and advantage create conflict	Address conflict by creating an arena to forge divisive issues into shared agreements; bring HR staff to a common interest
Symbolic	With new management, the HR staff feel uncertainty, ambiguity and a lack of identity; their culture is changing, and some struggle to keep the old one	Develop something for the HR staff to bond to, e.g., core values, rebuilding trust, respect and use history

Conflict Resolution Tool #6: Appreciative Inquiry

As outlined in previous chapters, appreciative inquiry focuses on valuing what the collective group can do and envisioning where members of the group want to go. It assumes that discussion about strengths, successes, hopes, and dreams is itself a transformational process. Envisioning a different way of doing business together is a viable strategy to conclude a facilitation where people take into consideration all parties' hopes, desires, and goals, and create new strategies for working collaboratively.

The process of carefully crafting appreciative inquiry questions creates a joyfully focused state of mind as the person considers and answers them. Research has shown the following basic assumptions about appreciative inquiry: (1) what people focus on becomes their reality; (2) the act of asking questions of a group or individual influences the group or individual in some way; (3) people are more confident in transitioning to the future, which is not known, when they carry forward the best parts of the past, which is known; and (4) the language people use creates their reality (Orem, Binkert and Clancy, 2007).

Back to Case Study 6.2

Considering Case Study 6.2, would it be beneficial to utilize appreciative inquiry questions as part of resolving the conflict? In reviewing the options outlined in the reframed process for the HR, political and symbolic frames, this type of questioning may engage the HR staff and assist in developing a common agreement on several levels. Thomas decided to add this tool to his implementation plan.

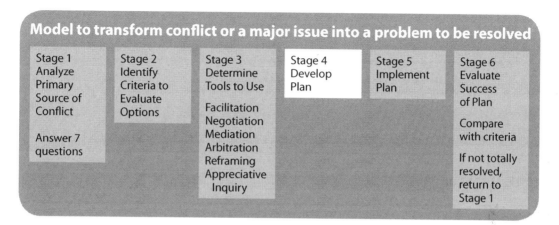

Model to transform conflict or a major issue into a problem to be resolved

Stage 1 Analyze Primary Source of Conflict	Stage 2 Identify Criteria to Evaluate Options	Stage 3 Determine Tools to Use	Stage 4 Develop Plan	Stage 5 Implement Plan	Stage 6 Evaluate Success of Plan
Answer 7 questions		Facilitation Negotiation Mediation Arbitration Reframing Appreciative Inquiry			Compare with criteria If not totally resolved, return to Stage 1

Stage 4: Develop a Plan to Resolve the Conflict or Issue

Following is a summary of how Thomas worked through the first four stages of the model to transform conflict into a problem to be resolved:

Stage 1: Analyze the primary source of the conflict: *The primary source of the conflict is the culture of the HR department—there are negative systemic issues that were in play for a long time.*

Stage 2: Identify criteria to evaluate options: *Thomas felt the following criteria must be satisfied in developing an action plan:*
- *contribute toward the HR staff feeling they are being listened to and valued*
- *provide an arena for the HR staff, including him, to honestly and in a forthright manner discuss issues and develop shared agreements*
- *rebuild trust among the HR staff, including him*
- *develop at least one ritual that indicates transition, captures the attention of the HR staff, and frames this experience*

Stage 3: Determine the tools to use:
- *Because the primary cause of the conflict is systemic issues that have existed for a long time, Thomas determined to utilize the facilitation method as a tool. Being involved in part of the conflict, he felt it was important to find a third-party facilitator considered neutral by the HR staff.*
- *The reframing tool was extremely helpful in outlining the complexity of the*

situation, with several promising options. Therefore, Thomas felt a multi-phase approach, using several options, would be optimal.

- *In addition, Thomas felt appreciative inquiry questions should be included to help the HR team learn about conflict and rebuild trust.*
- *Due to the purpose of the negotiation, mediation and arbitration tools, Thomas did not consider them.*

Stage 4: Develop the plan: *At this point, Thomas needed to discuss the process used and his ideas with at least one other person he trusted. When he began his position as the director of HR he was connected with a mentor, someone on campus who under-stood the culture, and knew how to address and work through conflict with positive outcomes. Thomas knew his mentor would be confidential, challenge his process, and help him develop the best plan possible.*

After discussing the conflict situation with his mentor and reflecting on it over the weekend, Thomas decided to use the facilitation, reframing and appreciative inquiry tools to develop a resolution. His mentor knew a person from another campus who was willing to facilitate a two-phase process to resolve the issues.

Model to transform conflict or a major issue into a problem to be resolved

Stage 1 Analyze Primary Source of Conflict	Stage 2 Identify Criteria to Evaluate Options	Stage 3 Determine Tools to Use	Stage 4 Develop Plan	Stage 5 Implement Plan	Stage 6 Evaluate Success of Plan
Answer 7 questions		Facilitation Negotiation Mediation Arbitration Reframing Appreciative Inquiry			Compare with criteria If not totally resolved, return to Stage 1

Stage 5: Implement the Plan

On Monday morning, Thomas met with the HR staff, telling them he understood there were issues and disagreements among people in the office, including him, since he became the director, and that he probably had not dealt with some of them in the best way.

He then explained that a neutral facilitator would lead a four-hour workshop dis-cussion around conflict and methods of resolution in one week. His expectations for the workshop included honest discussions among HR staff members that would contribute to rebuilding trust as a foundation for them to work together as an effective team.

To learn more about them and the history of the department, the four-hour workshop would be followed by several days of individual staff meetings with Thomas and the facilitator. He wanted everyone to feel comfortable in voicing their needs and feelings in an authentic manner.

Although no one had questions after his comments, Thomas noticed that for the rest of the week, there was a more relaxed environment in the office.

The first phase of the four-hour workshop included training and group discussion around conflict, and utilized information from previous sections of this chapter. All the HR staff members, including Thomas, participated in the workshop. The training was designed to promote discussion by the participants, keeping in mind the meeting guidelines they developed early in the workshop. Exhibit 6.4 outlines the agenda for their meeting.

Exhibit 6.4 Conflict resolution workshop agenda

1. Welcome
2. Introduce Facilitator
3. Summarize Agenda and Expected Outcomes
4. Develop Workshop Guidelines
5. Define Conflict
6. Discuss Types of Conflict
7. Discuss How Conflict Feels
8. Brainstorm Methods to Enhance Communication During Conflict
9. Next steps

As the discussion progressed in agenda item #7, first one staff member, then others, expressed openly what conflict looked and felt like. The room became quiet as one person at a time spoke from the heart, and often emotionally, about what conflict does to him/her.

At this point, the facilitator used appreciative inquiry questions to cause the HR staff to communicate even more openly and honestly about how they wanted to work together. He divided the staff into groups of two. Each person interviewed his/her partner using the following questions:

1. Describe a time when you were particularly grateful for an open, honest dis-

cussion that took place between you and another person—at work, or else-where in your life. Explain what made that discussion possible. Be specific as possible, and describe what it was about you, the other person, or the situation that opened the door for what took place.

2. If there was some type of pronounced shift in this discussion—from defensive or partial communication to openness and honesty—what made that shift possible? What was it about you, the other person or the people around you that enabled such a change?

3. What three small changes could you and your teammates agree to that would enhance the level of open and honest communication within the HR staff?

At the end of 20 minutes, the facilitator asked the groups to report their answers to question #3, and captured them on a flip chart. The answers included:

- in order to detach from emotions—individuals are given the ability to indicate the need for a "time-out"
- determine and share individual "triggers" to conflict as a way to know each other better
- agree to ask each other during disagreements if the parties are adhering to the "HR core values"
- use effective listening to understand all points of view
- paraphrase all points of view
- determine areas of agreement and build from there
- those in disagreement can use the Fist-to-Five method of coming to agree-ment/consensus—start with the issue and develop the resolution
- provide closure for any outstanding "debris" to provide for healing

Using the Fist-to-Five consensus-building tool, the HR staff members agreed to adopt these eight changes as part of working together as a team. When asked by the facili-tator if there was any outstanding "debris," it was apparent, especially in non-verbal behavior with eyes looking down and nodding heads, that some existed. The facilitator then explained the second phase of the facilitation, a meeting with each of the staff individually with Thomas and the facilitator.

The individual meetings were scheduled for 90 minutes each, to discuss any remaining "debris" and the following questions to rebuild trust and generate a founda-tion for the team to work together. During these meetings, Thomas gave his answers to these questions first.

1. Think about a time when you went through a process of rebuilding trust, within either the work or personal environment. Who was involved? What happened? What specifically did you and the others do to strengthen your

relationship? What did you learn from this process—about yourself, the other person, and trust?

2. Describe a time when members of the HR staff successfully reconciled difficulties or differences, rebuilding trust in the process. Who did what? How? What happened?

3. Reflecting on these and other experiences you have had in the past, what core factors contributed toward rebuilding trust? What do you bring to this team in its ongoing commitment to rebuilding trust?

Although several individual meetings began with a great deal of emotion as the staff person discussed situations that were upsetting, each expressed his/her feelings and needs, using the guidelines determined in the workshop. Thomas accepted each feeling and need and his part in them, and noted instances where he made mistakes.

For the final piece of the facilitation process, all HR staff members came together to share what each learned. The facilitator helped Thomas and HR staff members develop a plan to rebuild trust within the team and effectively address future conflict. The session ended with each member of the team affirming each other.

Model to transform conflict or a major issue into a problem to be resolved

Stage 1 Analyze Primary Source of Conflict	Stage 2 Identify Criteria to Evaluate Options	Stage 3 Determine Tools to Use	Stage 4 Develop Plan	Stage 5 Implement Plan	Stage 6 Evaluate Success of Plan
Answer 7 questions		Facilitation Negotiation Mediation Arbitration Reframing Appreciative Inquiry			Compare with criteria If not totally resolved, return to Stage 1

Stage 6: Evaluate Success of the Plan

In order to evaluate the success of the plan, Thomas and the facilitator first determined its outcomes, as listed below.

- There was closure to any outstanding "debris," and a deep healing for the staff and for Thomas.
- The staff felt valued by Thomas taking the time to meet with them and to know each of them at a deeper level.
- Thomas learned more about each staff member—what motivated them; their

goals, strengths and weaknesses; how to approach them with potential conflict, etc. He also gained tremendous insight into how to pull them together as a team.

- Thomas learned about himself and his leadership style and what to adjust to meet the needs of the HR staff.
- The stage was set for building a cohesive team with constructive conflict.
- Staff learned how to address conflict in a constructive way, instead of taking it outside the department or in the hallway behind the backs of others.
- Staff developed core factors they felt contribute toward rebuilding trust.

In comparing these outcomes with the criteria developed previously and listed again in Exhibit 6.5, Thomas determined these outcomes satisfy the first three evaluation criteria.. In fact, these outcomes surpassed Thomas' expectations for resolution of the conflict situation. In reviewing criteria point #4: "develop at least one ritual that indicates transition, captures the attention of the HR staff, and frames this experience." Thomas felt that the eight-point agreement to deal with future conflict served as a symbol to meet this criteria point.

Exhibit 6.5 Thomas' criteria to evaluate conflict resolution

Case Study 6.2 Criteria to evaluate conflict resolution

1. Contribute toward the HR staff feeling they are being listened to and valued
2. Provide an arena for the HR staff, including Thomas, to honestly and in a forthright manner discuss issues and develop shared agreements
3. Rebuild trust among the HR staff, including Thomas
4. Develop at least one ritual that indicates transition, captures the attention of the HR staff, and frames this experience

Case Study Questions:

1. Although the two-phase facilitation process resolved the conflict, what are possible additional alternatives for resolution?
2. The recruitment for the final open position in the HR department was in the interviewing stage. When the new employee begins, how should this person be "brought into the team"? Should any of the prior conflict and resulting rebuilding of trust be shared?
3. Using the criteria developed by Thomas to evaluate the plan, do you feel it was successful? Why or why not? Is there anything that could have been done

to improve the outcomes? Is there any ritual or symbol that could serve this criteria point better?

4. *For you, what core factors contribute toward rebuilding trust?*

To review discussion of recommendations for Case Study 6.2 questions go to **www.HR-higher-ed.com**

Case Study 6.3: Using the Negotiation Tool

An example of using the negotiation tool for resolving conflict is a situation that occurred between Diana, Director of HR, and an HR staff member who was a member of an HR department team. The team consisted of four HR staff involved in improving a critical service to stakeholders of the organization. The team was designing materials for an organization-wide training program, with training dates already publicized.

One week before the first training session, Bruce, a member of the team, approached Diana with a major problem. He and the two others felt that Sally was not completing her team responsibilities, and continually gave the others excuses for work not accomplished. They were concerned the materials and the training outline would not be completed in time. Two other team members requested that Bruce bring their concern to Diana.

Diana thanked Bruce for bringing the matter to her attention, and asked for an hour to think through the situation and consider alternatives. Bruce agreed. As Diana considered the situation and the remaining work to be completed, she, too, was concerned the team would not be ready for the training to begin in a week. Her criteria for evaluating the alternatives included the following:

- *the conflict be resolved soon*
- *the team continue to work together collaboratively on the project*
- *the materials and training outline be completed on time.*

Following are options Diana considered:

Scenario #1: Immediately talk with Sally to ask how preparations for the training are progressing. Issues with this alternative are that Sally may wonder why Diana is talking with her individually, and guess that a member of the team came to Diana to complain about her. Diana did not want any team conflict to impact the training.

Scenario #2: Bring together the entire team to discuss the progress of the work. Because three team members were aware that Bruce had talked with Diana, the meeting could become uncomfortable and tense. Because Diana was not a member of the team, again Sally may feel someone complained about her.

Scenario #3: Begin the facilitation process by talking with each member of the team individually to get perspectives on the issue and cause. Diana felt there was not enough time in the next week to resolve this situation using the facilitation approach, and still get the work completed in time for the training. The facilitation would take time away—both emotionally and physically—from the effective and efficient accomplishment of the project.

Scenario #4: Negotiate with Bruce on a short-term resolution, and then use the facilitation process in several weeks to resolve it. This alternative met Diana's criteria the best.

Diana met with Bruce, telling him she was very glad he approached her with this issue, noting his conscientiousness toward the project and understanding how awkward this must be for him. She asked several questions about Bruce's perspective on the needs and concerns of the team members. She then explained that the two areas important to him and the others—completing the project on time and the continuing cohesiveness of the team—also were vital priorities for her.

Because of these priorities, she offered both a short- and a long-term solution. First, the other members of the team would take on additional tasks over the next week to complete the materials and training outline. With the receptionist assisting with their daily work, the three team members would have additional time to assist with Sally's project responsibilities. Then, in two weeks, Diana would begin the facilitation process to resolve the issue. Bruce agreed with this solution, as he felt his needs and those of the other two team members were met. He suggested that he call a team meeting for that afternoon, first to discuss the completion of the project, and second to develop an action plan to reassign project responsibilities for the next week.

In this situation, the supervisor is not involved in the conflict, although she has an "interest" in the outcome. Her department potentially could have to deal with a negative public relations issue within the organization. However, she is seen as a "neutral" third party.

Case Study Questions:
1) Are there additional criteria that Diana could have used for evaluating the alternatives?
2) Are there potential additional options for resolution that Diana did not consider?

Using the "Negotiation" Tool when the Supervisor "is" Involved in the Situation

Suppose the example in Case Study 6.3 involved the team pulling together materials for a report Diana needed to give to her boss and other administrators in a week.

Scenario #1: Diana tells Bruce that the materials must be completed in one week, and that if the team members need to work overtime to get that done, that is what they will have to do. Their responsibility as a team is to complete the work within the time frame. In this case, resolution was based on the party that has the most power, clout or resources. Although this type of resolution may resolve the issue in the short-term, it will result in continuing conflict among the team members.

Scenario #2: Suppose Bruce told Diana that it was not fair for him and the two others to work overtime when Sally was not doing her share of the work. They felt they were enabling Sally's lack of responsibility. This was not the first time Sally did not do her share—there was a pattern. This indicated Bruce put himself in an adversarial "position," or drew a line in the sand. To him, this was an integrity issue, and he was tired of Sally's irresponsibility and the team always having to bail her out.

Diana addressed this situation by moving Bruce away from his adversarial "position" and addressing his underlying "interests." She agreed with Bruce that there was an issue and thanked him for bringing it to her attention. Diana then discussed the importance of a team working together in an honest and collaborative way to achieve common goals, and acknowledged that Bruce and the other two team members had similar values. She knew he wanted the issue resolved, and could trust him to make sure that his needs and values would be included in the subsequent facilitation process for long-term resolution.

Scenario #3: Suppose that in addition to the current issue, Bruce came to Diana with a complaint of sexual harassment against Sally. Legally, Diana must deal with the complaint situation as soon as possible. Bruce knew this and used this situation to impact their negotiation.

Scenario #4: Diane focuses on changing people's behavior and improving their relationships. Suppose Diana empowered the members of the team to address and resolve conflict situations themselves. Knowing that all teams eventually engage in disagreement and conflict, when the team was charged to work together, Diana would lead a discussion around conflict, what it may look like, the causes, and methods for resolution. She could recommend that the team utilize several books or Internet sites that provide more information on teams and conflict. She helped the team develop a plan to address conflict when it occurs.

It is evident that this type of negotiation takes more time than the others, but in the long term, the behavior and relationships within the team are transformed. The team members improve a multitude of skills: a sense of leadership, autonomy, respect for the perspectives of others and recognition of the value of others' concerns.

On the other hand, through the conflict resolution process, Diana may discover that Sally has a performance problem. In this case, as Sally's supervisor, she needs to work with Sally to improve her performance. Diana also may learn that Sally is experiencing intrapersonal conflict because of a personal situation, and needs to work with Sally to facilitate alternatives for effective resolution.

Case Study 6.4: HR Staff Member Intrapersonal Conflict

Ellen is the director of the HR department of a comprehensive university with approximately 1,600 employees, and an additional 1,800 part-time student employees. The HR staff members enjoy the stability her presence brings to the office. Two years ago, the director, who was in the position for 25 years, retired. The new director hired left after a year, leaving a part-time interim person in charge of the department until Ellen was hired.

During the first month in her new position, Ellen met with the HR staff to develop department core values and complete a current task-responsibility chart. For several months, she worked with groups in the department to develop flow charts of all major processes. This helped her to understand work flows and procedures, and especially to get to know the staff at a deeper level.

The recruitment process for the department receptionist position recently concluded, with the new person hired a month ago. With the help of the other HR staff, Ellen developed an orientation and training plan that covered the next two months. The department was fortunate that two other staff in the office had been in this position, and could help train Sandra, the new receptionist. Although Sandra's major responsibilities included serving as the department's receptionist, she also hired, trained and supervised several student employees, served as an administrative assistant to the director, and provided clerical assistance to other staff in the department. Ellen considered this position the "hub" of the department.

The layout of the department includes seven individual offices that line the two exterior walls, and two cubicles in the center of the office space. Ellen's office is an exterior walled office that is the furthest distance from the receptionist area. Unless she walks through the office or in the work area, she cannot hear what is happening in the front reception area. Richard's office is located in one of the central cubicles.

For several months, Ellen suspected that Sandra and Richard, the student employment and payroll coordinator, did not always get along well. Several other HR staff told her that Richard often interrupted Sandra while she was talking with a student customer, and at times shouted, over the wall of his cubicle, an answer to a student's payroll or employment question.

Several days ago, Richard stormed into Ellen's office after lunch, complaining that Sandra did not complete a work assignment he gave her, which included making copies for training that began in an hour. He said that Sandra did not do the work intentionally to make him look bad. In his tirade, he said that Sandra continued to give incorrect information to student employees and he was tired of dealing with her incompetence.

Ellen knew that Sandra was at lunch, and an HR student employee was at the reception desk. She walked with Richard to the reception desk and asked the student to make the copies immediately. She then told him she would follow up on his complaints as soon as possible.

Yesterday, Ellen overheard Sandra talking with a student hired by the English Department. Suddenly Richard shouted from his cubicle, "Sandra, this is the third time you gave that incorrect answer! Aren't you listening to me when I correct you?!!" Ellen heard him leave his cubicle and move to the reception area, complaining in a loud voice. In front of the student and another HR student employee, he again told Sandra she was wrong and gave the student employee the correct information. Afterwards, he returned to his cubicle, muttering under his breath.

Ellen realized she needed to deal with the conflict situation between Richard and Sandra as soon as possible to keep it from escalating. In reflecting on the situation, she wrote the following notes:

1. Richard has been in his role as student employment and payroll coordinator for about ten years. Prior to that, he was a financial specialist in the library for seven years.

2. The previous HR director, in the position for many years, allowed the HR staff to resolve their own issues. There was a definite hierarchy in the department, with some staff favored by the director. Richard was one who was favored.

3. Although Sandra is short and petite, she is strong of character, possessing a good work ethic. Her previous work experience was with a local retail chain. In the short time she has been in the position, she has provided a great deal of needed structure to the work of the HR student employees, including the development of a new process for the other HR staff to request that work be done by her or the HR student employees.

4. Richard is tall and stocky. Ellen learned that he needs to improve his time management and customer service skills, having received email complaints from several people who hired students in the academic colleges. She planned to discuss this when they met for his annual performance review in a month.

As Ellen's mentor, help her by discussing the following questions to address this situation.

To download the Conflict/Issue Analysis Worksheet go to **www.HR-higher-ed.com**

Case Study Questions:

1. *What is the primary source(s) of the conflict?*
2. *Identity criteria to evaluate the success of the options you have chosen. Why did you choose them?*
3. *Which tool(s) do you recommend using to resolve the conflict? Why did you choose them?*
4. *Develop your detailed plan for resolution.*

To review discussion of recommendations for Case Study 6.4 questions go to **www.HR-higher-ed.com**

Summary

Although there are many definitions of conflict, Sandra Cheldelin and Ann Lucas in their book, *Academic Administrator's Guild to Conflict Resolution* (2004), describe it best, using the following characteristics:

1. Expressed disagreement occurs between at least two people or groups who have an interdependent relationship.
2. The parties differ around goals, methods, values, or all three.
3. The interaction between the parties involves behaviors designed to defeat, reduce or suppress each other.
4. Each party acts to gain an advantage over the other in an effort to "win."

Causes of conflict include: differing viewpoints, personality, structure of the department or organization, poorly defined responsibilities, inequality in treating people, competition over scarce resources, clashes of values, human drives for success, recognition, power, attacks on personal characteristics and the initiation of significant change.

Conflict need not be destructive; it can be constructive when it produces change, leads to unity of purpose, and promotes collaboration. Addressing conflict in creative ways can enhance problem solving, clarify decision-making, and strengthen the HR staff as a team. Conflict can improve team members' understanding of each other, increase their skills in working together in extremely productive ways, and generate synergy and engagement.

Constructive conflicts encourage open discussion and allow full exploration of each person's needs, concerns, values, and interests, which are the essential ingredients of authentic communication. In addition, conflict can be constructive by providing individuals an opportunity to release pent-up emotions. A model to transform conflict into a problem to be resolved includes the following stages:

1. Analyze the primary source of the conflict
2. Identify criteria to evaluate options
3. Determine tools to use
4. Develop a resolution plan
5. Implement the plan
6. Evaluate success of the plan

Major Themes

Reframing conflict through utilizing the symbolic and HR frames serves as one method in Case Study 6.2 to resolve long-standing conflict.

Leadership of Change is a major thread in this chapter, showing a process for the HR director to empower HR staff members to shape their environment, develop their conflict resolution skills, and approach conflict as an opportunity to create an improved workplace.

Note that many of the questions utilized in Case Study 6.2 are based on **Appreciative Inquiry**.

Evaluation of "Your" HR Department's Chapter 6 Outcome

Outcome Desired: Prepare the HR staff to deal with conflict and resistance to change in positive ways.

Change: Develop the HR staff into a team that works together within a trusting and respectful environment

Key Indicators of Success: (check if "yes")

☐ The HR staff acknowledge and openly discuss conflict issues

☐ There is a process within the department to resolve conflict issues in a productive manner

☐ HR staff exhibit department values in addressing conflict issues

☐ Many conflict issues are resolved at the individual level, not needing the input of the HR director

☐ Conflict issues are dealt with as soon as they appear, however minor they appear to be

☐ Conflict resolution skills are included in the department's core competencies and performance evaluation process

Potential Barriers to Change: (check if "needs attention")

☐ One or more HR staff are uncomfortable with conflict, or are unable to or refuse to address conflict

☐ One or more HR staff feel it is the director's job to deal with conflict

☐ The previous culture in the department included conflict avoidance

☐ One or more HR staff utilize conflict to accomplish personal agendas

Chapter 7

Discover Value and Obtain Support

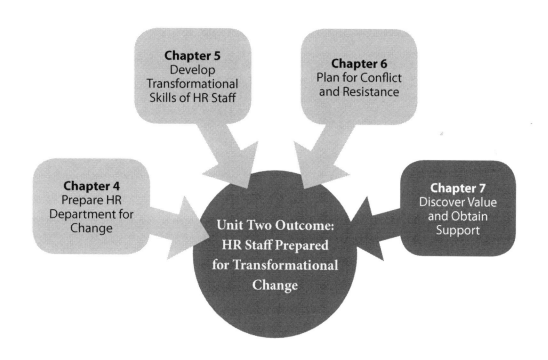

Although the chapters in Unit One outline challenges to higher education and rationale for change, a sound business case often is not enough. The need for change must be "seen" and "felt" by people so that they can become emotionally charged to make change happen. Integrating emotion and logic is at the core of successful change. People need to "see" and "feel" the negative outcome if nothing changes, in addition to the rewards and opportunities of change.

The first three chapters of Unit Two focused on the new HR paradigm and its transformative roles. Then, through presentations, discussions, training, development plans and opportunities for self-reflection, the transformational skills of the HR staff are raised to higher levels. Figure 7.1 outlines the process for learning what key constituents value about the HR function, and to develop a plan to obtain support for the HR paradigm change.

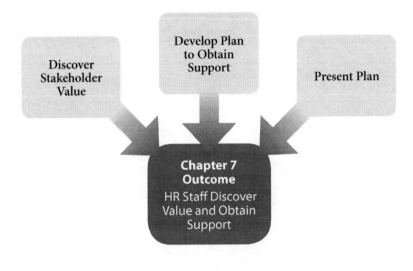

Figure 7.1 Model for discovering stakeholder value and obtaining support for HR paradigm change

Discover Stakeholder Value

Stakeholder value means that HR practices, procedures, programs and professionals provide positive outcomes for faculty, staff, student employees and administrators of the institution. Employees must feel they, personally, are receiving something worthwhile from an HR department initiative.

As HR professionals, we deliver stakeholder value through the multiple roles we play and the core competencies we utilize in our work. In their book, *The HR Value Proposition*, Ulrich and Brockbank (2005) summarize their years of research to show what the HR function must know to add value to the organization. A key outcome of their research reveals that making a strategic contribution accounts for almost half of HR's total influence on the institution's performance. Factors that influence a positive strategic contribution include: culture management, fast change and strategic decision-making. Other outcomes that positively impact performance—but at a lower degree—are personal credibility, HR delivery, business knowledge and HR technology.

> … making a strategic contribution accounts for almost half of HR's total influence on the institution's performance.

Why Does Stakeholder Value Matter?

When HR professionals begin to evaluate their services or potential new projects with the value of stakeholders in mind, the following outcomes occur:

The HR function:

1. becomes proactive instead of reactive
2. moves from implementing "best practices" to delivering "value-added" HR practices
3. is recognized by all stakeholders as bringing value to the table
4. is perceived as helping supervisors and managers accomplish their goals
5. emerges more quickly as a full strategic partner
6. allows HR staff to develop capabilities that enable the institution to compete better now and in the future
7. produces changes that are influenced heavily by realities in the external and internal environment;
8. is built for efficiency and effectiveness
9. achieves measureable and valuable results

The institution:

1. The HR function enhances the institution's efficiency and effectiveness.
2. The HR function creates sustainable competitive advantage for the institution, serving as a partner to compete in a changing and challenging environment to accomplish its vision and mission.

Consequently, "influence with impact occurs when HR professionals start with the beliefs and goals of the receivers." (Ulrich and Brockbank, 2005, p 4). Instead of acting on their own beliefs, goals and actions for what should happen in the institution, HR professionals ask the following questions:

- Who are the key stakeholders we serve?
- What are their goals, values and issues?
- What is important to them?
- What do they want?

Getting answers to these questions directs those in the HR function to acquire the knowledge and skills necessary to align HR activities with stakeholder value.

Why Involve the HR Staff in Identifying Stakeholder Value?

Although those leading the change initiative may understand the need to move the HR function to the transformative model, in developing an "urgency for change," it is vitally important to include the HR staff in the process of gathering information from key campus constituents.

> … it is vitally important to include the HR staff in the process of gathering information from key campus constituents.

Adult learning focuses on applying facts and transforming information into action. When adults understand "why" they should learn, they accept "what" they should learn more readily. For example, HR staff members who have done primarily transactional work in their careers need to understand the challenges facing higher education, and how these impact the HR function and their individual responsibilities. Hearing directly from key stakeholders about what is important to them and how the HR department can contribute toward that helps HR staff members become more open to change.

Most HR staff want to do good work and add greater value. Including them in identifying stakeholder value allows each person to enumerate what HR value means, how it is created, and why it matters. Some HR staff members may be reluctant to do so, thinking they will hear complaints about the HR department and services offered. It may be helpful to frame the context of these interviews as "non-personal." Although complaints or weaknesses about the HR function may be heard, the HR staff members should consider themselves as being "trusted" by constituents to give them honest information that will help strengthen the work they do.

Including Stakeholders in Evaluating HR Deliverables

In their article, Doing Less With Less, Vaillancourt and Brantley (2009) present a model to engage stakeholders in conversations to help evaluate the value and long-term impact of HR deliverables. The value of this process includes reducing the need for transactional HR work and freeing time for HR professionals to focus on transformational work.

Obtaining the input of stakeholders regarding current HR deliverables—especially in an environment of increasingly scarce resources—is crucial. Whether this is an outcome of the work in chapter 18 or in this chapter is not important—the timing depends on your specific situation. If you decide to include this as part of determining stakeholder value, refer to chapter 18, "Stakeholder Input on Current HR Programs."

Methods to Identify Stakeholder Value

We discuss three methods for identifying stakeholder value: one-on-one interviews, focus groups and surveys. Table 7.1 describes each method, with its benefits, weaknesses and process to implement.

Table 7.1 Methods to identify stakeholder value

Description	Benefits	Weaknesses	Process
One-on-one Interviews: meetings with people individually, or with several at one time, to learn facts and opinions about a specific topic	• the interviewee can address his/her concerns and opinions directly • miscommunications can be resolved quickly • provides in-depth information • obtain "facts" plus any insight behind the facts	• the amount of time taken to interview people individually • cannot use data gathered to "generalize"	1. Determine objectives 2. Prepare for the sessions 3. Determine whom to invite 4. Develop agenda with questions 5. Develop background for purpose of interviews and focus group sessions 6. Conduct interviews and focus groups 7. Close by summarizing information learned 8. Summarize information from all sessions 9. Develop report 10. Communicate results to all participants
Focus Groups: group interviews where 8-12 people discuss prepared questions on a specific topic	• obtain "facts" plus any insight behind the facts • elicits many points of view • provides for good conversation on a given topic • provides themes or perspectives • provides spontaneous, unexpected elements	• not a reliable technique for determining an individual's authentic point of view due to "social norms" • cannot use data gathered to "generalize" • need more than one focus group to elicit diverse points of view	
Surveys: a set of questions designed to elicit information from a large number of people	• results can be generalized to make predictions about data gathered • can elicit information from a large number of people easily • can analyze results statistically to give objective data	• correct methodology must be used to analyze data • poorly designed questions impact results • not testing the survey instrument	1. Determine major decision points or what needs to be discovered 2. Determine if another method than surveys is optimal 3. Develop questions; use open-ended questions sparingly 4. Test the survey with a pilot group 5. Determine method to conduct survey, e.g., hard-copy, email, website 6. Analyze results 7. Present results

Prior to choosing the "best" method to identify stakeholder value from the three listed above, we need to consider the questions in Table 7.2.

Table 7.2 Checklist to determine best method to identify stakeholder value

Factor to Consider:	Yes	No	Best Tool if "Yes"
1.Determine answers to questions plus insight into emotions, contradictions, tensions and what is not said			Interview, focus group
2.Determine answers to questions in order to generalize or make predictions about the topic on a large scale			Survey
3.Desire quantitative data to analyze statistically to provide objective outcomes			Survey
4.Elicit additional information not directly addressed in the questions			Interview, focus group
5.Determine an individual's "reliable" point of view			Interview, survey
6.Elicit information that paints a portrait of combined perspectives of a specific group			Focus group
7.Elicit as many points of view as possible			Focus group, survey
8.Generate spontaneous, unexpected conversation to encourage participants to open up, think deeply, and consider alternatives on the topic			Focus group
9.Desire in-depth information from a single individual			Interview
10.Desire qualitative information			Interview, focus group

Case Study 7.1: An Example to Identify HR Stakeholder Value

Jacque was an HR director at several higher education institutions over her professional career. In her current position, she led the effort to identify what is valued about the HR function among supervisors, administrators, and faculty and staff members prior to developing revised HR vision and mission statements and evaluating existing HR deliverables.

STEPS TO DETERMINE STAKEHOLDER VALUE FOR THE HR FUNCTION

Step 1: **Determine project objectives/best methods**
Step 2: **Prepare for the interviews and focus group sessions**
Step 3: **Determine interviewees and invitees to focus groups**
Step 4: **Develop agenda and questions**
Step 5: **Develop background**

Step 6: **Conduct interviews and focus groups**

Step 7: **Summarize information learned from each meeting**

Step 8: **Summarize information learned from all meetings**

Step 9: **Develop a report**

Step 10:Communicate results to all participants

Back to Case Study 7.1

Step 1: *Determine project objectives/best methods. The HR staff members agreed to the following objectives for this project:*

- *elicit qualitative information from diverse groups of employees*
- *provide an environment for open-ended conversations to obtain information outside the given questions*
- *identify key constituents needed to support an HR paradigm shift, and obtain their in-depth value of the HR function*
- *form the foundation for building trusting relationships with stakeholders*
- *identify HR deliverables valued by stakeholders*
- *resolve any misconceptions about the HR function*

In reviewing Table 7.2 to evaluate alternative methods based on these objectives, they decided to utilize a combination of the one-on-one interviews and focus groups. They felt the survey method was not applicable to the objectives for this project.

Step 2: *Prepare for the interviews and focus group sessions.*

- *determine length of each interview and session*
- *schedule dates, times and locations for the focus group sessions*
- *order refreshments for the focus group sessions*

Step 3: *Determine interviewees and invitees to focus groups. Jacque knew that she and the HR staff needed the support of the president's cabinet and other key constituents for the HR paradigm shift. Therefore, she recommended interviewing people one-on-one in the following roles to obtain in-depth information on their perspective of stakeholder value for the HR function:*

- *deans of all academic colleges*
- *vice presidents/chancellors*
- *president/chancellor*
- *CIO*
- *other cabinet members*

Jacque decided to call each of these individuals personally to schedule a one-hour interview in their office, and to explain the objectives for the meeting.

In designing focus group sessions, Jacque understood the importance of inviting people with similar characteristics to a single session. Her research and experiences indicated that a group with highly different characteristics would decrease the quality of the data, because individuals tend to censor their ideas when with people who differ greatly from them in status, education, or job responsibilities. Therefore, the HR staff agreed to conduct multiple 90-minute focus group sessions on the same topic, with people invited to a single focus group session from each of the following employee categories:

- directors of major units or departments
- faculty, including those in a department chair role
- administrative staff
- support staff
- ad hoc teaching staff

To ensure that 8-12 individuals attend a specific session, approximately 20 were invited via an email, with a follow-up hard-copy invitation. Invitees were asked to confirm their attendance.

Step 4: *Develop agenda and questions.* Exhibit 7.1 illustrates the agenda for both the interviews and the focus group sessions. Jacque included each HR staff member in at least one interview and one focus group. Because several served as meeting facilitators in the past, they acted as a co-facilitator of a focus group session with Jacque. Others helped with note-taking.

Exhibit 7.1 Agenda of one-on-one interviews and focus groups

1. Welcome
2. Review of agenda
3. Review of goal of the meeting
4. Review of meeting guidelines (focus groups only)
5. Introductions
6. Discussion questions
7. Summary
8. Next steps

For assistance in developing meeting guidelines, refer to chapter 9.

Jacque and the HR staff members developed the questions detailed in Exhibit 7.2.

Exhibit 7.2 Questions for interviews and focus groups:

1. *What are your current major issues or problems in accomplishing your responsibilities?*
2. *From your perspective, what are the causes of these issues?*
3. *What are the current strengths of the university's HR function?*
4. *What does it mean to you for the university's HR function to be "transformative or strategic"? What will be different? What additional programs or services will exist?*
5. *How can the university's HR function improve or change to deliver increased value to you? What would you like to see more or less of from HR staff members?*

Step 5: *Develop background.* *At the one-on-one interviews, spend a few initial minutes discussing neutral topics to establish a connection with the interviewee. Then, although the invitations indicated the purpose of the interviews and focus group sessions, repeating that as part of the agenda focuses people to the task at-hand. The major points in the purpose statement include an explanation of the following:*

- *project objectives*
- *stakeholder value*
- *why the HR department wants to understand stakeholder value*
- *the HR paradigm shift and how it will be implemented*
- *next steps*

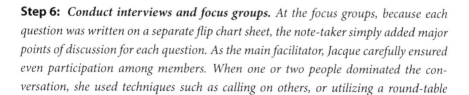

To review the PowerPoint presentation utilized by Jacque go to **www.HR-higher-ed.com**

Step 6: *Conduct interviews and focus groups.* *At the focus groups, because each question was written on a separate flip chart sheet, the note-taker simply added major points of discussion for each question. As the main facilitator, Jacque carefully ensured even participation among members. When one or two people dominated the conversation, she used techniques such as calling on others, or utilizing a round-table* *approach, going in one direction around the table, giving each person a minute to answer a question.*

For each interview, Jacque provided the questions in advance. During the meetings, the note-taker summarized the responses to each question before moving to the next one. During most of the interviews, follow-up questions were asked to elicit more information on the topic.

At the conclusion of each interview, Jacque asked each person if he or she thought the interview covered all the areas of concern, and if there were issues that were not discussed. In addition, she inquired if there was anything about the interview that could be improved.

Key quotations in response to questions by interviewees or focus group participants were written on the flip chart or in discussion notes to utilize later in the report or presentations.

Step 7: *Summarize information learned from each meeting.* As part of building strong relationships, at the conclusion of each interview, Jacque explained to the interviewees or focus group participants that the information learned would be summarized, and incorporated into a report to be shared with them and the entire HR staff. In addition, periodic updates regarding progress made in the HR paradigm shift would be shared.

Immediately after each interview or focus group session, Jacque and the note-taker wrote down any observations, such as the following: What was the participation like for each group? Were there any surprises during the meeting? Were there any emotional responses? Did people differ on their perspective? Did anyone seem uncomfortable about a topic of discussion?

Step 8: *Summarize information learned from all meetings.* After the first several interviews and focus group sessions, Jacque and the note-taker reviewed the information learned and sorted it into logical categories or themes, which provided structure for summarizing successive meetings. These major themes included the following:

1. *Strengths of the HR function*
2. *HR programs to improve or add*
3. *HR elements that create value*

Step 9: *Develop a report.* Jacque and the HR staff members developed a succinct summary report with the following components:

1. *the objectives of the meetings, with a summary of the background to the project*
2. *the positions interviewed one-on-one*
3. *the number of focus group meetings, with participation in each*

4. *the agenda, with questions*
5. *summary of themes (listed in Exhibit 7.3)*
6. *next steps (listed in Exhibit 7.4)*

The next steps focused on the "value" of specific goals or priorities expressed during the interviews and focus group sessions, and included specific, simple and valued actions to generate "quick wins."

Exhibit 7.3 Summary of themes from interviews and focus group sessions

1. Elements of the HR function valued by stakeholders:
- *two-way communication regarding transactional activities*
- *employee advocacy—representing employee interests*
- *personal credibility of HR staff members*
- *administrative support delivery that genuinely serves and cares for employees*

2. HR programs determined to be strengths:
- *retirement counseling*
- *benefit sessions for finalists for faculty, staff and administrative positions*
- *efficient and effective recruitment and hiring policies, practices and training*
- *self-service HR systems*
- *mentoring programs for professional development*

3. Transformational HR programs to improve or add
(in order of number of times discussed):
- *training for managers to ensure they have the necessary skills, knowledge and abilities to effectively supervise employees and deliver institution goals; facilitate discussions with major units to develop strategic goals*
- *all-university staffing plan*
- *metrics or measures of performance to indicate how HR deliverables impact university strategic goals*
- *onboarding program for new faculty and staff*
- *employee leadership/succession plan*
- *comprehensive employee wellness program*
- *assist with reorganization of departments/units, work process design, etc.*
- *HR strategic plan*
- *facilitate a university-wide discussion to improve reward systems for faculty*

Exhibit 7.4 Next steps

1.   Discuss summary report with HR staff members and the vice president for administration
2.   Develop HR department mission and vision statements (within one month)
3.   Improve key internal HR department processes and determine if any HR programs need to be eliminated (within three months)
4.   Develop HR strategic plan with priority goals (within six months)

Step 10: *Communicate results to all participants.* Within a week of the final focus group session and interview, the PowerPoint summary report was placed on the HR department website. A "thank-you" email sent to all participants provided the link to the report.

Jacque states in the email she would continue to communicate updates as she and HR staff members worked through the "next steps" document. She was very satisfied with the results of the interviews and focus group sessions. It was apparent the HR staff members enhanced their perspective on what it means to be a transformational HR function. In addition, hearing from the stakeholders themselves about the elements that are valued increased the motivation and energy of several staff to continue to improve their transformational skills. Jacque's supervisor, the vice president for administration, was pleased with the results, and asked her to make a presentation to the cabinet members at the next meeting.

Develop a Plan to Obtain Support for the HR Paradigm Shift

By discovering stakeholder value in the HR function, the needed information is available to develop a plan to obtain support and commitment for transformational change. This plan essentially serves as a "communication plan" to inform the supervisor and members of the cabinet about the HR paradigm shift, and to obtain the support needed as the process unfolds.

The information in Unit One is organized so much of it can be used in the communication plan. In addition, the detailed examples provided from the interviews and focus group sessions clarify and give improved meaning to "transformational human resources."

Components of the Plan

The communication plan must be polished, succinct and professional. Although the first draft can be written by the leader of the change initiative, the HR staff members must be involved in revising and making recommendations to improve the plan. The plan includes the following components:

1. Detail the need for a changed HR paradigm. Information from Unit One and from interviews and focus group sessions can serve as the basis for describing the "urgency for change."

2. Present the vision of how the HR transformation will impact the university in a meaningful and worthwhile way. Build support for this vision by describing valued examples given during the interviews or surveys, especially from cabinet members. Include the topic of the HR function creating "value," providing solutions to their issues.

3. Describe the process to move the HR function to the strategic level of the university. Highlight the major steps in the change process with a potential timeline to completion. Give specific examples of potential quick wins that excite, get attention and are "valued."

4. Consider any potential substantive and/or political concerns to gaining support. Address those in your plan.

5. Your supervisor and cabinet members typically will be concerned about two issues: How will the HR paradigm shift contribute toward accomplishing the university's strategic goals? How will their constituents react to it? This is where the report on identifying stakeholder value will strengthen the plan. Outline the benefits to the university's supervisors, managers and employees with a move to HR becoming transformational.

6. Include key indicators of success for measuring the progress of the project.

Although not included in the communication plan itself, identify specific people that need to commit and support this project. These individuals must be kept informed about progress of the paradigm shift.

It is vitally important to determine if there are any individuals who might be resistant to HR transformational change, for what reasons and how strongly. This is where initial interviews of key administrators, leaders and constituents will help to identify any resistance to the plan. Brainstorming potential ways the transformation will create value for each level will provide tools to address any resistance.

> It is vitally important to determine if there are any individuals who might be resistant to HR transformational change, for what reasons and how strongly.

In planning to address any resistance, focus on "interests" not on "positions." Although taking a position involves a "win-lose" scenario, staying focused on interests can provide a "win-win" outcome. Refer to Exhibit 7.5 as a reminder of the difference between interest and position.

Exhibit 7.5 "Interests" versus "Positions"

Taking a "position" usually means having a particular viewpoint from which there is little movement. It can be extremely difficult for someone who takes a position on an issue to change his or her mind. For example, assume that one of the people on the Cabinet takes the position that HR should focus on other outcomes instead of becoming transformational and strategic. Instead of continuing with a discussion of what that change looks like to that person, it is more effective to focus on his or her reason, need or goal that underlies the position. The question, "Why?" is powerful in uncovering real reasons. Discovering the "interest" involves understanding what is behind the position, which then offers alternatives to satisfy the person's need or goals.

In addition, plan for reducing any resistance by continuing to focus on "stakeholder value," which includes knowing the "value" of any constituent who may resist the HR paradigm shift.

Present the Plan to Obtain Support

After drafting the communication plan, discuss it with your supervisor to get his/her support and recommendations for improvement. Your supervisor may request that you give a presentation of the plan to the entire cabinet, either at that point or in the future as your plan unfolds and benefits begin to appear.

To review the PowerPoint presentation of a sample communication plan go to **www.HR-higher-ed.com**

Summary

Stakeholder value means that HR practices, procedures, programs and professionals provide positive outcomes for faculty, staff, student employees and administrators of the institution. Employees must feel they personally are receiving something worthwhile from an HR department initiative. As HR professionals, we deliver stakeholder value through the multiple roles we play and the core competencies we utilize in our work. Three methods for identifying stakeholder value are one-on-one interviews, focus groups and surveys.

The steps to determine stakeholder value for the HR function consist of the following:
1. determine project objectives
2. choose method(s) to collect information
3. prepare for data collection by determining length of sessions, scheduling dates, times and locations of the sessions, determining means of data collection, etc.
4. determine participants
5. develop agenda, questions and background information
6. conduct sessions
7. summarize information learned
8. determine if project objectives are met
9. develop report
10. communicate results

By discovering stakeholder value in the HR function, the needed information is available to develop a plan to obtain support and commitment for transformational change. This plan serves as a communication plan to inform the supervisor and members of the cabinet about the HR paradigm shift, and to obtain the support needed as the process unfolds. Components of the plan include the following:
1. detail the need for a changed HR paradigm
2. present the vision for how the HR transformation will impact the university
3. describe the process utilized for the HR paradigm shift
4. consider and address any potential substantive concerns to gaining support
5. include key indicators of success for measuring the progress of the HR paradigm shift

Obtaining the input of stakeholders regarding current HR deliverables—especially in an environment of increasingly scarce resources—is crucial. Whether this is an outcome of the work in chapter 18 or in this chapter is not important—the timing depends on the specific institution and situation. This process is summarized in chapter 18.

Evaluation of "Your" HR Department's Chapter 7 Outcome

Outcome Desired: Your supervisor and other cabinet members see and feel the need for change

Change: An urgency is developed for the HR function to move from transactional to transformational

Key Indicators of Success: (check if "yes")

☐ HR staff understand the components of stakeholder value

☐ Key constituents support the HR paradigm shift

☐ Your supervisor and other cabinet members support the need for change

☐ Your supervisor and other cabinet members ask hard questions, taking the time to understand the meaning of change

☐ Your supervisor and other cabinet members expect a thorough implementation plan

☐ Your supervisor and other cabinet members want continual communication about progress of the change

Potential Barriers to Change: (check if "needs attention")

☐ Your supervisor and cabinet members do not see or feel that the rationale for change is compelling

☐ Rationale for change does not include both internal and external data

☐ An organizational culture that avoids confrontation

☐ An organizational or department structure that supports narrow functional goals

Unit Two Summary

As shown below, we made a great deal of progress in Unit Two to prepare for transformational change. We understand the components of the new HR paradigm, along with the external and internal forces driving these changes. Knowing that change often causes conflict issues, we discussed conflict and methods of resolving it. We developed a process to raise the skill level of the HR staff through developing employee core competencies, assessment of skills, and individual development plans. The HR staff members are involved intricately in discovering stakeholder value in the HR function, and developing the plan to obtain support for the HR paradigm shift.

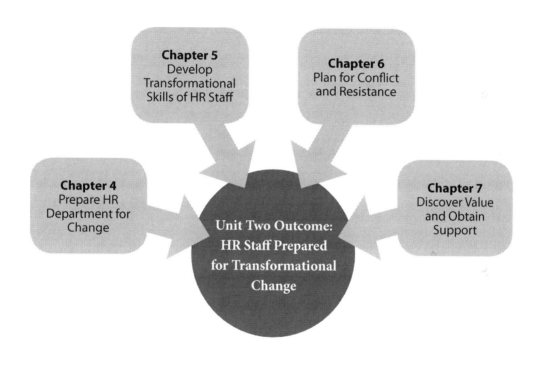

Unit Two model for preparing the HR department for change

Throughout Unit Two, we have used case studies as a method to practice the knowledge and skills described in the chapters. Although recommended answers to the case studies are provided on the website, there definitely are additional ways to deal with each situation. We encourage you to facilitate these discussions in your department, and email us the additional answers for us to include on the website. We will give your HR department the credit it deserves!

How are administrators, supervisors, and the HR function itself impacted by the concepts explored in Unit Two?

This unit definitely "builds the foundation" in preparing the HR department for change. The first difference noticed by stakeholders after the initial changes to the HR function, is increased value offered by HR staff. The department developed core values that focus on providing value to stakeholders. The skills of the HR staff are noticeably enhanced. They facilitate focus group sessions, and ask more questions about the needs and expectations of stakeholders, and how those can be satisfied.

How long does this process take? It depends on the HR staff and where each is individually in his/her acceptance of change and transition. As the HR director, you may need to work more closely with some staff than with others to encourage the development of skills. Some HR staff may leave the department, no longer feeling a "job-interest alignment." This provides an opportunity to utilize the HR recruitment brand outlined in Unit Three in recruiting and hiring new employees.

Unit Two Outcome Desired: HR Staff are Prepared for Transformational Change

Chapter 4 Outcome: Increased HR staff knowledge and understanding of the HR paradigm shift and the need for improved transformative skills

Key Indicators of Success: Check (x) if "yes"

- [ ] All HR staff understand the need for change
- [ ] All HR staff ask hard questions, taking time to understand the meaning of the change
- [ ] All HR staff "see" and "feel" the need for change
- [ ] All IIR staff support the need for change on a day-to-day basis
- [ ] All HR staff understand transactional versus transformational work
- [ ] All HR staff actions reflect HR department core values
- [ ] All HR staff discuss potential changes among themselves
- [ ] All HR staff develop enhanced long-term perspectives

Chapter 5 Outcome: Improved HR staff level of transformational skills

Key Indicators of Success: Check (x) if "yes"

- [ ] HR staff participate openly and positively building their individual development plan

- [ ] The development plans include goals, time lines and action plans
- [ ] Periodic one-on-one meetings occur between the HR director and individual staff to evaluate progress of their development plans
- [ ] The development plans include a clear method for measuring success of the goals
- [ ] All HR staff are committed to accomplishing their development plans
- [ ] Open and honest communication occurs between the HR director and all HR staff

Chapter 6 Outcome: *Improved conflict management skills for HR staff*

Key Indicators of Success: Check (x) if "yes"

- [ ] All HR staff acknowledge and openly discuss conflict issues
- [ ] There is a process within the department to resolve conflict in a productive manner
- [ ] All HR staff exhibit department values in addressing conflict issues
- [ ] Many conflict issues are resolved at the individual level, not needing the input of the HR director
- [ ] Conflict issues are dealt with as soon as they appear, however minor they appear to be
- [ ] Conflict resolution skills are included in the department's core competencies and performance evaluation process

Chapter 7 Outcome: *Your supervisor and other cabinet members see and feel the need for change*

Key Indicators of Success: Check (x) if "yes"

- [ ] All HR staff understand the components of stakeholder value
- [ ] Key constituents support the HR paradigm shift
- [ ] Your supervisor and other cabinet members support the need for change
- [ ] Your supervisor and other cabinet members ask hard questions, taking the time to understand the meaning of change
- [ ] Your supervisor and other cabinet members expect a thorough implementation plan
- [ ] Your supervisor and other cabinet members want continual communication about progress of the change

Unit Three

Become Catalysts for Change

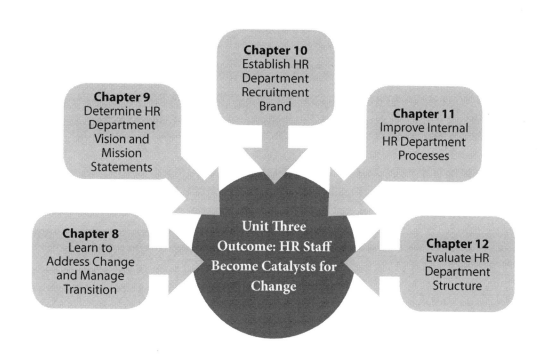

Unit Three Model for developing the HR staff to become catalysts for change

In Unit Three, together we learn about change and transition, work through the processes of improving the HR department functions, establishing an HR department recruitment brand, and evaluating the structure of the HR department. Developing more efficient and effective internal processes will continue to improve the transformative skills of all HR staff, and free time for involvement in additional change initiatives external to the department.

The books, *Leading Change*, by John Kotter (1996), and *The Heart of Change*, by John Kotter and Dan Cohen (2002), introduce the following eight steps to successfully initiate organizational change.

Step 1: Establish Urgency for Change

Step 2: Build Guiding Team(s)

Step 3: Develop the Vision and Strategy

Step 4: Communicate for Buy-In

Step 5: Empower Action

Step 6: Generate Short Term Wins

Step 7: Consolidate and Continue Change Initiatives

Step 8: Anchor New Culture

In our HR paradigm change process, so far we have touched on the first six steps of this change process. The first step in the change process is to establish the urgency for change, developed in the first two units of this book. We build the HR team, change step two, in chapters 4 through 7, by improving their conflict resolution and other transformative skills. We involve them intricately in the work of creating HR core values, HR core competencies, and individual development plans.

Discovering stakeholder value in the HR function and developing a plan to obtain support for the HR paradigm change in chapter 7 clarifies the direction of change for the HR staff. This third step then motivates them to take action in the right direction. In addition, the work of chapter 7 is included in step four in the change process.

Step five in the change process enables the HR staff to take action in moving to work in a transformative way. Although we began this effort in Unit Two by involving them in developing core values, core competencies and a plan to obtain support for the HR paradigm change, in Unit Three we move to a deeper level of action through improving internal HR functions.

In Unit Two, we also created short-term wins regarding the HR paradigm shift, step six in the change process, and Unit Three continues this effort through improving internal HR functions. Steps seven and eight, sustaining the change effort and incorporating the change within the HR department culture, are addressed in Units Four and Five.

The work of Unit Three incorporates steps four, five and six of Kotter's change process, and continues with steps two and three, building the skills, strengths and vision of the HR staff.

Learn to Address Change and Manage Transition

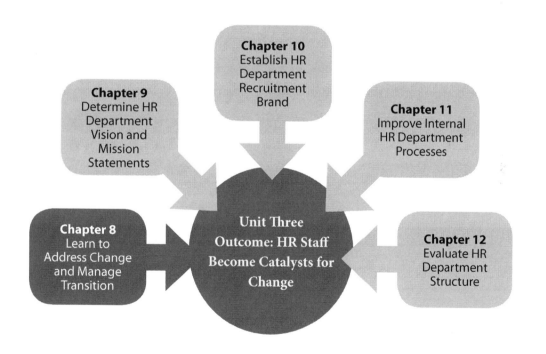

Chapter 8 Learn to address change and manage transition

As an advocate of professional development, the HR leader role must be intricately involved in the learning process. Although it is extremely valuable for individuals to learn through attending conferences, workshops and seminars, or work toward an academic degree, having actual on-the-job experiences intensifies the learning process. Multiple methods of learning can be highly beneficial in the organizational change process.

We all have returned from a workshop or seminar highly motivated by the experience, only to have none of the learning impact our workplace. The folder of workshop materials, filed in a desk drawer, is soon forgotten because of other work priorities.

We challenge you to try a new method of learning together: reading and discussing a common book. At this point, a book such as *Managing Transitions: Making the Most of Change*, by William Bridges (2003), or a similar book on change and transition, is the optimal choice.

There are at least two alternatives in discussing the book. One is to schedule one-on-one meetings each month with each staff member, where you will discuss 2-5 questions from the readings. A second is to schedule one longer staff meeting each month, to discuss the chapter readings and questions as an entire staff. If any staff are resistant to change, it may be best to meet with each staff member individually, and still meet with the entire staff monthly.

Figure 8.1 delineates the model to address the change and manage transition to a transformative HR paradigm.

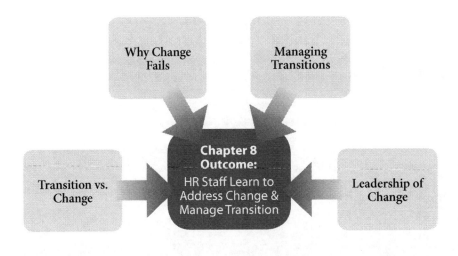

Figure 8.1 Model to address change and manage transition

Transition versus Change

Change and transition do not mean the same thing. In an HR paradigm shift, the "change" is the new transformative culture, whereas the "transition" is the process of getting to this new culture. The change is situational and normally occurs at a point in time; the transition can be highly emotional for those involved. In many cases, the transition period is the most difficult for people, with the major role of the leader being to help people through this transition if the change is to work.

Let us discuss the "change" and when it starts. It is fairly easy to understand when the change of moving to a new computer system starts, as there is normally a "start date" when the old system is taken down, and a new system, or several modules of it, is operational. However, the start date for the change to a new culture or way of doing things cannot be pinpointed as easily. Regardless, a start date is necessary in moving people through the transition period.

> In an HR paradigm shift, the "change" is the new transformative culture, whereas the "transition" is the process of getting to this new culture.

As shown in Figure 8.2, the transition process comprises three stages. In our case, these stages include the ending of a culture that is primarily transactional, the period in-between when the old culture is gone but the new culture is not fully developed (Bridges calls this the "neutral zone"), and the beginning of the new transformational culture (Bridges, 2003).

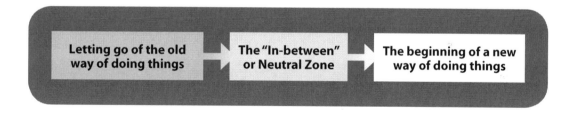

Figure 8.2 Three stages of the transition process

Why Change Fails

Many reasons exist for why a change initiative fails or never gets started. The major ones follow:

1. One or more of the people involved do not understand or move through all three stages of the transition process.

2. One or more steps of the eight-step change process is not built into the foundation for change.

3. Change is an iterative process. at times, one or more steps need to be revisited, but are not.

4. Although sufficient data are gathered to indicate urgency for a change initiative, the leader does not provide any compelling emotional situation to allow people to "see and feel" the need for change.

5. The structure of the department or organization is not evaluated for effectiveness.

6. Specific systems that hamper change, e.g., weak training programs or performance management processes, are not identified and strengthened.

7. Identifying and strengthening skills of the HR staff is not done.

8. Resistance to the change initiative, including helping those without a "good fit" to move on, is not dealt with.

9. The leader of the change initiative does not understand the role of leading and managing transition and change

Throughout this chapter, we use the case study of the HR function at American University (AU), a medium-sized private university, to illustrate the importance of the first four reasons why a change initiative fails.

Case Study 8.1

Dennis, the current HR director, has extensive experience in organizational development through working in the HR function in both the private and public higher education sectors. Dennis's supervisor, the vice president of administration, strongly supported the HR paradigm shift from transactional to transformative work.

In his first three months as the HR director at AU, Dennis spent time with each HR staff member, learning his/her responsibilities and understanding the culture and history of the department. Through his own facilitation and the assistance of a staff member from another department, the HR department updated its core values, and HR core competencies were in place.

Dennis was about to have his first one-on-one meeting with an HR staff member regarding the book, Managing Transitions. *His goals included determining where each person was in the transition process, and enhancing his/her learning about change and transition. He decided to discuss the book individually with each staff member and then bring that information to an entire HR staff meeting for a summary discussion. Dennis was excited about these meetings and anxious to begin the process of improving internal HR processes. He hoped it would not take long to discuss transitions and develop a transition plan.*

Dennis asked each staff member to prepare individual answers to the following questions before discussing them in their one-on-one meetings:

1. For you personally, what do you see "ending" with the change to a transformative HR culture?
2. As an HR staff member, what will identify the "ending" time?
3. What will be the duration of the "neutral zone" for you?
4. What will a new beginning in HR look like to you?
5. What will help you to move through the phases of the transition?

After meeting individually with each HR staff member, Dennis realized he had a problem: several long-time staff indicated that they were very unclear about the HR paradigm change, especially about what would end and what would begin. In fact, two staff members indicated their job responsibilities and how they perform their jobs would not change at all. They felt their processes could not change.

Dennis thought back to the materials they read and discussed regarding the external forces driving the HR paradigm shift. He and the staff discussed these forces thoroughly, along with the results of his interviews with campus leaders on stakeholder value in relation to the HR function. Had he missed something?

Over the next few days, Dennis reflected on this situation, and decided to review the change steps in Kotter's book, Leading Change (1996) prior to talking with his mentor. When reading about the first step, developing urgency for the change initiative, the answers became clear:

- He had not provided a situation where the HR staff members emotionally could see and feel the need for change.
- He had not included the HR staff in his interviews with stakeholders.
- They had not discussed at a deeper level what transformative work looked and felt like.
- Many of the HR staff members did not understand the difference between change and transition.

Dennis realized that understanding the transition process was intricately connected to the first step in the change process. At the next week's extended HR staff meeting, Dennis was ready. The agenda consisted of the three main items and appreciative inquiry questions summarized in Exhibit 8.1.

As Dennis distributed the agenda and note pads, he explained that during the first 15 minutes of the meeting, they would individually answer the first question, writing each answer on a separate note. For example, if there were 15 different changes in answering question one, then 15 different notes were posted on the flip chart titled "Changes." The notes with 1-3 positive outcomes from question two were posted on a second flip chart titled "Positive Outcomes," etc.

The seniority of the HR staff members was 2 to 23 years, and as individuals

Exhibit 8.1 Extended HR staff meeting agenda topics

1. Past changes within the HR department
   a. What changes have you experienced within the HR department?
   b. For you personally, what are 1-3 positive outcomes from one of these changes?
   c. Which of these positive outcomes can potentially relate to the new HR paradigm shift?

2. Transformational versus transactional work
   a. Review HR department Task-Responsibility Chart

3. Three phases of the transition process
   a. Using one of the recent examples in #1a above, how were the three phases of transition worked through? What went well and what issues arose?

answered the first question the flip chart soon filled with multiple notes that were posted on top of other notes. Next, Dennis asked each staff member to share one "positive" change experience. As stories were told, other individuals nodded in agreement or smiled knowingly. One person's story included the resignation of the previous HR director, which caused ripples of laughter. The magnitude of changes experienced related to personnel, technology, processes, policies, and physical workspace. Illustrating the enormous number of changes the HR staff collectively experienced, and telling their stories, engaged them emotionally.

At that point, Dennis pointed to the remaining parts of the first question and asked each staff member to relate a positive outcome resulting from a change, and then to explain how that outcome could relate to the new HR paradigm shift. As staff members related their thoughts, Dennis summarized them on another flip chart. During this step in the process, staff members felt comfortable enough with each other to ask detailed follow-up questions such as: What will that mean?; How will that happen?; How do you know?; How do you feel about that? The conversation was extremely authentic and personal, with individuals helping others work through emotions.

Eventually, one staff member asked, "So what is the next step? Can we have a discussion about what transformational work we already do?" Dennis smiled and handed each person a copy of the Task-Responsibility Chart they completed a few months ago, containing the primary and back-up responsibilities for each person in the department. He said, "We will review each HR responsibility on this chart and indicate if it is transactional or transformative."

The results were what Dennis expected. The majority of the responsibilities were transactional, in that they focused on what the department did instead of what was *delivered, and in most cases reacted to events happening instead of being proactive. As a group, next they discussed the difference between transactional and transformative work. Dennis gave them a summary sheet of his interviews with campus leaders, outlining what they valued from the HR function and the changes they needed as part of the HR paradigm shift.*

Dennis concluded the discussion of the first two agenda items by saying, "I realize I made a major mistake by not including you in my meetings with stakeholders to determine what they value about the HR department. I apologize for that. However, it is evident that they want more from us than what we currently deliver. We need to develop a transition plan to provide stakeholder value and to work in different ways. Next week, we will have a special staff meeting to begin this process. In the meantime, we'll work through the remaining agenda item before ending this meeting."

In response to the third question, one person brought up the situation a year ago—before Dennis moved to AU—where the position with responsibility for faculty recruitments, hiring, tenure, and renewal and promotion functions, moved from the provost's office to the HR department. As people discussed aspects of this move, Dennis summarized them on a flip chart under their appropriate headings of Endings, Neutral Zone, and New Beginning. Other staff contributed several similar transition examples, with the result that people were much more comfortable with the meanings of these three phases of the transition process.

Throughout the next week, the staff members discussed "Dennis's value proposition" and the flip charts of posted notes from the meeting left in the conference room. Dennis heard laughter and comments like, "How did you ever get through that change? Did you ever consider leaving the department? Do you believe that Dennis apologized to us? That is the first time I can remember an apology from my boss!" Several people teased him about being the first "good" HR director they had in years!

Managing Transitions

As explained earlier, barriers to change can include not adding an emotional component to the urgency for change, one or more people involved not moving through all three stages of the transition process, and not understanding that change is an iterative process, with the need at times to revisit earlier steps. In our case study, Dennis realized all of these barriers existed, and as a leader understood he must deal with them before moving forward. It is vitally important to recognize that the path to change and through transition is not always a straight line. Successful transition and change initiatives often include the "two steps forward, one step backward" approach.

Tools to Assist in Managing the Transition Period

Leading people through the transition period can be easier utilizing the tools as outlined in Exhibit 8.2 (Bridges, 2003). Although specific tools are indicated for each transition phase, because these phases are interrelated, the tools can enable progress through other stages.

Exhibit 8.2 Tools to help manage transition (Bridges, 2003)

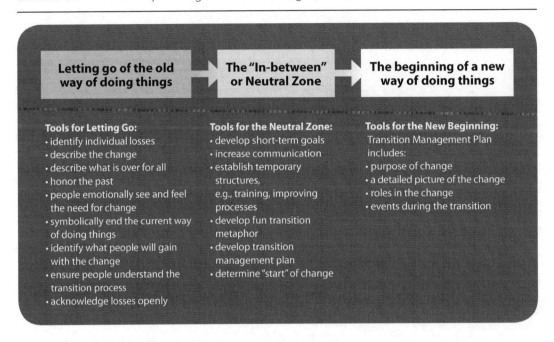

A major component of successfully moving through the phases of the transition period is to increase communication by utilizing the tools described in Exhibit 8.2. Dennis began this process by reading and discussing the *Managing Transitions* book together with the HR staff as a method to increase communication and help people understand the transition process. He then facilitated a meeting to allow the HR staff to emotionally see and feel the need for change, while allowing them to honor the past.

> A major component of successfully moving through the phases of the transition period is to increase communication…

The next step in managing the transition process is to involve the HR staff in developing a transition management plan, which addresses the process of the change on a personal level and starts where people currently are in the transition, and moves them forward step by step. The transition plan is designed to help people let go, negotiate the neutral zone, and engage their hearts and heads with the change itself.

Described in Figure 8.3 are the benefits of having the plan and involving the HR staff in developing it. These benefits include elements that strengthen the HR department in multiple ways.

Figure 8.3 The benefits of a transition management plan

First, the HR staff members develop a deeper awareness of the three phases in the transition, and this knowledge prepares them to deal with issues that develop during the transition. Communication within the team strengthens as they discuss one-on-one and with each other their individual "endings," the "neutral zone," the "new beginning," and the timing of these stages. In addition, they discuss recent changes in the HR department within this model, and point out things that could have been done better. Essentially, the HR staff members develop a tightly-knit team in learning how to work through transition together, discuss their anxieties regarding the change, and provide advice to the HR director regarding the transition.

Another benefit is assessing the readiness of the HR department for the change. Any weaknesses within the department are identified and strengthened. Methods are developed to increase innovation. One idea to create a fun environment and label the transition period is for the HR staff to brainstorm a fun metaphor to describe the neutral zone. An example is using the acronym *NEON* for the transition period to a transformative culture. This acronym stands for *Not Employing Outdated Notions*, referring to thinking and working in new and innovative ways.

During a transition period, it is vitally important to provide a consistent message from the HR staff to the campus community. The plan includes components to provide communication to the most effective campus opinion makers. Establishing temporary systems, such as training on business process improvement and team building, provides structure during the neutral zone phase of the transition.

It is important during the transition, when the HR staff members are between the old and the new way of doing things, to provide short-term goals, and roles or "parts" in the transition.

Back to Case Study 8.1

Dennis realized that some of the HR staff did not yet understand what needed to change in the HR function and why, or what the "picture" of the change looked like. He decided to continue meeting individually with the HR staff each month and to dedicate the majority of the weekly staff meetings in the next month to develop the key components of the transition management plan.

At the next staff meeting, Dennis facilitated a discussion of the following questions provided to staff members in advance. After the last meeting, most of the staff members were ready to describe their emotions regarding the potential HR paradigm shift.

1. What emotions did you feel when you heard peers sharing stories of change and its positive outcomes?

2. When reviewing our Task-Responsibility chart, what were you thinking when you saw that most of our HR responsibilities are transactional?

3. What struck you the most when you reviewed the summary of my interviews with key campus leadership?

4. As you consider a changed culture in the HR department, what will that look and feel like for you?

5. What do you see as your role during the transition period?

To Dennis's surprise, the first three questions generated discussion about the "endings" people personally felt after the last staff meeting. Feelings were mixed. Some individuals were frustrated that the department continued to work in transactional ways. Others were angry because their work was no longer appreciated by employees. Still others were confused and wondered when employees began to want changes. Exhibit 8.3 summarizes some of the endings expressed.

Dennis asked those who were in the department for many years to describe some of their best memories and interactions with employees as a method to continue to honor the past. There were stories like, "Oh yeah, I remember him, he always had a few jokes to tell when he came into the office!" "Remember that international employee who threw a big party and invited us when she gained citizenship!" "Remember that supervisor who would come into my office and talk forever while he signed his employees' timecards? We actually developed a plan where the receptionist called me after 15 minutes to give me an excuse to leave!" "Remember when an angry and intoxicated employee cornered you in your office, and we had to call campus security?"

Exhibit 8.3 Losses people felt with moving to a changed culture

- *a familiar way of doing my work*
- *frustration with not understanding the need for change*
- *not feeling my work is valued any longer*
- *being the new person in HR and "not knowing" current processes*
- *knowing I have the skills and knowledge to do the work I've always done*
- *knowing what employees expect of our department, and of me*

Dennis moved to question four about the change. He realized people needed more detail than, "transformative work," and "HR paradigm shift," as these terms did not tell them what would be different and how the change would impact them on a day-to-day basis. After a great deal of discussion and flip-charting of answers, their "picture" of the change is summarized in Exhibit 8.4.

Exhibit 8.4 HR staff detail their "picture" of the change

- *more efficient processes and ways of doing business*
- *special programs are developed by the HR department in partnership with others on campus*
- *different jobs and responsibilities within HR; revised position descriptions*
- *more campus training done by HR, e.g., assessing employee performance, dealing with difficult employees, recruiting basics, legal issues*
- *one-on-one sessions on retirement planning*
- *work with supervisors on potentially restructuring versus recruiting same position*
- *HR department goals everyone is responsible for*
- *using metrics to evaluate processes and programs*
- *the HR director a member of the president's cabinet*
- *expanding our skills sets*
- *being viewed by constituents as providing valued service*
- *potential for promotion*

With this collective discussion and list describing what it would look and feel like to work within a transformative HR culture, Dennis saw sparks of recognition in people's faces, along with increased excitement as they expressed their personal vision of the change. The last question continued to motivate people as they brainstormed potential roles during the transition period. These roles are outlined in Exhibit 8.5.

Exhibit 8.5 HR staff roles during the transition period

- *active participant or facilitator in business process improvement*
- *lead or participate in special task groups, e.g., document imaging, recruitment technology*
- *strengthen transformative skills*
- *work to accomplish transition management plan*
- *document history of transition and change process*

Dennis then moved the discussion to when the transformational culture—or the change in how the HR staff worked—would start. Normally, each change has a definitive date when it begins, which can be very different than the new beginning phase of the transition. He wanted to ensure the HR staff understood the difference.

On a flip chart, he listed items that indicate the start of the change: revised internal to HR department processes, updated HR staff position descriptions, HR staff working with external constituents in new ways. Together, the HR staff determined it would take approximately six months to get to this point, and set that date as the "start date" for the change. They understood that date could change, depending on their work in redesigning processes.

Next, Dennis divided the staff into groups of two or three, and asked them to discuss the following questions and write their answers on one of the five flip charts labeled: Endings, Neutral Zone, New Beginning, HR Staff Gain, Advice for HRD. Note these questions are similar to those Dennis first asked as he met one-on-one with each HR staff member in discussing the book, Managing Transitions.

1. *How will you personally know when you have let go of the old ways of doing things?*
2. *For you, what will be the duration of the neutral zone?*
3. *When will your heart and head be engaged in the change? (This is the new beginning phase of the transition.)*
4. *What will you gain from the change?*
5. *What advice do you give to the HR director about the transition?*

From the discussion of the third question, "When will your heart and head be engaged in the change?" the HR staff understood the possibility that some of them would not be present in the new beginning phase of the transition at the actual "start" of the change itself.

A summary of the answers, listed in Exhibit 8.6, indicate the HR staff better understand the HR paradigm shift and are ready to carry out the transition plan. At this point, Dennis could move ahead and complete the transition management plan with the HR staff. Although they had a rocky start, the HR team now could "feel" and "see" the change.

Exhibit 8.6 Back to the endings, neutral zone, new beginning

Question #1: How will you personally know when you have let go of the old ways of doing things?
- *I have a new self-identity in how I do my work and how others see me.*
- *It has already happened for me.*
- *We have improved the major processes I work with and I understand them thoroughly.*
- *We have developed the transition management plan and I see the details of the transition.*
- *I do not know yet.*

Question #2: For you, what will be the duration of the neutral zone?
- *At this point I can see the end of the neutral zone.*
- *We finish redesigning the processes I am responsible for.*
- *I do not know yet.*
- *The neutral zone is already done for me.*

Question #3: When will your heart and head be engaged in the change?
- *When the processes I'm responsible for are improved, in place and I'm comfortable with them.*
- *When my skills improve so that I feel comfortable working with others in different ways.*
- *I can stop saying, "What does transformative work mean?"*
- *I am there!!*
- *I do not know yet.*

Question #4: What will you gain from the change?
- *increased knowledge and training*
- *considered a trusted partner by campus constituents*
- *ability to change processes and create better ways of doing my job*
- *a potential promotion*
- *I do not know yet.*

Question #5: What advice do you give the HR director for the transition?
- *provide support to us with the extra work involved in the transition*
- *help keep us on the positive side; have fun*
- *develop and use a transition plan*
- *make sure we have "T" to the "third power," or "time, technology, training"*
- *plenty of communication within the HR team*

Develop a Draft of the Transition Management Plan

It may seem like it took a long time to get to where we develop the purpose of the change along with the rest of the transition management plan. Remember, the phases of the transition are not always linear. The path depends on where each HR staff member is in the process of letting go, moving through the neutral zone, and engaging in the change. What is important is that each barrier listed in this chapter in the "Why Change Fails" section is worked through to completion.

Next, Dennis developed the following goals for the plan:

- *Prepare the HR staff to engage their "hearts" and "heads" with the paradigm shift.*
- *Continue discussions with the HR staff—both individually and within the team as a whole—regarding the transition and change.*
- *Engage the HR staff in developing and implementing the steps of the plan.*
- *Develop the HR staff to be "agents of change."*

Table 8.1 describes the draft plan template Dennis provided the HR team for their next meeting. The HR staff together worked through each item of the draft including the change purpose, and made changes, additions and other recommendations. They inserted a timeline showing when each item should be completed, and used the com-

Table 8.1 Draft transition management plan

Item	Responsibility	Timeline	Comments
Change Purpose: Due to the current crisis in higher education, HR needs to serve its constituents in ways that align with the strategic plan of the university.	HR Team		Revise both the "purpose" and the "picture" as needed
Describe the "Picture" of change	HR Team		Refer to Exhibit 8.4
Describe HR staff roles during the transition	HR Team		Refer to Exhibit 8.5
Train HR team on improving business processes	HRD		
Begin improving internal HR processes	HRD and HR team		
Identify weaknesses of the HR department and strengthen them	HR project team		
Brainstorm a fun metaphor for the transition	HR team		
Develop methods to increase innovation	HR project team		
Provide support for HR team	HRD		
Celebrate all successes	HR team		
Communicate within HR department	HRD and HR team		
Communicate to campus leaders	HRD		
Update position descriptions	HRD		

ments section to indicate where the item was in the process of completion.

Although the "purpose" and a "picture " of the change, along with HR staff roles, were discussed and developed, Dennis understood the importance of revisiting these topics periodically, as each could change in the perspective of individual staff members. Table 8.2 summarizes the four major barriers Dennis faced in the initial move of the HR department to a transformative culture, and identifies the tools he used to work through these barriers. Note that when Dennis provided situations for the HR staff to "see and feel" the need for the change, they understood the need for change at a deeper level and were able to engage more with the phases of transition.

Table 8.2 Case Study 8.1 summary of barriers to change

Barriers to Change	Tools Used
1. One or more of the eight steps in Kotter's process for change is not built into the foundation for change.	Change Step 1: provide a compelling emotional situation for change: • increased communication with HR staff by discussing previous changes, their positive outcomes, and how those could relate to the current change; shared summary of stakeholder value interviews • apologized for not including the HR staff in the interviews • reviewed Task-Responsibility chart Change Step 3: develop a vision for the change • developed a "picture" of what the change will look like • brainstormed what individuals will "gain" with moving to the vision
2. Although sufficient data are gathered to indicate urgency for a change initiative, the leader does not provide any compelling emotional situation to allow people to "see and feel" the need for change."	• refer to Change Step 1 above • reviewed the Task-Responsibility chart for difference between transactional and transformational work • encouraged telling of "stories" to honor the past
3. One or more of the people involved do not understand or move through all three stages of the transition process.	• increased communication through reading common book, one-on-one discussions of the book, extra staff meetings to discuss change and transition • discussed past changes and transitions and how those impacted people personally • discussed individual "losses and gains" with the change • discussed individual "roles" during the transition • established temporary structures such as training for business process improvement and team-building • determined the "start" of the change • developed the transition plan with the HR staff
4. Change is an iterative process; at times, one or more steps need to be revisited, but are not.	• discussed the three phases of transition in more detail • included a process in the transition plan to continually review the change purpose, picture and roles as perspectives of HR staff change

Leadership of Change

First introduced in Unit Two, leadership of change is a continuing thread throughout this book. At this point in the transition, eleven key components can be identified as being priority for the leader of change. These are listed in Table 8.3, which also indicates the chapters where these topics are discussed.

Table 8.3 Key components of leadership of change

Key Leadership of Change Component	Discussed in Chapter
1.Building trust and respect between the leader and the HR team	8
2.Building trust among the HR team	8, 11
3. Challenging the HR team during the process improvement stage	11
4. Encouraging risk-taking and innovation	11
5. Continuing to develop the skills of the HR staff members	Units Two – Five
6. Empowering the HR staff to enable action	Units Two – Five
7. Evaluating the HR department structure for effectiveness	12
8. Dealing with any resistance to change	6, 11,13,19
9. Accomplishing the transition management plan	8
10. Providing support for the HR team during the transition	8
11. Role modeling desired behaviors and skills	8

Building Trust and Respect

It is extremely important, as the leader of a change initiative, to have the trust and respect of those people you are leading through a transition toward a change. Especially in a culture change, which is more difficult for people to grasp than a change that can be "seen," is it important for people to have trust in the leader. Trust is a complex topic, as it is so personal. Having trust in someone depends on a person's past experiences with that particular person. Did that person show he/she could be trusted through his/her actions and words? If there is distrust from past experiences, it can be difficult to regain trust. In addition, a person's past experiences with trusting people outside of the current workplace experience impacts his/her ability to trust.

Back to Case Study 8.1

> *From our case study, because Dennis is fairly new in the HR director position at AU, he has not had a great deal of time to build trust, or for that matter distrust, with the*

HR staff. Listed in Exhibit 8.7 are tools he can use to build trust with the HR staff as they move through the transition.

Exhibit 8.7 Tools to build trust

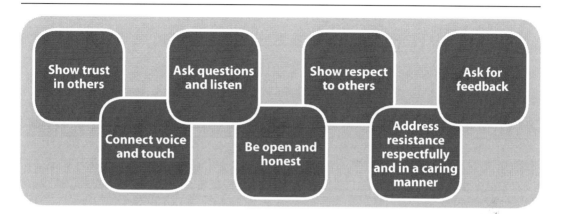

Tool 1 Show trust in others: *Dennis needed to show trust in each HR staff. Note that during the discussions about the transition process, some answered, "I do not know." Dennis did not pursue more details in front of the entire HR staff. He trusted that whether it occurred during his one-on-one meetings or during a staff meeting, more details would be shared. Showing trust links with showing respect, something all people want and deserve.*

Tool 2 Connect voice and touch: *Connect voice and touch means Dennis needed to do what he said he would do. What he says or promises the HR staff must equal his actions. If something occurred that impacted this, he needed to communicate the circumstances immediately to the HR staff or the person involved.*

Tool 3 Ask questions and listen: *Dennis needed to listen, ask questions, listen, and then listen some more. People working through transition need to feel they are heard, and can communicate essential barriers that need to be addressed. By listening to the HR staff as he asked them the initial questions about the transition, Dennis realized he needed to back up a few steps. Again, this contributed toward people's trust in him. If he had not done this, but had continued in the process he designed, a lack of trust would have become part of the foundation of the transition.*

Tool 4 Be open and honest: *Being open and honest about his feelings and weaknesses regarding the transition and change meant people did not have to guess Dennis's* *feelings, and potentially misconstrue them. People normally engage very quickly with someone they can relate with. When Dennis facilitated the discussions regarding the endings, neutral zone, new beginnings, roles, etc., sharing his feelings and needs with the others contributed toward the trust factor. This included being honest when the news is not good news, and apologizing when applicable.*

Tool 5 Show respect to others: *Showing trust links with showing respect, something all people want and deserve.*

Tool 6 Address resistance respectfully and in a caring manner: *Addressing resistance to change means addressing a situation with an individual in a respectful and caring manner. These are always difficult situations, but it may motivate the person to become engaged in the transition. An appropriate first question is, "This is what I've noticed about you, and to me it means…. What is your perspective?" Then follow-up questions, "What advice can you give me to improve the transition process? What can I do to help you engage in this transition?" Do not argue with the person; give only your perspective and the facts of the change. Many times, this type of conversation is needed to let people know the change really will happen, no matter if they drag their heels or not.*

Tool 7 Ask for feedback: *Asking for feedback goes hand in hand with listening and asking questions. When people are unsure of what the change means to them and how they will get there, asking for their feedback builds their sense of control and self-confidence. Again, this was one of Dennis's strengths as he communicated with the HR staff.*

Often during a transition and change, people will bring up past situations that were handled badly and did not work, or a leader they did not trust. Not only will these situations be brought up, but they also will be repeated many times during the course of the transition. Again, to gain trust, the leader's role during these situations is to be respectful and caring. Listen and let the person vent. Do not argue. That will only make the person more agitated. Remember that in the long run, it is important to "get these skeletons out of the closet" to increase the likelihood that individuals can let them go.

Finally, building trust results in earning the respect of those people involved in the transition and change.

Providing Support for the HR Team during the Transition

Note that this item, listed in the transition management plan in Table 8.1, should be the responsibility of the leader in any change effort. In addition to contributing toward building trust for the leader, providing support for the HR team during the transition increases the likelihood of successful change. Providing support can mean different things, depending on the situation. It could mean emotional support, helping to solve problems that arise, support for the change itself with administrators and other constituents, resources such as additional staff or funds, recognizing and managing stress, providing training and other experiences to improve skills, communicating more, etc.

Back to Case Study 8.1

In our case study, the HR staff listed this topic when Dennis asked for advice. Several employees indicated they did not have the time to participate in redesigning processes and still get their work done. They indicated that in order for ALL HR staff to take the necessary time to redesign HR processes, they would need additional staff support or the ability to work overtime when needed. Dennis asked them to provide a list of the types of responsibilities a temporary employee could take on during the business process improvement phase. Subsequently, Dennis's request for a temporary employee and for funding for overtime during this period was approved by his supervisor.

Role Modeling Desired Behaviors and Skills

Part of developing trust is to connect voice and touch: doing what you as the leader said you would do. This includes role modeling the behaviors and skills you tell others are important in the vision of the changed HR transformative culture. Your actions will speak louder than your words. HR staff will watch your behavior closely.

The symbolic frame means giving up symbols that might remind people of the old culture and developing new symbols that communicate the new culture. In our case study, the old HR culture included silos, where different functions worked and made decisions separately. Although the department was renamed the HR Department (formerly the Personnel Office) several years ago, the culture remained the same in how people worked and were structured. Dennis brought together an "HR team" to develop an HR vision, mission, values, core competencies, and recruitment brand. The team concept was expanded as the department improved its internal processes.

As the leader of the change effort, you may feel like you have a great deal of responsibility, and along with needing to be a role model, your load can become heavy. Remember that there probably are others within the HR staff who can be role models and who also understand and "know" what the changed HR paradigm entails. Allow them to utilize their skills and knowledge to become role models and further their skills as a leader.

Case Study Questions

1. What could Dennis have done differently to improve the transition process for the HR staff members?
2. In what ways did Dennis use symbolism throughout the case study? Do you have ideas for additional symbolic events that could be used at this point?
3. What events, activities or rituals could symbolically signify the "ending" of the

old transactional culture?

4. *Why is documenting the history of the process an important role during the transition?*

5. *Consider a change initiative in the recent past in your HR department. Were all three phases of the transition dealt with thoroughly and positively? What could have been done better?*

To review discussion of recommendations to Case Study 8.1 go to **www.HR-higher-ed.com**

Summary

In moving from a transactional HR function to one that is transformative, this chapter introduces the eight steps involved in successfully initiating organizational change by John Kotter. The first eight chapters of this book incorporate aspects of steps one through six. The eight steps comprise the following (Kotter, 1996):

Step 1: Establish Urgency for Change

Step 2: Build Guiding Team(s)

Step 3: Develop the Vision and Strategy

Step 4: Communicate for Buy-In

Step 5: Empower Action

Step 6: Generate Short-Term Wins

Step 7: Consolidate and Continue Change Initiatives

Step 8: Anchor New Culture

Change and transition do not mean the same thing. In an HR paradigm shift, the "change" is the new transformative culture, whereas the "transition" is the process of getting to this new culture. The change is situational and normally occurs at a point in time, while the transition can be highly emotional for those involved. In many cases, the transition period is the most difficult for people, with the major role of the leader being to help people through this transition if the change is to work.

The transition process comprises three stages: the ending of a culture that is totally transactional, the period in-between when the old culture is gone but the new culture is not fully developed (Kotter calls this the "neutral zone"), and the beginning of the new transformational culture.

The major reasons a change initiative fails are the following:

1. One or more of the people involved do not move through all three stages of the transition process.
2. One or more steps of the eight-step change process is not built into the foundation for change.
3. Change is an iterative process. at times one or more steps need to be revisited, but are not.
4. Although sufficient data are gathered to indicate urgency for a change initiative, the leader does not provide any compelling emotional situation to allow people to "see and feel" the need for change.
5. The structure of the department or organization is not evaluated for effectiveness.
6. Specific systems that hamper change, e.g., weak training programs or performance management processes, are not identified and strengthened.
7. Identifying and strengthening skills of the HR staff is not done.
8. Resistance to the change initiative, including helping those without a "good fit" to move on is not dealt with.
9. The leader of the change initiative does not understand the role of leading and managing transition and change.

A major component of successfully moving through the phases of the transition period is to increase communication by utilizing tools described in a transition management plan. The outcomes include: the HR staff are prepared to deal with transition issues, the HR staff become a tightly knit team, HR department readiness is evaluated and improved, communication is improved to and within the HR team, and temporary systems are created for the transition.

Major Themes

Leadership of change is a continuing thread throughout this chapter. The following eleven key components, discussed in detail in this chapter and in other chapters, are identified as priority for you as the leader of change:

1. building trust and respect between the leader and the HR team
2. building trust and respect among the HR team members
3. challenging the HR team during the business process improvement stage
4. encouraging risk-taking and innovation
5. continuing to develop the skills of the HR staff members
6. empowering the HR staff to enable action
7. evaluating the HR department structure for effectiveness
8. dealing with any resistance to change
9. accomplishing the transition management plan
10. providing support for the HR team during the transition
11. role modeling desired behaviors and skills

Evaluation of "Your" HR Department's Chapter 8 Outcome

Outcome Desired: Learn to address change and manage transition

Change: Knowledge of the phases of the transition process enable the HR staff to move forward through the transition process

Key Indicators of Success: (check if *"yes"*)

☐ HR staff understand the details regarding transition versus change

☐ Communication within the HR team is strengthened

☐ The HR staff openly discuss their anxieties and other feelings regarding the change

☐ A transition management plan is developed, with involvement of the HR staff

☐ HR staff understand the change and when it will begin

☐ HR staff, either within the team or one-on-one, discuss their endings

☐ HR staff identify things they will gain with the change

☐ A consistent message is provided regarding the change

☐ The HR director provides the type of support needed by the HR staff

☐ The HR director builds mutual trust and respect with the HR staff

Potential Barriers to Change: (check if *"needs attention"*)

☐ One or more of the people involved do not move through all three stages of the transition process

☐ The leader does not provide a compelling emotional situation to allow people to "see and feel" the need for change

☐ The leader does not facilitate discussions regarding transition and the change

☐ There is open or underlying resistance to change that is not positively resolved

☐ The leader does not recognize that transition can be an iterative process

☐ Individuals do not understand how the change will impact them, or what they will gain from the change

☐ A transition management plan is not created

☐ Individuals do not understand their role during the transition

Determine Human Resources Department Vision and Mission Statements

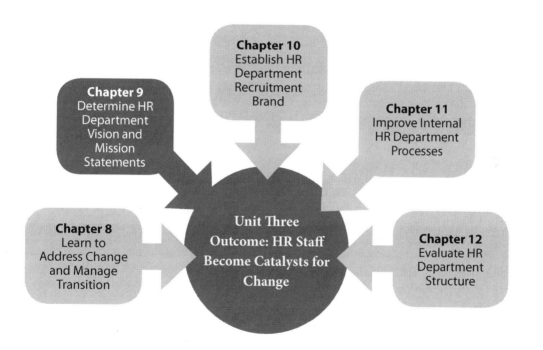

Chapter 9 Determine HR department vision and mission statements

Leadership of Change

In his book, *Leadership Jazz*, Max DePree (2008) describes the role of a watercarrier in an American Indian tribe as one of the most important and respected positions. Water, like air and food, is essential for survival.

What does it mean to be a watercarrier in a current-day institution of higher education? Betty has served in the role as a payroll and benefits specialist at Western Comprehensive University (WCU), a campus of a state university system, for almost 30 years. One day an employee complained that her health insurance had refused to cover a charge for $1,500. In researching this, Betty discovered that this charge was covered under the employee's insurance plan—contrary to what the company relayed to the employee.

Betty called the System benefits office, that agreed with the insurance company that the charge was not covered. Undaunted, Betty wrote a lengthy letter, with attached documentation, to the System director of benefits. A week later, the director personally called Betty to agree with Betty's determination, and to commend her for her persistence in support of the employee.

What made Betty so persistent? She felt that the consequences of her behavior were personal. Her level of integrity and commitment to the employee extended and strengthened her relationship with that employee, and ultimately strengthened the quality of WCU.

What transforms potential watercarriers into actual ones? Think of qualities such as compassion, building relationships, commitment to problem-solving, a passion for the way in which things ought to be done, humor, a sense of history, the ability to teach, and an unshakable commitment to the vision of the organization.

Betty understood the significance of the history, the values and the culture of WSU. She understood that people, relationships, values and beliefs are most important to an organization, and lived those daily in the workplace. When WSU created an outstanding performance award for support staff, Betty's peers and WCU's top administrators chose Betty to be among the first group to receive it. She stood on the stage, along with faculty and administrative staff, to receive her award in front of 500 peers.

Mario, the director of HR and Betty's supervisor, understood her contribution as a leader. Shortly after Mario's arrival at WCU, he recognized that Betty was far ahead of other HR staff in identifying the need for a broader vision and mission for the HR function. Mario, knowing that an obvious requirement for doing good work as a leader is to learn the perspective of "followers," acknowledged he could learn a great deal from Betty to help transform the HR function to the new paradigm.

Mario also expected a great deal from Betty in transforming the HR function. In her role as a watercarrier, he expected her to:

- challenge him in his role as director
- help determine, implement and perpetuate the quality of an institution's goals and strategies
- take responsibility for achieving personal goals in transforming the HR function
- take ownership and be engaged in areas consistent with her responsibilities and accountabilities

- make a commitment to change
- understand the contributions of others and accept the authenticity of each member of the HR staff
- take responsibility for developing constructive relationships
- work as a "builder," not a "taker"

Who are the watercarriers in your HR department? Who have the potential to assume this role? In leading the transformation of the HR function in your institution of higher education, it is important to recognize the significance of the watercarrier role within this process—that it serves both as a leader and as a follower in portraying the symbolic frame within the change process. One of your responsibilities is to empower and coach others to serve in the watercarrier role.

> … it is important to recognize the significance of the watercarrier role within this process—that it serves both as a leader and as a follower in portraying the symbolic frame within the change process.

In this chapter, we outline a process to bring the HR staff together into a cohesive team, developing a strategic focus for the future. Figure 9.1 illustrates the process we utilize to revisit the core values and develop the HR department's vision and mission statements.

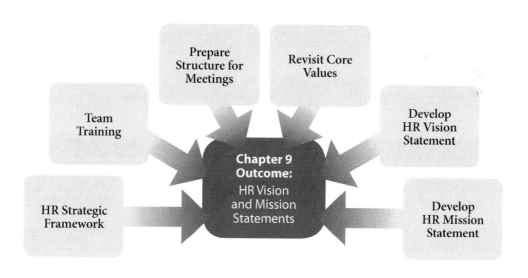

Figure 9.1 Determine HR department vision and mission statements

HR Strategic Framework

The major purpose of the HR strategic framework, composed of mission, vision, core values, core competencies, goals and strategic plan, is to weave together, into one configuration, initiatives for renewing the department and providing value to all stakeholders in the organization. Strategy formulation serves three purposes: (1) articulates a future direction for the HR department; (2) allocates resources; (3) proclaims promises that reflect commitments to multiple stakeholders. Strategy implementation then occurs when department practices align with the university's strategic framework.

Figure 9.2 outlines the HR strategic framework. Although we develop the HR strategic plan in Unit Five, creating the vision and mission statements now provides a tool to continue integrating the HR staff into a team with a common purpose. In addition, through this process, the HR staff expand their skills and perspectives.

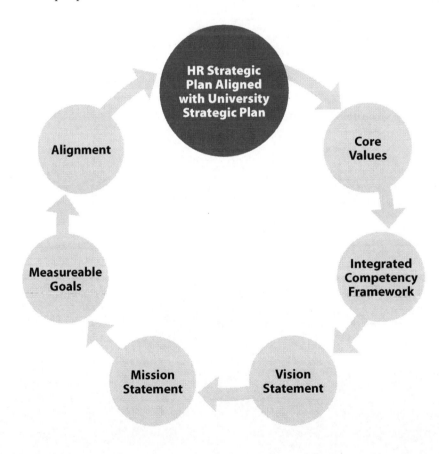

Figure 9.2 HR strategic framework

Team Training

Prior to bringing together the HR staff to revisit the values and develop vision and mission statements, it is important to begin the process of uniting them as a fully-functioning team, working toward the same goals.

Why a Team? The Importance of "Building" a Team

Because a department's strategy focuses on accomplishing both short- and long-term goals and objectives, it is important for all HR staff to participate in developing the department's vision and mission statements. Although there are times when the HR director needs to make the ultimate decision, it is more appropriate in this situation to obtain the ownership of all HR staff members in developing the vision and mission statements. Their engagement in the process contributes towards successful implementation.

Perhaps in the past, the HR staff members were organized into functional "silos," and are not used to working together as a team. These individuals may have different skills, backgrounds, experiences and knowledge of HR. They may have communicated and shared information, but they may not have worked together toward common goals in a highly structured manner. Alternately, the HR staff members may have worked together well in the past, but a new person was hired, which definitely changed the dynamics of the team.

Or, perhaps the HR staff currently work well together. In this case, instead of discussing the information in this section, you may decide that team members review what currently is working well for them, detail any challenges in working together, and brainstorm how they can improve working together.

> *To download the sample Team Evaluation Tool to customize for your department go to* **www.HR-higher-ed.com**

There are many methods to begin "building or re-building" the team to work together differently. We describe one method that has worked for us in building teams, both in and outside of HR, and organization-wide. It can be varied to suit the situation and culture of the department.

STEPS FOR ONE METHOD TO BUILD TEAMS

Step 1: **Schedule a one-hour meeting to discuss teams using the information in this section.**

Step 2: **Explain how important it is for everyone to work together as a team in transfor-ing the HR function.**

Step 3: **After conveying your message about the person, ask that person to reach into a bag to select a symbol of teamwork.**

Step 4: **The person whose name you picked now selects a name from the bowl, and the process continues until all individuals have had a turn.**

Step 5: **Finish the activity by explaining there are three "rules" with the boas (or other teamwork item).**

Step 1: **Schedule a one-hour meeting to discuss teams using the information in this section.** All HR staff need to participate. Spend the first 30 minutes discussing this information.

Step 2: **Explain how important it is for everyone to work together as a team in transforming the HR function.** Use any information from Unit One or Two that is pertinent: changing the HR paradigm, changing HR staff roles, developing a new vision and mission in order to begin moving forward, etc.

Indicate that it is important to share when you appreciate the work others do, to thank them for assisting with a project or work responsibility, etc. Then describe an activity where you will take a piece of folded paper out of a bowl, read the name of the HR staff member written on the paper, and then tell that person, in front of the others, what you most appreciate about working with him/her. (An alternative is to convey a recent example of when this person provided great customer service—to either internal or external customers. You may have other suggestions about what to say about the person whose name is chosen.)

Step 3: **After conveying your message about the person, ask that person to reach into a bag to select a symbol of teamwork.** One idea is to fill a bag with vibrantly colored "boas," of the kind used during "Mardi Gras" celebrations or other parties. This will lend a sense of humor to the event.

Step 4: **The person whose name you picked now selects a name from the bowl, and the process continues until all individuals have had a turn.**

Step 5: **Finish the activity by explaining there are three "rules" with the boas (or other teamwork item).** First, they can exchange theirs with another HR staff member if both agree. Second, the item must remain visible in each person's workspace. Third, when a new person is hired into the department, the same process will be used to "bring the person" into the team.

The positive outcomes from this activity are phenomenal. It is amazing to see how people become engaged and respond—both during the meeting and afterward. For several weeks, the level of humor in the physical office is elevated. People relate to a common event, with a visual they can point to. This activity serves symbolically as a ritual, and the "item" serves as a visual symbol of what occurred. Visitors to the HR department ask about the boas, and a staff member describes proudly what happened. You may recall from chapter 5 that the symbolic frame focuses on loss of meaning and the importance of creating new symbols and common ground. This type of activity does just that.

Characteristics of an Effective Team

One outcome of an effective team is that the members "learn" together by thinking insightfully about complex issues, developing open and trusting dialogue around these issues, and encouraging each other to raise the most difficult, subtle, and conflict issues essential to the team's work. Each team member brings his or her unique skills, perspectives and ideas to the team, similar to a jazz band where each member plays his or her own instrument, and with the leadership of the conductor, the band generates beautiful music. Other outcomes can include:

- Members trust each other—earned over a period of time.
- Members feel free to express themselves; other members do not try to intimidate.
- All members participate and are listened to.
- The goals of the team are clear to all, shared by all; everyone is involved.
- The atmosphere is to solve problems, not symptoms of problems.
- Leadership responsibility is shared, with different team members being leaders at different times.
- The culture of the team is to try new and innovative things.
- Unusual ideas are accepted and used, not ignored or criticized.

Roles of Individual Team Members

Both "task" roles and "team" roles are necessary for a team to be effective. All team members are responsible for both roles. Just as the name describes, task roles are about getting the job done. The team goal or charge needs to be accomplished, the meeting agenda must be developed, and discussions must focus on the agenda. Task roles require skills in organization, providing structure, and developing action item charts, minutes of meetings, and procedures for accomplishing goals.

Team roles include working well together toward the common goal, everyone participating and listening to each other, dealing with differences effectively, and cultivating a positive climate among team members. Team roles require additional skills in self-management, confronting conflict effectively, listening, awareness of others and reaching out to include others.

How many of you dislike being on a team because you're always the "recorder"? On a well functioning team, this role rotates each time the team meets, so one person does not have this responsibility permanently. While being a recorder, it often is difficult to participate in the team discussions because you are too busy taking notes. Refer to Exhibit 9.1 for tips on what to record from a meeting

In addition to the recorder, a second individual role is the team leader. This person is responsible for leading meetings, selecting methods and procedures, and providing follow-up on critical items. This person keeps participants focused on the agenda. If a team member brings up an important topic that is not on the agenda, the team leader places the item on a flip chart called a "parking lot." This item remains on the flip chart, and is not discussed until the team agrees to move it to a future agenda item.

Exhibit 9.1 What to record from a team meeting

Agree on a standard format for meeting minutes
Date and time of meeting
Names of attendees
Agenda Items
Process/procedures used for each item
Main points made in the discussion
Action taken, decisions made
Assignments to be completed between meetings
Items to be carried over to future agendas

Developing Meeting Guidelines

We all have been part of teams or groups where people are late for meetings or interrupt each other during discussions, or there is not a focused agenda, or one person dominates the conversation, or the meeting runs longer than the pre-arranged time period, or action items are not accomplished when agreed upon, etc. All these issues frustrate participants and cause disengagement and problems in obtaining the objectives of the team.

Meeting guidelines are agreements among team members about how they will work together to reduce frustrations and create a positive environment. Setting guidelines for team meetings will clarify expectations, guide team members in decisions about how to handle difficult situations, and reduce the likelihood that conflict will occur. Prior to the first meeting it is helpful to provide team members with the planning worksheet outlined in Exhibit 9.2. The time taken by team members to consider and discuss meeting guidelines will be valuable as the team works to accomplish its objectives.

Team "Charge" or Objective

Each team is brought together for a reason, to accomplish an objective that may be short- or long-term, multi-faceted or simple, difficult or easy to accomplish. But all teams need a "charge." In most cases, this is given to them by a supervisor or administrator who is not a member of the team, although the "convener" may lead the team initially or facilitate the process of accomplishing the team objective. In the charge to develop a department's vision and mission statements, the department head can either serve as the facilitator or bring in someone from outside the department.

Exhibit 9.2 Meeting guidelines planning worksheet

1. *How can we ensure we do not interrupt one another?*
2. *How can we demonstrate we are listening to and understanding differing points of view?*
3. *How can we ensure everyone in the group participates?*
4. *How can we make sure no one dominates the group?*
5. *How do we want to handle disagreements and conflict?*
6. *How can we ensure we look at a problem from all angles before solving it?*
7. *What meeting attendance guidelines do we want to establish?*
8. *How can we ensure team members accomplish their assignments in a timely manner?*
9. *How can we ensure we start and end our meetings on time?*
10. *What other guidelines might be appropriate for our team?*
11. *How do we want to rotate routine task roles such as recording the minutes of team meetings?*

Prepare Structure for the Meetings

The methodology in Case Study 9.1 borrows heavily from the successful process used by the Director of the Department of HR and the HR staff at the University of Wisconsin Milwaukee in developing their HR strategic plan. The HR director gave us permission to share his team's process and outcomes as part of a case study for this chapter.

Case Study 9.1

> *Throughout the remainder of this chapter, we will use the case study of Mario, the HR director at Western Comprehensive University (WCU), as he planned the development of an overall HR strategic plan, aligned with the university's strategic plan. He prepared to facilitate meetings with the HR staff to develop a department vision and mission statement, and revisit the core values, because one staff member was hired recently.*

STEPS TO PREPARE STRUCTURE FOR MEETINGS

Step 1: Determine membership of workshops
- all HR staff (or) Planning team

Step 2: Determine workshop agendas
- meeting roles and guidelines
- purpose and expected outcomes

- methodology and context
- definition of "strategic"

Step 3: Determine documents needed
- sample vision and mission statements
- accountability reports
- president/chancellor objectives

Back to Case Study 9.1

Step 1: *Determine membership of workshops.* With 10 HR staff members in the department, Mario chose one option for bringing them together. Because the number of staff was small and all wanted to participate fully in the process, Mario decided on a series of three half-day workshops over several weeks. (A second option was to choose a planning team from the larger HR staff to develop recommendations to bring to the entire HR staff for their input. If the second option were chosen, a full day retreat would be scheduled, with a small planning team chosen by the HR staff to provide a variety of views, perspectives and demographics.)

Step 2: *Determine workshop agendas.* Mario, as the convener of the team, developed draft agendas for each workshop. The first day included the purpose and expected outcomes, developing roles and guidelines, and an overview of the methodology that would be used to obtain the outcomes. He called these "tentative" agendas because he was open to having any HR staff member suggest additions or changes to the agenda at the beginning of each workshop. Exhibit 9.3 summarizes the draft agenda for the first workshop.

Exhibit 9.3 Draft agenda for day one workshop

7:30am	Continental Breakfast
8:00	Housekeeping
8:15	Team-building Exercise
8:45	Outline Agenda, Expected Outcomes of Workshops
9:00	Develop Roles and Guidelines
9:45	Break
10:00	Overview Methodology Used
10:15	Context Discussion
10:30	Revisit Core Values
11:00	Vision Presentation
Noon	End for the Day

Step 3: *Determine documents needed. Bring the applicable documents listed in Exhibit 9.4 to the second and third workshops. Other than the statements from peer institutions, these include documents outlining the strategic direction of the university, which can be used to ascertain alignment of the HR department's mission and vision when they are developed. Mission and vision statements from peer institutions serve as examples during the brainstorming stage.*

Exhibit 9.4 Potential documents for workshops

Existing mission/vision statements for HR department
Mission/vision statements from peer institution(s)
University's stated vision, mission, values, objectives, initiatives
President/Chancellor's stated goals, initiatives
Budget proposals
Accountability reports
State of the university/college addresses
Annual reports

First Workshop

Due to Mario's detailed planning for the first workshop, the meeting was energizing for all participants. All HR staff participated in developing the guidelines and roles for the series of three workshop sessions, as outlined in Exhibit 9.5. In particular, they liked having guidelines for working together, and knowing they possessed the ability to use them during the meetings.

Although Mario discussed the definition of "strategic" with the HR staff in previous meetings, it worked well during this workshop to set this context as a framework for the subsequent conversations. The HR staff understood that "strategic" means possessing a broader perspective than just "operational," or the day-to-day activities of a department. They were empowered to develop a framework to create change within their HR department, to move the HR function from being primarily transactional to transformational.

They knew that within the broader context, this strategic framework must align with the overall organization's framework. As Mario described the process they would use during the next workshops to revisit the core values and develop their vision and mission, they were anxious to get started.

Exhibit 9.5 Outcomes of first planning workshop

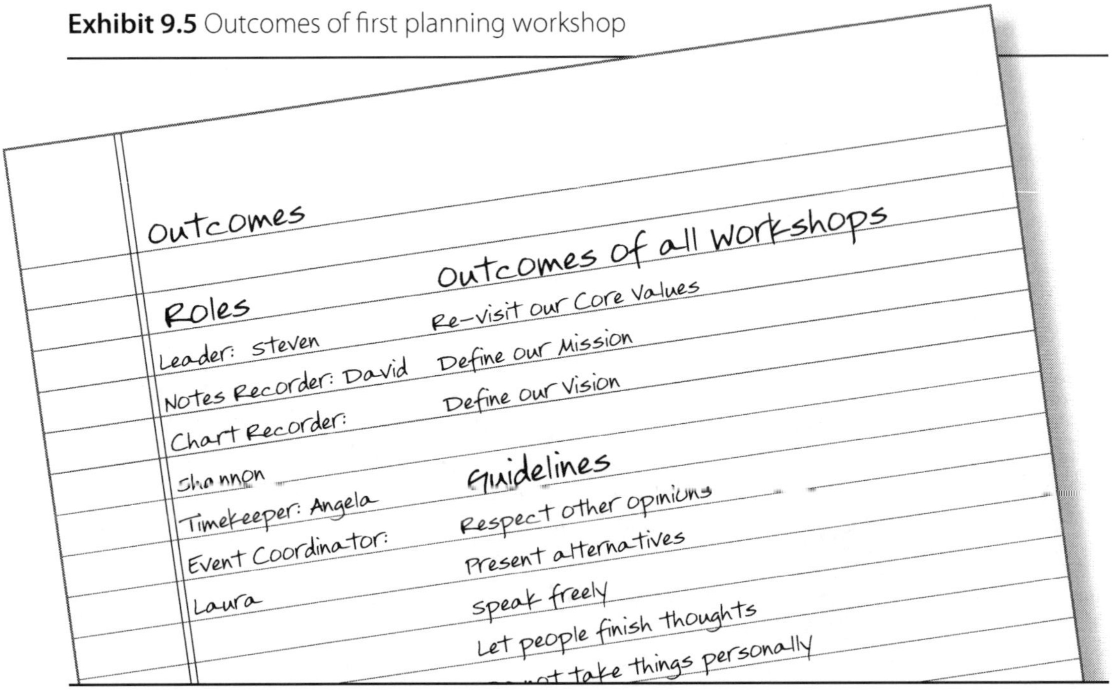

Outcomes

Roles

Leader: Steven

Notes Recorder: David

Chart Recorder:

Shannon

Timekeeper: Angela

Event Coordinator:

Laura

Outcomes of all workshops

Re-visit our Core Values

Define our Mission

Define our vision

Guidelines

Respect other opinions

Present alternatives

speak freely

Let people finish thoughts

...not take things personally

To review suggestions for increasing participation among team members go to **www.HR-higher-ed.com**

Revisit Core Values

As shown in Figure 9.2 earlier in this chapter, core values are a crucial component of a department's strategic framework. Because there was a new staff member in the HR department, Mario decided to revisit the current core values, to ensure they continue to inspire and shape the actions of all HR staff.

During the agenda item for revisiting the core values of integrity, equity, consistency, professionalism, generosity of spirit and collaboration, Mario asked the following three questions to facilitate a discussion: For each core value,

1. Does it continue to be a quality considered worthwhile by all the HR staff; does it represent the HR staff's highest priorities and deeply held driving forces?
2. Are there any values we need to add to the grouping of core values?
3. How does the current definition continue to inspire us on a day-to-day basis?

These questions generated a meaningful discussion, with the resulting agreement that the current core values continue to inspire and motivate them to improve the work place. Mario ended by asking the HR staff to share recent examples of living these core values. These examples worked beautifully in transitioning to his presentation on visioning.

Develop HR Vision Statement

One powerful way in which a leader can pull together the HR staff as a team is by including them in developing a vision of the department's core purpose. The vision addresses the challenges of the present and the hopes and values of the HR staff. A vision is particularly important in a time of crisis, change and uncertainly. When people are in transition, when they are confused and uncertain, or when they feel despair, they desperately seek meaning and hope.

A vision statement outlines where a department wants to be in three to five years. It includes aspirations for the future, incorporates personal visions, and motivates people to work toward goals. It articulates a compelling, common purpose for the department, engages hearts and minds, and creates pride among the HR staff. In our case of moving the HR department to the new paradigm, the vision statement will contain clearly defined outcomes and results of the HR transformation.

Where does such a vision come from? One view is that a leader can create a vision and then persuade others to accept it. Another view is that leaders discover and articulate a vision that already is there. However, leadership is a two-way street. An optimum method is to bring together the department members and engage them in a process where, together, the leader and the staff develop a common vision. As part of a discussion for a potential vision statement, a symbolic leader can embed his or her vision within a story—a story about "us" and "our" past, present and future, and encourage others to do the same.

In most cases, the past is regarded as a time when things were good. The present can be a time of trouble, a challenge, or a crisis—a critical moment when choices are required and things will change—sometimes drastically. The future is considered a dream of how things can return to a "greatness" that often links to the past. By involving story-telling as part of the discussion of a vision statement, a symbolic leader respects and uses history to link new initiatives to the values, stories, and heroes of the past.

Back to Case Study 9.1

> *To prepare for day two of the workshop, Mario asked all HR staff members to bring to the workshop a story from his/her past experiences working in the HR department. The topic could include a fun event, a humorous, sad or motivational story, what it was like to work with a particular person, a customer or peer who impacted them the most, etc. As shown in Exhibit 9.6, Mario placed this on the draft agenda after*

summarizing the events of the day one workshop. He planned to use these stories to transition to the visioning process.

Exhibit 9.6 Draft agenda for day two workshop

7:30am	Continental Breakfast
8:00	Review Day One/Choose Recorders for Today
8:15	Stories from the Past
8:45	Visioning
9:45	Break
10:00	Visioning
11:00	Mission Presentation
Noon	End for the Day

In addition, the documents in Exhibit 9.7 were available at the meeting.

Exhibit 9.7 Excerpts from WCU documents relevant to developing a vision

WCU Mission Statement
"provide a wide array of degree programs, a balanced program of applied and basic research, and a faculty who are active in public service."

2008/09 Strategic Initiative
"Communicate our need to grow research while maintaining access and diversity."

2009/10 Strategic Initiative
"Improve student retention/graduation, renew state investment in budget, comprehensive campaign, improve WCU image, Research Growth Initiative."

2010/11 Strategic Initiative
"Expand research, footprint, and partnerships."

System Accountability Report 2010/11
Goal IV *"provide a learning environment"*
Goal V *"provide guided research, mentorships, and access"*
Goal VI *"efficient and effective stewardship of resources"*

STEPS COMPRISING THE VISIONING PROCESS

Step 1: Individuals separately complete questions 1-6 on the Vision Statement Worksheet (Exhibit 9.8).

Step 2: Brainstorm as a team a "cover story" and "headlines" that describe the outcomes from the visioning process. Consider that they could appear in a newspaper, presentation, brochure, report, or website.

Step 3: Brainstorm "quotes" by administrators or the media.

Step 4: Brainstorm "words" to be part of the vision statement.

Step 5: Draft a one-paragraph vision statement from the information in steps 1-4 above.

Exhibit 9.8 Vision Statement Worksheet

EXAMPLE TOOL: Developing an HR Vision Statement

A Vision Statement is:
- a clear picture or description of where and what the department members want to be
- articulates a compelling common purpose
- describes aspirations for the future without necessarily specifying the means to accomplish the desired ends
- is a statement of department members' ambition
- accounts for department values
- presents the best view of your future
- motivates staff to work towards goals
- defines the department as interesting, active, attractive, and exciting
- embraces continuous improvement and learning
- describes what you are trying to do
- incorporates personal and multiple visions
- grows and evolves over time

The **vision statement** is a statement that expresses the MIND/HEART/SPIRIT of the department. It is a statement that will identify what we want to improve, maintain, and enhance with regard to the work we must do. It is a benchmark to be used as we make decisions.

Remember to use your heart; be optimistic and idealistic, but realistic. Give a strong image of what you would like the future to look like within the human resources function.

It is five years from now, and the HR department is functioning perfectly and has accomplished the mission and initiatives in its strategic plan. Assume that you have total control, sufficient resources, and no constraints. Strive to envision an ideal program for your department. Assume that you and your colleagues have been hired to initiate a human resources function from scratch for your institution
...have your current staff, but that no one has been assigned a role or job. What would
...you create if you could start from scratch? Using the following
...(as if this activity was occurring right now).

To download a template of this Vision Statement Worksheet to customize go to **www.HR-higher-ed.com**

Back to Case Study 9.1

Step 1: *Individuals separately complete questions 1-6 on the Vision Statement Worksheet (Exhibit 9.8).* After story-telling and summarizing relevant strategic information from the university and system level, Mario gave all HR staff the visioning worksheet in Exhibit 9.8 and asked them to complete questions 1-6 individually, taking as much time as needed.

Step 2: *Brainstorm as a team a "cover story" and "headlines" that describe the outcomes from the visioning process. Consider that they could appear in a newspaper, presentation, brochure, report, or website.* Mario facilitated the conversation of a potential "cover story" with "headlines," summarized in Exhibit 9.9, that resulted from the HR staff completing the exercise.

Exhibit 9.9 Cover Story and Headlines that describe the realization of the vision

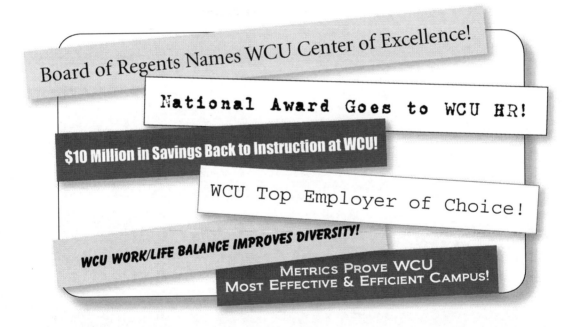

Step 3: *Brainstorm "quotes" by administrators or the media.* Mario facilitated the brainstorming by HR staff of "quotes" by administrators or the media that signify the successful outcomes from the new HR department vision. These are listed in Exhibit 9.10.

Exhibit 9.10 Quotes that signify the successful outcomes of the HR department vision

> **Senator:** "WCU proves good steward of state funds!"
>
> **Chancellor:** "The HR department continues on its journey of innovation and delivering stakeholder value!"
>
> **System President:** "WCU HR best practices duplicated at other campuses!"

Steps 4-5: *Brainstorm "words" to be part of the vision statement, and draft a one-paragraph vision statement from the information in steps 1-4 above. During the brainstorming of words to include in the vision statement, several HR staff suggested that instead of developing a vision statement in sentence or paragraph form, they use what they have developed thus far to choose strategic concepts that describe their vision for the future. Mario and the others agreed, with their final vision outlined in Exhibit 9.11.*

Exhibit 9.11 WCU HR department vision

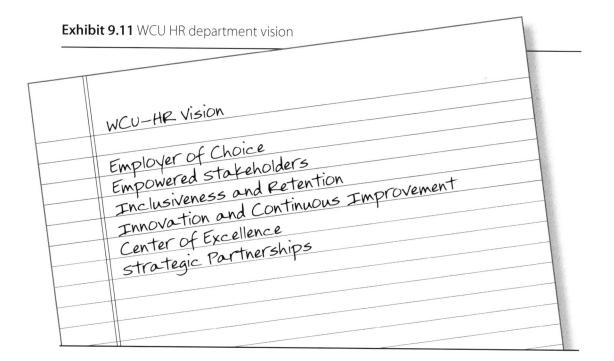

WCU–HR Vision

Employer of Choice
Empowered stakeholders
Inclusiveness and Retention
Innovation and Continuous Improvement
Center of Excellence
Strategic Partnerships

Develop HR Mission Statement

A mission statement for HR describes the basic nature and concept of the department in a meaningful way. Although it can include the stakeholders who are affected by the work of the department and outline their needs, it definitely describes the principle products and/or services provided. Exhibit 9.12 outlines the draft agenda for the third and final workshop.

Exhibit 9.12 Draft agenda for day three workshop

7:30am	*Continental Breakfast*
8:00	*Review Day Two/Choose Recorders for Today*
8:15	*Mission Methodology Presentation*
8:45	*Mission Statement Discussions*
9:45	*Break*
10:00	*Mission Statement Discussions*
11:00	*Evaluation of Core Values, Vision and Mission Statements—aligned with those of the university?*
Noon	*End for the Day*

STEPS TO DEVELOP A DEPARTMENT MISSION STATEMENT

Step 1: HR staff members individually complete the Mission Statement Worksheet

Step 2: HR staff members, as a team, brainstorm key words or phrases they would like to see in the mission statement

Step 3: Develop the mission statement

Step 4: Ensure the mission statement is aligned with that of the university

Back to Case Study 9.1

Step 1: *HR staff members individually complete the Mission Statement Worksheet. After presenting the process and context for developing a mission statement, Mario gave the HR staff the document in Exhibit 9.13 to complete individually.*

Step 2: *HR staff members, as a team, brainstorm key words or phrases they would like to see in the mission statement. After all HR staff completed the mission statement worksheet, Mario facilitated the brainstorming of potential key words or phrases for the mission statement.*

Exhibit 9.13 Mission statement worksheet

EXAMPLE TOOL: Developing an HR Mission Statement

A Mission Statement:
- Describes the basic nature and concept of the department
- Tells the world who you are and what you do
- A broad, succinct, *meaningful* statement for the existence of the department
- Is a focal point for identifying your purpose
- Describes principle products, services, clients, and markets
- Helps to define the boundaries of the department within the university
- Guides strategy formation, establishes standards for organizational performance, and shapes standards for individual ethical behavior
- Provides guidelines for operational planning, budgeting, organizational development, and staffing
- A working document that should be used to guide and manage operations

1. What products and/or services do we provide?
2. What are our major inputs?
3. Who are our customers/constituents, internal and external?
4. What are the needs of our customers/constituents?
5. What do our customers/constituents value?
6. What is unique about our department?

Directions:
1. Answer questions 1-6 individually
2. As a team, brainstorm key words or phrases you'd like to see in your department's mission statement:
3. Develop the mission statement
   We are . . .
   alignment with the mission statement of the institution.

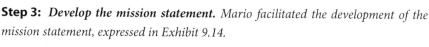

To download the complete mission statement template to customize for your department at **www.HR-higher-ed.com**

Step 3: *Develop the mission statement.* Mario facilitated the development of the mission statement, expressed in Exhibit 9.14.

Step 4: *Ensure the mission statement is aligned with that of the university.* Mario facilitated a discussion to ensure that the HR department's core values, vision and mission statements aligned with those of the overall university.

Exhibit 9.14 HR department mission statement

> ***Western Comprehensive University HR Department Mission***
> *"Foster a campus culture that attracts and inspires individual excellence, success and alignment with the University's overall mission"*

Developing the HR Strategic Plan

At this point, the HR department's core values and vision and mission statements were completed. However, as illustrated in the HR strategic framework in Figure 9.3, steps remain to complete the entire HR strategic plan. Completing this process is discussed in Unit Five.

Why not complete the process now? Although it may work for some HR departments to move right into developing the remainder of the HR strategic plan, in most cases it is best to continue to build the skill level of the HR staff, so that they are ready to become full partners in developing the strategic plan. How do we know? Because we have tried to continue, with negative outcomes including:

- The HR staff have not reached the skill level needed to partner in implementing the HR plan, and they are left behind.
- Although the campus community buys into the HR strategic plan, stakeholders look solely to the HR director for implementation of the initiatives and goals. The HR director cannot and should not attempt to implement the HR strategic plan alone.
- The HR strategic plan loses momentum and impact.
- The HR staff do not feel empowered and part of the entire process, and the gains made previously are eroded.

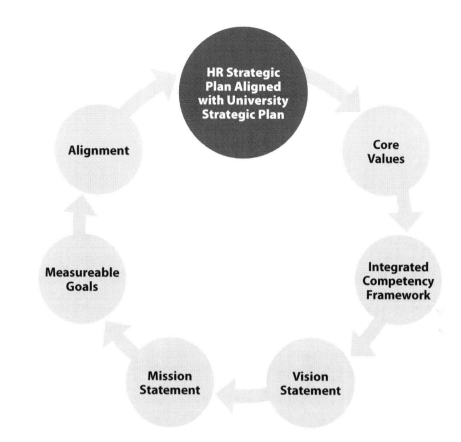

Figure 9.3 HR strategic framework

Summary

The major purpose of the HR strategic framework, composed of mission, vision, core values, core competencies, goals and strategic plan, is to weave together, into one configuration, initiatives for renewing the department and providing value to all stakeholders in the organization. Strategy formulation serves three purposes: (1) articulates a future direction for the HR department; (2) allocates resources; (3) proclaims promises that reflect commitments made to multiple stakeholders. Strategy implementation then occurs when department practices align with the university's strategic framework. Although we develop the HR strategic plan in Unit Five, creating the vision and mission statements now provides a tool to continue integrating the HR staff into a team with a common purpose. In addition, through this process, the HR staff members expand their skills and perspectives.

Prior to bringing together the HR staff to revisit the values and develop vision and mission statements, it is important to begin the process of uniting them as a fully functioning team, working toward the same goals. One outcome of an effective team is that the members "learn" together by thinking insightfully about complex issues, developing open and trusting dialogue around these issues, and encouraging each other to raise the most difficult, subtle, and conflict issues essential to the team's work. The following summarizes key components to build a highly effective team:

1. developing team roles and task roles
2. developing meeting guidelines
3. working within a team charge or objective

A vision statement outlines where a department wants to be in three to five years. It includes aspirations for the future, incorporates personal visions, and motivates people to work toward goals. It articulates a compelling, common purpose for the department, engages hearts and minds, and creates pride among the HR staff. In our case of moving the HR department to the new paradigm, the vision statement will contain clearly defined outcomes and results of the HR transformation.

One powerful way in which a leader can pull together the HR staff as a team is by distilling and disseminating a vision, a persuasive and hopeful image of the future.

A mission statement for HR describes the basic nature and concept of the department in a meaningful way. Although it can include the stakeholders who are affected by the work of the department and outline their needs, it definitely describes the principle products and/or services provided.

Major Themes

Leadership of change continues as a major theme in this chapter. In leading the transformation of the HR function in your institution of higher education, it is important to recognize the significance of the watercarrier role in this process—it serves both as a leader and as a follower in portraying the symbolic frame within the change process. One of the leader responsibilities is to empower and coach other HR staff members to serve in the watercarrier role.

Evaluation of "Your" HR Department's Chapter 9 Outcome

Outcome Desired: HR department vision, mission and core values are aligned with those of the institution

Change: A shared mission, vision and core values that integrates the work of the HR staff and inspires them to take steps in the right direction

Key Indicators of Success: (check if "yes")

- [ ] The vision is clear, challenging, compelling, focused and achievable
- [ ] The vision describes an outcome that appeals emotionally to the HR staff
- [ ] All HR staff are involved in at least part of the process
- [ ] All HR staff "buy into" the vision, mission and core values
- [ ] All HR staff begin/continue to exhibit the behaviors that need to be added, removed or improved in order to accomplish the vision and mission
- [ ] Cabinet members support the HR department's vision, mission and core values, and acknowledge it is aligned with those of the institution
- [ ] HR staff can express the vision and mission in their own words
- [ ] HR staff discuss the vision and mission in meetings, within decision-making situations, and in communicating with those external to the HR department

Potential Barriers to Change: (check if "needs attention")

- [ ] The vision is NOT clear, challenging, compelling, focused and achievable
- [ ] The vision does NOT appeal emotionally to one or more HR staff
- [ ] All HR staff are NOT involved in at least part of the process
- [ ] One or more HR staff exhibit behavior that is contrary to that needed to accomplish the vision and mission
- [ ] Cabinet members feel the HR department's vision, mission and core values are NOT aligned with those of the institution
- [ ] One or more HR staff do NOT take the department's vision, mission and core values seriously
- [ ] HR staff do NOT have a clear understanding of the behaviors that are expected in order to accomplish the vision and mission

Establish Human Resources Department Recruitment Brand

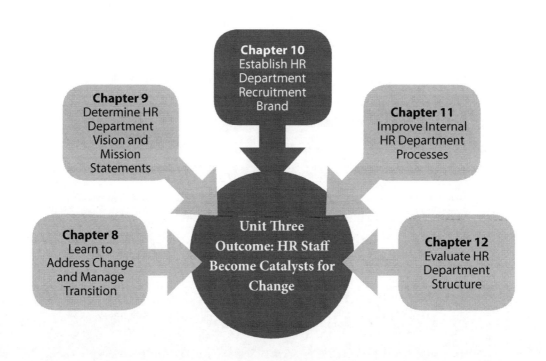

Chapter 10 Establish HR department recruitment brand

Our job as an HR professional is to create an institution that constantly improves through developing the people we employ. We ensure our higher education institution can attract, hire, retain and develop faculty and staff needed to accomplish the mission and vision in times of competitive change. As we HR practitioners continue to rethink our role and that of the HR department, we must balance the demands of the roles outlined in chapter 5: strategic partner, organizational design specialist, HR partner, HR specialist, employee advocate, and leader.

As part of the "leader" role, we need to strategically develop an HR department recruitment brand. All HR departments and institutions of higher education have a recruitment brand, sometimes referred to as an employment brand. But few recognize the importance of deliberately and strategically shaping this brand—the perception of the unique employment experience we provide—to attract and retain the best faculty, staff and administrators.

Why include this topic at this point in the process of transforming the HR function? Strategically developing a recruitment brand is extremely critical as we move the HR function to the new paradigm and have the opportunity to hire new HR staff due to retirements, transfers or resignations. We want to ensure the HR department stands for something meaningful as an employer, and that potential job seekers and employees know what that "something" is. Without a deliberate recruitment brand in place well in advance of a recruitment, we face the situation of hiring an employee without the needed transformational skills and competencies.

> Without a deliberate recruitment brand in place well in advance of a recruitment, we face the situation of hiring an employee without the needed transformational skills and competencies.

Recruitment brands are utilized in the private sector and serve as an example of a strategic tool that can be modified and implemented in higher education to play a critical role in both attracting and retaining talented individuals. Although it is optimal for the overall university to have a deliberate recruitment brand, in reality most do not.

In this chapter, we focus on developing a brand for the HR function. Ultimately, as part of the HR strategic plan, Unit Five includes developing a recruitment brand for the overall institution. At that time, the HR recruitment brand is revisited to ensure alignment. Figure 10.1 outlines the major sections of this chapter.

Case Study 10.1

Throughout this chapter, we will work with the case study of Adele, a fairly new HR director. Adele had been in her position for approximately six months when a long-term HR assistant retired. Because she valued professional development of HR employees and promotion from within whenever possible, Adele promoted the HR department receptionist into the HR assistant position.

Adele planned the recruitment of the receptionist position. Because the HR staff

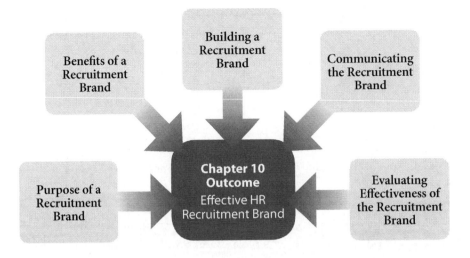

Figure 10.1 Model for developing an HR recruitment brand

are non-represented support and administrative employees, her recruitment choices were: (1) Recruit on-campus for those interested in transferring to the HR department; (2) Conduct an open recruitment, where on-campus employees, those at other campuses within the system, and non-university employees can apply.

Adele strongly felt that the receptionist position was one of the most vital in the department. This person "was the HR department" to internal administrators and employees, and was the first person external individuals saw. Therefore, customer service skills were extremely important. In addition, this position hired, trained and supervised the HR department student employees, was the administrative assistant to the director, assisted other HR staff in completing their responsibilities, and managed workflow processes within the department.

Adele acknowledged that the person in this position faced a steep learning curve relative to the HR topics, and decided to recruit internally to the university. This option meant the potential employee would have a broad knowledge of university functions and would not need to learn those.

After the recruitment deadline, Adele learned that only five people were interested in the position. Because the university employed more than 350 support and administrative staff eligible to transfer to this position, having only five candidates surprised her. In evaluating these five candidates, Adele felt only three possessed the required *skills and abilities, including the core competencies, required for the position. The HR manager scheduled interviews with the three candidates, to include a group interview with four of the current HR staff, followed by a one-on-one interview with Adele.*

Adele utilized the interviews to describe the vision, mission and values of the HR department, and their progress toward developing the HR strategic plan. She emphasized her philosophy of growing and developing employees, and working toward employment goals that satisfy the needs of both the HR staff member and the department and university. Adele felt strongly that while working in a university, employees must be supported in their educational goals, and set aside a portion of her HR annual budget for tuition reimbursement. Currently, three of the HR staff were taking classes toward either a bachelor's or a master's degree.

After the interviews, Adele met with the HR staff involved in the interviewing to obtain their feedback. They overwhelmingly felt that only one of the candidates, Susan, met the requirements and was a strong fit for the department. Adele agreed, but after conducting the reference checks, was concerned that Susan was weak in several skill areas. In addition, Susan was working toward a bachelor's degree and needed to take classes during the day, which was an issue due to the responsibilities of the position. During the interview, she indicated that if she obtained the position, she would schedule her classes during her lunch breaks and schedule student employees to work during that time. Susan's current supervisor indicated she often used excessive sick days.

Adele was in a difficult situation. She wanted to have someone in the permanent position as soon as possible, as the new academic year would begin in one month. Then the department would be inundated with new faculty, staff and student employees needing to complete their hiring and benefit paperwork. A new external recruitment for the position would take three to four months, and she would need to hire a temporary person in the meantime. Despite her instinct to the contrary, Adele decided to hire Susan.

Purpose of a Recruitment Brand

The main goal of creating a strong recruitment brand is to attract and retain employees having a strong "fit" with the department and university, uniquely differentiating our department from others within the university. In essence, the purpose of a recruitment brand for the HR function is to become an "employer of choice." Developing and continually improving our recruitment brand is a long-term effort that encompasses each step of the employee life cycle: recruitment, hire, onboarding, development, promotion, retention and engagement.

To be competitive in today's recruitment marketplace and to prepare for future growth, we must sell our department while attracting the right candidates. Therefore, the recruitment brand needs to convey the benefits of committing to work in the HR department, connecting both rationally and emotionally with potential and current employees. To maximize the recruitment brand, this process must be included during the first steps of the recruitment.

The HR department recruitment brand captures and expresses what it is like to work in our department, especially what is good about being a part of the HR staff. Although "word of mouth reputation" is always present—important in its own right—it may not be complete or even accurate. Developing a recruitment brand is a more sophisticated and integrated effort to create and deliver a credible and honest message about being an employee in the HR department at our institution. It is not just a vision or a promise; it needs to be consistent with reality, so honesty is the key component.

> The HR department recruitment brand captures and expresses what it is like to work in our department, especially what is good about being a part of the HR staff.

Proactively developing and communicating a recruitment brand is especially vital when the HR function is moving to a new paradigm. During this process, we want to ensure that both current and potential employees have the correct and complete picture of what it is like to work in the HR department, and what the department stands for. Figure 10.2 describes the benefits of an effective recruitment brand.

Benefits of a Recruitment Brand

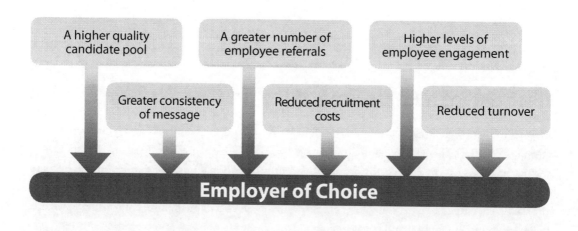

Figure 10.2 Benefits of an effective recruitment brand

A Higher Quality Candidate Pool

Including our HR recruitment brand in the initial stages of the recruitment process provides obvious benefits, with the most important outcome being a higher quality candidate pool. The "drivers" of this outcome include the following:

1. motivates target candidates—those with the right fit—to become applicants
2. enhances public relations among current employees through increased and accurate "word of mouth" communication
3. enables those involved in the recruitment to accurately explain the mission, culture, values and goals of the HR department
4. increases attraction of people not actively searching for a new position, but drawn to the expressed culture and values
5. allows applicants to screen themselves in or out of consideration by providing better information
6. increases the number of candidates who match the position requirements, meet or exceed the expectations of the HR director, and relate to the department's culture, vision and values

Greater Consistency of Message

When "selling" to applicants during the hiring process, whether by the director, HR staff members, or current employees who serve as referrals, the message has greater consistency.

A Greater Number of Employee Referrals

An individual's perspective of a work environment is real to him/her, even if it is based on inaccurate information. Utilizing a recruitment brand provides a greater likelihood for current employees to serve as effective ambassadors for the HR department, resulting in better word of mouth reputation.

Reduced Recruitment Costs

The major costs to recruit include those that are both quantitative and qualitative. Quantitative costs consist of dollars for advertising, pre-hire checks such as calling references and doing background checks, paying someone in the interim to perform the job responsibilities, and purchasing recruitment technology to create efficiency in the recruitment process.

In many cases, the qualitative cost of time spent on the recruitment is more important than money. Other HR staff may need to take on additional duties during the interim, time spent on planning the recruitment, screening and interviewing the candidates and performing pre-hire checks takes people away from other job responsibilities. In addition, most of us have experienced recruitments that have failed and need to be re-done, which is emotionally and physically draining.

Utilizing a recruitment brand can provide for a shorter time to fill open positions, reduced recruitment costs—both in money and time, a lower rate of offers rejected, and decreased metrics such as time-to-fill and cost-per-hire.

Reduced Turnover of HR Staff

Improved awareness and clarity of expectations about the HR department's values and culture lead to better alignment with and commitment to its goals, mission and vision, causing higher employee retention.

Higher Levels of HR Employee Engagement

Developing and implementing an HR department recruitment brand strengthens internal department understanding of working towards the mission and vision. By participating in the development of the brand, and serving as a communicator of the brand, HR staff members more clearly engage in the described culture because it resonates with their personal values and goals.

Back to Case Study 10.1

> Adele hired Susan, the internal candidate for the receptionist position in the HR department. Susan immediately engaged in the position, quickly learning the responsibilities of her position and the major functions of the department, a result of goals developed during her several performance evaluations the first six months. In addition, Adele felt Susan needed to strengthen her skills regarding several of the HR department core competencies, especially customer service, innovation, partnership and leadership.
>
> Although Susan performed adequately as a receptionist to the department, she made it very clear to Adele that she was interested in other positions. Susan was within a year of obtaining her bachelor's degree and felt strongly she was capable of more demanding responsibilities. Although Adele offered Susan opportunities to learn other aspects of the HR function in addition to giving her other responsibilities, it became more apparent that Susan was not happy in her receptionist position. Within six months, Susan increasingly disengaged from others on the HR team, and other HR staff complained to Adele that Susan was not accomplishing her responsibilities.
>
> Susan told Adele that she planned to transfer to another position within the university at her first opportunity. Susan indicated she was very unhappy in the receptionist position and did not want to wait until another position opened up in the HR department.
>
> Initially, Adele was very disappointed about this. However, in reflecting on the situation, she understood she was being given a chance to plan a more effective recruitment for the position when and if it became open. Not knowing how long it would take Susan to find another position, Adele immediately researched recruitment options. Being a member of a national organization for HR professionals in higher education,

Adele read an article in the monthly newsletter about the benefits of developing a recruitment brand, along with steps in the process.

Adele read that the disadvantages of not having an effective and proactive recruitment brand included the following: not attracting the type of employee that will be happy working in the department, less qualified candidates, more costly and time-consuming recruitments, shorter employee retention, and reduced engagement of employees. This described the prior recruitment for the receptionist position, causing Adele to continue her research on the topic.

Building a Recruitment Brand

Steps to Build an Effective Recruitment Brand

   Step 1: **Define objectives and project scope**
   Step 2: **Conduct an assessment process**
         a. Develop questions to gather information
         b. Organize and conduct focus group process
         c. Evaluate information from focus group sessions
   Step 3: **Develop employer distinctive attributes**

Back to Case Study 10.1

   Step 1: *Define objectives and project scope. Adele preferred to jump immediately into the assessment process of this project, but understood the importance of first defining the objectives and project scope. She knew that the university would benefit from having an overall recruitment brand, and felt that this should be a goal in the HR strategic plan to be developed next year. In the meantime, working through the process of implementing a successful HR department recruitment brand could serve as an excellent model for the university branding process. Therefore, the immediate project scope related to only the HR department.*

   The potential objectives for the project encompassed the following:
   - *establishing an employee referral program*
   - *decreasing staff turnover rates*
   - *increasing numbers of candidates*
   - *reviewing and updating the website or improving the limited term employee program to appeal to graduates of the university*
   - *improving candidate quality and fit to the department*
   - *reducing recruitment costs*

Upon reflection, Adele determined the following goal for the project: "improving candidate quality and fit to the department." Several of the other potential objectives could contribute toward accomplishing this main goal.

In her next one-on-one meeting with her supervisor, the vice president for administrative services, Adele laid out the benefits of developing and implementing an HR department recruitment brand, along with her objective for the project. Her supervisor supported her plan and recommended Adele meet with the other vice presidents to discuss her plan, and obtain their thoughts on current perceptions of the HR department and culture, leadership vision, and the important HR distinctive attributes.

Step 2: *Conduct an assessment process.* At the next HR staff meeting, Adele presented this project. She described a recruitment brand, its direct benefits to the HR department and the steps to develop a brand. Because the HR staff numbered 12 people, Adele asked volunteers to form a team to conduct the assessment process, develop draft employer distinctive attributes, and then bring these to the entire HR staff for further discussion. Six of the HR staff volunteered to be part of this team.

At their first meeting, team members, led by Adele, brainstormed the steps to accomplish their goal. Adele gave all team members materials to read on recruitment brands, and excitement filled the room and the discussion was animated. Adele was pleased that those who volunteered for this project encompassed all functions within the HR department—payroll, benefits, recruitments, training, and technology. Serving on this team definitely would improve the team skills of these staff members.

The assessment steps agreed to at this first meeting were the following:
   a. Develop questions to gather information
   b. Organize and conduct focus group process
   c. Evaluate information from focus group sessions

Step 2a: *Develop questions to gather information.* Because Adele had used appreciative inquiry in the past to successfully obtain feedback from stakeholders, she explained the questioning and listening process to others on the team. They decided to brainstorm appreciative inquiry questions targeted to those currently working in the HR department, and others targeted to employees outside the department. They understood that the key to this project's success was to open up conversations with all levels of employees throughout the university. They also determined this process served as a great opportunity to communicate the new vision, mission and values of the HR department, and set the stage for developing the HR strategic plan.

The questions outlined in Exhibit 10.1 were designed to gather the following information:

1. *What do current university employees (including the HR staff) value about their work and workplace?*
2. *What factors cause a person to stay in a job and a workplace?*
3. *What attributes do internal and external employees value about the HR department?*

Exhibit 10.1 Focus group questions

---

1. *What 3-5 factors do you value about working in your current department?*
2. *Looking into the future, name 3-5 attributes that would cause you to stay with your current department. These are the factors that make up your "dream job."*
3. *Consider a situation in which your experience with the HR department was extremely rewarding and positive. Specifically, what about the situation contributed toward it being a rewarding and positive experience?*
4. *What characteristics or attributes of the HR department contribute toward it being a good place to work?*

Step 2b: *Organize and conduct focus group process. The team decided to conduct five campus focus group sessions over two weeks, to include faculty and staff from throughout the university. Adele facilitated a separate HR staff focus group, and other HR staff members on the team facilitated the focus groups for external employees. Adele was charged with interviewing each vice president one-on-one. In addition to an all-employee email stating the purpose, times and locations of the meetings, specific individuals were invited to attend, e.g., those who had relationships with HR staff and understood the move to the new HR paradigm. The agenda for the one-hour focus group sessions is outlined in Exhibit 10.2.*

Step 2c: *Evaluate information from focus group sessions. All focus groups were highly attended. Participants were engaged and enjoyed asking each other the questions and sharing stories. Adele and the other HR staff facilitators were excited that the participants were interested in the changes taking place within the HR function. Participants especially liked that they were being asked for their feedback and would receive information on the outcome of the focus groups.*

In addition, Adele noted that HR staff serving as facilitators improved their self confidence and skills speaking in front of a group. Several used the experience to reach out to participants to begin relationship-building.

Exhibit 10.2 Focus group agenda

1. *Welcome. Discuss handout on new HR paradigm, vision, mission and values of HR department. (10 minutes)*
2. *Discuss handout on definition of recruitment branding, benefits, process to develop. (10 minutes)*
3. *Working in groups of 2-3, ask each other the questions listed on the handout. The person asking the questions briefly summarizes the answers on the post-it notes provided, using one post-it for each question. When finished, place each post-it on the corresponding flip chart. (30 minutes)*
4. *Thank them for participating, discuss how their feedback will be used, and answer any questions. (10 minutes)*

The team documented and organized the data obtained from the focus groups and Adele's meetings with the vice presidents into the segments shown in Exhibit 10.3. Attributes unique to attracting a person to the HR department are listed on the left, and those unique to retaining an individual in HR are on the right. The five attributes in the center—called a department's "distinctive attributes"—are common to both attracting and retaining a person.

Step 3: ***Develop employer distinctive attributes.*** Next, Adele and the sub-team brought the results of the focus groups to the entire HR staff, presenting the process used and the outcome for discussion. The entire HR staff agreed with the five common attributes. They determined these were the HR department distinctive attributes—the five messages the HR staff wanted others to know about their department. These then became the HR department "recruitment brand" or image.

The discussion then turned to whether these attributes were currently strong within the HR department or whether any need to be improved. Although they determined that several needed to be improved and asked the sub-team to work with Adele to develop a plan of action, they agreed all five could be utilized in future recruitments as the HR department recruitment brand.

Exhibit 10.3 Draft HR department employer distinctive attributes

attraction attributes	career and progression opportunities	retention attributes
learning environment		high performance rewarded
autonomy	integrity	trust in leadership
helping others		mentoring
respect	job-interest alignment	opportunity for innovation
flexibility of work hours		flexibility
collaborating with others	empowerment	reputation of office
teamwork		vision and long-term strategy
fit with department culture	work-life balance	supervisor as coach

Communicating the Recruitment Brand

The plan to communicate the HR department recruitment brand needs to include how the benefits of working in the HR department match the employment needs of current employees working throughout the university, and those working externally.

STEPS TO COMMUNICATE THE RECRUITMENT BRAND

Step 1: Identify target candidates
Step 2: Select potential media and tools to convey branding efforts
Step 3: Get buy-in to the plan from supervisor
Step 4: Pilot the message

Back to Case Study 10.1

Step 1: *Identify target candidates. Adele and the sub-team determined that the communication plan should focus on both university employees and the general public for the following reasons:*

1. *Future HR department employees may work elsewhere within the university.*
2. *Current university employees could communicate the HR department recruitment brand and future recruitments to their families, friends and neighbors.*
3. *Community members researching open positions within the university would learn the HR department recruitment brand.*
4. *Student employees may consider permanent employment with the HR department.*

Step 2: Select potential media and tools to convey branding efforts. How we communicate our distinctive attributes is up to us. The message can be implemented and executed in many ways—visual, written, verbal, etc. Most important is that the "what it is like to work for the university HR department" message is clear and consistent in all that we do—recruitment communications and otherwise. Remember, we do not need to be involved in a recruitment to communicate our recruitment brand. In fact, the communication should be in place long before any recruitment begins in order for potential employees to know and connect with the brand.

Back to Case Study 10.1

Adele and the sub-team brainstormed potential media and tools to communicate the recruitment brand for the short-term, and decided on the following:

1. *Develop and disseminate an HR department newsletter that includes a section on what it is like to work in the department, have HR staff write columns, highlight HR staff and others throughout the university who have partnered with HR in a specific activity.*
2. *Use a video on the website to feature HR department employees, highlighting their unique perspective on any or all of the distinctive attributes.*
3. *Use a video on the website to highlight a "day in the work life" of employees, showing an HR staff member working and interacting with colleagues, both internal and external to the HR department.*
4. *Develop a slogan, e.g., "Making a Difference for Midwestern State University."*
5. *Develop a program to involve university employees in spreading the word about the HR department recruitment brand.*
6. *Reinforce the recruitment brand in a neutral way when HR staff attend HR department or university-wide events.*
7. *Develop brand recognition and specialized names for specific employment systems or positions within HR, e.g., Career Opportunity Program (limited term employee program), The Dream Team (a name for the HR staff to denote job-interest alignment or work-life balance), The Honor Corps (for the payroll-benefits specialists), etc.*

Step 3: *Get buy-in to the plan from supervisor.* *Using the five distinctive attributes and the media and tools described above, Adele and the sub-team drafted a detailed action plan with a timeline to roll out the HR department recruitment brand. Table 10.1 outlines an example action plan. The entire HR staff recommended a few minor changes and enjoyed brainstorming several other specialized names to add to those in #7 above. Adele's supervisor supported the recruitment brand and communication plan, and asked her to present it at the next weekly meeting of the president's cabinet.*

This presentation generated many questions, especially the idea of developing an overall university recruitment brand.

Step 4: *Pilot the message.* *The first stage of the communication plan included highlighting one HR staff member each week in a video placed on the HR website. These received a great deal of recognition from other campus employees, with numerous positive comments and questions coming to those HR staff highlighted. It was apparent this tool captured the attention and interest desired.*

Table 10.1 Example action plan template for HR department videos

Action Item	Who Responsible	Timeline	Completed (x)	Comments
1. Develop HR department slogan	All HR staff	Within one week	X	• Slogan to be used in newsletter and videos
2. Work with Media Services to arrange for and complete videos in December	Brent from Sub-team of Sally, Brent, Linda, Jodi	October 15		• Need to schedule dates for each HR staff to be video-taped
3. Determine topics for videos and communicate to HR staff	Sub-team	November 1		• Utilize brand recognition and specialized names
4. Choose HR staff order of introducing videos	Sub-team	November 1		
5. Work with HR staff members on text for videos	Sub-team	December 1		
6. Announce videos to campus community	Sub-team	First video placed on web in January; others one week apart after that		
7. Determine process to evaluate effectiveness of videos	Sub-team	January		

Evaluating Effectiveness of the Recruitment Brand

In this step, we want to create a process to continually measure and evaluate the effectiveness of communicating our branding effort. This ensures that the expectations the expectations of future employees are better aligned with the reality of what it is like to work in the HR department. Plus, we all know that what gets measured gets done. Potential metrics to track to test the effectiveness of the recruitment brand are:

1. Attraction: number of job applicants, number of "hits" to job postings on the web or elsewhere, number of "hits" to view the job description, quality of job applicants, length of time to fill job openings, candidate acceptance rate, learning how candidates find out about the opening, increased positive perception of the HR department among university employees, increased positive perception of employment with the HR department among applicants or potential applicants.

2. Retention: turnover of new hires, turnover of veteran employees, employee satisfaction and engagement.

Case Study Questions

1. *What are the strengths and weaknesses of Adele using the HR department project team to work on first identifying, and then improving the distinctive attributes?*

2. *Outside of HR staff meetings, the receptionist told other staff external to HR the distinctive attributes are not accurate. She complained that she was hired into the wrong position—she really did not want another receptionist job—and then was promised career progression—which has not happened. How should Adele deal with this situation?*

3. *Although the entire HR staff felt the five distinctive attributes were true for the HR department, two of them—career and progression opportunities and job-interest alignment—needed to be improved to align with current employee goals. Discuss methods that could be used to improve them.*

4. *Brainstorm other media and tools that can be used to communicate a department's recruitment brand internally to the organization, and externally to the general public.*

5. *Do you agree with Adele's objective for the HR department recruitment brand of "improving candidate quality and fit to the department?" If you do, what metric(s) should be used to evaluate success of the branding effort? Would another objective be more valuable to the HR department?*

To review discussion of recommendations for Case Study 10.1 go to **www.HR-higher-ed.com**

Summary

All HR departments and institutions of higher education have a recruitment brand, sometimes referred to as an employment brand. But few recognize the importance of deliberately and strategically shaping this brand—the perception of the unique employment experience we provide—to attract and retain the best faculty, staff and administrators. Although this chapter concentrates on developing an HR department recruitment brand, ultimately as part of the HR strategic plan, Unit Five includes developing a recruitment brand for the overall institution.

The benefits of an effective recruitment brand, for the HR department as well as the broad university, comprise the following: a higher quality candidate pool, greater consistency of message, a greater number of employee referrals, reduced recruitment costs, reduced turnover, and higher levels of employee engagement. An effective recruitment brand also serves as a distinctive advantage for a department or university.

There are three steps to build an effective recruitment brand: define the objective and project scope, develop an assessment process to gather and evaluate information from focus groups, and develop employer distinctive attributes.

Finally, developing a plan to communicate the HR department recruitment brand needs to include how the benefits of working in the HR department match the employment needs of current employees working throughout the university, and those working externally. The plan components include: identify target candidates, select potential media and tools, get supervisor buy-in and pilot the message.

Major Themes

We focused on the **HR frame** in this chapter, with its emphasis on understanding people. We empowered HR staff by having them participate in developing the department recruitment brand. They were able to influence their immediate work environment and the factors that impact them. We invested in them by giving them time to gain experiences with focus groups and develop relationships with stakeholders to determine value.

Leadership of Change was a major thread in this chapter, showing a process for the HR director to empower HR staff members to shape their environment, develop plans to improve their workplace, and cultivate relationships with stakeholders to create value through innovation and collaboration. In addition, reflecting on Kotter's eight-step change process, implementation of an HR recruitment brand definitely corresponds to steps five and six: empower action and generate short-term wins. It also provides a model for the university to utilize when the timing is right.

Note that the questions in Exhibit 10.1 for the focus groups are based on **Appreciative Inquiry**.

Evaluation of "Your" HR Department's Chapter 10 Outcome

Outcome Desired: Develop an effective HR department recruitment brand

Change: HR staff utilize and improve transformative skills in working as a team

Key Indicators of Success: (check if "yes")

- [ ] One or more HR staff take on leadership roles
- [ ] More HR staff are willing to take initiative and risks
- [ ] More HR staff are innovative in their thinking and work
- [ ] HR staff assume the responsibility to contribute time and effort to develop the brand
- [ ] Issues and problems are identified and acted upon rapidly
- [ ] Feedback and suggestions are offered spontaneously
- [ ] There are more informal conversations regarding a recruitment brand
- [ ] HR staff actively work together to accomplish the project

Potential Barriers to Change: (check if "needs attention")

- [ ] One or more HR staff show a reluctance and/or lack of motivation to participate
- [ ] People are frustrated
- [ ] There is a high level of skepticism among the HR staff about this change effort
- [ ] One or more HR staff micromanage the team's activities
- [ ] One or more HR staff withhold information from those who need it
- [ ] Progress on this initiative is too slow
- [ ] HR staff feel they are not being given the resources to accomplish this project
- [ ] HR staff feel they are not being rewarded for working on what they call "these extra projects"
- [ ] One or more HR staff believe the HR director should be doing the work and making the decisions on this type of project

Improve Internal Human Resources Department Processes

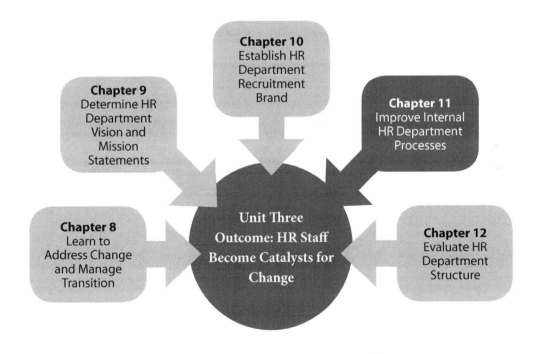

Chapter 11 Improve internal HR department processes

In reviewing the eight-stage change process, chapter 11 encompasses three of these stages: (1) continuing to build the guiding team by providing business process improvement projects for the HR staff to work on together as teams; (2) enabling action by empowering HR staff to redesign internal HR processes to be more efficient and effective; and (3) contributing toward short-term wins with the redesigned processes.

The work in this chapter comprises a crucial juncture in the HR paradigm shift. Because the outcome of the work is visual and will change work processes, it will motivate most individuals to continue to move forward proactively, and potentially cause others to resist the changes, or to leave the HR department. It inevitably will create conflict.

Consequently, the role of the leader is central in continuing to move proactively through the transition process. This chapter must include additional discussions around building trust and managing conflict and resistance as part of working as a team. In addition, the HR team must be empowered to take risks and become innovative in proactively redesigning internal processes. Figure 11.1 lays out the model to improve internal HR department processes. The outcomes for this chapter are more effective and efficient internal HR processes that provide increased value to stakeholders and continued HR staff skill development.

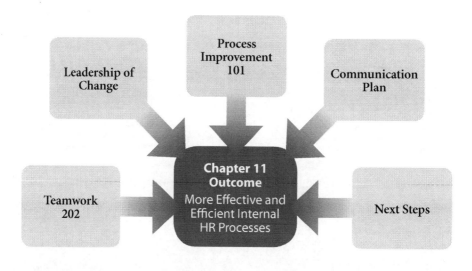

Figure 11.1 Model to improve internal HR department processes

Teamwork 202

In chapter 9, the following team concepts were introduced as we prepared to develop HR department vision and mission statements, and revise the core values:

- benefits of working as a team
- characteristics of an effective team
- roles of team members
- what to record from a team meeting
- meeting guidelines
- a team charge
- a meeting agenda
- methods for increasing participation during meetings
- methods to evaluate the team

Before moving further, it is essential to discuss these and additional elements of an effective team with the HR staff.

Case Study 11.1

We return to the case study of Dennis in his role as HR director at American University, a medium-sized private university. With the change being the move to a transformative HR culture, in chapter 8 Dennis led his HR team through the process of discussing change versus transition, and together developing a transition management plan.

Dennis brought the entire HR team together to discuss aspects of an effective team, and how these could be incorporated into working together on improving internal HR processes. He previously gave the assignment to research—either on the internet or using other sources—the components of building an effective team as detailed in Figure 11.2.

A positive environment in working together includes organizational and personal values and principles such as the department vision, mission, values and core competencies, a specific charge or objective, trust among team members, active participant involvement and participation, and effective decision-making.

The roles and responsibilities of team members include the "team" role, which effectively and positively addresses how the team works together, resolves conflict that arises, increases the participation of team members, and builds trust among them. The "task" function includes accomplishing the charge or objective of the team within the environment of the department's vision, mission, values, core competencies and guidelines determined by team members, and operational items such as following agendas, accomplishing action items, and getting the work done.

Dennis conveyed to the HR staff that their research and additional reflection

Figure 11.2 Components of building team effectiveness

should enable them to discuss the following topics during a staff meeting:
1. *stages in team formation*
2. *methods they can use to continue building trust among the HR team*
3. *identify potential "barriers" to the team successfully and effectively working together toward the common goal, and how to minimize these barriers*
4. *methods to help the team resolve and learn from conflict when it arises—and it will*
5. *methods that each individual can use to help the team work better together*
6. *determine how their teamwork can be evaluated for successfully and effectively working together*
7. *purpose of a "parking lot"*
8. *determine ways the team can celebrate its successes*

Assignment *11.1: Give the HR team the same assignment as Dennis's, and facilitate a discussion of the topics listed above.*

Leadership of Change

The leader's roles in improving internal HR processes includes those shown in Figure 11.3.

Figure 11.3 The leader's roles in improving internal HR processes

Serve as Coach and Integrator

The role of the leader in business process improvement can be compared to a basketball coach. In basketball, the efforts of the players are highly reciprocal as each player depends on the effort of all the others. Anyone can handle the ball, attempt to score, or serve in a defensive or offensive capacity. Team members are always on the move—sometimes in a predetermined direction, and other times in totally spontaneous ways. The game is a group effort, with relationships among team members that include trust and knowing each other well enough to anticipate each other's moves.

Before a game, the role of the basketball coach is a mentor, leader and trainer, preparing the game plan and ensuring that individual players know key plays and understand the competition. During a game, the role is an integrator, periodically reinforcing team cohesion and interdependence, helping players coordinate plays, challenging them to utilize their collective ability to make decisions that fit the situation, and dealing with issues the team cannot resolve on its own. After a game, the role is a motivator, providing the team with support and recognition.

Although the leader of the HR business process improvement project is the person giving the "charge" or objective to the HR team, he/she also can serve as the coach of the process and an integrator to form team cohesiveness. The leader prepares the game plan, trains the HR staff, gives them the information needed to accomplish the goal, empowers them to make effective and efficient decisions, and challenges them to redesign processes in innovative ways.

During the actual meeting, the leader in a "coaching role" means that he/she can serve as a facilitator to capture information on a flip chart or other resource for the purpose of redesigning the current processes and any potential changes. The leader keeps track of topics that can be part of a future meeting, in a "Parking Lot" or by listing future discussion items. The benefits of the leader serving in this role are significant:

1. In most cases, the leader does not know the entire process being redesigned, and this role will walk him/her through the process.
2. Because the leader does not know the details, he/she will ask numerous follow-up questions about details of the process that other staff may take for granted.
3. The leader serving as a "recorder" frees up time for everyone on the team to participate fully in the discussions.
4. The leader serving in this role for at least the first business process improvement project role-models desired behaviors to those who will assume this role for future projects.
5. The leader can influence the project's flow by challenging the HR staff and asking that tough question, "Why?" again and again.

Empower the HR Staff

Empowering employees means creating an environment in which people can have an impact on decisions and actions that affect their jobs. It is all about giving them real power. This process clears the way for employees to use "their" skills and knowledge, with the outcome that employees are helped to own their work and take responsibility for their results. Essentially, a manager moves from being a "controller" to being a leader, coach, skill developer, team-builder and coordinator.

> Empowering employees means creating an environment in which people can have an impact on decisions and actions that affect their jobs.

What are mechanisms that limit or stall employee empowerment? Outlined in Figure 11.4, these mechanisms are prevalent in higher education cultures due to their highly centralized and bureaucratic organizational structures.

The leader's role is to eliminate, or at least diminish, these barriers—one by one—in order to empower employees. Within our HR paradigm change, we have addressed the lack of needed skills by the HR staff since chapter 5. With improving internal HR processes, we are laying the foundation for dealing with the remaining barriers

Essential features to increase empowerment of the team are the following:

1. Clearly identify the team's purpose and goals as a method for members to be clear about how much autonomy the team has.
2. Clarify the team's authority. This point expands on #1 above. Are there parameters within which their recommendations or decisions must fit?
3. Ensure that all team members face similar outcomes for the results of the team.

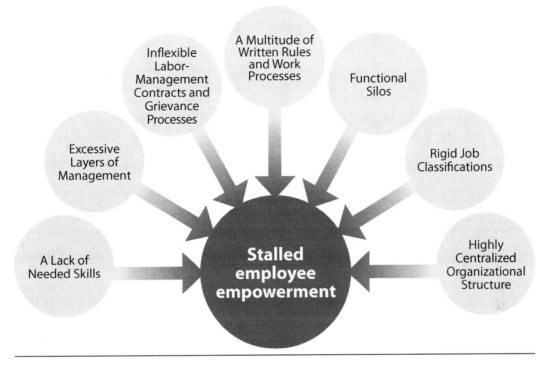

Figure 11.4 Mechanisms that limit or stall employee empowerment

4. Provide the team with support and recognition.
5. Help the team to develop team-based competencies such as group decision-making, group problem-solving, and dealing with conflict.
6. Reward and recognize empowered behavior exhibited by the team.

Challenge the HR Staff

A major role of the leader during business process improvement is to challenge the thinking of the HR staff about why processes are structured in the current way. Questions like the following can open the discussion and allow individuals to rethink old ways of doing things:

"Why is this step being done?"
"What is the outcome of this step?"
"How does this step help the customer?
"Why does this step include a hand-off to...?"
"What is missing in this step?"
"Is there a waste of time (or materials or technology) in the way this step is being done?"

In concert with challenging the HR staff, the leader must encourage risk-taking and innovation in the process of designing more efficient and effective internal HR processes. For individuals for whom change is difficult, talking about a revised process as a "pilot" provides a safe opportunity to challenge traditional approaches and encourage new ideas and risk-taking. This includes setting a specific time line for using the revised pilot process, and developing criteria to evaluate its success and a process to make improvements if necessary.

In addition, involving the HR staff in researching internal HR processes at other higher education institutions in order to benchmark best practices provides a challenge to traditional thinking. Knowing that peers successfully work using different processes can encourage risk-taking. Finally, a leader who demonstrates a willingness to take risks sets the tone for the HR staff.

Resolve Conflict if Necessary

Although it is optimal for the HR team itself to resolve conflict and issues, in the early stages of empowering individuals, it may be necessary for the leader to take on this role. We include more on this topic when we continue with our case study.

Process Improvement 101

Why improve processes? First, it is important that all individuals involved in a process understand how and why it is being done the way it is. Second, evaluating the current process and discussing alternate methods of accomplishing it improves the HR staff's skills of decision-making, innovation, risk-taking, and working together within the environment of the department's vision, mission, core values and core competencies. The HR staff take ownership and responsibility for the outcome of their work. After business process improvement begins and short-term wins prevail, it is very likely that internal processes will continue to be improved periodically as individuals engage more deeply with the process and become empowered.

… this process is conducted in an environment that includes the HR department's vision, mission, core values, and core competencies.

Process Improvement Basics

A model for business process improvement is outlined in Exhibit 11.1. Note that this process is conducted in an environment that includes the HR department's vision, mission, core values, and core competencies. Our goal is to develop more effective and efficient internal HR processes within and

Exhibit 11.1 Model for business process improvement

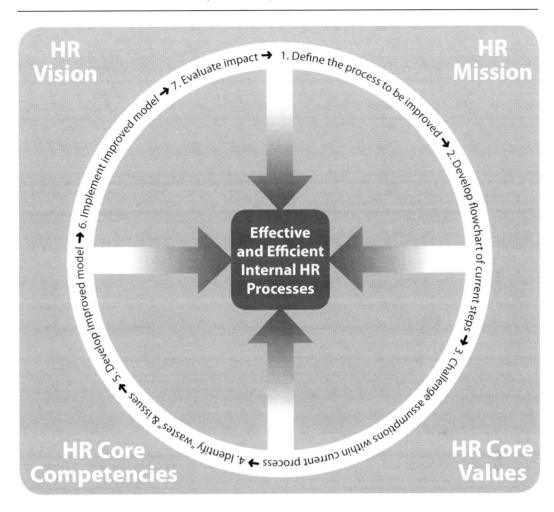

aligned with this environment. These seven steps in the process are explained in more detail in Table 11.1, which includes the outcome of each step.

Table 11.1 Detailed steps for improving internal HR processes

Step	Activity	Outcome
1. Define the process to be improved	• develop a list of key HR activities as processes (e.g., recruitments, hires, contracts, terminations, renewals, retirements, new benefits, etc.) • prioritize key processes (e.g., which need to be improved the most) • involve subject matter experts • choose the first project to improve; define where it begins and ends	Prioritization of processes to improve
2. Develop flowchart of current process	• list each step or activity in the current process, using one sticky note for each step; use a verb to start the step description • for each step or activity, determine if anything cannot be changed due to an existing constraint • for each step or activity, identify who does it, where and how • for each step or activity, identify any hand-offs • for each step or activity, identify key measurements related to process (e.g. cost, quality, materials, time, corrections, waiting/delay, extra processing, motions/movement/hand-offs) • sequence the current steps • add appropriate symbols and arrows	Flowchart of current process identified Each step or activity on one sticky note with: verb, any existing constraint, who does it, where and how, any hand-offs, key measures
3. Challenge assumptions within the current process	• challenge each "step or activity" in the current process: • why is it being done • why is it being done there • why is it being done then • why is it being done this way • why does that person do it • who benefits from the step or activity; does it provide customer value • challenge current policies and practices behind a process	Identification of potential far-reaching improvements in the process
4. Identify "wastes" and issues	• identify wastes such as time, quality, materials, hand-offs, corrections, waiting/delay, extra processing, extra motions/movements • determine any "problems" in current process • explore alternative methods • cut across functional silos • incorporate technology when appropriate	Identification of potential parts of the process to improve
5. Develop improved model	• integrate separate processes when appropriate • draft new process flowchart showing each "activity" • assess potential impact of new process (use key measurement(s) identified in step #2)	Development of new improved process
6. Implement improved model	• develop implementation plan with timeline; who is responsible for each step of the plan • conduct pilot testing if appropriate • anticipate and address potential problems	Implementation of new improved process
7. Measure impact or metrics; evaluate new process	• determine impact—efficiencies and effectiveness—before and after business process improvement • measure impact, both in the short-term and the long-term • evaluate process for potential changes	Impact communicated to stakeholders; evaluation determines if additional changes are to be made

Back to Case Study 11.1

> *Dennis was very excited about being at this point in improving business processes. As part of step 1, the entire HR staff brainstormed a list of all the major internal processes in the department, indicated in Exhibit 11.2.*

Exhibit 11.2 Major internal HR processes

- **faculty and administrative staff hiring***
- **support staff hiring***
- *faculty and administrative staff recruitment*
- *support staff recruitment*
- *faculty and administrative staff promotion, salary equity, renewal, tenure, salary administration*
- *support staff promotion and transfer*
- *administrative and support staff reinstatement*

- **FMLA***
- **403(b)***
- *immigration*
- **benefit changes***
- *payroll changes*
- *retirements and resignations*
- *leave accounting*
- **performance evaluations***
- *grievances and complaints*
- *terminations*
- **student employment/hiring***
- *student payroll*

**Prioritized processes for improvement*

From the list in Exhibit 11.2, the HR staff identified seven key processes that either had problems or provided the opportunity for the most improvement. Dennis recommended the HR staff break into two teams, one to improve the faculty and administrative staff hiring process, and the other to improve the same process for support staff. Each team comprised those individuals who dealt with stages of the hiring process for their particular employee group. Because there was only one benefits specialist, that person was on both teams. The receptionist was added to both teams. The teams set up weekly meetings over the next several months.

During each team's first meeting, they revisited the HR department vision, mission, core values, and core competencies and developed meeting guidelines. They were very concerned about everyone participating thoroughly, so Dennis asked the temporary employee to attend both meetings as the recorder. They also identified the importance of team members completing action items within the time lines agreed upon, and stated this as one of the guidelines. The teams gave themselves names reminiscent of the employee group each served: Support Staff Team, Faculty Team. First, we will follow the work of the Faculty Team, utilizing the steps in Table 11.1.

Step 1:   **Define the process to be improved**

The team determined that the process for hiring a faculty member begins with the receipt of an appointment form from the department, and ends when the hired person chooses his/her benefits.

Step 2:   **Develop flowchart of current process**

This involves listing each step or activity in the current process, using one sticky note for each. Each sticky note contains:

- a verb to begin the step description
- any existing constraints that would impact a potential change
- identify who does it, where and how
- identify any hand-offs
- identify key measurements (e.g., cost, materials, quality, time, corrections, waiting/delay, extra processing, motions/movement/hand-offs, etc.)

Listed in Exhibit 11.3 are the steps in the current process of hiring a faculty member brainstormed by the Faculty Team and captured by Dennis on a flip chart. The team detailed "each" step or activity on a separate sticky note. The Faculty Team determined

Exhibit 11.3 Steps in hiring faculty

1. Receive paperwork from department.
2. Review paperwork for completion and accuracy.
3. Contact department if problems with paperwork.
4. Obtain signatures from provost and budget offices.
5. **Request contract letter from IT*.**
6. Prepare contract packet.
7. **Send contract packet to faculty member via postal mail*.**
8. Receive completed contract materials from faculty; check for accuracy and completion.
9. Contact faculty if need more information.
10. Obtain signature from Provost on signed faculty contract.
11. Send signed contract sent to Faculty.
12. Enter appointment information into the human resources system (HRS).
13. Enter payroll information into HRS.
14. Enter information into IT program for faculty email, campus directory, network and other IT access.
15. **Develop personnel file*.**
16. Develop benefits file.
17. Develop payroll file.
18. Conduct group benefits orientations.
19. Collect benefits paperwork; check for completion.
20. Enter benefits into HRS.
21. File all materials into personnel file.

* See Exhibit 11.4 for examples of sticky notes.

that the list of steps shown in Exhibit 11.3 is the accurate sequence of the events. The three
highlighted and starred steps in Exhibit 11.3 are provided as examples in Exhibit 11.4.

Exhibit 11.4 Details of three steps in hiring faculty

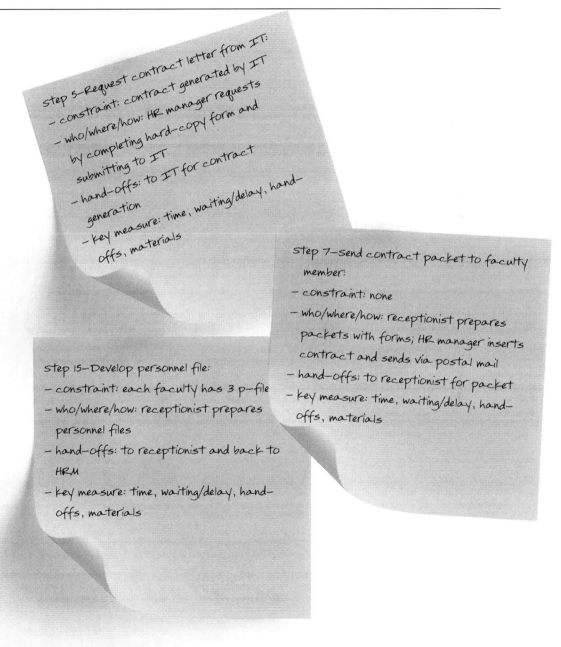

step 5—Request contract letter from IT:
– constraint: contract generated by IT
– who/where/how: HR manager requests
  by completing hard-copy form and
  submitting to IT
– hand-offs: to IT for contract
  generation
– key measure: time, waiting/delay, hand-
  offs, materials

step 7—Send contract packet to faculty
  member:
– constraint: none
– who/where/how: receptionist prepares
  packets with forms; HR manager inserts
  contract and sends via postal mail
– hand-offs: to receptionist for packet
– key measure: time, waiting/delay, hand-
  offs, materials

step 15—Develop personnel file:
– constraint: each faculty has 3 p-file
– who/where/how: receptionist prepares
  personnel files
– hand-offs: to receptionist and back to
  HRM
– key measure: time, waiting/delay, hand-
  offs, materials

Exhibit 11.5 illustrates the flowchart of the first seven steps in the current process of hiring faculty.

Exhibit 11.5 Flowchart of the first seven steps in hiring faculty

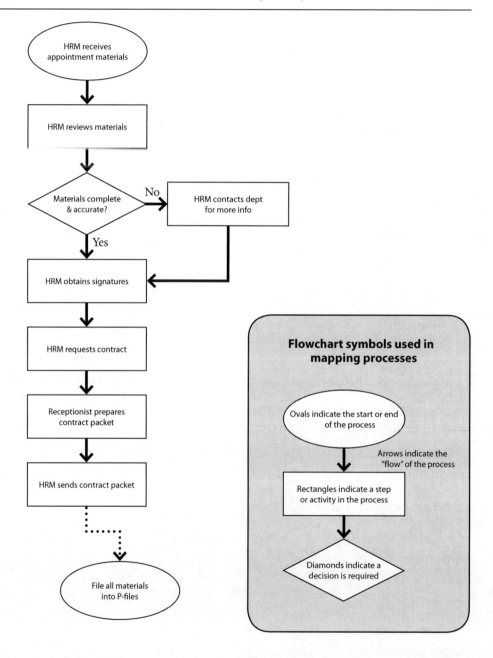

Step 3:   **Challenge assumptions within the current process**

During this step in business process improvement, the Faculty Team challenged each step in the process of hiring a faculty member. They identified eight steps in the process that were especially problematic, and listed them in Table 11.2.

Step 4:   **Identify "wastes" and issues**

For each step, they determined its issue(s) and constraints or key measure(s). They then spent the next several weeks brainstorming each step to develop alternatives to create greater efficiency and effectiveness with the process. Team members indicate that the recommended revisions need to be valued by those people impacted by the process, e.g., department chairs, department administrative assistants, deans, new faculty members. Their recommended revisions were included in the table.

Table 11.2: Problematic steps in the process of hiring faculty, with recommended revisions

Step	Issue	Constraint or Key Measure	Recommended Revision
4. Obtain signatures from provost and budget offices	Paperwork often sits for several days in each office before signed	HR does not have control over timing of signatures/ time, waiting/delay, hand-off	Department obtains needed signatures prior to submitting paperwork to HR
5. Request contract letter from IT	May take 1-3 days for IT to run program that generates contracts; IT must make changes to contract template when needed	HR does not have control over timing of contracts being run, or timing of revisions to contract template; waiting/delay/time, hand-off	Faculty Team bypass IT program by developing contract templates with aid of campus attorney; merge template with new faculty information to obtain contract
7. Send contract packet via postal mail to new faculty member	Faculty member is often between addresses	Time for contract to be received by faculty member, completed and returned	Faculty Team develop process to email contracts to new faculty; place employment documents on website for ease of downloading and completion
10. Obtain signature from provost on signed faculty contract	Contract often sits for several days before signed	Time, waiting/delay, hand-off	Provost's electronic signature is placed on the contract that is emailed to new faculty
11. Send signed contract to faculty member	Copy is made of signed contract and mailed to faculty member	Time, extra processing, motions/movement, cost	New faculty member keeps own copy of emailed contract
15 Develop personnel file 16 Develop benefits file 17. Develop payroll file	Three files for one faculty member are created and filed in separate locations	Hand-off, extra processing and materials	Receptionist copied when contract emailed to new faculty member; prepares a personnel file with 3 sections-appointments, benefits, payroll—gives to HRM

During the several weeks that the Faculty Team brainstormed alternatives, they kept track of the number of days it took to process the hiring of a new faculty member. Fortunately, the Faculty Team worked on this project in late winter and the departments recruiting new faculty were busy making offers and completing appointment paperwork. The team determined that, on average, the process to hire a new faculty member could be reduced by five days with the changes indicated in Table 11.2.

The Faculty Team members worked well together on this first project. At one point, the HR manager was not convinced they could bypass the IT program and create the contracts themselves. She had used the current process for many years, and felt the recommendation was too complicated to develop. However, other team members offered to work with her to develop the new process, and try it as a pilot for three months. If the new process did not meet the criteria for increased efficiency and value to stakeholders, they would re-evaluate the project.

Step 5: **Develop improved model**

With the recommendations for process changes from the Faculty Team, Dennis knew he needed to talk with three people: the provost, the budget director, and the IT director. His conversation with the IT director went very well. The program used to generate the new faculty contracts was very old and recently crashed while generating contracts. The programmers were busy on other high priority projects and were not able to spend time re-coding this program.

Dennis's conversation with the budget director began very differently. At first, he did not like the idea that departments would bring their forms directly to his office for signature. He liked the current process, as it was very efficient for his staff. However, after they discussed the issues with the current process and the need to improve stakeholder value, the budget director had a different suggestion. Because his office signed off on the recruitment itself, and each dean was responsible for his/her budget, why did his office need to sign the appointment paperwork? Dennis indicated that to his knowledge, there was never a situation when the budget office did not approve the hire. They agreed that beginning immediately, the budget office did not need to sign the appointment form for new faculty hires.

With this knowledge, Dennis met with the provost, explaining the situation and the decision by the budget and IT directors. Although the provost acknowledged that she signed off on the recruitment paperwork and therefore knew the departments that were hiring, she liked to sign the appointment paperwork so that she learned who was being hired. Dennis suggested that the HR manager could copy the provost's Office on the emailed contract, and the provost liked that idea. Before their conversation ended, she also agreed to provide her electronic signature for the contract itself. The provost was impressed that the new process was developed with one of the goals being increased value to stakeholders.

As another method to reduce the timeline, the provost suggested the hiring department be able to email the appointment documents, including those scanned with signatures, to the HR department instead of sending the hard-copy documents through inter-campus mail. Dennis liked that idea and said he would bring it to the Faculty Team for discussion.

In exchange for these process changes, the provost asked Dennis for a report on the new process after three months. She wanted him to develop criteria to evaluate the new process, to include quantitative and qualitative measures. That is just what Dennis wanted to hear, and he planned to give this project to the Faculty Team as a way to evaluate the changes.

Step 6: *Implement improved model*

The Faculty Team members were ecstatic when Dennis told them about the positive outcomes of his meetings. They really liked the idea of the hiring department emailing scanned documents to them instead of sending the hard-copy materials. They were motivated to begin making the changes immediately, and scheduled a meeting to develop an implementation plan and timeline. Dennis approved that the team members could work the overtime needed to develop the changed process.

They then discussed that each faculty member had three personnel files, one each for appointment, benefit and payroll paperwork, and that each file was physically located in a different space in the HR department. The Faculty Team decided to make "one" personnel file for each faculty member, with three sections. With that decision, Dennis approved that the receptionist hire a student employee to work during the summer to combine the files of current faculty.

Finally, Dennis suggested the entire HR team celebrate its accomplishments by having lunch together—which he would pay for.

Exhibit 11.6 contains a list of the revised process for hiring new faculty. According to step five in business process improvement, this also should be accompanied by a new process flowchart showing each activity. Note the "call-out" box that assesses the potential impact of the new process. These criteria will become "metrics" in the plan to evaluate the revised process.

Step 7: *Measure impact or metrics; evaluate new process*

The Faculty Team developed metrics to evaluate the new process three months after it was put into place. The quantitative criteria included: number of days to hire a new faculty member, reduced number of hand-offs, reduced cost, reduced processing time, reduced waiting/delay time. Qualitative criteria included: increased access to

Exhibit 11.6 Revised steps in faculty hiring

1. Receive paperwork from department via email
2. Review paperwork for completion and accuracy
3. Contact department if problems with paperwork
4. Create contract from templates
5. Email contract with letter containing links to employment documents to faculty member; copy provost office plus receptionist
6. Receive completed contract materials from faculty; check for accuracy and completion
7. Contact faculty if need more information
8. Enter appointment information into HRS
9. Enter payroll information into HRS
10. Enter information into IT program for faculty email, campus directory, network and other IT access
11. Develop combined personnel file
12. Conduct group benefits orientations
13. Collect benefits paperwork; check for completion
14. Enter benefits into HRS
15. File all materials into personnel file

Note:
- steps are reduced from 21 to 15
- hand-offs of paperwork are reduced from 10 to 4
- waiting/delay/time is reduced in 8 steps
- processing is reduced in 4 steps
- costs are reduced in 5 steps

employment paperwork (put forms and information on HR website), satisfaction with new process by department chairs, department administrative assistants, deans, deans assistants, and new faculty member.

Communication Plan

In chapter 7, we recommended interviewing leaders across the campus to obtain powerful testimonies for an HR paradigm shift. The interviews included our assurance to communicate periodically with the interviewees regarding progress made in the transformation. At this point in the process we have communicated periodic progress only to the leader's supervisor and/or the cabinet members. There are numerous reasons for and benefits of developing a communication plan for the HR paradigm shift:

1. demonstrates progress is occurring
2. gives credibility to the effort

3. *builds support for the effort*

4. *develops a base foundation for stakeholder understanding of the change*

5. *evaluates the level of understanding and acceptance of the vision*

6. *builds commitment to the vision*

7. *influences stakeholders to think and act in accord with the vision*

8. *determines stakeholder value in the HR function*

9. *seeks stakeholder feedback and questions*

10. *follows-up on stakeholder feedback and questions*

11. *detects resistance to the vision and determines how to deal with it*

12. *prepares stakeholders to absorb and engage in the change*

When/Who /What Message/How

To whom, when and how the message is communicated, and the content of the message are dependent on the phase in the change process. Table 11.3 offers suggestions for each aspect of the communication plan.

Transition Monitoring Teams

An effective method for communicating the message is to utilize transition monitoring teams (TMTs). A TMT is a small group of people chosen from a wide cross-section of the university. A TMT meets periodically and serves as a method for the HR staff to facilitate communication to campus stakeholders regarding the change initiative, and to obtain their feedback. When used effectively, TMTs:

- provide feedback to the HR staff on plans or communications before they are announced to the entire campus
- provide feedback to the HR staff on the understanding and commitment of stakeholders
- demonstrate to stakeholders that the HR staff value their opinions
- offer a mechanism for generating ideas
- increase HR knowledge of stakeholder values and interests
- gain stakeholder investment in the outcomes of the change
- secure stakeholder "influence" in the communication plan to the campus
- provide access to the employee "grapevine" to correct misinformation and rumors
- improve the skills of HR staff who facilitate TMT discussions

Back to Case Study 11.1

The Faculty Team made great strides in improving the faculty hiring process, and looked forward to the day the pilot program began. The Support Staff Team also finished improving the process for hiring support staff. Although their processes were not as complex as

Table 11.3 Details of a communication plan

When: Phase of the Change Process	Who	What Message	How
Develop vision of HR paradigm shift	Cabinet, HRD supervisor, key influencers	INFORM-LISTEN: Communicate the vision	In-person interviews, presentations or meetings
Develop HR department vision, mission, core values, core competencies, HR recruitment brand	All stakeholders	INFORM-LISTEN: Updated focus of HR department in order to provide value to stakeholders	Verbal, written or in-person interactions with stakeholders, email, website
Improve internal HR processes	Cabinet, HRD supervisor, key influencers	INFORM-LISTEN: Purpose and outcomes of improved HR processes	In-person meetings, newsletter, transition monitoring teams (TMTs)
Evaluate HR department structure	Cabinet, HRD supervisor, key influencers	INFORM-LISTEN: Purpose and outcomes of evaluating and potentially changing HR department structure	In-person meetings, newsletter, TMTs
Focus HR staff externally	Cabinet, HRD supervisor, key influencers, all supervisors	INFORM-LISTEN-ENGAGE: Purpose and outcomes of focusing externally	In-person meetings, emails, newsletter, TMTs
Improve external HR processes	Cabinet, HRD supervisor, all stakeholders	ENGAGE-COLLABORATE: Purpose and outcomes of improving external HR processes; seek involvement on teams; seek ownership	Email, TMTs, newsletter, website
Develop HR strategic plan	Cabinet, HRD supervisor, all stakeholders	ENGAGE-COLLABORATE: Purpose and outcomes of developing an HR strategic plan; seek involvement on teams; seek ownership	Email, TMTs, newsletter

those for faculty, they did make changes that reduced time and hand-offs. These included emailing an offer letter to the person being hired—similar to that for faculty—along with placing the employment documents on the HR website for ease of access.

More Business Process Improvement

During a staff meeting, the two teams shared their work and accomplishments. The excitement, indicated by laughter and joking, was at a high level. Dennis noted that several staff members were subdued, and made a sticky note to discuss with all staff members during their one-on-one monthly meeting where they were in the transition process.

Although the Faculty Team expected to be busy over the next month redesigning their processes, Dennis knew the Support Staff Team's work was almost finished. He suggested that they review several other processes for improvement: the support staff promotion, transfer and reinstatement processes. Although these were less complicated than hiring a new support employee, similar revisions could create greater stakeholder value without a great deal of extra time or effort by the team.

The payroll specialist on the Support Staff Team volunteered to serve as the facilitator for this second team project. She recently enrolled in an online masters program in leadership and training, and saw this as an opportunity to improve her skills. With her serving as the team facilitator, Dennis decided to not attend the team's meetings, but to ask the payroll specialist to update him after each meeting on the team's progress.

Resistance to Change

Some people have more problems dealing with change than others. They may take it personally. They may internalize their frustrations and feelings. Outwardly, they may seem aligned with the change—up to a point. Then something happens that causes their emotions to become external and they fight the change in various ways.

Leaders need to watch continually for signs of resistance to change and then deal with them immediately and effectively if the team cannot. Signs of resistance include not wanting their processes to change, not accepting a change in their responsibilities, emotional eruptions and conflict within the department, and disengagement from working with others to redesign processes.

> Leaders need to watch continually for signs of resistance to change and then deal with them immediately and effectively if the team cannot.

Back to Case Study 11.1

As the meetings of the Support Staff Team progressed, the payroll specialist indicated to Dennis that Donna, the benefits specialist, was increasingly resistant to making changes to any of her benefit processes. Donna reasoned that her services were very valued by stakeholders—she had many emails and notes of appreciation that indicated that. Yes, she understood that some of the tasks she did were "extra" and could be eliminated, but these contributed toward the value she provided. She also understood that some could be done more efficiently, but she already worked overtime and said she had no time to work on redesigning processes that may not be valued by employees.

When challenged by team members to have others take on some of her responsibilities, Donna indicated very forcefully that the benefits could not be separated—it just would not work with more than one person doing employee benefits. Finally, Dennis learned Donna did not attend the last two meetings of the team, saying she had too much work to spend time in meetings.

Dennis met with Donna one-on-one the next day. He told her what others on the team had communicated to him, and asked her for her perspective. Donna was very blunt in stating that she had no time for redesigning benefits processes. She understood the value of that being done with other processes, but the current processes worked very well for her and the university's employees. She also brought up that she continually needed to work 5-10 hours a week in overtime, and did not have time for these extra meetings.

Dennis then indicated that it was time to bring together a Payroll and Benefits Team to review those processes, in particular FMLA, 403(b), benefit changes, and payroll changes. He knew there were particular issues with FMLA and student payroll. He thought members of the team would comprise those HR staff involved in benefit and payroll functions for any employee: faculty, administrative staff, support staff, or student employee. This included four HR staff: Donna as the benefits specialist, the faculty/staff payroll specialist, the administrative/support payroll specialist, and the student payroll specialist.

When Dennis countered her arguments with the idea that redesigning benefit processes could limit the need for her to work overtime, Donna took this personally and became very upset. Dennis gave her time to vent and compose her emotions. He then calmly told her that she was a valuable member of the HR department, and her work was appreciated and respected by the university's employees.

The fact remained that the various benefits processes needed to be improved, as did all processes in the department, and most of her overtime eliminated. In addition, he explained to Donna that a major weakness of the department, and a disservice to employees, was that there was no back-up in the benefits area when she was absent. He wanted her to proactively and positively engage in improving processes. Dennis asked her if she could do that. She paused and then replied that she did not know. When Dennis asked when she could give him an answer, she told him the next Monday. It was Thursday, and he scheduled a meeting with her for Monday.

On Monday morning, Donna called in sick; and did the same for the next four days. She always left a message on Dennis's phone at 6am, an hour before he came into the office. A week later, Donna came into work at 7am, walked into Dennis's office and *handed him her retirement letter. She gave three month's notice. She indicated she no longer felt valued and did not like the direction the department was headed. Dennis accepted her resignation and said he would get back to her as soon as he developed a succession plan.*

Having worked at other universities as the HR director, Dennis understood that some departments organized the benefits work around one or more staff who served as payroll "and" benefits specialists. Early that morning, he met with the three staff who served as payroll specialists. He explained that Donna decided to retire, and that he would take on the FMLA and 403(b) benefit responsibilities for three reasons: (1) their processes needed major revisions, and because both currently had issues with legal implications, he needed to take on those immediate responsibilities; (2) as a new direc-tor, managing these programs would connect him closer with faculty and staff; and (3) this would reduce the amount of time other staff needed to spend on employee benefits.

He then asked them about their workload and interest in taking on benefits responsibilities. He suggested the advantages to each were the following:

1. *Potential long-term opportunities included promotion in title and salary.*
2. *Benefits work entailed greater confidentiality and intimacy with employees than payroll work. Most HR benefits staff developed close relationships with employees as they learned about medical issues, issues with family members, concerns about retirement, etc.*
3. *Working within the benefits function required additional skills and would chal-lenge them to grow professionally and personally.*
4. *Because he planned to bring together a payroll and benefits team to improve those processes, they would be involved intricately with the opportunity to create increased efficiency and value for employees.*

All three agreed to take on the benefits function for their specific segment of employee. They were excited about the idea of forming a "payroll and benefits" team that worked together to improve these HR processes. They especially felt that having a team that backed up each member during his/her absence from the office provided significant value to campus constituents.

Dennis led the discussion to schedule a timeline over the next three months for Donna to train them in benefits responsibilities.

Implementing Transition Monitoring Teams
Dennis realized he should have developed a plan earlier to communicate the HR para-digm change and timeline to key campus influencers. He did interview campus leaders initially to communicate the change and get their input, but since then, he was busy

working internally with the HR staff. Now he began to hear comments like, "What is going on in HR? People are talking about process changes and are excited about what they are doing. How will this impact me? I do not understand what is going on." Dennis hoped he had not waited too long to communicate, and therefore lose the trust and support he needed as the HR paradigm shift was implemented.

In a recent HR staff meeting, others brought up this same confusion by people across the campus. One of the staff suggested they develop a transition monitoring team (TMT) process, as William Bridges described in his book, Managing Transitions (2003). Before the meeting was over, they agreed to the following methods to implement TMTs:

1. Consider a TMT to include an existing team or committee. This gave them access to key administrators such as vice presidents, deans, directors of major campus divisions, and shared governance.
2. Develop a list of potential members of a TMT, to include faculty, administrative staff and support staff across campus considered to be influencers. People who may resist the change publicly or privately must be involved.
3. Each HR staff member serves as a facilitator of a TMT of their choice.
4. Develop a "template" to communicate a consistent message to the TMT, and manage and follow through on feedback received from the TMT.

Case Study Questions

1. Regarding all the work in this chapter, what were the major mechanisms used by Dennis that enabled successful business process improvement?
2. What could Dennis have done to provide for even better outcomes of improving the faculty hiring process?
3. What alternative methods could Dennis have used to deal with Donna's resistance to change?
4. Should Dennis have tried to convince Donna not to retire?
5. Use the 6-stage model for transforming conflict or a major issue into a problem to be resolved, outlined in chapter 6, to work through the process of dealing with Donna's resistance to change. Did Dennis use this model? What alternative methods for dealing with Donna's resistance does using this model reveal?
6. What are potential problems when a communication plan is not developed and implemented at the appropriate times?

To review discussion of recommendations for Case Study 11.1 go to **www.HR-higher-ed.com**

Summary

It is important that all individuals involved in a process understand how and why it is being done the way it is. Evaluating a current process and discussing alternate methods of accomplishing it improves the HR staff's skills of decision-making, innovation, risk-taking, and working together within the environment of the department's vision, mission, core values and core competencies. The HR staff take ownership and responsibility for the outcome of their work. After business process improvement begins and short-term wins prevail, it is very likely that internal processes will continue to be improved periodically as individuals engage more deeply with the process and feel their empowerment.

Business process improvement is conducted in an environment that includes the HR department's vision, mission, core values, and core competencies. Our goal is to develop more effective and efficient internal HR processes within and aligned with this environment. The seven steps for improving processes are:

1. Define the process to be improved
2. Develop flowchart of current steps
3. Challenge assumptions with current process
4. Identify "wastes" and issues
5. Develop improved model
6. Implement improved model
7. Evaluate impact or performance metrics of improved process

Major Themes

Leadership of Change is central in continuing to move proactively through the transition process. This chapter includes additional discussions around building trust and managing conflict and resistance as part of working as a team. In addition, the HR team must be empowered to take risks and become innovative in proactively redesigning internal processes.

In improving internal HR processes, the leader's roles includes the following: serving as coach and integrator, empowering HR staff, challenging HR staff and resolving conflict if necessary. Mechanisms that limit employee empowerment and must be eliminated, or at least diminished, include:

1. Highly centralized organizational structure
2. Rigid job classifications
3. Functional silos
4. A multitude of written rules and work processes
5. Inflexible labor-management contracts and grievance processes
6. Excessive layers of management
7. A lack of needed skills

Evaluation of "Your" HR Department's Chapter 11 Outcome

Outcome Desired: More effective and efficient internal HR processes

Change: HR staff members are empowered to take risks and become innovative in proactively redesigning internal department processes; the team is strengthened and empowered to take action, with short-term wins as a result (change steps 2, 5, 6)

Key Indicators of Success: (check if "yes")

☐ HR staff give up their own "agenda" to develop a better one

☐ HR staff choose to be more excited about the team's success than about personal success

☐ A spirit of teamwork exists within the department environment, where individuals seek to build up those around them and be open and honest in the process

☐ Increased trust exists between team members

☐ Team members have open and honest discussions regarding problems, issues, and progress toward their goal(s)

☐ Team members understand and believe in the importance and urgency of the change effort

☐ Team members stay on track regarding their approach and direction

☐ New ideas are proposed and tested

☐ Issues and problems are identified and acted upon quickly

☐ Feedback and suggestions for improvement are identified and acted upon quickly

☐ The level of activity relating to change increases as people become more engaged in the process

☐ Some resisters become supporters; some supporters become actively engaged

☐ Important achievements are recognized and celebrated

☐ Redesigned processes include metrics for evaluation

☐ More HR staff are moving through the "neutral zone" toward the "new beginning"

☐ Increased support for the change from people in positions of power and influence

Evaluation of "Your" HR Department's Chapter 11 Outcome, *continued*

Potential Barriers to Change: (check if *"needs attention"*)

- [ ] Resistance to the change increases and negatively impacts the work of improving processes
- [ ] One or more team members refuse to participate in subtle ways
- [ ] One or more team members withhold information from the rest of the team
- [ ] There is skepticism about the change from one or more team members
- [ ] Progress on improving HR business processes is too slow
- [ ] Many ideas for improving processes are generated, but few are acted upon
- [ ] Team members avoid dealing with problems
- [ ] People are frustrated
- [ ] Business process improvement efforts are given a low priority by one or more HR team members
- [ ] One or more HR staff members do not feel a sense of urgency to achieve the goal
- [ ] Conflict erupts among team members
- [ ] Trust is low among team members
- [ ] One or more team members do not work within the environment of the HR department vision, mission, or core values
- [ ] People are working long hours
- [ ] People do not feel they have been given enough training in order to improve processes
- [ ] People do not feel that the "leader" demonstrates the type of behavior, skills, and attitudes needed to attain the changed HR paradigm
- [ ] People do not feel the "leader" has removed work activities that divert them from accomplishing the goal
- [ ] People do not feel they are being rewarded for doing the extra work of improving processes
- [ ] Key influencers complain that they are not kept informed on the progress of the change

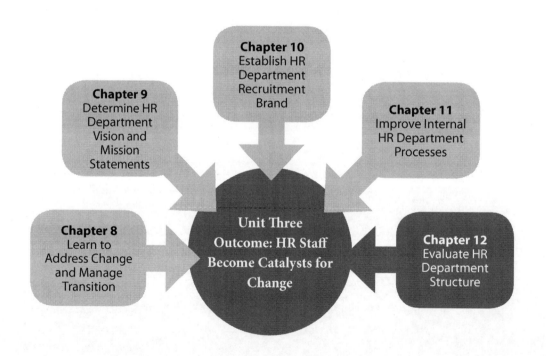

Evaluate Human Resources Department Structure

Chapter 12 Evaluate HR department structure

Within the context of Unit Three, the outcome of chapter 12 is an HR department structure aligned with the department's vision, mission, goals, current environment, technology and tasks. One of the barriers to encouraging urgency for change is a structure that focuses staff's attention on narrow functional goals, e.g., measuring performance on their functional responsibilities instead of on broad department goals or process measures. The wrong department structure hinders the ability of staff to accomplish its vision and mission in the following ways:

- reduced empowerment and decision-making
- inadequate communication among staff in different functional areas
- different focus and priorities among functional areas in the department

> The wrong department structure hinders the ability of staff to accomplish its vision and mission…

The department structure serves as a road map for formal expectations and interactions among the HR staff, and between HR staff and stakeholders. Structure has two components: (1) "allocate" work among employees by specifying positions or roles; (2) indicate how employees need to "coordinate" their work among these roles. Methods for coordinating and allocating work can include:

- employee knowledge or skill
- product or service
- place or geographical area
- time
- customers or clients
- process or flow of work

In many cases, we do not evaluate structure and positions and how they coordinate until someone leaves the department, and sometimes not even then. Especially within higher education, we

> Structure has two components: (1) "allocate" work among employees by specifying positions or roles; (2) indicate how employees need to "coordinate" their work among these roles.

become accustomed to one basic structural design—maybe because it has been used for decades and we are oblivious to any alternatives. Sometimes people have so much invested in that structure that they are afraid of the potential changes—perhaps they will lose authority, control, expertise or recognition. In addition, if the sense of urgency has not been established solidly, people resist structural change.

Figure 12.1 outlines the process for evaluating the structure of the HR department. The outcome of this process contributes toward the accomplishment of two steps in Kotter's eight-step change process: aligning the department structure with the vision, and enabling action by changing the infrastructure to remove significant and immediate barriers to the change.

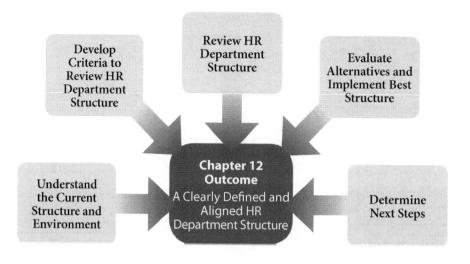

Figure 12.1 Model to evaluate the HR department structure

Understand the Current Structure and Environment

STEPS TO TAKE PRIOR TO REVIEWING THE CURRENT STRUCTURE OF THE HR DEPARTMENT

Step 1: Understand the current environment in which the HR department exists

Step 2: Develop current HR department vision and mission statements and goals aligned with those of the university

Step 3: Understand current HR department tasks, processes, technology and structure

Step 1: **Understand the current environment in which the HR department exists.** The current external environment and the challenges it brings to higher education institutions, including the HR function, is described in Unit One and can be updated for your specific institution. In addition, the current environment includes the structure of the university itself.

The typical structure for most not-for-profit higher education institutions is a bureaucracy, summarized in Figure 12.2. This structure is essentially flat and decentralized, with strategic and other important decisions made at the administration or strategic level. This top level normally has few employees compared to the rest of the institution, and includes cabinet members (chancellor or president, vice

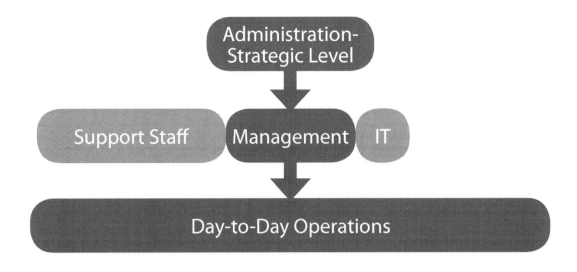

Figure 12.2 Organization of a typical not-for-profit higher education institution *(Bolman and Deal, 2003)*

presidents), deans, associate deans, and directors of major units, e.g., library, athletics, etc. Both the technology, or IT, section, and that of the support staff for administration and management sectors, are very small compared to those in the private sector. Few managerial or supervisory levels exist between administration and faculty/staff. The operating core, where day-to-day operations are controlled, is large relative to the other structural parts.

Resulting from this structure, including how work is allocated and coordinated and decisions are made, the institution responds slowly to external change. It is difficult to promote an urgency for change or accomplish a new vision when there are multiple focuses and priorities among people in different functional areas, and a lack of coordination exists.

Step 2: Develop current HR department vision and mission statements and goals aligned with those of the university. This should have been completed as part of the work of chapter 9.

Step 3: Understand current HR department tasks, processes, technology and structure. As part of chapter 11, the HR staff evaluated and improved all business processes.

Within not-for-profit higher education, the typical HR department structure lies between all positions reporting to the director, and that described in Figure 12.3. Because it also serves in an administrative assistant role, the receptionist position reports to the director. Benefits and payroll employees report to an HR manager or assistant director with knowledge of these tasks, policies and laws.

In some institutions, the equity and affirmative action role reports to the HR director, and in others it reports to the chancellor or president. Regardless of the structure, those in the HR department have some responsibilities for both equity and affirmative action.

Because institutions of higher education typically have employees segmented according to support staff, faculty, ad-hoc instructional staff and administrative staff, many processes differ, e.g., recruitments, promotion, hiring, etc. As a result, these functions are separated within the HR department.

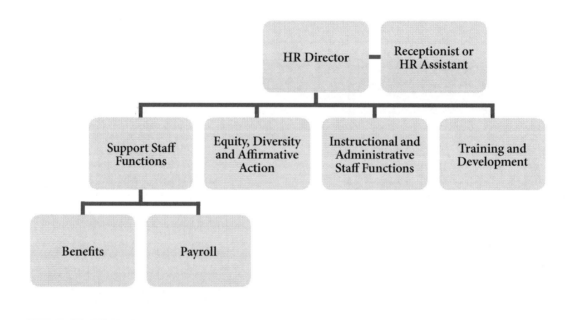

Figure 12.3 Typical HR department structure in not-for-profit higher education

… successfully restructuring depends on how well the new model aligns with the department and its environment, technology, tasks, processes, ability to accomplish its vision, mission and goals, and on the effectiveness of the process used for determining structure.

As with the overall higher education institution, this is a hierarchical structure that can result in functional silos, reduced communication and reduced speed of change, causing levels of authority, control and power. It essentially makes it difficult to accomplish the vision of the department.

In the short-term, restructuring a department can produce confusion and resistance. In the long term, successfully restructuring depends on how well the new model aligns with the department and its environment, technology, tasks, processes, ability to accomplish its vision, mission and goals, and on the effectiveness of the process used for determining structure. Many efforts to restructure become problematic, as those involved have an incomplete picture of the current situation. With knowledge of the current situation, we can develop criteria and a process for reviewing the current structure.

Case Study 12.1

> In our last chapter, Dennis and the HR teams reviewed HR internal processes. The Faculty Team developed an improved process for hiring faculty and administrative staff, which is in the implementation stage. The Support Staff Team implemented changes to the support staff hiring process that improved efficiency, and incorporated those changes into other processes, e.g., promotion, transfer, reinstatement, etc. Donna, the benefits specialist, decided to retire, with her responsibilities moved to a Payroll-Benefits Team responsible for managing the succession of benefits responsibilities and generating greater efficiencies. Dennis planned to redesign and recruit for the open position after the process of evaluating department structure was completed.
>
> Exhibit 12.1 outlines the current organization chart of the HR department at American University, including the changes with Donna's retirement.

Exhibit 12.1 American University HR department structure

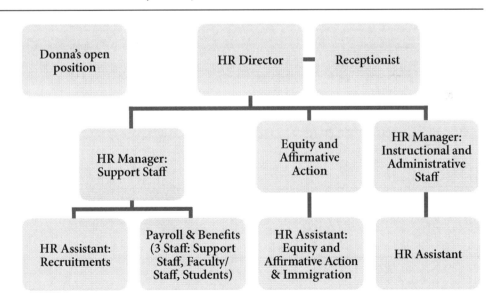

This department's formal organization chart indicates work is coordinated through "type of customer and services offered," and work is allocated to HR employees through "services offered and process or flow of work." For example, recruiting, hiring, and promoting support staff is completed by one HR manager and his HR assistant, and the same functions for instructional and administrative staff are completed by a different HR manager and HR assistant. Each HR assistant's responsibilities include only a portion of each employment "process" for that employee group. Each payroll and benefits staff member is responsible for a specific employee group.

During a recent staff meeting, Dennis and the HR staff discussed that although this chart shows reportage, it brings up several questions, such as:

1. *Is there a need for HR staff working with different employee groups to communicate? If so, how do they communicate?*
2. *How does the HR manager for instructional and administrative staff communicate with payroll and benefits when a new person is hired?*
3. *Are there informal methods for communication among groups? If so, do they provide for effective communication among HR staff?*

Dennis knew that prior to beginning the process to review the HR department's structure, he and the HR staff needed to understand all current HR processes, with their strengths and weaknesses. He expected the teams to work through improving all internal HR processes in six to eight weeks.

Develop Criteria to Evaluate HR Department Structure

In their book, *Reframing Organizations*, Bolman and Deal (2003) discuss eight dilemmas that must be resolved during the restructuring process. Essentially, these can serve as "criteria" in evaluating a department's structure. After reflecting on each of them to consider if they relate to restructuring the HR department, we integrate them into the following six criteria:

1. policies and procedures
2. workload of HR staff
3. gaps in allocating work
4. defining responsibilities
5. coordinating work
6. HR department strategic focus

First, are policies and procedures too loose or too tight? Are decisions made according to strict rules, with no deviations? Do HR staff lack the flexibility to be creative or innovative in working with customers? Does the structure promote inconsistency and favoritism in decision-making?

Second, what is the workload across employees? Are some overworked, and do others not have enough to do? Do some people always leave work when the office closes, do others consistently work late or skip their lunch hour? Are some HR staff bored, spending work time on personal pursuits or socializing excessively? Do HR staff serve on several university-wide committees or teams?

Third, are tasks clearly assigned? Do important tasks fall through the cracks and cause problems for customers? Are any tasks allocated to more than one person? Is there conflict over how a specific task needs to be completed? Is unnecessary data kept manually or can it be obtained through technology?

Fourth, are staff members unclear about their tasks and responsibilities? Do they take on tasks they personally prefer? Do people follow rigid job descriptions instead of focusing on stakeholder value? Do you hear, "That is not my job," or "You'll have to wait until next week to resolve this issue," in response to a stakeholder question or problem?

Fifth, is there too much or too little coordination among HR staff? Are HR staff distracted by unnecessary coordination of work? Are many approvals of work required in business practices? Are there unnecessary meetings to share information that could be done more efficiently? Are mistakes made because HR staff are not sharing vital information?

Sixth, are HR staff unclear about personal goals versus department goals? Do staff have individual goals aligned with the department goals? Do they know the department or university goals?

These six criteria comprise the tool to evaluate the current structure of the HR department.

Review HR Department Structure

Back to Case Study 12.1

> After the HR teams finished their first round of improving internal business processes, Dennis met with them to discuss reviewing the department structure. He shared what he learned from his research, and presented the evaluation tool. Discussion erupted as the HR staff engaged first in understanding the six criteria, then in relating examples of each in the department. Table 12.1 summarizes the evaluation tool along with the discussion of the HR staff, followed by further explanation and decisions for each criterion.

Criteria 1: Policies and Procedures

> The HR staff collectively felt the structure was too tight. They indicated they "always" worked according to the department and university rules and policies, and could not challenge them or work around them. They also heard stakeholders say that HR was very bureaucratic and that there were too many rules and policies. Many of these "rules" were internally driven, for example, the mid-month payroll option. Normally

Table 12.1 Case study completed tool to evaluate department structure

Criteria		Comments	Needs Improvement (Yes/No)
1. Policies and procedures			
Too loose-not sufficient structure for consistency and fairness ⟷	Too tight-not responsive to stakeholder value	Policies and procedures are too tight, not responsive to stakeholder value	Yes
2. Workload of HR staff			
Employees under-worked ⟷	Employees over-worked	Since HRS implementation, employee workload is inequitable	Yes
3. Gaps in allocating work			
Gap in assigning tasks ⟷	Overlap in assigning tasks	Relevance of continuing to keep manual data and reports	Yes
4. Defining responsibilities			
Lack of clarity ⟷	Strict definition	Rigid job descriptions impact stakeholder value; reallocate work to provide for effective back-up procedures	Yes
5. Coordinating work			
Too little coordination ⟷	Too much coordination	Too little coordination causes issues that impact stakeholders and HR department	Yes
6. HR department strategic focus			
Focus is on personal goals ⟷	Focus is on department goals	Focus primarily on personal goals	Yes

this was used to pay someone only when a HR staff member made a payroll mistake. Otherwise, the employee needed to wait until the next normal monthly or bi-weekly payroll to be paid. For example, if payroll paperwork was received in the HR department after the deadline for the normal payroll cycle, the faculty member had to wait almost an additional month to be paid.

HR staff heard informal verbal complaints by supervisors and managers, who felt the rules and policies provided barriers instead of value to them as stakeholders. In addition, adding to the bureaucratic image of the department, HR staff did not work *creatively with customers to accomplish their goal, but steadfastly adhered to which-ever policy defined the process.*

Decision: *Evaluate and revise HR department and university policies and procedures to focus on delivering stakeholder value; offer flexibility for HR staff to be creative in resolving stakeholder issues, while providing consistency and fairness.*

Criteria 2: Workload of HR Staff

Although some HR work is cyclical, such as recruitments due to employee retirements, transfers or resignations, the HR staff agreed that since the implementation of the new HRS, some of them were overworked and some could take on more responsi-bilities. With Donna's retirement, several took on additional benefits responsibilities, and stream-lined those for greater efficiencies. In particular, the process for recruiting support staff had not changed dramatically with the new HRS, whereas many other HR department processes now comprised employee self-service components. Large numbers of support staff retirements during the last year added to the workload issue.

One of the services Donna had provided was benefits orientations to finalists for faculty and administrative positions as part of their on-campus interview. The Payroll-Benefits Team expanded the service to finalists for all recruitments—if desired by the supervisor—and developed a process where all team members were involved in giving the orientations. This change was immediately valued by stakeholders.

Decision: *Reallocate HR tasks and responsibilities among HR staff members*

Criteria 3: Gaps in Allocating Work

The HR staff did not see any unassigned tasks that fell through the cracks, not con-sidering services that currently were not offered by the HR department, e.g., wellness program, leadership training, supervisor training, etc. Many of the HR staff manu-ally kept track of various data and reports generated from their work processes. This prompted the HR managers to consider that much of the data they kept manually either could be found in the new HRS or was redundant or not necessary. Each offered to work with their HR assistants on a process to evaluate data kept by them and provide a report to Dennis.

Decision: *Evaluate data and reports to determine relevance to HR work effectiveness and efficiency.*

Criteria 4: Defining Responsibilities

HR staff had tightly configured position descriptions, with a lack of discernable "back-

up" of responsibilities. For example, when a staff member was ill or on vacation, he/she returned to work and faced an overflowing "in" basket, email and phone messages. This negatively impacted the HR staff member plus customers: the staff member needed to schedule vacations around payroll or benefit time lines, and then upon return to work needed to work overtime to catch up; the customer needed to wait to have his/her HR request filled—which often impacted his/her payroll and benefits.

While working through the HR "task-responsibility" chart together, the HR staff noted that each person had a different idea about what being a "back-up" meant. The Payroll-Benefits Team had discussed this topic during their formation, resulting in team members addressing this responsibility differently. Those responsible for payroll backed each other by doing a different payroll each cycle. Those responsible for benefits had an area of expertise, but any differences in benefits among employee groups were easy to learn. Especially with the implementation of the new HRS, the payroll and benefits responsibilities involved more self-service and almost no manual work other than running the payroll and checking edit and discrepancy reports.

Decision: As part of reallocating tasks and responsibilities, develop a "back-up" process that provides for stakeholder value.

Criteria 5: Coordinating Work

The HR staff quickly agreed that coordination and communication among HR staff within different business functions improved since they formed the Payroll-Benefits Team and began reviewing business processes. However, it continued to be weak in several areas, especially in the recruitment function and between the HR managers and those involved in payroll and benefits. Recently, it became apparent that several supervisors used this lack of coordination to evade current policies. Better channels of coordination and communication between HR staff members needed to be implemented.

Decision: Restructure the HR department to improve coordination and communication among the HR staff.

Criteria 6: HR Department Strategic Focus

While the HR teams were improving business processes, Dennis reviewed each of their position descriptions, especially those taking on benefits responsibilities, intending to update them. None of the HR staff had a personal development action plan that included accomplishing department or university goals. Consequently, their annual performance evaluation included only accomplishments of the responsibilities detailed in their position description.

Although the HR department now had a new vision, mission and core values,

Dennis had not met with the staff to evaluate their skills and create a development plan with goals. Many felt they did not have an opportunity to work toward department goals. Dennis agreed to meet with each of them one-on-one over the next month to begin the individual development plan process.

As a result, the HR staff agreed that although some were adhering to department goals, others did not yet have the chance to move to this paradigm. Overall, this criteria point was an issue and not yet operationally aligned with the vision and mission, environment, technology and tasks.

Decision: *Develop individual personal development action plans to include department goals; revise the annual performance evaluation process.*

Exhibit 12.2 summarizes the decisions resulting from reviewing the current HR department structure.

Exhibit 12.2 Case study decisions resulting from reviewing current HR department structure

1. *Evaluate and revise HR department and university policies and procedures to focus on delivering stakeholder value*
2. *Offer flexibility for HR staff members to be creative in resolving stakeholder issues, while providing consistency and fairness*
3. *Reallocate HR tasks and responsibilities*
4. *Evaluate data and reports to determine relevance to HR work effectiveness and efficiency*
5. *Develop a "back-up" process that provides stakeholder value*
6. *Improve coordination of work among HR staff*
7. *Create individual development plans to include department goals*
8. *Revise annual performance evaluation process to include goal-setting*

Note that the presence of issues when evaluating structure indicates that the current department structure—how work is allocated and/or coordinated—is out of alignment with one or more of the following items. We utilize these items in evaluating an alternative structure for the HR department.

- the department vision, mission and goals
- current environment, including stakeholder value and institution strategy
- available technology
- department tasks and processes

Evaluate Alternatives and Implement Best Structure

Back to Case Study 11.1

> One of the Payroll-Benefits Team members indicated how well their team shared the payroll and benefits responsibilities, along with creating a plan to back-up each other. They also developed an agreement or charter for how they work together, share information and make decisions to meet the needs of their stakeholders. She suggested that the HR department change to coordinating work based on teams similar to the Payroll-Benefits Team.
>
> With that comment, Dennis wrote "HR Teams" at the top of a flip chart, with "Payroll-Benefits Team" below. He reminded everyone that "structure" included both allocating work and determining how to group people into working units to coordinate the work. He noted that the Payroll-Benefits Team currently coordinated work based on "services offered"—payroll, benefits, retirement counseling—and allocated work within the team by "type of customer." He asked the staff to propose other potential teams.
>
> Soon the flip chart included the "Staffing Team," composed of four HR staff involved in recruiting employees: faculty, ad-hoc instructional staff, administrative staff, support staff and temporary employees. The manager of equity and affirmative action proposed a third team, the "Equity and Affirmative Action Team," composed of three positions, the HR director, Equity and Affirmative Action manager, and HR assistant. A fourth team suggested was the "Performance Management Team," responsible for evaluation, promotion, tenure, renewal, and salary equity functions.
>
> Two HR department teams currently working to improve internal business processes for faculty, ad-hoc instructional staff, administrative staff and support staff were not considered potential "long-term" teams for purposes of coordinating work.
>
> Dennis asked, "Does this alternative offer alignment with the department's vision, mission and goals, environment, technology, and tasks?" The following points summarize their conclusion that this alternative does offer alignment with those elements.
>
> 1. **The updated HR department vision and mission statements and goals** focus on stakeholder value and alignment with the university's strategy. Working within a team structure allows HR staff to discuss creative and innovative methods to deliver value and align current policies and procedures consistent with this focus. In addition, the alignment reduces barriers to HR staff effectively completing their tasks, and allows for the needed flexibility to function in a transformational paradigm.
>
> 2. **The current university environment** demands transactional services that are timely and can be trusted, along with transformational deliverables valued by stakeholders. This environmental change demands that a department also

change. A team structure provides for "back-up" support in addition to a vehicle for the professional development of team members.

3. **The new HRS includes state-of-the-art technology** and comprehensive employee self-service. Consequently, it created the need for a flatter, more flexible and more decentralized department structure—re-defining roles and coordination of work. A team structure better suits the HR paradigm shift.

4. **Continuous improvement of the HR department internal and institution-wide tasks and processes** requires the ability to work together as teams. An HR department earns recognition, respect and loyalty by sharing its knowledge with stakeholders to help them reach their own goals more effectively. This is transformational HR work at its best.

Utilizing the team concept, the HR staff brainstormed the three alternative structure models outlined in Table 12.2.

Table 12.2 Alternatives for coordinating and allocating work among HR team members

Alternative	Teams	Description
1. Coordinate based on "type of customer"; allocate based on "service offered"	• Support Staff • Faculty and Ad Hoc Instructional staff • Administrative Staff/students	• Each team has an "expert" in staffing, payroll-benefits, equity and affirmative action and performance management for that employee type • most similar to the current model • Involves training team members in all parts of a process
2. Coordinate by "service offered"; allocate by "type of customer"	• Staffing • Payroll-Benefits • Equity and Affirmative Action • Performance Management	• Each team member can perform all the functions of the specific services offered for all employee types, e.g., a Staffing Team member can lead a recruitment for a faculty or support staff position; a Payroll-Benefits Team member can place a new student on the payroll, manage the faculty payroll or explain benefits
3. Coordinate based on "area within the university"; allocate based on "HR staff member knowledge or skill"	• Academic Affairs • Student Affairs • Administrative Services/President/Foundation	• Each team member serves as an "expert" in a specific function, but is a "generalist" in all other functions • Each team contains "experts" in all functional areas

After discussing each alternative, Dennis decided to end the staff meeting and resume discussions a week later. During that time, the HR staff members informally talked about and reflected on these options.

During their subsequent meeting, one staff member pointed out that the alternatives comprised substantial training and change. After extensive discussion, an HR staff member suggested they utilize alternative #1 as a pilot for six months, using that time to train all team members on all parts of the team's functional processes. At that time, they would discuss the potential for moving to alternative #2.

Dennis then asked, "Do you agree to structure the work of the HR department according to alternative #1 listed on the flip chart? Fist-to-Five?" All but one of the HR managers raised either four or five fingers. Dennis asked him what needed to change so that he would totally support this alternative. The HR manager voiced his concern about how the work would be allocated among each team—how would his job responsibilities change?

Dennis was prepared for this question. To answer, he asked the members of the Payroll-Benefits Team to explain how they had allocated the payroll and benefits work, and adjusted each of their roles to accommodate back-up responsibilities. When they finished, he added that he did not know at this point how responsibilities would be re-aligned. He preferred to talk with each person to get input, and then to talk together as a team. He explained that his top priority was to provide value to stakeholders, and that they all needed to keep that in mind as they moved forward to restructure.

Dennis again asked the question. This time all hands showed either four or five fingers. He felt a few staff agreed to restructure into teams through peer pressure, and decided to schedule his one-on-one meetings as soon as possible to begin discussions of re-aligning responsibilities.

In addition, Dennis indicated that each team needed to develop an agreement or charter, similar to that of the Payroll-Benefits team, to describe how the team will work together, share information, and make decisions that provide value to stakeholders.

Determine Next Steps

Dennis prepared the draft action plan summarized in Table 12.3 to accomplish the restructuring details. Specific responsibilities and deadline dates were discussed and agreed to during a staff meeting.

Case Study Questions

1. What are potential topics to include in a team agreement or charter?
2. Knowing the staff in your HR department, what issues would erupt during a re-structuring process? What are potential methods for dealing with them?
3. What are potential symbols or rituals to accompany a re-structuring?
4. How can we best communicate re-structuring and re-alignment of responsibilities to stakeholders?

Table 12.3 Draft action plan to accomplish HR department restructuring

Action Item	Who Responsible	Deadline Date	Comments
1. Evaluate and revise HR department and university policies and procedures to focus on delivering stakeholder value	Dennis recommends teams to HR staff		Teams to include representatives across the university
2. Offer flexibility for HR staff to be creative in resolving stakeholder issues, while providing consistency and fairness	Dennis		Also will be an outcome of action item #1
3. Reallocate HR tasks and responsibilities according to alternative #1	Dennis with individual HR staff		
4. Evaluate data and reports to determine relevance to HR work effectiveness and efficiency	HR managers with their team members		
5. Each team develops a "back-up" process that provides stakeholder value	Each team		
6. Improve coordination among HR staff—implement "team" structure	All HR staff		Develop criteria to evaluate new model
7. Create individual development plans to include department goals	Dennis with individual HR staff		
8. Revise HR department annual performance evaluation process to include goal-setting	Dennis with HR staff		
9. Each team develops its "charter or agreement"	Each team		
10. Develop training program for team members	Dennis with each HR manager		
11. Evaluate pilot and recommend next steps	All HR staff	6 months	
12. Redesign and recruit for the open position	Dennis		
13. Revise HR department organization chart	All HR staff		

> *To review discussion of recommendations for Case Study 12.1 go to* **www.HR-higher-ed.com**

Case Study 12.2 ~ available only on website:

> *To review discussion of recommendations for Case Study 12.2, a discussion on revising the HR department organization chart focused on stakeholder value, go to* **www.HR-higher-ed.com**

Summary

The department structure serves as a road map for formal expectations and interactions among the HR staff, and between HR staff and stakeholders. Structure has two components: (1) "allocate" work among employees by specifying positions or roles; (2) indicate how employees need to "coordinate" their work among these roles. Methods for coordinating and allocating work can include:

- employee knowledge or skill
- product or service
- place or geographical area
- time
- customers or clients
- process or flow of work

In many cases, we do not evaluate structure and positions and how they coordinate until someone leaves the department, and sometimes not even then. Especially within higher education, we become accustomed to one basic structural design—maybe because it has been used for decades and we are oblivious to any alternatives. Sometimes people have so much invested in that structure that they are afraid of the potential changes—perhaps they will lose authority, control, expertise or recognition. In addition, if the sense of urgency has not been established solidly, people resist structural change. A model to evaluate the HR department structure comprises the following steps:

1. uunderstand the current structure and environment
2. develop criteria to review HR department structure
3. review HR department structure using the criteria
4. evaluate alternatives and implement best structure
5. determine the next steps, to include an action plan to accomplish restructuring

Criteria to evaluate department structure include: policies and procedures, workload of HR staff, gaps in allocating work, defining responsibilities, coordinating work and HR department strategic focus.

Evaluation of "Your" HR Department's Chapter 12 Outcome

Outcome Desired: A clearly defined and aligned HR department structure

Change: The infrastructure is changed to remove significant and immediate barriers to the change by aligning the HR department structure with the vision (change steps 3, 5)

Key Indicators of Success: (check if *"yes"*)

- [ ] HR staff innovate to provide value to stakeholders
- [ ] Significant changes are seen in the way business is conducted
- [ ] Some tasks are no longer done, and/or insignificant data is no longer kept
- [ ] Coordination and communication are improved among functions
- [ ] People are moved to act according to the department vision and mission
- [ ] Position descriptions align responsibility with authority
- [ ] Department structure aligned with vision, mission, environment, tasks and technology
- [ ] Traditional thinking is challenged in order to provide increased value to stakeholders
- [ ] HR staff demonstrate willingness to take risks
- [ ] HR staff feel the department structure makes the change initiative achievable
- [ ] HR staff actively help each other find ways to make the change initiative a success

Potential Barriers to Change: (check if *"needs attention"*)

- [ ] Functional silos continue to exist, reducing coordination and communication
- [ ] HR staff continue to focus on personal goals, not on department goals
- [ ] People become frustrated in their attempts to accomplish the vision
- [ ] There is a high level of skepticism about the change effort
- [ ] HR staff show a reluctance or a lack of motivation to participate in the change effort
- [ ] Change efforts are given low priority
- [ ] HR staff do not feel they are being rewarded or recognized
- [ ] Position descriptions are so detailed that they do not provide flexibility in performing tasks and responsibilities
- [ ] HR staff feel they are not receiving the necessary training to improve the skills needed to accomplish successful change

Unit Three Summary

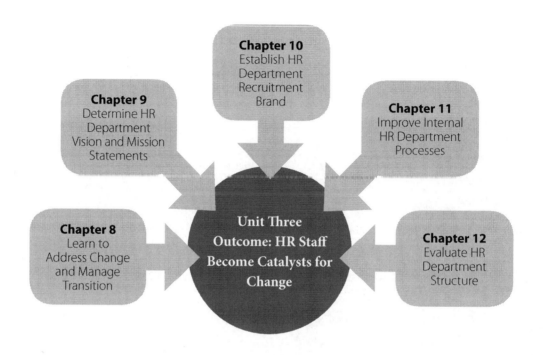

Unit Three model for developing the HR staff to become catalysts for change

Unit Three included a great deal of subject and experiential learning by the HR staff moving toward the changed HR paradigm of transformational work. So far, we have dealt with the ideas of transition versus change and determined where each HR staff member is along the transition continuum. Some may continue to struggle with letting go of the past, others are in the neutral zone and do not totally understand the change and the need for it, still others are already at the new beginning—experiencing the results of being empowered to innovate to improve value to stakeholders.

The HR staff learned the basics of improving processes and formed teams to redesign internal HR processes to become more effective and efficient. Some teams may lead this effort better than others, again because of where their members are in the transition process. Some HR staff are motivated in this process, others are resistant, and one or two people may have left the department. There were some "quick wins" on some teams, which motivated members to continue to move forward.

We led the process of evaluating the structure of the HR department to ensure it is aligned with the department vision and mission, current environment, technology and tasks. In some cases, we re-structured, which continues to motivate some staff and cause further resistance by others. The information in chapter 6 on conflict management continues to serve as a resource on how to use that conflict and resistance to promote positive resolutions.

An important question is, "Where are we in the process of moving the HR function to the strategic level of the university?" As shown in the figure below, Phase 1 prepares the HR professionals for transformational change. This includes transitioning the HR staff to the new HR paradigm, discussing conflict and methods of resolution, assessing and developing plans to increase the skill level of employees, developing the HR staff into a cohesive team, motivated to work in different ways, and developing a new HR vision, mission and values aligned with those of the organization.

Model for HR transformation within higher education

Phase 2 develops the HR staff to become catalysts for change through developing more efficient and effective internal and external HR processes. This phase includes the HR staff learning and utilizing various business process improvement processes while working as equal members of a team. In addition, evaluating the HR department structure determines whether it accomplishes its vision and mission, and provides value to stakeholders.

As the transformation progresses, stakeholders may notice that common transactional functions are completed faster, with more focus on valued outcomes. The HR staff may reach out to them with improved methods. Examples include a new hiring and training process for limited term employees, and assistance in the evaluation of skills of candidates for permanent positions.

Because of regular updates by the HR director on the progress of the HR transformation, and "in the trenches" stories from their constituents emphasizing the change in HR, members of the administration have increased trust in the process. They see their expectations of the transformation fulfilled in the short-term.

We have accomplished the work of these first two phases of the HR paradigm shift, and are ready to move forward to Phase 3, described in detail in Unit Four.

Unit Three Outcome Desired: HR Staff Become Catalysts for Change

Chapter 8 Outcome: *Learn to address change and manage transition:*

Key Indicators of Success: Check (x) if "yes"

☐ HR staff understand the details regarding transition versus change

☐ Communication within the HR team is strengthened

☐ HR staff openly discuss their anxieties and other feelings regarding the change

☐ A transition management plan is developed with participation by the HR staff

☐ HR staff understand the change and when it will begin

☐ HR staff, either within the team or one-on-one, discuss their endings

☐ HR staff identify things they will gain with the change

☐ A consistent message is provided to the HR staff regarding the change

☐ HR director provides the type of support needed by the HR staff

☐ HR director builds trust with the HR staff

Chapter 9 Outcome: *HR department vision, mission and core values are aligned with those of the institution*

Key Indicators of Success: Check (x) if "yes"

☐ The vision is clear, challenging, compelling, focused and achievable

☐ The vision describes an outcome that appeals emotionally to the HR staff

☐ All HR staff are involved in at least part of the process

☐ All HR staff "buy into" the vision, mission and core values

☐ All HR staff begin/continue to exhibit the behaviors that need to be added, removed or improved in order to accomplish the vision and mission

☐ Cabinet members support the HR department's vision, mission and core values, and acknowledge they are aligned with those of the institution

☐ HR staff can express the vision and mission in their own words

☐ HR staff discuss the vision and mission in meetings, within decision-making situations, and in communicating with those external to the HR department

Chapter 10 Outcome: Develop an effective HR department recruitment brand

Key Indicators of Success: Check (x) if "yes"

☐ One or more HR staff take on leadership roles

☐ More HR staff are willing to take initiative and risks

☐ More HR staff are innovative in their thinking and work

☐ HR staff assume the responsibility to contribute time and effort to develop the brand

☐ Issues and problems are identified and acted upon rapidly

☐ Feedback and suggestions are offered spontaneously

☐ There are more informal conversations regarding a recruitment brand

☐ HR staff actively work together to accomplish the project

Chapter 11 Outcome: More effective and efficient internal HR processes

Key Indicators of Success: Check (x) if "yes"

☐ HR staff give up their own "agenda" to develop a better one

☐ HR staff choose to be more excited about the team's success than about personal success

☐ A spirit of teamwork exists within the department environment, where individuals seek to build up those around them and be open and honest in the process

☐ Increased trust exists between team members

- [ ] Team members have open and honest discussions regarding problems, issues, and progress toward their goal(s)
- [ ] Team members understand and believe in the importance and urgency of the change effort
- [ ] Team members stay on track regarding their approach and direction
- [ ] New ideas are proposed and tested
- [ ] Issues and problems are identified and acted upon quickly
- [ ] Feedback and suggestions for improvement are identified and acted upon quickly
- [ ] The level of activity relating to change increases as people become more engaged in the process
- [ ] Some resisters become supporters; some supporters become actively engaged
- [ ] Important achievements are recognized and celebrated
- [ ] Redesigned processes include metrics for evaluation
- [ ] More HR staff are moving through the "neutral zone" toward the "new beginning"
- [ ] Increased support for the change from people in positions of power and influence

Chapter 12 Outcome: A clearly defined and aligned HR department structure

Key Indicators of Success: Check (x) if "yes"

- [ ] HR staff innovate to provide value to stakeholders
- [ ] Significant changes are seen in the way business is conducted
- [ ] Some tasks are no longer done, and/or insignificant data is no longer kept
- [ ] Coordination and communication are improved among functions
- [ ] People are moved to act according to the department vision and mission
- [ ] Position descriptions align responsibility with authority
- [ ] Department structure aligned with vision, mission, environment, tasks and technology
- [ ] Traditional thinking is challenged in order to provide increased value to stakeholders
- [ ] HR staff demonstrate willingness to take risks
- [ ] HR staff feel the department structure makes the change initiative achievable
- [ ] HR staff actively help each other find ways to make the change initiative a success

Unit Four

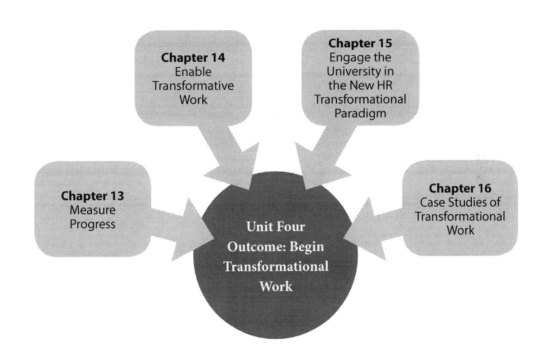

Unit Four model for beginning the transformational work of HR

Our interviews with key campus constituents in chapter 7 provided testimonies for how the HR department can deliver increased value to stakeholders, and included examples from both transactional and transformational work. The following example describes the values of key stakeholders compiled during one-on-one interviews at one university.

Example of stakeholder value for the HR function

Transactional Work	Transformational Work
• HR has knowledge of faculty markets	• HR engages in strategic conversations with key administrators
• HR provides personal, credible service	• HR leads the development of a university recruitment brand
• HR processes/policies are effective in helping accomplish stakeholder goals	• HR leads the development of a university leadership brand
• A single point of contact	• HR facilitates a campus discussion of the faculty/staff reward structure
• Timely communication	• HR serves as a facilitator for organizational and cultural transitions
	• HR serves as a conduit or facilitator to bring together administrative units to focus on an issue
	• HR leads changes in drafting more effective position descriptions

Learning what is valued by constituents allows the HR function to:

1. configure the roles of the HR staff according to stakeholder value
2. develop the appropriate skills of the HR staff
3. understand the external and internal environment within which the HR function works
4. develop practices and policies that deliver value
5. engage stakeholders in the HR paradigm shift

This has comprised our work so far in moving to a transformational HR paradigm. We must keep in mind that what is "valued" by our constituents will consist of both transactional and transformational points.

The outcome of Unit Four is the beginning of transformational work external to the HR department. This work encompasses the following components: (1) creation of more efficient and effective "external" HR processes; (2) continued development of the HR staff's transformational skills; (3) changed campus perspective of HR staff; (4) improved relationships and partnerships among HR staff and campus constituents; and (5) increased stakeholder value.

Although the HR staff may be ready to begin developing the HR strategic plan process, this unit contains key activities and should not be skipped for the following reasons:

1. We need to "step back" and measure our progress to determine if we are where we need to be in the transformation process.

2. As the leader of the HR function, YOU cannot do all the transformative work demanded by the HR paradigm shift. The HR staff must be involved in transformative work and be seen by campus stakeholders in this role. (The work of the HR staff to this point has been mainly internal to the department; their perception by external stakeholders needs to include transformative activities.) Therefore, the transformational skills of the HR staff need to be developed, with activities and experiences external to the HR department.

3. The HR staff must be involved in transformational activities that are external to the HR department in order for the HR paradigm shift to be woven into the culture of the department.

Measure Progress

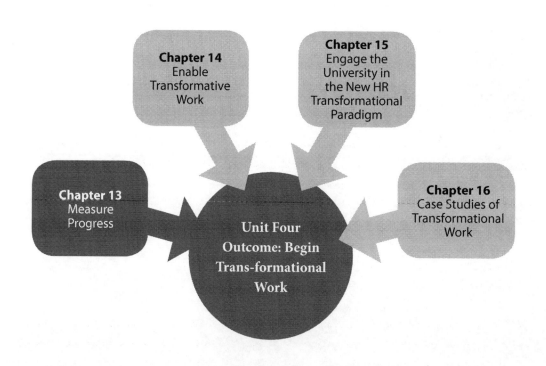

Chapter 13 Measure progress

Figure 13.1 Model for regrouping, refining and consolidating gains

Lead Change

Our roles in leading the change effort are vitally important at this juncture. We have accomplished some quick wins, and the majority of the HR staff are motivated to continue moving forward. We are impatient to continue. If we look at this metaphorically—we as the leader are the driver of a Greyhound bus—we need to make sure all the passengers are on board, we all are going to the same destination, we have the correct road map to get there, the bus is in good mechanical order, and our boss continues to support us driving this bus. Figure 13.2 outlines the seven major roles of the leader at this point in the change process.

Step 7 in the *Heart of Change Field Guide* by Dan Cohen (2005) does an excellent job of explaining the roles of the leader. Essentially, we must reflect on our progress to discover potential areas to strengthen before moving forward.

Step Back to Reflect

We need to reflect on what has happened since our change initiative began, and determine steps in the change or transition processes that need strengthening. Following are questions to begin the discussion:

1. What have we learned from our short-term wins?
2. What could we have done better?
3. Are we continuing to move forward toward a transformational HR paradigm? What indicates this?

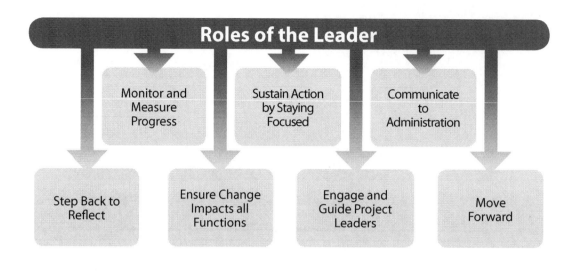

Figure 13.2 Roles of the leader

We need to pull the HR staff together to reflect on what has happened since our change initiative began, and determine steps in the change or transition processes that need strengthening.

4. Has our progress on the change initiative helped us to move forward through the neutral zone of the transition process? How?

5. Are there any "systems" within the HR department that are not aligned with the new HR paradigm?

6. How can we take what we have learned to positively impact our future direction?

As a result of this discussion, there may be issues we need to deal with prior to moving forward. There may be HR staff who continue to resist the change initiative. There may be systems within the HR department that need to be redesigned, such as those for recognizing and rewarding performance. Take the necessary time to work through and resolve any issues. Document what all HR staff have learned that can be used to move forward, and display these in a prominent place, e.g., staff meeting agenda template, note pads, etc.

Monitor and Measure Progress

Any new initiative or process needs to have one or more simple metrics that can be used to measure the progress of the initiative, and if the initiative accomplishes the goal or purpose. We recommend using the least possible number of metrics, and each needs to be easily understood and measured.

In the case study in chapter 11, Dennis and the Faculty Team developed four metrics to evaluate the redesigned faculty hiring process: time, waiting/delay, hand-offs, materials. Through a spread sheet of all faculty hired, these metrics are simple to measure and to understand. They can serve as a powerful tool when communicating improved processes to administrators, stakeholders, and the HR staff themselves.

Similar metrics can be defined for the change initiative of moving to a transformational HR paradigm. We need to ask ourselves, "What will it look like to work within a transformational HR paradigm?" In addition, chapter 5 reminds us how the HR function works differently in a transformational than a transactional culture. Brainstorming with the HR staff can offer a few of the following metrics, plus indicate where staff members are in the transition process:

> Any new initiative or process needs to have one or more simple metrics that can be used to measure the progress of the initiative, and if the initiative accomplishes the goal or purpose.

- being proactive, not reactive, in accomplishing work
- focusing on delivering HR practices valued by stakeholders
- creating relationships among those within and external to the department
- collaborating with others within and external to the department
- developing HR functions based on value to stakeholders
- contributing toward accomplishing the vision, mission and goals of the HR department
- strengthening skills, e.g., core competencies of change or transition management, coordinating and partnering, creating stakeholder value, innovating, etc.
- increasing numbers of HR staff reaching the "new beginning" stage of the change initiative

Ensure Change Impacts all Functions

It is human nature to work more closely or concentrate on areas within a department that are more successful than others. It is more motivating to work with individuals who are excited about the change and engaged thoroughly in the effort than with those who are not. Now is the time to evaluate whether there is equal change within all functions of the department. The role of the leader includes:

- continue to remove barriers to the change initiative moving forward
- manage resistance and priorities
- provide guidance to the project teams to enable decisions to be made that are aligned with the vision of the change

Sustain Action by Staying Focused

As the leader, we must continue to walk the talk and serve as a role model. In addition, remember the importance of symbols and rituals to convey the new ways of doing things in the transformational culture. Soliciting ideas during a staff meeting can provide many interesting discussions, helping everyone to focus strategically.

Although there continues to be many initiatives that fall to the HR function, the change initiative needs to remain a top priority. Maintain the sense of urgency, help the HR staff to remain in touch with the purpose of the change and show commitment for the change through day-to-day actions, e.g., expressing impatience when things are not completed in a timely manner, working on a Saturday to complete a key strategic task because it is important to be ready for staff review and editing, etc. We must choose staff members to lead the project teams, offer support or resources if needed, and identify any leaders who need to be removed from managing a project.

Engage and Guide Project Leaders

After accomplishing a few short-term wins, we have a much better idea who within the HR function are moving the change initiative forward, and who are holding it back. We need to consider carefully who we will ask to lead the project teams. The leader of the change initiative does not have the time or energy to serve in this role with all the teams. The best case scenario is that all the staff can serve in this role, but realistically we know that not everyone develops skills within the same time frame.

Communicate to Administration

Supervisors and other administrators may want quick results, and do not understand the amount of time and energy needed to achieve a paradigm shift. This is where the communication plan developed in chapter 7 becomes extremely important to implement. Update your supervisor on a consistent basis, and ask to present to the cabinet when major progress is made.

Move Forward

With a re-vitalized sense of purpose, lead the HR staff to the next step of the change initiative: begin to weave the new behaviors into the culture of the department. We address this phase in Unit Four.

Evaluate Skill Improvement

Chapter 5 provides a framework for evaluating the skills of HR staff. If you completed this process with the result that all HR staff have an action plan for improving their skills, now is the time to meet one-on-one to evaluate their progress and determine a revised action plan.

If you have not done this employee self-assessment and evaluation process, DO IT NOW before proceeding further with the change initiative. The items in an individual's action plan can serve as metrics to signify progress in his/her professional development. In addition, through this process we can discover conflict or resistance issues and deal with them accordingly. We use what we learn in measuring current projects to create improved evaluation methods for future projects.

Measure New Processes

As mentioned earlier in this chapter, one of the roles of the leader is to monitor and measure progress of the change initiative. We need to work with each of the project teams, first to develop metrics, and then to evaluate each project's progress using the metrics. We use the results to either redesign the project to be better aligned with its goal, or to determine that the project is accomplishing its goal.

Move Forward

At this point, many in the HR function have made progress in shifting behavior and improving skills to fit the transformational HR paradigm. These new behaviors need to be woven into the fabric of the HR culture if they are to be sustained over the long-term. Case Study 13.1 focuses on: personnel issues, leadership of change, measuring progress of paradigm change, and alignment of HR department systems.

Case Study 13.1

It was a busy six months in the HR department, and Dennis looked forward to bringing the HR staff together to evaluate the work done. He assigned the temporary employee and several student employees to serve customers in the HR department, and scheduled a morning retreat off-campus for the other staff, followed by lunch together. The retreat agenda, shown in Exhibit 13.1, was distributed to HR staff members in advance.

Dennis felt it was very important to celebrate both their collective accomplishments over the last six months and to regroup and reflect on what they have learned. Attending a morning retreat off-campus followed by lunch was considered by HR staff as recognition for work well done, and an aura of excitement and laughter filled the air.

Dennis thought long and hard about how he could recognize each individual HR staff member for his/her work done over the past six months. At times, it was not easy when conflict or resistance to change cropped up, but each person contributed at

Exhibit 13.1 HR department retreat agenda

7:30am   *Continental Breakfast*
8:00am   *Goal of retreat:*
         Celebrate!
         Refine our Path
8:10am   *Celebrate!*
         Summary of timeline
         Summary of team accomplishments
         Summary of additional department accomplishments
9:00am   *Regroup and Reflect*
         What we have learned so far
         What we could have done better
9:30am   *BREAK*
9:45am   *Progress toward a transformational HR culture*
10:15am *Identify and discuss barriers that stand in the way of continuing*
         success, e.g., systems within the HR department not aligned with
         a transformational HR culture
11:00am *How we can take what we have learned to positively impact*
         our future direction

least one accomplishment. He decided to begin the "Celebrate!" part of the retreat by personally thanking each person for one unique contribution.

He began with Heather, the first person to enthusiastically agree to take on benefits responsibilities with Donna's retirement. As he thanked her in front of all the HR staff, Heather beamed and nodded in gratitude. In turn, Dennis thanked each person. People really got into the moment by clapping for the person Dennis thanked, or saying, "We second that!" or "Amen to that!" To his surprise, when Dennis finished, one of them shouted, "And we thank you for providing us with a temporary employee to help us with our work during this transition period!" It was a great method for beginning the retreat.

Dennis then displayed a flip chart with the timeline of activities since they began their discussions on change and transition. He wanted to remind people of the context in which they had worked over the last six months. He was amazed when he prepared for this retreat—that they had participated in training on: working as teams, change versus transition, and business process improvement. They had discussed where each person was in the transition process, improved multiple internal HR processes successfully, developed a communication plan and restructured the HR department into teams.

In turn, Dennis asked each team leader to summarize his/her team's accomplish-

ments, which he wrote on a second flip chart. Following that, he facilitated a discussion and listed additional accomplishments in the department.

Because everyone concentrated on the flip charts during the discussion, they did not realize that Linda, the vice president of administration and Dennis' supervisor, had entered the room. She walked to the front of the room, and, in an emotional tone, told them how proud she was of the work they had done, and that this really was a celebration.

She conveyed that the entire president's cabinet supported the work they were doing, and reminded them they were breaking new ground in moving the HR department to the strategic level of the university. She said this was an opportune time to convey discussions she and Dennis had regarding a pool of money to be used to recognize and reward their performance in moving forward to accomplish the HR paradigm change. She let Dennis describe the details, but wanted them to know she and the others on the cabinet recognized and supported the work being done.

After she left, Dennis deviated from the retreat agenda to describe the draft recognition plan referred to by Linda. Some individuals had taken on additional responsibilities and now could be evaluated for a potential re-titling or promotion. In addition, he had developed a draft plan for one-time bonus checks, based on performance and improvement of skills. Within the next month, he intended to meet one-on-one with each person to review his/her individual action plan, evaluate it for progress, and revise it for the next six months. The key ingredient to his request to Linda for bonuses included the progress on the action plans. With that, it was time for the break.

After the break, several people had questions about the bonuses. It was apparent people were surprised by the announcement, and the room buzzed with conversation during the break. Several questioned if the dollar amount of the bonus would be the same for everyone who received one, and Dennis shook his head, "No." Whether a person received a bonus, and the amount, were determined by each individual's performance according to his/her action plan.

One person asked why Dennis had not told them about this when they developed the action plans. He responded that he had approached Linda about it just last week. Although bonuses had never been given in the HR department, he felt there were no methods to reward and recognize performance. He indicated that at next week's staff meeting, he would share the evaluation tool he had drafted to get their feedback prior to the individual meetings.

They then moved back to the agenda item, "Regroup and Reflect." It was apparent to Dennis the discussion was being taken seriously. He asked each question listed in Exhibit 13.2, then wrote their comments across several flip charts. A summary of their answers to several questions is shown in Exhibit 13.3.

Dennis concluded the retreat by asking each person to vocalize what he/she

Exhibit 13.2 Regroup and reflect questions

Regroup and Reflect Questions
1. *What have we learned so far?*
2. *What could we have done better?*
3. *Are we making progress toward a transformational HR paradigm?*
   What indicates this?
4. *Are there any barriers that stand in the way of continuing success with the*
   change initiative?
5. *How can we take what we have learned to positively impact our future direction?*

most looked forward to in working toward the transformational HR paradigm. Lunch was then served. All in all, he felt the retreat went well. He was happy that Linda was able to recognize and thank the HR staff for their hard work and accomplishments. It was important they knew administrators supported them and provided needed resources. Dennis saw that the announcement of bonuses got their attention; he expected some were concerned whether or not they would receive one.

Realizing his role as a change leader was important, Dennis subsequently met with each of the HR teams to charge them with monitoring and measuring the progress of their initiatives. He wanted to integrate their information in order to develop a communication to administrators and other key stakeholders. Soon the HR staff needed to begin working on projects that impacted those external to the department, and he needed to communicate progress thus far on the change initiative.

In addition, Dennis knew he needed to work on two major topics: (1) evaluate HR staff members on their progress toward goals in their action plans; (2) ensure that change impacts all functions within the IIR department equally. Both topics influence the HR paradigm change in similar, and equally important, ways.

Dennis reflected that an HR staff member not progressing in attaining his/her action plan goals probably is not deeply engaged in any change initiative. If that person is leading one of the project teams, the team may be risk-adverse, not very innovative and slow to make decisions. His concern encompassed two people, the manager for equity and affirmative action, and the HR assistant for staffing.

… an HR staff member not progressing in attaining his/her action plan goals probably is not deeply engaged in any change initiative.

Exhibit 13.3 Answers to three regroup and reflect case study questions

Question 1 What have we learned so far?
—we know more than we thought we did
—it is motivating to find steps in processes that can be
  eliminated or made more efficient
—as a team member, we each contribute strengths that
  make the team stronger
—I did not realize there were so many hand-offs in the
  ~~~tly~~ hiring process
  ~~~~~~ improve processes is important for
  ~~~~~~~~ tient and not skip

Question 2 What could we have done better?
—increase risk-taking
—manage meetings more effectively by staying with the agenda
—as team members, work through conflict or resistance
  better; we are still in the forming stage where some members
  do not feel confident speaking up

Question 3 Are we making progress toward a transformational
  HR paradigm?
Yes!! As an HR team, collectively we are moving to a
  transformational HR culture, shown by:
—redesigning processes with stakeholder value in mind
—restructuring the department with the change vision in mind
—we are becoming more proactive
—we are beginning to focus on what is "delivered"
—we are developing relationships and collaborati~~
—we a~~~~~~~ toward the ~~~

Howard had been the Director of Equity and Affirmative Action, reporting to the president of the university, for many years. About two years ago, he became embroiled in a major academic department conflict situation that caused political fallout for the president, who subsequently took a job in another state. The new president moved Howard's reportage to the HR director. Howard was unhappy about this change, and felt it was a demotion.

Dennis knew Howard to be fair-minded and ethical, well liked by many campus constituents for his efforts toward diversity. At the same time, Howard remained bitter about what he called his "demotion," and Dennis had not had time to get to know him since he became the HR director. Howard had improved several of his skills in the past six months, especially those relating to innovation, creative thinking, coordinating and partnering. He wasn't yet where he needed to be, but there definitely was progress in his skill development. Dennis felt, with the right situations and experiences, Howard could become a good leader.

Thinking back to the book, Reframing Organizations (Bolman and Deal, 2003), and the idea that one can look at a situation in different "frames" or ways to resolve it more effectively, Dennis decided to deal with the situation in the HR frame. The HR frame focuses on the needs and skills of individuals, emphasizes an understanding of people, with their strengths, weaknesses, emotions, desires and fears. This frame views people as an investment: we want to hire the right people, keep them, invest in them, empower them and promote diversity.

He thought about how to create a performance management system that would result in Howard becoming more engaged in the HR paradigm change. He decided to talk with Howard in their one-on-one evaluation meeting about his interest in co-leading the Staffing Team. The work of this team would be crucial to the success of the HR paradigm change. The team needed to be comprised of HR staff plus key campus constituents external to HR who utilize its policies and procedures. Its work included understanding current policies and revising them to provide increased value to stake-holders, while continuing to adhere to state and federal employment laws. He liked the idea of Howard and him co-leading this team.

Melissa, the HR assistant for support staff, had been working in the HR department for about ten years. Early in his position, Dennis felt Melissa was doing a great job. She knew how to talk about strategy, customer service, and empowerment, and wanted to take on more responsibilities. Soon he realized she was not "walking the talk." She continually made mistakes that she blamed on others, made promises to supervisors in the recruiting process that she could not keep, and at times lost her temper with other HR staff.

The HR manager she reported to had tried everything he knew to encourage her to develop her skills, take responsibility for mistakes and manage her emotions better. Dennis and the HR manager had several discussions with her, and Melissa felt she was improving. However, several recent mistakes were brought to Linda, Dennis' boss, and the situation became political. In this situation, methods from the HR frame had been used for several years, but had not improved Melissa's performance. In a recent conversation, Dennis was honest with her, telling her she needed to find another job because her performance had not improved and she was no longer a good fit for the department.

Melissa was devastated, and said she would improve. But that did not happen. Dennis determined that he would try one more tactic to encourage her to exit from the HR department gracefully before he terminated her. He planned to remove her from all teams, take away the new responsibilities she had asked for, and leave her with only low level tasks involving support staff recruitments. In fact, the more he thought about the situation, the more he felt it may be better to give all her current responsibilities to the temporary employee, who was quick to learn and possessed the necessary skills to accomplish the work effectively. That would leave the most mundane tasks in the department for Melissa to do.

This would be difficult, but Dennis was determined to remove all barriers to the success of the HR paradigm change.

Case Study Questions

1. What are the implications for Dennis' decision to deal with Melissa? What alternatives could he have considered?

2. What are the implications for Dennis' decision to deal with the situation with Howard? What alternatives could he have considered?

3. Has Dennis addressed all the roles of a leader of change at this point in the change initiative? If not, what has he missed?

4. What advice can you give Dennis about how to decide on his bonus recommendations for the HR staff?

5. How can Dennis and the others on the HR team take what they have learned so far to positively impact their future direction?

6. What are examples of "systems" within the HR department that may not be aligned with a new HR paradigm, and therefore hamper progress of change?

7. Was there a change situation in your professional career where this step on regrouping, refining and consolidating gains was not done? What was the outcome?

8. Although it was beneficial in the retreat for Dennis to summarize the timeline, team and department accomplishments, it would have been helpful at the end of the retreat to brainstorm a list of projects that currently are underway or that need to be in the pipeline. What tool(s) are valuable for this purpose?

To review discussion of recommendations for Case Study 13.1 go to **www.HR-higher-ed.com**

Summary

Following are the key roles of the leader at this point in the change process:

1. step back to reflect
2. monitor and measure progress
3. ensure change impacts all HR functions
4. sustain action by staying focused
5. engage and guide project leaders
6. communicate to administration
7. move forward

Chapter 5 provided a framework for evaluating the skills of HR staff members. If you completed this process with the result that all HR staff have an action plan for improving their skills, now is the time to meet one-on-one to evaluate their progress and determine a revised action plan.

Major Themes

Our role in **leading the change effort** is vitally important at this juncture. We have accomplished some quick wins, and the HR staff are motivated to continue moving forward. If we look at this metaphorically—we as the leader are the driver of a Greyhound bus—we need to make sure all the passengers are on board, we all are going to the same destination, we have the correct road map to get there, the bus is in good mechanical order, and our boss continues to support us driving this bus.

Evaluation of "Your" HR Department's Chapter 13 Outcome

Outcome Desired: Regroup, refine and consolidate gains

Change: Do not let up, broaden the effort to accomplish the change initiative (change step 7)

Key Indicators of Success: (check if "yes")

- ☐ Project leaders monitor and measure the progress of their project
- ☐ Project teams revise processes if needed
- ☐ New projects are initiated
- ☐ Leaders emerge from the HR staff
- ☐ Stakeholders recognize new processes that provide value to them
- ☐ HR staff are revitalized to continue with the change initiative
- ☐ Administrators are talking about the success and progress of the change
- ☐ Symbols and/or rituals are in place to remind the HR staff of the change
- ☐ HR staff are motivated to move forward with the change initiative

Potential Barriers to Change: (check if "needs attention")

- ☐ Other projects become priority in the long-term
- ☐ Department resources are committed to other projects in the long-term
- ☐ Administrators feel the change is taking too long
- ☐ Key HR staff members are resistant to change
- ☐ HR staff feel the change initiative is moving too fast
- ☐ HR staff feel overworked and not valued for their efforts on the change initiative

Chapter 14

Enable
Transformative Work

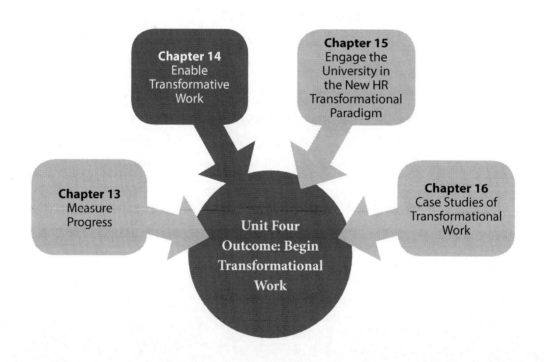

In today's age of technology with HR systems that offer self-service within the functions of staffing, benefits, and payroll, HR can add value by providing continuing, equitable and credible administrative support. Employees look for personal service that is responsive and builds trust in the HR function. When they have transactional questions, employees value a single point of contact that gives timely and accurate answers.

At the same time, the HR paradigm shift expects professionals to work in transformative ways. How does the HR function structure itself to provide value within both transactional and transformative needs? Table 14.1 summarizes the differences between HR transactional and transformative work.

Table 14.1 Transactional versus transformative work

FROM: HR Transactional work	TO: HR Transformative/Strategic Work
Creates efficiency through standardization, automation and consolidation	Aligns vision, mission and goals of HR with strategy of the organization
Mostly reactive	Proactive
Focus is on what we do	Focus is on what we "deliver"
Work with employees	Create relationships/collaborate
Implement best HR practices	Deliver value-added HR practices
Build HR functions for efficiency	Build HR functions for stakeholder value

Transformative work in an HR department consists of aligning goals of the HR department with the strategic goals of the organization. As indicated in Table 14.1, the work is primarily proactive—based on creating relationships and collaboration, and focused on the work or value "delivered" to stakeholders.

In our case study discussion of structure in chapter 12, we determined that a team structure was best aligned with the current environment, tasks, technology and mission/vision. Our case study described a move from one person handling all benefits work to a team responsible for backing up each other. Within the team environment, how do we align the seemingly inconsistent values of "a single point of contact," "timely answers" and "transformative work"?

Figure 14.1 delineates the agenda for chapter 14, which provides a model for integrating these stakeholder values. We describe three teams, the HR Collaboration Team, the HR Partner teams and the Process/Program teams. With each team, we outline the following:

1. the issue
2. team description

> Within the team environment, how do we align the seemingly inconsistent values of "a single point of contact," "timely answers" and "transformative work"?

3 team purpose

4. process for working together

5. examples of transformative work by the team

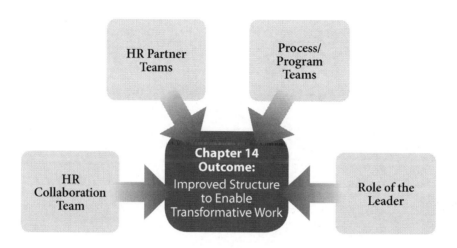

Figure 14.1 Model to enable transformative work

HR Collaboration Team

The Issue

The HR department is normally not the only function within the university that deals with HR issues or has knowledge of potential issues. Others are the provost and vice president's office, the equity and affirmative action function, the safety function and legal counsel. Each department normally reacts to issues brought to it.

As we all know, HR work can become complicated, with a major issue impacting several functions in complex and multiple ways. Issues can involve recruitments, discrimination and harassment situations, grievances and complaints, situations with employment practices (tenure, renewal, promotions, salary equity, etc.) or conflict situations within departments. An employee may contact multiple departments to obtain the result wanted. An issue not resolved effectively and timely can spread exponentially to other departments or higher levels within the university.

Team Description

Team membership depends on the university and its structure and culture. Normally, the HR director, equity and affirmative action director/manager, and associate provost positions comprise the membership. Others can be included when appropriate. Each person brings to the team his or her unique knowledge, experiences and relationships that provide the team with a greater potential to resolve issues effectively. Working together as a team to resolve these issues provides improved and more timely problem-solving than working singly on the issues brought to each function.

Team Purpose

The goals of the team are not to make decisions, but include the following:

1. share information that may provide the responsible person with a broader view of the situation
2. bring a situation to the position responsible for resolving it
3. assist with evaluating potential resolutions to a situation
4. resolve common issues effectively and timely
5. build the foundation of relationships for developing and implementing the HR strategic plan
6. reduce gaps or overlap in service to stakeholders
7. improve coordination to provide increased value to stakeholders

Process for Working Together

Obviously, many issues enforce confidentiality. Because each position works within this context, sharing appropriate information includes confidentiality. The team can determine to meet weekly, biweekly or monthly, depending on whether there is information or issues to discuss.

Examples of Transformative Work

Example 1: Academic Department Conflict

Several team members learned, from different sources, of a conflict occurring in an academic department. The conflict had several dimensions, impacted large numbers of faculty and staff including individuals external to the university, and existed for six months. The team previously developed and trained a campus mediation team to deal with conflict issues that could not be resolved informally. One of the Collaboration Team members talked with the department chair to learn more about the conflict, and brought that information back to the other team members. The result was that the mediation team was charged to mediate the conflict, with positive results. Because the issue was dealt with quickly and effectively, it did not spread or cause deeper conflict.

Example 2: Salary Equity

A female faculty member met with representatives of several offices, alleging she was treated inequitably—and unlawfully—in a recent request for a salary equity adjustment. In comparing her salary and experiences with two other male faculty members, she felt her salary was inequitable.Not getting the answer she wanted, she met with the HR director, threatening to go to an attorney and sue the university for discriminating against her.

Because the HR director learned of this issue in a prior meeting with the HR Collaboration Team, she suggested a comprehensive audit of the faculty member's salary history, using data from the university's office of institutional research. The team agreed, and the associate provost obtained this information because the position reported to her. Using this data, the HR director convinced the faculty member some of her data were inaccurate, and she was satisfied—although not happy—with the result. A law suit, taking a great deal of time and effort, was avoided.

Example 3: Cancelled Recruitment

An HR Collaboration Team member learned of issues on a committee charged with recruiting for an administrative position. After talking with a majority of committee members one-on-one, the HR Collaboration Team felt discriminatory comments were made by several committee members during phone interviews of two candidates. The provost and vice president decided to cancel the current recruitment to avoid potential legal action from the candidates, and begin it again later. The HR Collaboration Team was asked to evaluate the process used to charge the committee and educate the members on discriminatory behaviors in an effort to avoid future situations of this type.

Example 4: Complaint Against Faculty Member

Several serious complaints against a faculty member came to the provost and vice president's office via the college dean. Although the associate provost was charged with investigating the complaints, the HR Collaboration Team was utilized to determine potential alternative actions. After a meeting with the HR director, the faculty member decided that retirement was her best option.

Example 5: Chapter 16 includes a comprehensive example of transformative work by an HR Collaboration Team.

HR Partner Teams

The Issue

In moving to a transformational HR paradigm, the issue can be described as how to align seemingly inconsistent stakeholder values within the HR function of "a single point of contact," "timely answers" and "transformative work."

HR Partner Description

Within the HR staff, each person serving as an "HR Partner" ultimately will be responsible for both transactional and transformational work, as described in Exhibit 14.1.

Exhibit 14.1 Description of one HR staff member's roles

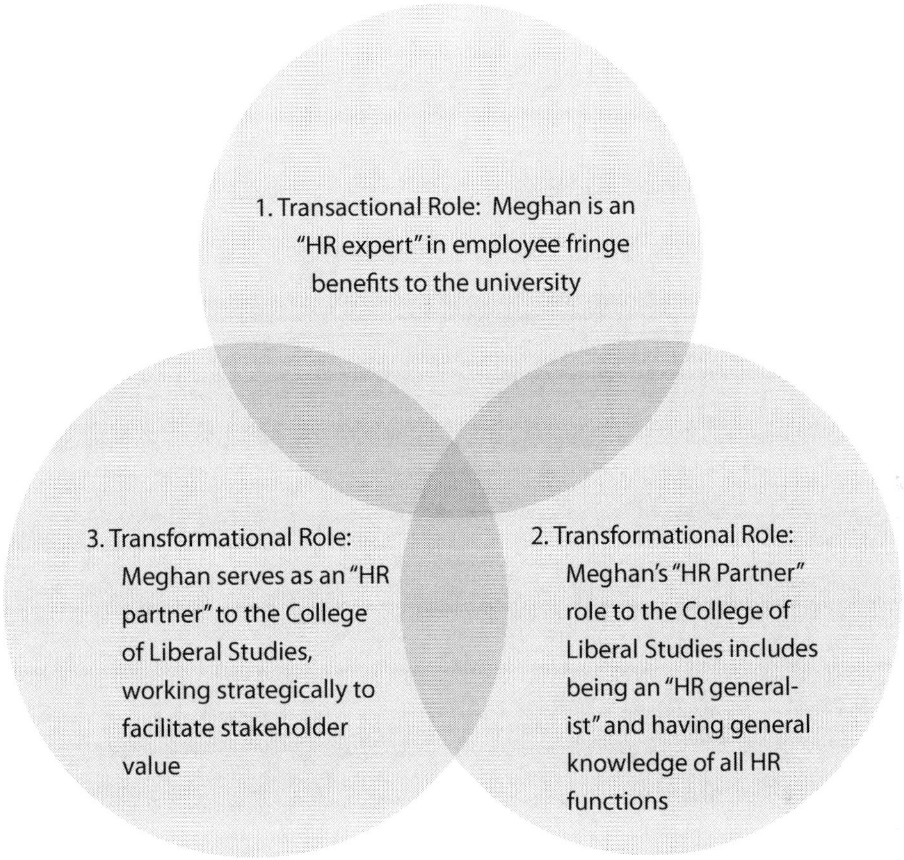

1. Transactional Role: Meghan is an "HR expert" in employee fringe benefits to the university

3. Transformational Role: Meghan serves as an "HR partner" to the College of Liberal Studies, working strategically to facilitate stakeholder value

2. Transformational Role: Meghan's "HR Partner" role to the College of Liberal Studies includes being an "HR generalist" and having general knowledge of all HR functions

Transactional work: Each HR staff serves as an expert for the university in a specific function, e.g., payroll, benefits, staffing, training, legal issues, etc.

1. In this transactional role, Meghan is an expert in fringe benefits to the university's faculty and administrative staff.

Transformational work: At the same time, each HR staff "partners" with a specific business unit within the university to serve as an HR "generalist" responsible for transformational work:

2. In this transformational role, each works directly with key administrators in his/her partner business unit to clarify strategy, perform organizational audits, deliver supportive HR strategy, and lead the HR function. Meghan is "partnered" with the College of Liberal Studies.

3. In this transformational role, Meghan can provide some degree of knowledge around other

HR functions outside of her expertise, referring questions and issues she cannot answer to another "HR expert."

In moving to the HR Partner model, the "HR central service function," potentially located at the HR reception area, serves as the single point of contact for timely answers relating to the self-service function of the HR system. The receptionist and all back-up staff are trained extensively to provide exceptional, accurate and timely service. Developing this function gives the needed time to HR staff to serve in the HR Partner role.

HR Partner Purpose

The purpose of the HR Partner model is as follows:
1. provides a single point of contact for employees using the self-service function of the HR system, e.g., designing benefits, recruiting for open positions, payroll issues such as entering time and leave information, obtaining employment documents such as W-2s and earnings statements, and changing employment information
2. provides time for HR staff to work with campus partners within a transformational context
3. allows the HR generalists to partner with campus business units to work in transformational ways
4. provides a means for HR staff to develop strong relationships with their campus partners
5. continues to strengthen the transformational skills of HR staff

Process for Working Together

1. Each HR staff is matched or "partnered" with a major business unit of the university, e.g., an academic college, library, student services department, athletics, student support services, facilities and grounds, outreach services, etc. The HR staff can propose a division of units that seems equitable to him/her. In most cases, it will include the "work load demands" of the unit.

2. After the HR Partner structure has been communicated to key university administrators, each HR staff uses a similar process to introduce him or herself to key constituents in the partner group, explains the HR partner process, and develops working relationships with managers and others. In an initial meeting, the discussion can center around:
   a. expectations for the relationship between the HR partner and key constituents
   b. how to coordinate their communication
   c. issues within the business unit that the HR partner can help to resolve

Exhibit 14.2 outlines a sample HR Partner working relationship document developed after the first meeting with Meghan and several staff within the College of Liberal Studies dean's office, and prior to a presentation at the college's meeting of all department chairs. Note that it indicates the expectations for the relationship, how to coordinate communication and potential issues to be resolved.

Exhibit 14.2 Sample HR Partner working relationship document

Meghan Thompson *is the HR Partner to the College of Liberal Studies. In this strategic role, Meghan serves as the HR professional to work with the dean, associate and assistant deans, dean's assistant, department chairs, administrative assistants to the chairs, and other key administrative staff to accomplish both transactional and transformational work valued by constituents.*

1. *Expectations for the relationship:*
   - *For questions or issues around HR topics related to their position responsibilities, administrators and support staff within the college/ department/unit will contact their HR Partner, e.g., contracts, recruitments, payroll, benefits, staffing, performance management, salary equity, promotions, etc.*
   - *For personal questions related to any of these topics, all employees utilize the self-service component of the HRS, or contact the HR "Help Desk" for assistance.*
   - *If the HR Partner needs to, he/she will bring in an HR subject matter expert to work with the specific situation.*
2. *Communication:*
   - *We agree to respond to each other's phone calls or emails within 24 hours.*
   - *If absent from work, the HR Partner notifies key constituents of whom to contact.*
   - *We agree to meet with key constituents bi-monthly or more often to work through projects or issues.*
   - *Issues that impact other business units or the entire university will be brought to the HR staff for discussion.*
3. *Potential issues to work on together:*
   - *timeline and content for ad-hoc instructional contracts*
   - *contracts for faculty with "split" appointments*
   - *training and development needs*
   - *reorganization of departments or units*
   - *development of an improved performance evaluation form and process for ad-hoc instructional staff*
   - *development of an improved onboarding process for ad-hoc instructional staff*
   - *performance issues*
   - *FMLA/ADA issues*

Examples of Transformative Work

Example 1: Ad hoc Compensation Policy

Proactively work with the partners in the university's liberal arts college to design an equitable compensation policy for ad hoc instructors.

Example 2: Department Chair Training

Proactively work with the partners in the university's business college to develop and offer training for department chairs.

Example 3: Staffing Plan

Proactively work with the partners in the adult access and continuing education unit to perform a staffing audit and recommend a staffing plan that is aligned with the unit's vision and mission.

Example 4: Restructure Residence Life

Proactively work with the managers in the residence life unit to restructure based on current needs.

Example 5: Chapter 16 contains a comprehensive example of transformative work by an HR Partner Team

Implementing the HR Partner Structure in Stages

In most cases, the HR Partner structure must be implemented in stages due to the level of knowledge and skills needed by the HR staff. This structure means that the staff not only must possess transformational skills, but also have knowledge of other HR functions beyond their area of expertise.

A major training program must be developed. In the meantime, one HR staff member can be matched with another HR staff member who possesses the requisite knowledge. For example, an HR staff member with knowledge of staffing and organizational change can accompany another HR staff member who does not yet have this knowledge to a Partner meeting.

Process/Program Teams

The Issue

There are processes external to the HR department that impact its work and the work of the entire university, especially processes for recruiting and hiring faculty and staff. These processes can be inefficient and ineffective and the result of doing business in the same way for many years. To work in a transformative way, the HR department can proactively bring together people to evaluate and improve these processes using the methods described in chapter 11.

Team Description

Team membership needs to include those most involved and impacted by the process to be evaluated and improved. For example, a team of 9-12 people to evaluate and improve the recruitment process needs to include those in the following positions:

1. the administrative staff in major business units with the responsibilities for the recruitment paperwork, e.g., department administrative assistant, dean's assistant, etc.
2. people involved in the recruitment function from various employee groups, e.g., supervisor or manager, faculty member, department chair
3. representatives from administrative offices involved in the process, e.g., budget office
4. representatives from the HR function with responsibilities for the process

Team Purpose and Process for Working Together

A process or program team is tied to a particular process enhancement or program development and implementation. One goal is to evaluate and improve a chosen process so that it is more efficient and effective for all involved. A second goal includes developing a program for a major unit or the entire university that contributes toward stakeholder value and includes alignment with the university's strategic plan. The team disbands after the improved process or program is implemented and evaluated.

Examples of Transformative Work

Example 1: Faculty and Administrative Staff Recruitment Process

A team improving the recruitment process for faculty and administrative staff determines that members on search and screen committees need training in developing more effective position descriptions, and evaluating and interviewing candidates.

Example 2: Contracts for Ad Hoc Instructional Staff

A team from the college of liberal studies proposes changes to contracts for ad hoc instructional staff because of issues with multiple individual contracts.

Example 3: Recruitment Brand

The university president charges an institution-wide team to develop a recruitment brand for the entire university.

Example 4: Faculty and Administrative Staff Hiring Process

In addition to identifying issues with transactional processes, the work of a business process improvement team ultimately discovers other issues associated with the particular process being evaluated. A team improving the hiring process for faculty and administrative staff identifies the need for an onboarding program for new faculty and staff. The HR staff member serving as the team's facilitator works with the HR director to create a second team to address and resolve this issue.

Example 5: Chapter 16 includes a comprehensive example of transformational work of a process team.

Roles of the Leader

We are at a point in our change process where there is a great deal happening. Multiple teams are working on internal and external HR processes. HR staff are beginning their role as an HR Partner and developing relationships with key constituents in their partnered university unit. Within this context, the work of the leader encompasses tasks outlined in Exhibit 14.3

Exhibit 14.3 Roles of the leader in enabling transformative work

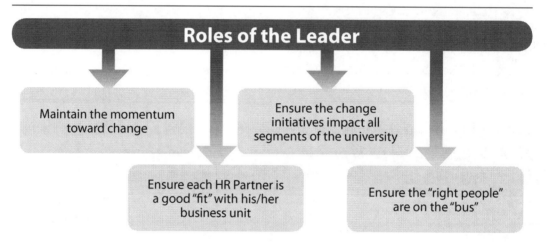

Maintain the Momentum toward Change

If you look at the transformational change process as a wagon wheel, the leader is the "hub," as shown in Figure 14.2. In this position, the leader knows about all activities currently underway and any completed or planned. As the center of all activity, the leader is aware of progress toward goals, any conflict or disruption on a team, and barriers to progress.

The leader serves as a role-model by continuing to convey commitment to the change by providing resources when needed, approving policy changes, and aligning department reward structures with the change. In addition, the leader takes on the HR Partner role and is matched with a key business unit of the university.

The leader monitors and guides change initiatives by developing a process to communicate with the HR Partners on their progress in developing relationships and working in transformative ways.

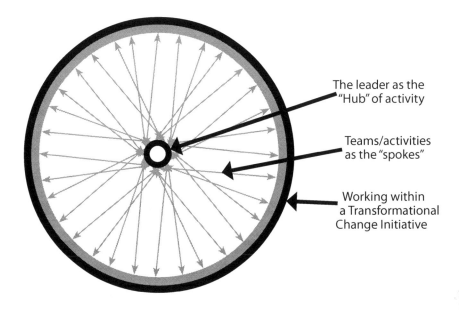

Figure 14.2 The leader as the hub of activity

Similarly, the leader develops processes to communicate with HR staff serving as facilitators of process or program teams.

As discussed more extensively in chapter 15, the leader develops and implements a communication plan to ensure key campus constituents are aware of the changes taking place in the HR function.

Most importantly, as indicated by the arrows in Figure 14.2 pointing in both directions—to and from the teams/activities—the leader listens, listens, and continues to listen to HR Partners, members of process or program teams, and key campus constituents.

Ensure each HR Partner is a good "fit" with his/her Business Unit

A crucial piece of the HR Partner model is the "fit" or relationship between the HR staff member serving as the Partner, and the key constituents in the business unit. The leader must facilitate the relationship process and choose the HR Partner carefully. One strategy is to match an HR staff member with a business unit where he or she already has built relationships and credibility, or has an interest in learning more about that unit.

On-going development of the HR Partner's relationship skills is paramount to a successful partnership. The leader serves as both coach and mentor in his/her own role as an HR Partner.

Ensure the Change Initiatives Impact All Segments of the University

The case studies outlined in chapter 16 are examples of change initiatives that impact all segments of the university. The leader must ensure the initiatives are aligned with the vision, mission and goals of the university.

Helping to identify constituents who are passionate about the topic and inviting them to become members of an initiative that interests them are key roles of the leader. Similarly, as described in the third case study in chapter 16, neglecting to invite key campus "influencers" to become members of a process or program team can cause major team dysfunctions and produce political barriers that hinder the accomplishment of the goal.

Ensure the "Right People" are on the "Bus"

We have come a long way in our move from a primarily transactional HR culture to a transformative culture. As an HR department, we spent a great deal of time and energy on this effort. What if one or more of the HR staff just are not able—or do not want—to learn and utilize transformative skills within a new HR paradigm? What are our options?

First, as the leader, we *MUST* address the situation. Dealing with someone who does not "fit" in a position is crucial to the reputation of the HR department and the change initiative itself. Getting the right people in job positions is mandatory to accomplish our mission and vision effectively. In addition, "how we deal" with an HR staff member who is in the wrong job or struggles with mastering the essential functions of his/her position within a transformative HR workplace will be watched carefully and role-modeled by the rest of the institution.

> Dealing with someone who does not "fit" in a position is crucial to the reputation of the HR department and the change initiative itself.

In many cases, an employee is not a good fit for the following reasons:

1. There was a lack of an assessment of the skills, abilities and values needed for the position at the time of hire.
2. The person has been in the position for some time and lacks the interest or skills to move to a transformational HR workplace.
3. Previous performance issues were not dealt with effectively, or at all.

If we have not skipped any steps in the process for transformational change, at this stage it should not be a "surprise" if an HR staff member is not a good fit for his/her responsibilities. In working through the process in this book, we would have identified this much earlier during one of the following phases:

1. developing an urgency for change
2. assessing this person's skills, competencies and required knowledge, and mutually creating a

personal development plan to improve specific areas

   3. including the person:

     a. on at least one team to improve an internal HR business process,

     b. in establishing the HR recruitment brand and evaluating the HR department structure,

     c. in revising the HR department vision, mission, core values and core competencies,

     d. in developing a transition plan for the HR paradigm shift,

     e. in identifying stakeholder value and developing the communication plan to obtain cabinet support for the HR paradigm change;

   4. meeting with the person periodically to review progress of his/her personal development plan and revising it if necessary

If we identified problems with the staff member's progress, we should have had one or more conversations where we:

1. talked with the person authentically about the situation, listened to what he/she said, gave him/her a chance to develop a solution to the problem, and discovered ways to deal with the situation.

2. revised the person's development plan to include potential training and other professional experiences

3. discussed work interests to potentially realign the person's job responsibilities to build on his/her strengths and interests

4. provided additional coaching or assessments to identify potential other work environments of interest

5. developed a mutually agreed-upon plan of action and timeline for review

6. documented the situation.

As a result of these conversations, we may have changed the job responsibilities of the employee, and the problem was resolved. The person may have transferred to another position within the university after acknowledging he/she was no longer a good fit in the HR department. Perhaps the revised plan and/or additional coaching resulted in substantial improvement. By definition, a transformation or paradigm shift requires people to change their behaviors. What if, at this change in our paradigm shift, our efforts do not cause change?

If all our efforts fail, we must show compassion and respect by offering meaningful alternatives to those who cannot perform effectively in the new HR paradigm. That is when we talk with them about alternatives, which can include:

1. transferring to another position within or external to the university that suits their values, interests and abilities;

2. taking a leave of absence to evaluate options;

3. evaluating options they may have in mind; and

4. working with a member of the institution's career services staff to seek other employment.

In a caring manner, we must clearly communicate the behaviors or results expected and give examples of where his/her performance is weak. We must indicate that while he/she continues to be an HR staff member, we will initiate a progressive performance evaluation process with ramifications of a potential termination. Our knowledge of how employment-at-will concepts are interpreted and applied in our state, along with any institution policies or procedures, are critical at this point to avoid a legal case of "wrongful termination."

Although this type of situation is always difficult to deal with, keep in mind that the cost of doing nothing is high. Employees who do not fit within the workplace or have performance issues create a high level of relationship tension within their sphere of influence in the HR department and in dealing with stakeholders. Other high performing employees may leave or disengage, customers do not value interactions, or the HR team becomes dysfunctional. Ultimately, the HR paradigm shift does not happen, and our reputation with key constituents deteriorates.

Summary

In today's age of technology, with HR systems that offer self-service within the functions of staffing, benefits, and payroll, HR can add value by providing continuing, equitable and credible administrative support. Employees look for personal service that is responsive and builds trust in the HR function. When they have transactional questions, employees value a single point of contact that gives timely and accurate answers.

At the same time, the HR paradigm shift expects professionals to work in transformative ways. How does the HR function structure itself to provide value within both transactional and transformative needs? A team environment aligns the seemingly inconsistent values of "a single point of contact," "timely answers" and "transformative work." This chapter outlined a process and benefits of developing an HR Collaboration Team, HR Partner teams and process/program teams.

An HR Collaboration Team normally consists of the HR director, equity and affirmative action director/manager, and associate provost/president positions. Others can be included when appropriate. Each person brings to the team his/her unique knowledge, experience and relationships that provide the team with a greater potential to resolve issues effectively.

Within the HR staff, each person serves as an "HR Partner" and ultimately is responsible for both transactional and transformational work. Each HR staff serves as an expert for the university in a specific transactional function. At the same time, each HR staff "partners" with a specific business unit within the university to serve as an HR "generalist" responsible for transformational work. In moving to the HR Partner model, the "HR central service function," potentially located at the HR reception area, serves as the single point of contact for timely answers relating to the self-service function of the HR system.

Processes external to the HR department, such as those for recruiting and hiring faculty and staff, often are inefficient and ineffective and the result of doing business in the same way for many years. To work in a transformative way, the HR department can proactively bring together people to evaluate and improve these processes using the methods discussed in chapter 11. A process or program team is tied to a particular process enhancement or program development and implementation. When the process has been improved and the new program implemented and evaluated, the team has finished its work and can be disbanded.

Major Themes

We are at a point in our change process where there is a great deal happening. Multiple teams are working on internal and external HR processes. HR staff are beginning their role as an HR Partner and developing relationships with key constituents in their partnered university unit. Within this context, **Leadership of Change** encompasses these tasks: maintaining the momentum toward change, ensuring each HR Partner is a good "fit" with his/her business unit, ensuring the change initiatives impact all segments of the university and ensuring the "right people" are on the "bus."

Evaluation of "Your" HR Department's Chapter 14 Outcome

Outcome Desired: Improved structure to enable transformative work

Change: Make the new behaviors stick by weaving them into the culture of the department; broaden the effort to accomplish the HR paradigm shift (change steps 7, 8)

Key Indicators of Success: (check if "yes")

☐ HR Partners are motivated to work with key constituents in transformational ways

☐ HR Partners feel they are receiving appropriate training for their transformational role

☐ Conflicts within teams are being managed timely and positively

☐ Teams are able to determine priorities and progress toward goals

☐ The urgency for change continues to be a motivation for moving forward with the work

☐ HR staff or others are being rewarded and compensated for being instrumental in the progress of the change initiative

☐ HR staff continue to be trained on their transformational role

☐ New projects and initiatives are introduced

☐ Additional "leaders" emerge from the HR staff

☐ Reward and recognition structures are changed to be aligned with the change initiative

☐ All initiatives appear to be well coordinated

Potential Barriers to Change: (check if "needs attention")

☐ People miss meetings and/or do not accomplish action items

☐ Planned changes are delayed

☐ Recommendations from teams are not acted upon, but are "shelved"

☐ HR staff complain they are overworked

☐ The morale of HR staff drops

☐ The change initiatives are not well coordinated

☐ Reward and recognition structures are not changed to be aligned with the change initiative

Evaluation of "Your" HR Department's Chapter 14 Outcome, *continued*

- ☐ Successful changes or improvements have not been seen in the last 3 months
- ☐ HR staff do not feel competent to serve as an HR Partner
- ☐ HR staff are not being given the appropriate resources to accomplish their work
- ☐ Complaints from a campus business unit about an HR Partner come to the leader of the change initiative

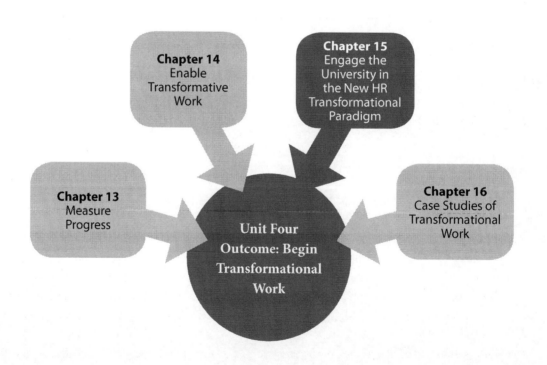

Chapter 14
Enable Transformative Work

Chapter 15
Engage the University in the New HR Transformational Paradigm

Chapter 13
Measure Progress

Chapter 16
Case Studies of Transformational Work

Unit Four Outcome: Begin Transformational Work

Chapter 15 Engage the university in the new HR transformational paradigm

Chapter 11 initially addressed the development of a communication plan to convey progress regarding the HR paradigm shift to those external to the HR function. We indicated that the message, its purpose, the audience and how it is communicated are dependent on the specific phase of the change process.

With the HR staff's move to focus on improving external HR processes and beginning transformative work, the details of the communication plan must be aligned with its purpose: to inform, to listen and especially to engage supporters. The outcome of chapter 15 is to engage key constituents in the HR paradigm change. A model to accomplish this outcome is summarized in Figure 15.1.

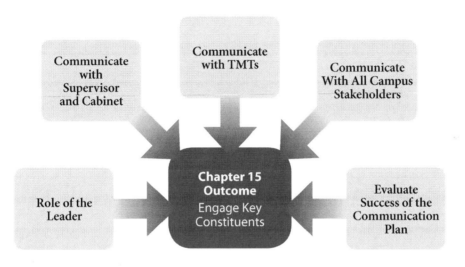

Figure 15.1 Model to engage key constituents

Role of the Leader

A key component of engaging people is first to inform them of information in a way that will motivate, excite and inspire them emotionally. The information must contain an aspect of what is valued in their work or personal life. The next steps are to: listen, answer questions, listen, provide examples, ask for feedback, listen, act on the feedback and provide the results of the feedback. The cycle continues as shown in Figure 15.2.

The involvement and leadership of the person leading the change initiative is critical to the success of engaging constituents. This is the primary role of the leader at this point in our change process. We utilize the details of a communication plan, as outlined in chapter 11, to provide examples to obtain the outcome of engaging constituents.

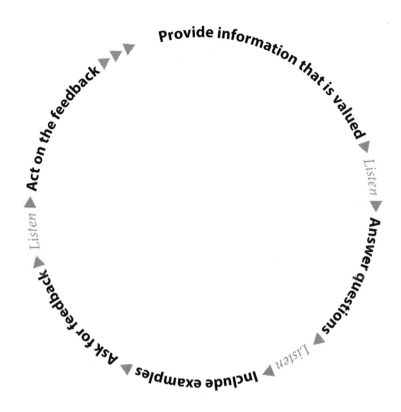

Figure 15.2 Cycle of generating engagement

Communicate with Supervisor and Cabinet

Our interviews with key campus constituents in chapter 7 provided a basis for learning the value of the HR paradigm shift for these individuals. This "value or interest" now is utilized in the communication plan to continue to engage our supervisor, cabinet members and others in the change initiative. Table 15.1 contains an example of a plan to communicate to our supervisor and cabinet at this juncture.

For the top administrative group, the value of the HR paradigm shift is normally the development and implementation of an HR strategic plan aligned with that of the university. That "value" becomes the focus for how we present our communication to this group.

Because we have periodically informed our supervisor and cabinet about the progress of our change initiative, there is less information to share now. This information needs to include the primary successes and accomplishments since we last updated them.

Remember the PowerPoint presentation from chapter 7, where we outlined the vision of the

Table 15.1 Example plan to communicate with supervisor and cabinet

Value: HR strategic plan aligned with that of the university

Message	What Information?	How to Communicate?
Inform	Reinforce the vision of a transformational HR paradigm	• in-person presentation to supervisor
	Developed HR Collaboration Team—proactively resolved major campus issue: discuss metrics	• supervisor provides updates at every other cabinet meeting
	Implemented HR Partner model to work with supervisors to implement university core competencies: discuss metrics	• hard copy summary of PowerPoint presentation
	Brought together campus team to improve student employment process: discuss metrics and provide comments from supervisors	
	At request of college dean, brought together campus team to improve faculty/staff reward structure: give progress	
Listen and ask questions	Ask for feedback and listen to perspective; additional "value" perspectives?	• in-person presentation to supervisor
	Debrief HR staff or teams on feedback	• supervisor provides updates at every other cabinet meeting
	Include feedback in change activities	• hard copy summary of PowerPoint presentation
Engage	Ask for their support	• provide email or in-person update on follow-through
	Follow through on feedback	

HR paradigm shift, its benefits to the university, the organizational change process used to become a transformational HR function and the expected outcomes? This presentation can be updated to show "Here's what we promised…." and "These are our accomplishments…."

Communicate with Transition Monitoring Teams

A transition monitoring team (TMT) is a group of 8-12 university faculty and staff with the purpose of serving as a conduit for communication about the HR paradigm shift. A facilitator from the HR staff informs the TMT about progress of the change initiative, engages them in dialogue, finds out what is important to them, and asks for advice. In essence, the TMT serves as a "two way street" in that participants are provided information and asked for feedback.

In communicating with a TMT, we can:

- learn what is valued about the change initiative
- discover issues to resolve proactively
- obtain feedback on plans or processes

Types of Transition Monitoring Teams

A current team, committee or group formed for other purposes can serve as a transition monitoring team. Examples are: president or chancellor's administrative team, provost's staff, student affairs directors, facilities management supervisory team, faculty or staff governance or advisory groups, etc. Requesting to communicate about the HR paradigm shift during a regularly scheduled meeting enables direct communication to multiple groups of key campus constituents.

> Key campus influencers can be invited to be part of a transition monitoring team that exists only until the change initiative is completed or evaluation feedback is no longer needed

Key campus influencers can be invited to be part of a transition monitoring team that exists only until the change initiative is completed or evaluation feedback is no longer needed. People who are prime "influencers" throughout the university—those who are respected and listened to by others—need to be on the team. They can be faculty, instructional staff, administrative staff, support staff, department chairs or supervisors.

We may not always agree with them or like their tactics for influencing, but identifying and inviting them to be part of a TMT is essential to the success of the change initiative. It is much better to learn about any major issues, feedback or negative political situations early and be able to respond to them, than to learn about them after the change initiative has been implemented. In many cases, members of a TMT engage and support the change initiative early, and positively influence the support of others.

Again, in working with a transition monitoring team, it is vital to inform, listen to learn of value or interest, act on their recommendations, gain their investment in the outcome, listen, and secure their engagement and influence. Table 15.2 offers a sample plan to communicate with transition monitoring teams. The value statement expressed in Table 15.2, "HR leads the development of a university leadership brand," is an example of an "interest" that was expressed by many members of TMTs in earlier conversations.

Communicate with all Campus Stakeholders

This may be the first time we have conducted information sessions for all campus stakeholders to learn about the changed culture within the HR function. We need to start at the beginning. Table 15.3 offers a sample plan to communicate with all campus stakeholders. The value statement expressed in Table 15.3, "HR serves as a facilitator for organizational and cultural transitions," is an example of an "interest" that was expressed by key campus constituents in earlier conversations.

Table 15.2 Example plan to communicate with transition monitoring teams

Value: HR leads the development of a university leadership brand

Message	What Information?	How to Communicate?
Inform	Reinforce the vision of a transformational HR paradigm	• in-person presentation • emails • hard copy of a PowerPoint summary
	Present progress of the team that is in the process of improving faculty/staff recruitment; how TMT members can be involved	
	Developed HR Partners; give purpose and current project of working with supervisors to implement university core competencies; provide training dates for core competencies, new performance evaluation process and development plans; provide "supportive comments" from supervisors	
	Brought together campus team to improve student employment process: provide results with dates for training	
	At request of college dean, brought together campus team to improve faculty/staff reward structure: provide process and how they can be involved	
Listen and ask questions	Ask for feedback and listen to perspective; additional "value" perspectives?	• in-person presentation • emails • hard copy of a PowerPoint summary
	Debrief HR staff or teams on feedback	
	Include feedback in change activities	
Engage	Ask for their support	• provide email or in-person update on follow-through
	Follow through on feedback	

Evaluate Success of the Communication Plan

How will we know our efforts to engage key campus constituents are successful? Table 15.4 contains a checklist for each group communicated with: supervisor and cabinet, transition monitoring teams, and all campus stakeholders. An apparent lack of any of these criteria may indicate weaknesses in our communication plan that need to be addressed.

We have come a long way and have worked very hard toward accomplishing the HR paradigm change. We have developed the knowledge and skills of the HR staff regarding transformational work, led them through experiences internal to the HR department to enhance their skills and self-confidence, built trust and respect among the HR staff, and have moved their work external to the HR department. This work, and our communication of it, engages and energizes campus stakeholders, with the outcome being a changed HR culture cascading throughout the university.

Chapter 16 presents three comprehensive case studies of transformational work that can set the stage for developing the HR strategic plan.

Table 15.3 Example plan to communicate with all campus stakeholders

Value: HR serves as a facilitator for organizational and cultural transitions

Message	What Information?	How to Communicate?
Inform	Explain the new HR transformational paradigm, using examples to capture their interests and value	• in-person presentation to focus groups
	Give examples to show how the change can impact them personally and collectively	• emails
	Present progress of the team that is in the process of improving faculty/staff recruitment; how they can be involved	• HR newsletter • HR website for PowerPoint summary
	Developed HR Partners; give purpose and current project of working with supervisors to implement university core competencies; provide training dates for core competencies, new performance evaluation process and development plans	
	Brought together campus team to improve student employment process: provide results with dates for training	
	At request of college dean, brought together campus team to improve faculty/staff reward structure: provide process and how they can be involved	
Listen and ask questions	Ask for feedback and listen to perspective; additional "value" perspectives	• in-person presentation to focus groups
	Debrief HR staff or teams on feedback	• emails
	Include feedback in change activities	• HR newsletter • HR website for PowerPoint summary
Engage	Ask for their support—how do they want to be engaged?	• provide email or newsletter update on follow-through
	Follow through on feedback	

Table 15.4 Sample checklist for evaluation of communication plan

University Group	Evaluation Criteria	Successful (x)	Needs More Work (x)
Supervisor and Cabinet	Issues are brought early to members of the HR Collaboration Team or the HR Partners		
	The HR function has an improved knowledge of constituents' value or interests		
	Increased campus discussions/dialogue around the topic of transformational HR; success stories are brought to HR		
	Success stories told by supervisors and others are being repeated		
	Increased advocacy for the new HR paradigm		
Transition Monitoring Teams	People are inspired to join existing teams		
	Issues are brought early to members of the HR Collaboration Team or the HR Partners		
	The HR function has an improved knowledge of constituents' value or interests		
	Increased campus discussions/dialogue around the topic of transformational HR; success stories are brought to HR		
	HR staff are requested to give updates on new HR paradigm to campus group or departments		
	Success stories told by supervisors and others are being repeated		
	Increased advocacy for the new HR paradigm		
	Supervisors can express to their department members how the new HR paradigm positively impacts them		
	More excitement among employees and supervisors to address and resolve issues by partnering with HR		
All campus stakeholders	People are inspired to join existing teams		
	Issues are brought early to members of the HR Collaboration Team or the HR Partners		
	The HR function has an improved knowledge of constituents' value or interests		
	Increased campus discussions/dialogue around the topic of transformational HR; success stories are brought to HR		
	HR staff are requested to give updates on new HR paradigm to campus group or departments		
	Success stories told by supervisors and others are being repeated		
	Increased advocacy for the new HR paradigm		
	Supervisors can express to their department members how the new HR paradigm positively impacts them		
	More excitement among employees and supervisors to address and resolve issues by partnering with HR		

Summary

Utilizing a communication plan to continually convey progress regarding the HR paradigm shift to those external to the HR function is crucial at this point. The message, its purpose, the audience and how it is communicated are dependent on the specific phase of the change process. With the HR staff's move to focus on improving external HR processes and beginning transformative work, the details of the communication plan must be aligned with its purpose: to inform, to listen and especially to engage supporters.

A key component of engaging people is first to inform them of information in a way that will motivate, excite and inspire them emotionally. The information must contain an aspect of what is "valued" in their work or personal life. The next steps are to listen, answer questions, listen, provide examples, ask for feedback, listen, act on the feedback and provide the results of the feedback, continuing the cycle where appropriate.

Therefore, normally communication plans for different segments of stakeholders are slightly different. For example, because cabinet members may value the implementation of the HR strategic plan aligned with that of the university, their communication plan focuses on that value, and a communication plan targeted to stakeholders who value the development of a university recruitment brand focuses on that value.

Major Themes

Leadership of Change includes developing a checklist for evaluating the various communication plans.

Evaluation of "Your" HR Department's Chapter 15 Outcome

Outcome Desired: Engage key constituents

Change: Implement communication plan to obtain commitment and support of key constituents (change step 4)

Key Indicators of Success: (check if "yes")

- ☐ People are inspired to join existing teams
- ☐ People bring issues to members of the HR Collaboration Team or HR Partners
- ☐ HR function has an improved knowledge of what is valued by constituents
- ☐ Increased campus discussions and dialogue around the topic of transformational HR
- ☐ HR staff are requested to give updates on the new HR paradigm to campus groups or departments
- ☐ Success stories by supervisors and others are being repeated
- ☐ Constituents provide feedback and success stories without being asked
- ☐ Increased advocacy for the new HR transformational paradigm
- ☐ Open positions in the HR department bring increased applications by people with the needed transformative skills
- ☐ Supervisors can express to their department members how the new HR paradigm impacts them in positive ways
- ☐ Faculty and staff understand the differences between transformative and transactional work
- ☐ More interest among employees and supervisors to address and resolve issues, as they feel supported by the HR function

Potential Barriers to Change: (check if "needs attention")

- ☐ Sending inconsistent messages
- ☐ An overload of information in any single message, or using multiple forms of communication that causes people to "opt out" of engaging in any communication
- ☐ Not providing a communication method to engage people
- ☐ Not listening when feedback is given by constituents
- ☐ Not taking action on the feedback given by constituents

Case Studies of Transformational Work

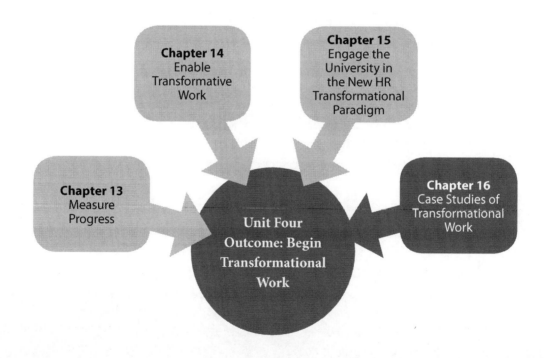

Chapter 16 Case studies of transformational work

Unit Four's outcome is the beginning of HR transformational work. Setting this stage in Unit Four allows us to become a strategic partner in Unit Five to develop and align the HR strategic plan with that of the university.

Chapter 16 presents three comprehensive case studies based on actual experiences within a university setting. Together, these case studies illustrate models for how HR professionals can partner with and engage constituents to deliver results that are highly valued. In addition, these case studies highlight the successes and challenges that faced the implementation teams.

As outlined in Figure 16.1, this chapter builds on the model expressed in chapter 14, with one case study pertaining to the work of the HR Collaboration Team, a second to the work of the HR Partners, and a third to the work of a campus-wide team improving an HR process.

Each case study is separate from the others, and follows the "template" of the eight-step change process as described by John Kotter in his book, *Leading Change* (1996).

Figure 16.1 Comprehensive case studies to illustrate transformational work

Role of the Leader

The fundamental and crucial role of the leader during any change initiative is to ensure that the implementation plan includes the eight-step change process. In the three case studies that follow, the method in which the change process emerges either contributes toward the success of the initiative or causes problems for the implementation team.

- Case Study 16.1 fails to infuse major cultural change within the university due to a lack of an

- integrative vision in the early steps of the project.
- Case Study 16.2 accomplishes culture change, mainly as a result of discovering stakeholder value and following the change process.
- Case Study 16.3 includes challenges that negatively impact the result of the project, which could have been avoided if greater attention had been paid to the change process itself.

The fundamental and crucial role of the leader during any change initiative is to ensure that the implementation plan includes the eight-step change process.

We explain each case study using the eight-step change process as a template in order to encourage you to use this process when developing an implementation plan for any change initiative, no matter how small or simple it may appear. Thinking through each of these steps will point out potential challenges, and ensure greater cultural change as an outcome.

HR Collaboration Team: Developing Leaders

Case Study 16.1

Background

With the support of her vice president and president's cabinet, Leslie, the HR director, has spent the last year developing the transformative skills of the HR staff and leading the HR paradigm shift, concentrating on activities internal to the HR department. They developed department core values, new vision and mission statements, and an integrated core competency framework resulting in the following core competencies for the HR department: collaboration and partnership, communication and personal effectiveness, customer orientation, achievement orientation, self-awareness and professional development, and leadership.

Knowing that the HR department is normally not the only function within the university that deals with HR issues or has knowledge of potential issues, Leslie built a working relationship with the associate vice president for academic affairs. Together with the assistant director of HR, responsible for staffing and equity, they formed a team to deal with common issues effectively and timely. Each person brought to the team his/her unique knowledge, experiences and relationships that provided the team with a greater potential to resolve issues effectively. Working together as a team to resolve these issues provided improved and more timely problem-solving in the last year.

Consequently, they decided to formalize their working together as a team by defining their purpose and goals, as outlined below.

Purpose: *Share information in order to resolve common issues effectively and timely*

Goal 1 *reduce gaps or overlap in service to stakeholders*

Goal 2 *improve coordination to provide increased value to stakeholders*

Goal 3 *build the foundation of relationships for developing and implementing the HR strategic plan*

During a weekly meeting, they discussed the outcome of a situation in one of the academic colleges. Leslie shared her frustration that academic department chairs were not provided training in areas such as the role of department chair, conflict resolution, effective communication and problem-solving, etc. Rob, the associate vice president for academic affairs, agreed, having been a department chair for three years prior to his current position. Theresa, the assistant director of HR, added that the longer a conflict situation existed, the more difficult it was to resolve in a productive manner. As a result, several departments in each of the four academic colleges provided difficult environments for faculty and department chairs, with low retention rates for newly hired faculty in these departments. Rob initiated the idea of a faculty leadership series, targeting faculty currently in administrative or leadership roles, and faculty interested in a future leadership role. They decided to reflect on this topic and address it again in a month, and Theresa agreed to research leadership programs at peer institutions.

At the next meeting, Theresa shared the results of her research, and the draft of a plan for a faculty leadership series. The draft plan included the goals and rationale for the program, and alignment with the university's strategic plan. The draft leadership program consisted of a series of seminars offering nine topical areas to be delivered as a pilot in January, May and August of the next year. Each seminar consisted of a two-day session. Participants were divided into small groups, with each group containing an experienced chair, director, or leader, in order to have "topical discussions" that allowed participants to learn from each other.

Expectations included participants spending time outside of the sessions reading several books, completing self-assessments, and working on their team goals. Topics to be presented and discussed included: creating effective leadership styles, the role of a department chair, becoming a respectful communicator, nurturing a successful work environment, developing institutional decision-making skills, developing conflict resolution skills, creating and managing transitions, developing teams, and systems thinking.

After an animated discussion, Theresa agreed to make enhancements to the draft plan, include a budget, and utilize it as a proposal to present first to the provost and vice president for academic affairs and vice president for administration and finance, and then to the entire cabinet. As a result, their proposal was approved by the cabinet, with the necessary resources obtained from the provost and vice president's office and through a grant from the Sloan Foundation. Rob, Leslie and Theresa implemented their plan.

Step 1: Establish Urgency for Change

An email and hard copy of the description of the Faculty Leadership Series was sent to all faculty, including those on tenure-track, tenured, and already in department chair or other administrative positions. Instead of describing the issues and urgency for change, the material included the "benefits" of participating in the series of workshops. Within two weeks, 28 faculty members registered for the program.

Step 2: Build Guiding Team(s)

Team members comprised Leslie, Rob and Theresa, members of the HR Collaboration Team.

Step 3: Develop the Vision and Strategy

The vision or goal statement: Develop consensus-building and leadership competencies among department chairs, academic program directors, sub-departmental managers, and faculty interested in administrative leadership and development.

The program components aligned with the mission, vision, core values and several strategic directions included in the university's strategic plan.

Step 4: Communicate for Buy-In

The program vision, strategy, alignment with the university's strategic plan, and program components were communicated via email to all faculty and administrators in the academic colleges, and included the following metrics:

- *An initial survey will be given to participants to measure knowledge of leadership.*
- *Before the program begins, participants will develop personal goals for their intended outcomes of the leadership program. Participants will be surveyed at the end of the program in August to determine if the goals were met.*
- *Evaluations will be done at the end of each seminar and at the end of the program, and will be used to improve future seminars.*
- *An end-of-the-program evaluation in August will determine whether the goals of the program were accomplished.*
- *A post-training survey will be done approximately six months after the program was completed.*

Step 5: Empower Action

The environment within the seminars proved to be conducive to sharing issues and information among faculty representing all four colleges. It was apparent they were serious about the seminars and appreciated the ability to discuss issues within their small groups and then within the larger group.

Step 6: Generate Short-Term Wins

During the last seminar in August, three teams worked throughout the morning on a campus issue important to them. The groups presented their issues to the president after lunch, and obtained his support for resolving them.

Evaluations indicated the program was a huge success and greatly valued by participants, who wanted it to continue each year. However, internal funding was not available at that time.

Step 7: Consolidate and Continue Change Initiatives

Staff Leadership and Development Program

A new president arrived at the beginning of the next academic year. It was apparent to her that the 350 support staff on the campus did not feel "valued." In discussing this with Leslie, the president suggested that Leslie work with a team to develop various programs, including a leadership and development program.

Leslie, Rob and Theresa worked together to develop the proposal, which was approved by the cabinet and implemented the next academic year, with 30 participants. Similar to the faculty leadership program, the staff development and leadership program included a strategic vision, alignment with the university's strategic plan, nine four-hour seminars throughout the academic year on team building, communication styles, stress and taking care of yourself, anatomy of a leader, how to be an engaged leader, conflict resolution, diversity, handling change, and a call to leadership. In addition, each participant was part of a mentor circle group as a means to further personal development. The program was so successful, the cabinet decided to continue it annually.

The Leading From the Middle Supervisor Leadership Series

During the first year of the Staff Leadership and Development Program, the HR Collaboration Team discussed issues pertaining to the weak skills of supervisors, especially related to conflict management, performance evaluation, and developing department core values, vision, mission, and goals aligned with those of the university. Much of their time lately was filled with resolving conflict within departments and between supervisors and those who report to them.

Together, they developed a proposal for a comprehensive development and leadership program for supervisors of support and administrative staff, to include a mentoring component. As with the other training programs, it had a strategic vision and was aligned with the university's strategic plan. It included nine four-hour sessions during the academic year, with topics on team-building, servant leadership, systems thinking, developing people and teams, creating and managing transitions, managing conflict, performance evaluation process, problem-solving tools, and creating a work environment conducive to success. More than the other training programs, this one was very action oriented, with assignments each supervisor needed to complete with his/her staff between sessions. The project was approved, and the cabinet made the necessary resources available.

As with the Staff Leadership and Development Program, this training program was highly valued by participants, their staff members and their supervisors. The cabinet approved the resources to continue it as an annual program.

The Leadership Fellow Program

While implementing the first Staff Leadership and Development Program, the HR Collaboration Team heard from both support and administrative staff that many applied for other positions throughout the university when they became available, but seldom was an internal person hired. The HR Collaboration Team discussed this, did research using the HRS database, and realized this was the case. During recruitments, managers and directors looked for candidates who had specific experience and skills in the position being recruited, paying less attention to transferable skills.

Leslie, Rob and Theresa wondered if a mentoring program or some type of "internship" experience could solve this problem. In reviewing the retention data for support and administrative staff, they found that more were leaving the university than in previous years. In talking with the cabinet, the president proposed a Leadership Fellow Program to include "internship" type positions for faculty, support staff, and administrative staff interested in working in another part of the university. For faculty, the program would comprise an administrative "internship." The Collaboration Team developed the proposal, subsequently approved by the cabinet, and were given resources to implement it.

… all the various leadership programs should have been integrated and aligned under one vision and model…

Through an application and interview process, four "Leadership Fellows" began internships the next academic year. They included one faculty member in the president's office, one administrative staff in the academic advising department, and two support staff, one in the HR department and the other in the budget/controller's Office. Although none of the "Interns" received additional salary, their home departments received the funding to hire a temporary employee to cover their responsibilities.

An evaluation of the program several years later indicated these "internship" oppor-

tunities increased the leadership and skill development of employees, and a large percentage were hired into permanent positions through the normal recruitment process.

Step 8: Anchor New Culture

Although successes in each of these programs generated short-term wins and eventually caused some culture change, the whole idea of leadership development and succession planning was not infused into the culture of the university. When resources became tight, several of these programs were "temporarily" discontinued. Why? What could have been done differently?

Although the university developed employee core competencies that included "leadership," they did not specifically link to business results or integrate throughout the entire employment process…

First, all the various leadership programs should have been integrated and aligned under one vision and model to include recruiting, on boarding, performance management, other training and development, succession planning and reward practices to build and reinforce key valued behaviors. The benefits of an integrated model, called a "leadership brand," include the ability to (Intagliata, Ulrich and Smallwood, 2000):

1. *identify and communicate key attributes of leadership that link to broad university "results"*
2. *identify and provide leadership role models within the university*
3. *provide direction for all leaders at all levels within the university*
4. *measure the extent to which leaders demonstrate these behaviors*
5. *provide goals for leaders to develop their capabilities*
6. *differentiate the university from its peers*

Although the university developed employee core competencies that included "leadership," they did not specifically link to business results or integrate throughout the entire employment process as illustrated above. As described in an article in HR Planning (Intagliata, Ulrich and Smallwood, 2000, p. 3), "Leadership brand occurs when leaders at every level are clear about which results are most important, develop a general consistency about how they will achieve these results, and build attributes that align with the achievement of these results…. Branded leadership creates a distinct leadership

… an integrative employee core competency framework can be built into a leadership brand that is integrated and aligned with the entire employment process.

culture that permeates the entire organization." In other words, an integrated leadership brand creates a competitive advantage for the university and is directly linked to business results. It is, therefore, highly valued and becomes a strategic priority for the university.

Although discussing the development of a university leadership brand is beyond the scope of this case study, an integrative employee core competency framework can be built into a leadership brand that is integrated and aligned with the entire employment process.

Second, specific program metrics—that tie directly to university performance measures—are crucial in measuring the success of how any program offerings contribute toward the accomplishment of university-wide strategy. For example, consider the situation when Gary Forsee became president of the University of Missouri System (UM System) in late 2007. Shortly after beginning in this position, he compiled a comprehensive set of 80 performance objectives and accountability measures for the UM System that encompassed five major categories: (1) teaching and learning; (2) research; (3) service and engagement: (4) economic development; and (5) developing and managing human, financial and physical resources.

Says Forsee, "Our accountability measures are derived from the strategy, vision and core values of the system as a whole, but are also designed to provide each of our four campuses with the flexibility to customize and tailor their metrics to fit their specific missions and goals. … Every single staff member, faculty member and administrator in the UM System has a role to play in helping to meet these goals" (80 Ways to Measure Success, 26).

The HR function, in leading the development of leadership and succession programs or a recruitment brand, can include metrics to evaluate these programs that tie directly to the success of these university performance measures.

Consider the performance management sub-categories under the fifth category, "developing and managing human, financial and physical resources": attract, develop and retain talented faculty and staff; sustainability and flexibility in resource management; replenishment of physical and financial assets; and stewardship. Specific UM System performance measures identified include: faculty and staff diversity by gender and ethnicity, tuition benefits used by staff, and faculty and staff turnover rates. The HR function, in leading the development of leadership and succession programs or a recruitment brand, can include metrics to evaluate these programs that tie directly to the success of these university performance measures.

Potential metrics could include the following:

- *increase retention of faculty by 15% in five years*
- *increase the percentage of female faculty by 20% in five years*

The success of these metrics could result from increased collegiality, mentoring of junior faculty and work-life balance within academic departments due to training of department chairs, improved training for mentors, conflict management training for all faculty and staff, development of a university-wide recruitment brand, etc. These results illustrate to the cabinet members the positive impact on university performance and the value of these programs. Remember, it is all about delivering stakeholder value.

HR Partners: University-Wide Core Competencies

Case Study 16.2

Background

Raymond was the director of HR at a small liberal arts college. As part of an HR paradigm shift to a transformative culture, the HR team participated in developing an integrated HR competency framework and restructuring the department, resulting in an HR Partner team model implemented with the following purposes:

1. *provide a single point of contact for employees using the self-service function of the HR system, e.g., designing benefits, recruiting for open positions, payroll issues such as entering time and leave information, obtaining employment documents such as W-2s, earnings statements, and changing employment information*
2. *provide time for HR staff to work with campus partners within a transformational context*
3. *allow the HR generalists to partner with their campus business units to work in transformational ways*
4. *provide a means for HR staff to develop strong relationships with their campus partners*
5. *continue to strengthen the transformational skills of HR staff*

The HR Partner model's success included the following multiple outcomes:

1. *strengthened transformational skills of the HR staff*
2. *increased partnerships and relationships among the HR staff members and constituents in colleges and departments*
3. *enhanced perception of HR staff members as transformational*

4. improved engagement of department chairs and supervisors with HR related work
5. consideration of the HR department first for assistance in problem-solving

As part of offering an initial Supervisor Leadership Series, a nine-month development and leadership program for supervisors of support and/or administrative staff, the 30 participants facilitated the development of their department's core values and vision and mission statements. Several invited Raymond or another HR staff member to facilitate these processes with their staff so they could serve as equal participants.

One of the Supervisor Leadership Series seminars dealt with effective performance evaluation forms and processes. Participants valued the simulation that accompanied a presentation of the process, where groups of three took turns being the supervisor, the employee, and an observer. Raymond and the HR staff spent several months developing a new performance appraisal form, and the supervisors felt it was a great improvement over the old one. Seminar evaluations indicated participants felt this topic was high priority and appreciated the insight and improved skills they gained.

During open discussions in the Supervisor Leadership Series, supervisors discussed problems that the HR department could assist with. Many did not have sufficient training to appropriately recruit, evaluate, hire, train and evaluate the performance of administrative or support staff reporting to them. Too often, a new staff member was determined to not be a good fit for the department, not have the requisite skills, or create conflict or dysfunction within the department. It was difficult to terminate this type of employee. Supervisors asked, "Is there a method to determine these attributes during the evaluation and interviewing stages of the recruitment?"

Raymond and the HR team members recognized that there was insufficient structure to support supervisors during the hiring and employment process. Several others on the team had received this complaint from their HR Partner in the past few months. Consequently, Raymond developed and presented a university-wide integrated employee core competency framework to the president's cabinet. After an extensive discussion, cabinet members determined that the framework provided definite advantages for the university, and the six employee core competencies identified by the HR department were those they valued for the broad university. They charged Raymond with implementation of the "next steps" listed in his presentation. Having the support of the president and cabinet to implement the integrated core competency model (discussed in chapter 5), they decided to utilize the Supervisor Leadership Series

> To review Case Study 16.2 powerpoint presentation on implementing university-wide core competencies, go to **www.HR-higher-ed.com**

as a pilot. During the next seminar, Raymond presented the model to participants, confirming the support of the president's cabinet and their role in the pilot to introduce and improve the model. Supervisors had the following alternatives:

1. Present the integrative core competency framework to their staff and utilize the six employee core competencies totally, with the same behavioral descriptors and wording. Use the PowerPoint presentation provided to explain the model to the staff. Place the core competencies into each staff member's position description. Evaluate the performance of each staff member utilizing the new form. Bring the results of implementing this process to a later seminar for discussion.

2. The same as option #1, except additional core competencies that pertain directly to work in the specific department are added. Behavioral descriptors are changed to reflect the work of the department more adequately.

3. The same as options #1 and #2, except Raymond or another HR staff member facilitates the presentation, and/or additions made to core competencies and behavioral descriptors.

Over the next six months the HR Partners evaluated the new recruitments of support and administrative staff, and kept in constant communication with the supervisors. Two outcomes were apparent:

1. Supervisors liked the core competencies as they gave them a method to determine "how" an individual accomplishes his or her work. They used behavioral interviewing questions during the interviews and reference checks to learn if the person already possessed the competencies. For those hired, they developed goals that included action items to improve a specific competency.

2. Supervisors talked with others about the benefits of utilizing employee core competencies, who then contacted the HR department to learn more about them.

Step 1: Establish Urgency for Change

The urgency for change definitely resulted from discussions by the Supervisor Leadership Series participants. They wanted change, and as soon as possible. They were a pilot group representing more than 150 supervisors with similar issues. Consequently, Raymond and the HR staff prepared and announced training for all supervisors of administrative and support staff regarding the core competency framework, the new performance evaluation form and the process of performance appraisal. In addition, they presented information sessions for administrative and support staff to learn about the new form with the core competencies.

Step 2: Build Guiding Team(s)

The guiding team consisted of the HR Partners facilitating the Supervisor Leadership Series seminars. The participants in the Series served as a "pilot team" to substantiate the benefits of the core competency framework. The president's cabinet was a "support team" and served as role models for the rest of the university.

Step 3: Develop the Vision and Strategy

The vision was to develop an employee integrative core competency framework to be used in recruitment, selection, professional development, career planning, evaluation and promotion. This framework aligned with the vision and mission of the HR department.

The strategy involved utilizing the HR Partner teams and providing presentations and training to all supervisors and staff.

Step 4: Communicate for Buy-In

The training for supervisors and information sessions for staff comprised the communication plan for the vision. Participants from the Supervisor Leadership Series served as role models and facilitators during the training, which greatly increased the buy-in for other supervisors. Each participant was given two books, The Performance Appraisal Question and Answer Book: A Survival Guide for Managers, by Dick Grote, 2002, and High-Impact Interview Questions: 701 Behavior-Based Questions, by Victoria A. Hoevemeyer, 2006.

The information sessions obtained buy-in for the new form and process, especially for many support staff who report to department chairs and have not had a performance evaluation for many years. They did not feel valued and looked forward to this process. Others appreciated that their supervisors attended training to make the evaluation process more thorough and equitable. Some indicated they actually completed their own evaluations in the past, with their supervisors just signing them.

Step 5: Empower Action

The training for supervisors, along with the two books, empowered them with the skills and structure to better recruit, hire, evaluate and develop individuals reporting to them. In addition, upon requests from several supervisors, the HR Partner teams prepared to offer training to supervisors and entire departments on addressing and resolving conflict. Listening to and addressing the needs of supervisors in the leadership series empowered action that continued to build.

Step 6: Generate Short-Term Wins

Although offering the training and information sessions could be considered short-term wins, the fact that most supervisors attended the training and 99.9% of administrative and support staff received a performance review was a major accomplishment. The skills of supervisors could continue to improve with training, but the majority of supervisors and staff bought in to the integrated core competency framework.

Step 7: Consolidate and Continue Change Initiatives

Although Raymond and the HR team members were excited about the outcomes so far, they knew they needed to embed the core competency framework further into the culture of the university. They developed a plan to meet with each department supervisor (not including department chairs in the academic departments) over the next six months. Based on the HR Partner model, they formed teams of two or three HR staff. Each team included a person(s) proficient in title classifications and restructuring, and a staff member needing more experience in those topics. For example, one team consisted of an HR manager with expertise in titling and restructuring for support staff, an HR assistant responsible for staffing temporary employees and university-wide immigration work, and Raymond, with expertise in organizational design and change.

As much as possible, the teams were assigned colleges or departments that contained "partners" of at least one of the HR team member because these relationships already were developed. The team members mentioned above had partners in the division of academic affairs, and thus were assigned that division for the core competencies project. The division consisted of departments such as the library, academic advising, admissions, registrar, academic support and adult learning. Each department head was contacted, and a meeting was scheduled to discuss the core competency model. The HR team:

1. *offered to facilitate a meeting for the entire department to discuss core competencies and add any department-specific competencies or behavioral indicators*
2. *proposed they assist by re-writing position descriptions for administrative and support staff in the department to include the core competencies*
3. *requested feedback on the current recruitment processes and forms to improve them*
4. *suggested other ways they could help, e.g., help evaluate the current structure of the department, evaluate how work was allocated within the department to suggest greater efficiency and effectiveness, etc.*

Although the HR staff planned to complete this project in six months, it actually expanded to more than a year. The extreme value of this project by supervisors meant the HR teams became intricately involved in changes within many of the departments.

Step 8: Anchor New Culture

Four HR teams were developed. One was assigned the division of academic affairs; the others developed separate relationships with the divisions of student affairs, foundation and alumni affairs, and administration and finance. Raymond took on the president's office. Although it took almost two years for the core competency frame-

work to be implemented throughout the entire university, the strategy in which the project was implemented served to advance the HR paradigm shift. When the HR strategic plan was offered to stakeholders for feedback, engagement was much more than expected.

In evaluating the metrics for this project, the HR team determined all were successful. The project contributed toward the following:

1. Relationships were improved between the HR department and supervisors.
2. There was a better fit of newly hired administrative and support staff with their department and university.
3. More development plans were completed for current and new staff.
4. Poor performance was dealt with more quickly and effectively by supervisors;
5. The retention of high performing staff was increased.

> … although the metrics for this program were accomplished, a weakness was that none of these metrics were tied directly to a university performance measure.

As in Case Study 16.1, although the metrics for this program were accomplished, a weakness was that none of these metrics were tied directly to a university performance measure.

HR Process Team: Improving Business Processes

Case Study 16.3

Background

With the student financial aid office restructuring to align with its updated mission statement, the HR department was requested to take responsibility for student employment. Although accountability for the student payroll function was in HR, the employment process—comprising all required documentation such as I-9s, W-4, direct deposit—historically existed in the financial aid office.

Rachelle, the HR director, agreed to move the student employment function to the HR department. Rachelle learned from the financial aid office director that there were multiple problems with the student employment function. These included inadequate completion of the legal employment documents by the hiring departments/units, and students beginning work prior to completing the documents.

Because of these problems, a major change made by Rachelle was to require the students to come to the HR department—instead of to the hiring department—to complete the employment documents. Otherwise, the same work authorization process was utilized to put students onto the payroll and timekeeping systems.

Step 1: Establish Urgency for Change

After six months, an evaluation of the current student employment process resulted in learning the following information:

1. Approximately 5,000 student employment work authorizations were processed each year, with 33% of student employees having more than one job. The majority of the authorizations were processed at the beginning of each academic semester—August/September, February and June. During these times, the student employment coordinator in the HR department needed the assistance of three other HR staff members to accomplish the work.

2. The HR department could not always process the work authorizations in the timely manner that supervisors and student employees expected so that the students could begin work when needed. Therefore, student supervisors were not happy with their inability to put the students to work as soon as possible. They did not value the new process.

3. An HR staff member(s) "touched" the documents for one student for one job at least two times, once for the legal employment documents, and once for the work authorization.

4. Communication among the supervisor, student employee and HR department was not always sufficient regarding employment documents, payroll and/or timekeeping.

5. The "lump-sum payment process," used to pay student employees once for specific work (instead of bi-weekly as work is accomplished), was cumbersome and prone to errors.

Rachelle realized changes must be made to the student employment process due to these issues that negatively impacted students and staff internal and external to the HR department.

Step 2: Build Guiding Team(s)

Trained in utilizing the LEAN tool for improving business processes, Rachel decided to assemble a campus-wide team to address issues within the student employment and payroll functions. The team consisted of the four staff in the HR department involved in student employment and payroll and five individuals from departments that hire many students each year: athletics, the library, residence life, student affairs, and the unit that managed a community student internship program.

In addition, the team included an employee from the university relations department not involved in any student employment functions, and a business consultant familiar with the LEAN process, currently serving as a member of the college of business advisory board. Rachelle planned to facilitate the business process improvement discussions, scheduled for four hours each morning over five consecutive days.

Step 3: Develop the Vision and Strategy

The overall vision for the project encompassed building a student employment process that provided greater efficiency and effectiveness for both the HR department and those hiring student employees. Specific goals—which also served as follow-up evaluation metrics—included the following:

1. *All students begin working within 48 hours after the HR department received the complete paperwork (student documentation plus work authorization).*

2. *A student's employment paperwork is touched by the HR department one time per student per job. Specifically, during the first year, the goal was for the HR department to touch a new student employee's paperwork "once" 50% of the time.*

3. *Reduce the number of miscommunications or touches among the student, HR department or employer by 50% for the next academic year.*

4. *Reduce the number of miscommunications or touches regarding payroll/time-keeping between the student, HR or employer by 50% for the next academic year.*

5. *Reduce the number of times students forget their user name or password by 50% for the next academic year.*

6. *Reduce the amount of time it takes HR staff members for the lump-sum process each pay period by 50%;*

7. *Reduce the amount of time it takes HR staff members to deal with errors, problems and questions per pay period by 50%.*

Step 4: Communicate for Buy-In

A crucial part of the LEAN process is to obtain the total support of the person who "charges" the team, in this case, the vice president for administrative services. Trained in the LEAN process, he was excited Rachelle planned to utilize this tool. Rachelle communicated the detailed description of the problem to the vice president, who relayed the information to others on the president's cabinet.

Two weeks prior to the start of the business process improvement work, Rachelle shared the detailed research on the current processes, issues and problems, and specific goals and metrics to those on the team, along with the project timeline as identified in Table 16.1.

To review Case Study 16.3 detailed issues and examples go to **www.HR-higher-ed.com**

Table 16.1 Student employment project timeline

Activity	Due Date	Comments
1. Communicate to the team the problem, goals, timeline, expectations	March 6	
2. Communicate project to all HR staff	March 6	
3. Do research necessary prior to event; prepare "start" facts	March 6	
4. Business process improvement project begins	March 27	Team meets 8am–noon each day
5A. Flowchart and define essential functions of the student work authorization process and the payroll process;	March 27	Vice president charges team
5B. Identify bottlenecks and problem areas for both work authorization and payroll processes		Do not discuss "solutions" on day 1
6. List bottlenecks and problem areas; eliminate "waste" from the process	March 28	
7. Make improvements to process; develop revised process in detail	March 29	
8. Revise process flowchart, forms; develop communication pieces to supervisors; develop timeline to implement	March 30	
9. Identify pilot test participants; develop any training needed; implement timeline for pilot process; determine when evaluation is done on new process	March 31	Offer open forum to other supervisors?
10. Celebrate achievements	March 31	Lunch together?
11. Follow-up evaluation of process changes; determine if goals are met		When conduct the pilot?
		When evaluate the pilot?

Step 5: Empower Action

The project opened with Rachelle's vice president charging the team with improving the student employment process. He confirmed that he supported their work and would "check-in" with Rachelle on their progress during the week.

Step 6: Generate Short-Term Wins

The team met, worked through the business process improvement project, including researching other "best practice" student employment programs at other universities, and recommended de-centralizing the hiring process to give more control and access to those hiring students. The vice president supported this move, as the expected outcomes of the new process more than satisfied the metrics. In addition, the recommendation included those departments hiring the most student employees. Those on the team determined they would comprise the "pilot" group to test the new process.

The HR staff developed and implemented training for the pilot group. Several months later, they interviewed those using the new process, and found the student supervisors were ecstatic about the new process. It more than met the metrics and their needs for hiring student employees. With the support of the vice president, Rachelle and the HR staff decided to expand the new process to the entire campus, to begin with hiring student employees for the fall semester.

Step 7: Consolidate and Continue Change Initiatives

Presentations to all employees who hired and supervised student employees explained the "urgency" for changing the process, details of the business redesign process, the involvement of those hiring many student employees, a description of the new process and how it would benefit them and the student employees, and the training offered during the summer. Members of the initial LEAN team and the pilot group attended the presentations to offer their support of the revised process. Most people hiring students were excited about the change and immediately registered for training.

As the communication plan regarding the change process was implemented, several staff from academic colleges believed they were being "delegated" work that they considered to be "HR work." Their departments hired only several students per year and did not value the new process. A key campus "influencer," a staff member from the college of liberal studies, used her influence with support staff in other academic departments to speak out against being "forced" to take on what they considered to be HR work.

This news reached the dean, who was leaving the university July 1. She used this information to align with the college's support staff against the initiative by scheduling a meeting with all college support staff and department chairs to rally against the HR department. In this meeting, the dean stated the college refused to utilize the new process, and many department chairs and support staff seem to attack Rachelle personally. They did not listen to the facts that showed the new process would save time and give those hiring students more control over the process, with students being able to begin work sooner.

The dean insisted that the revised process not move forward campus-wide. However, because the rest of the campus—other than the academic colleges—had already moved to the new process and felt it offered greater efficiency and effectiveness in hiring student employees, that did not happen. For the next month, while the dean remained in her position, Rachelle was forced to continue with the same process in the academic colleges.

After Rachelle met with the new interim dean, they decided to ask the support staff to designate a team of 6-8 support staff to work with Rachelle to resolve the conflict. Using the "HR frame," Rachelle and the team members reached a compromise. The support staff agreed to take on a portion of the new process, and the HR department would obtain the employment documents from the new student employees.

Step 8: Anchor New Culture

After a year, the revised process was anchored—and valued—in the culture of the entire university, except for the college of liberal studies. Several support staff moved to the new process on their own initiative, whereas 25 staff continued to utilize the compromise process.

Learnings from the Change Initiative

Several problems in how the student employment process first moved to the HR department and then was changed contributed to the inability to anchor the new process in the largest academic college. As a result, the situation became part of the political frame, where the vice president and Rachelle got little support from the academic colleges.

> Several problems in how the student employment process first moved to the HR department and then was changed contributed to the inability to anchor the new process in the largest academic college.

First, when the financial aid office maintained the program, those support staff in the departments hiring student employees completed the initial employment documents. Although there were problems with accurate completion of the documents, instead of bringing the entire process to the HR department—including the employment documents—training for the support staff could have been an alternative. They already completed the documents with the student and forwarded them to the financial aid office. With training, they could continue to complete them and forward them to the HR department. A year later, taking back this piece of the process was an issue with the staff in the academic colleges, who contended it was "HR work."

Second, in building the guiding team, step 2 of the change process, a support staff from one of the academic colleges could have been invited to be on the LEAN team. A perfect team member could have been the support staff considered a key campus influencer by his/her peers.

Third, in step 4 of the change process, communicate for buy-in, initial communication could have been broader to the campus regarding the business process improvement effort.

Fourth, including dollar amounts saved or hours saved by HR staff or student supervisors in the metrics for the plan would have contributed toward the value of the process.

Finally, many support staff in the academic colleges saw this change as just the beginning of decentralization of HR functions without additional resources to them. This became a "strategic campus issue," and should have been addressed in the HR strategic plan.

Case Study Questions

1. *In reading these three case studies, are there any "themes" that thread through each? If so, identify them.*
2. *Can you relate any of these case studies to your own experiences? If so, were any of the change steps missed or minimized?*
3. *Identify what you have learned from these case studies in initiating any change within your department or campus-wide.*

Summary

The fundamental and crucial role of the leader during any change initiative is to ensure that the implementation plan includes the eight-step change process. In the three case studies outlined in the chapter, the method in which the change process emerges either contributes toward the success of the initiative or causes problems for the implementation team.

- Case Study 16.1 fails to infuse major cultural change within the university due to a lack of an integrative vision in the early steps of the project.
- Case Study 16.2 accomplishes culture change, mainly as a result of discovering stakeholder value and following the change process.
- Case Study 16.3 includes challenges that negatively impact the result of the project, which could have been avoided if greater attention had been paid to the change process itself.

Unit Four Summary

In many respects, chapter 16 is a capstone of the activity of this unit. As captured in the graphic below, it describes the activities and accomplishments from the unit, and builds on them to move forward with the HR paradigm shift.

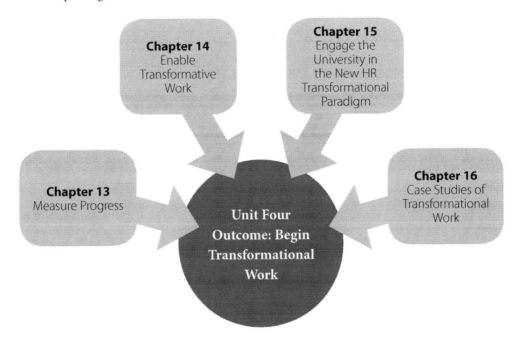

Unit Four model for beginning the transformational work of HR

An important question is, "Where are we in the process of moving the HR function to the strategic level of the university?" As shown in the following model, Unit Four has "set the stage" for transformational change by creating more efficient and effective external HR processes for improved customer value and relationship-building.

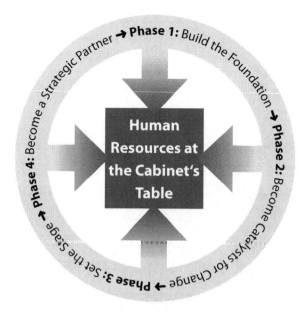

Model for HR transformation within higher education

The transformation of the HR function is changing the perspective of stakeholders in a positive way by the outcomes delivered. In addition, as stakeholder perspectives change, this motivates the HR staff to continue with their transformation. There is a definite alignment of synergy within the university. At this point, although the HR function always may have been considered to be credible, ethical, approachable and knowledgeable, the level of these perspectives increases as relationships are strengthened and built, and the HR staff are considered as adding increased value through innovation and broader thinking. All HR functions and practices are integrated with a unified strategic focus in that the same voice and vision are being projected throughout the university.

We have accomplished the work of these first three phases of the HR paradigm shift, and are ready to move forward to phase 4, described in detail in Unit Five.

Unit Four Outcome Desired: Begin Transformational Work

Chapter 13 Outcome: *Regroup, refine and consolidate gains*

Key Indicators of Success: Check (x) if "yes"

- ☐ Project leaders monitor and measure the progress of their project
- ☐ Project teams revise processes if needed
- ☐ New projects are initiated
- ☐ Leaders emerge from the HR staff
- ☐ Stakeholders recognize new processes that provide value to them
- ☐ HR staff are revitalized to continue with the change initiative
- ☐ Administrators are talking about the success and progress of the change
- ☐ Symbols and/or rituals are in place to remind the HR staff of the change
- ☐ HR staff are motivated to move forward with the change initiative

Chapter 14 Outcome: *Improved structure to enable transformative work*

Key Indicators of Success: Check (x) if "yes"

- ☐ HR Partners are motivated to work with key constituents in transformational ways
- ☐ HR Partners feel they are receiving appropriate training for their transformational role
- ☐ Conflicts within teams are being managed timely and positively
- ☐ Teams are able to determine priorities and progress toward goals
- ☐ The urgency for change continues to be a motivation for moving forward with the work
- ☐ People are being rewarded and compensated for being instrumental in the progress of the change initiative
- ☐ HR staff continue to be trained on their transformational role
- ☐ New projects and initiatives are introduced
- ☐ Additional "leaders" emerge from the HR staff
- ☐ Reward and recognition structures are changed to be aligned with the change initiative
- ☐ All initiatives seem to be well coordinated

Chapter 15 Outcome: Engage key constituents

Key Indicators of Success: Check (x) if "yes"

- [ ] People are inspired to join existing teams
- [ ] People bring issues to members of the HR Collaboration Team or HR Partners
- [ ] HR function has an improved knowledge of what is valued by constituents
- [ ] Increased campus discussions and dialogue around the topic of transformational HR
- [ ] HR staff are requested to give updates on the new HR paradigm to campus groups or departments
- [ ] Success stories by supervisors and others are being repeated
- [ ] Constituents provide feedback and success stories without being asked
- [ ] Increased advocacy for the new HR transformational paradigm
- [ ] Open positions in the HR department bring increased applications by people with the needed transformative skills
- [ ] Supervisors can express to their department members how the new HR paradigm impacts them in positive ways
- [ ] Faculty and staff understand the differences between transformative and transactional work
- [ ] More interest among employees and supervisors to address and resolve issues, as they feel supported by the HR function

Chapter 16 Outcome: Understand transformational work

Key Indicators of Success: Check (x) if "yes"

- [ ] Understanding that the eight-step change process is crucial for successful transformational work

Unit Five

Become a Strategic Partner

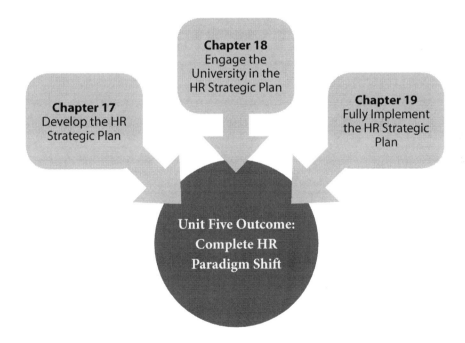

Chapter 18
Engage the University in the HR Strategic Plan

Chapter 17
Develop the HR Strategic Plan

Chapter 19
Fully Implement the HR Strategic Plan

Unit Five Outcome:
Complete HR Paradigm Shift

Unit Five model for completing the HR paradigm shift

In Unit Four, HR staff members reached outside the HR department to begin working in transformational ways with other campus constituents first to improve processes for efficiency and effectiveness, and then to serve in roles such as a strategic partner, organizational design specialist and leader to contribute toward a renewed and stronger university. Setting the stage in Unit Four allows us to become a strategic partner in Unit Five to develop and align the HR strategic plan with that of the university.

The outcome of Unit Five is the completion of the HR paradigm shift to a transformative culture. Where are we in the eight-step change process as described by John Kotter? Regarding the HR department and its staff members, we are at step seven—sustaining action toward building a solid foundation for the new transformational culture.

The chapters in Unit Five take us through change steps seven and eight, resulting in a changed culture where new behaviors are woven into the fabric of the HR department. In addition, campus stakeholders perceive the transformed culture, and collaborate with the HR staff to address and resolve issues confronting the university.

Although the work of these three chapters comprise the process for HR to become a strategic partner, we understand that your university culture and situation may be different. Therefore, you may advocate for a process that is similar, but less comprehensive. Knowing this, we identify seven essential steps that we feel *MUST* be included in order for the HR paradigm shift to integrate into the HR department culture. The following graphic outlines these steps—named "*Must Do steps*"— explored in more detail throughout Unit Five.

"Must Do Steps" to Complete HR Paradigm Shift

1. Review HR function
2. Assess external environment
3. Develop draft HR strategic plan to include SWOT
4. Align HR strategic plan with university plan
5. Develop metrics to evaluate plan
6. Obtain input from campus stakeholders
7. Involve stakeholders in action plan

"Must Do steps" in completing the HR paradigm shift

Chapter 17

Develop the Human Resources Strategic Plan

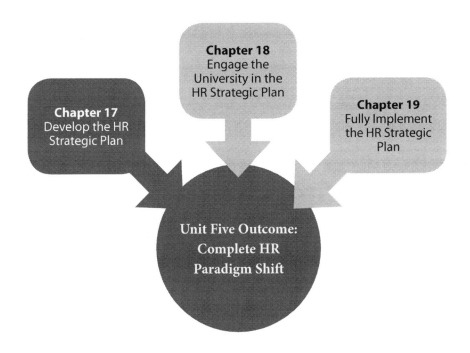

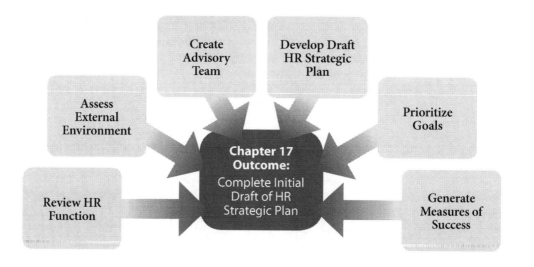

Figure 17.1 Model to complete the initial draft of the HR strategic plan

Case Study 17.1

Throughout Unit Five, we use the case study of Lisa, the HR director at National University, a medium-sized Ph.D. granting institution with approximately 15,000 students. A year ago, the current president facilitated a university-wide conversation to revise the mission statement, vision statement, core values, and strategic directions.

Since then, each academic college and major division developed its own mission and vision statements, core values and goals, and aligned them with those of the university. The president announced that the development of the following seven key operational plans comprises the university's next step in strategic planning:

1. *Academic program and student outcome plan*
2. *Enrollment management and student support plan*
3. *HR strategic plan*
4. *Facilities master plan*
5. *Information technology plan*
6. *Finance and budget plan*
7. *Advancement and relationship development plan*

Although Lisa had never developed a strategic plan, she was excited about the prospect of doing so. After attending a national conference regarding moving the HR function to the strategic level of the university, Lisa had worked with the HR staff to move to a transformative culture. She felt the HR staff were ready to move to this next phase of the new HR paradigm.

Lisa, James (the assistant director of HR responsible for equity, affirmative action, and staffing) and William (the associate vice president for academic affairs) formed the HR Collaboration Team to lead the establishment of the HR Strategic Plan. Lisa agreed to be the team leader. They first researched templates for a plan, resulting in the sample HR strategic plan template shown in Exhibit 17.1.

Exhibit 17.1: Sample HR strategic plan template

1. Executive Summary
2. Introduction and Vision for Change
3. HR Mission, Vision, Core Values
4. Environmental Scan/Forecast
   Demographics
   Technology
   Legal and Political
   Economy
   Labor Market
5. Internal Assessment
   Recruitment and Retention
   Equal Employment Opportunity and Affirmative Action
   Harassment and Discrimination Claims
   Promotions and Retirements
   Occupational Safety and Health Statistics
   Professional Development
6. Planning Assumptions
7. Overview of HR Function Services
   Staffing and Recruitment
   Job Assignment and Work Flow
   Promotion, Compensation, and Performance Support Policies
   Training and Development
   Labor Relations
   Diversity
8. HR Strategic Plan Goals and Recommended Action Steps

Review HR Function #1 Must Do

To understand the strengths and weaknesses of a university's HR function, the first step is to examine its policies, procedures, documentation, systems, and practices. The goal is not to point fingers, but to focus on analyzing and improving the HR function in order to support the university's mission and vision.

Who should conduct the review? Members of the HR Collaboration Team should lead this initial review: the HR director, the person responsible for the equity and affirmative action function, and the person from the provost and vice president's office responsible for HR functions. Other staff members within these offices definitely can participate as team members or in the gathering of data.

> To understand the strengths and weaknesses of a university's HR function, the first step is to examine its policies, procedures, documentation, systems, and practices.

The review includes research comprising the ten primary components of the HR function identified in Exhibit 17.2, with other categories added as needed.

Exhibit 17.2 HR function components to review

HR function review
→ *Mission, Vision, Culture*
→ *Leadership and Structure*
→ *Staffing and Recruitment*
→ *Job Assignment and Work Flow*
→ *Compensation and Benefits*
→ *Performance Management*
→ *Employee Development*
→ *Employee Relations*
→ *Diversity*
→ *Legal and Safety Issues*

Sample questions to help collect pertinent information for the ten components are included in the chapter 17 information on the website. Answering these questions will help to identify gaps in service or HR service(s) to improve. The focus is on the performance of each activity. Exhibit 17.3 includes a sample of these questions for the "staffing and recruitment" function.

1. *How many current employees do we have?*
2. *How many employees have supervisory responsibilities?*
3. *Have issues occurred related to classification of employees?*
4. *What are some of our future needs for staffing?*
5. *What are the procedures for hiring?*
6. *Does our university have a recruitment or employment "brand"?*
7. *What recruitment sources are used?*

To review sample questions for chapter 17 HR function review go to **www.HR-higher-ed.com**

Assess External Environment #2 Must Do

Factors in the external environment that may impact the university and the HR function must be defined and analyzed. We need to identify any external threats and opportunities that might influence the HR function or the university in successfully accomplishing its vision and mission. Examples of external forces that need to be researched and assessed include:

1. changing laws and regulations
2. changing demographics
3. changing economic conditions
4. political environment
5. technology innovations
6. competition

> Factors in the external environment that may impact the university and the HR function must be defined and analyzed.

Back to Case Study 17.1

> *Because most of the HR staff were inun-*
> *dated with work implementing a new module of the HRS, the HR Collaboration Team*
> *decided to split the gathering of internal HR function and external environment data*
> *among them. Lisa delegated much of the data collection around employee demograph-*
> *ics to the institutional research person in the HR department.*

Create Advisory Team

Lisa, William, and James decided to create an advisory team to provide input to the strategic plan from campus stakeholders. These individuals represented a cross section of the university's faculty and staff, and included middle and upper management and those responsible for HR functions. Using these criteria, the following positions were included on an advisory team of 10-12 members:

1. one academic dean
2. the staffing person in residence life
3. the dean's administrative assistant in the College of Arts and Sciences
4. a custodial or grounds supervisor
5. several faculty with knowledge of or experience in HR functions
6. an academic department chair
7. a director of a major administrative department
8. an ad hoc instructional staff member
9. a support or administrative staff member

Ten individuals across the campus agreed to participate as an HR Advisory Team member to accomplish the charge outlined in Exhibit 17.4. Lisa indicated a draft plan for the team to review could be ready within a few weeks.

Exhibit 17.4 HR Advisory Team charge

1. Oversee the development and implementation of the goals in the HR Strategic Plan
2. Involve the campus community in the improvement and implementation of the goals in the plan
3. Assist with the development of metrics to evaluate the outcomes of the goals in the plan
4. Provide advice and feedback on implementation of the goals in the plan
5. Evaluate the effectiveness of the implementation of the goals in the plan

Develop Draft HR Strategic Plan #3 Must Do

Notice in Exhibit 17.4 that the charge to the HR Advisory Team is NOT to "develop" the draft strategic plan or "gather" the data, but to "assist, oversee, provide and evaluate." It is the role of the HR function to gather data, research potential plan templates, draft an initial plan, and then bring that draft plan to the HR Advisory Team for their review and recommendations for changes.

Back to Case Study 17.1

> *After gathering the relevant information and data, Lisa, William, and James organized it into the categories identified in the sample HR strategic plan template shown in Exhibit 17.1 earlier in this chapter, and reviewed each major section according to the following:*
> - *noting differences between what we say we do and what we actually do*
> - *identifying gaps in service and/or issues with current services*
> - *determining strengths and weaknesses of the HR function*
> - *establishing external threats and opportunities*
>
> *Exhibit 17.5 displays the overview of strengths, weaknesses, opportunities and threats chart that resulted from this part of the discussion. Each rationale statement in the chart linked to data resulting from the assessment of the internal and external environments. They then drafted an initial HR strategic plan with draft goals based on identified gaps in service, improvements needed, and opportunities presented, and sent it to the HR Advisory Team members for their review several weeks prior to their first meeting. Exhibit 17.6 lists the goals recommended by the HR Collaboration Team (Lisa, William, James).*

Prioritize Goals

> *Over a period of several meetings, the HR Advisory Team discussed each section of the plan. Many members expressed surprise by the demographic data and number of retirements of faculty and staff expected over the next five years. Team members requested additional data for several sections of the plan. Because the charge to the HR Advisory Team included providing advice on implementing goals in the HR strategic plan, the next step was to prioritize the eight goals.*
>
> *After several meetings, HR Advisory Team members agreed to eliminate several goals, put one "on hold," and utilize the process identified in #3 below to prioritize the remaining goals.*

Exhibit 17.5 Overview of strengths, weaknesses, opportunities and threats

STRENGTHS

Training and support for recruitments

Salary equity processes

Promotion and classification change processes

Leadership programs for support and administrative staff

Mediation team to resolve conflict

Broad involvement on university wide teams

Increased numbers of female faculty

Mentoring programs for new faculty

Workshops on uses of technology in instruction

Implementation of HR Collaboration Team

Support of cabinet for HR paradigm shift

Improved processes for FMLA leave and "stop-the-tenure-clock"

WEAKNESSES

Lack of a university staffing plan

Wellness programs offered, but not integrated

Weak position descriptions

Weak performance evaluation processes

Supervisors need training to deal with performance issues of staff reporting to them

Onboarding for new faculty and staff

Work-life balance issues

Training for department chairs

Low number of faculty and staff of color

Lengthy and confusing recruitment processes

Knowledge of candidate evaluation and selection processes

Lack of university employee core competencies

Career progression opportunities

OPPORTUNITIES

Emerging technology for new HR systems

Increased stakeholder engagement with HR

Many HR staff value continued professional development

Cabinet interested in developing recruitment and leadership brands

Retirements in HR

HR vision, mission and goals aligned with that of the institution

Faculty, staff and administrative retirements

THREATS

Demand for increased accountability

Reduced budgets

Pressure to reduce costs

Less time for transformative work

Changing workforce demographics

Stakeholders demand deliverables that are valued

High number of employee injuries

Reduction in retention of high performing faculty and staff

Exhibit 17.6 HR strategic plan goals recommended by HR Collaboration Team

1. Develop a performance support plan for all employees of the university
2. Develop a university-wide recruitment and staffing program, with a university recruitment brand
3. Develop a career development and succession program, with a university leadership brand
4. Develop a university satisfaction survey to assess employee satisfaction with various aspects of their employment and guide HR policy decisions
5. Improve new employee onboarding
6. Improve renewal and promotion processes
7. Develop an integrated employee wellness program
8. Increase the diversity of faculty and staff in candidate pools

1. **Eliminate the following goals from the plan:**
   a. Goal #6: Improve renewal and promotion processes; they learned the governance groups have decided to work on this goal.
   b. Goal #7: Develop an integrated employee wellness program; the vice president of administration charged the HR department to integrate the campus components of this program to create an "umbrella" campus wellness team and program.

2. **Put "on hold" the following goal from the plan:**
   a. Goal #4: Develop a university satisfaction survey to assess employee satisfaction with various aspects of their employment and guide HR policy decisions; team members felt this survey could be conducted several years into the future.

3. **Follow the steps outlined below to prioritize the remaining five goals**
   a. Of the remaining five goals, the HR Advisory Team members determined they comprised two HR functional service areas, and combined them accordingly into the two major goals of staffing and development.
   b. The HR Advisory Team identified 19 sub-goals for these two major goals of staffing and development, delineated in Exhibit 17.7.
   c. Knowing they needed to prioritize the sub-goals in order to provide for "quick-wins," the HR Advisory Team determined that two variables— "resources needed" to accomplish the sub-goal, and the amount of "impact to the university in the short-term (1-3 years)" if the goal is accomplished—

Exhibit 17.7 Sub-goals for HR strategic plan goals

Goal #1: Staffing

1. Improve match between candidate pool and college and university needs.

2. Increase the diversity of applicants for faculty and ad-hoc instructional staff positions.

3. Improve match between candidate pool and department and university needs, goals and preferences for administrative staff.

4. Increase the diversity of applicants for administrative staff positions.

5. Increase efficiency in the recruitment process for administrative staff.

6. Create greater transparency and speed in the hiring process of support staff.

7. Increase the diversity of applicants for support staff positions.

8. Improve selection processes to optimize performance and commitment outcomes.

9. Decrease spending due to worker's compensation claims.

10. Increase efficiency in the appointment process for administrative staff.

11. Support the acclimation of new employees to their professional and social environment at the campus and department/unit levels.

Goal #2: Development

1. Improve supervisors', department chairs', and "line" managers' ability to create conditions that motivate employees, set goals for themselves and their employees, and complete performance evaluation of the employees they manage or supervise.

2. Support the creation of development plans for all employees, recognizing that faculty and instructional academic staff have different responsibilities than administrative and support staff.

3. Support the development and implementation of a career progression plan, recognizing that faculty and ad-hoc instructional staff have different responsibilities than administrative and support staff.

4. Ensure that flexibility in career tracks meets the needs of each employee group.

5. Offer leadership development training for individuals currently in leadership positions or seeking to enter leadership positions.

6. Offer training to increase appreciation and value of diversity of all types among all employee groups.

7. Offer continuous skill attainment, development and knowledge training for administrators, department chairs, team leaders, and supervisors.

8. Develop succession planning strategies for identifying and developing well-qualified employees, supervisors and administrators.

were important in the prioritization process. Resources needed for each sub-goal included money, time, people, space, materials, the university image, and training. The "impact" on the university in the first one to three years of the plan's implementation included the number of people impacted, *goodwill, publicity, improved education, improved governance, long-term employment, money, and improved atmosphere and climate.*

Although it took several meetings to work through the process of prioritizing the 19 sub-goals in the HR strategic plan, the HR Advisory Team members felt the process helped immensely to determine their next steps. As summarized in Exhibit 17.8, they then agreed to implement two goals and ten sub-goals during the first three years. They planned to review the remaining sub-goals in three years.

Exhibit 17.8 Prioritized goals and sub-goals to accomplish over 1–3 years

---

Goal #1: Staffing: to develop leading practices in the recruitment and retention of outstanding faculty, staff and administrators
1.   Create greater transparency and speed in the hiring process for support staff.
2.   Increase efficiency in the recruitment process for administrative staff and faculty.
3.   Improve selection processes to optimize performance and commitment outcomes.
4.   Decrease spending due to workers' compensation claims.
5.   Support the acclimation of new employees to their professional and social environment at the campus and department/unit levels.

Goal #2: Development: to develop leading practices in the development of faculty, staff and administrators to allow for employee mobility and succession planning
1.   Improve supervisors', department chairs', and "line" managers' ability to create conditions that motivate employees, set goals for themselves and their employees, and complete performance evaluation of the employees they manage or supervise.
2.   Support the creation of development plans for all employees, recognizing that faculty and ad-hoc instructional staff members have different responsibilities than administrative and support staff.
3.   Offer leadership development training for individuals currently in leadership positions or seeking to enter leadership positions.
4.   Offer continuous skill attainment, development and knowledge training for administrators, department chairs, team leaders, and supervisors.
5.   Ensure that flexibility in career tracks meets the needs of each employee group.

Generate Measures of Success

Goals are implemented all the time with successful outcomes. However, determining "in advance" of implementation how we plan to measure the outcome of a goal definitely contributes toward improving the credibility of the HR function in the eyes of stakeholders. In addition, having a sound measurement system improves decision-making by helping to focus on aspects of the HR function that create value, providing for the ability to make proactive rather than reactive decisions, and presenting a valid and systematic justification for allocating scarce university resources.

For each strategic goal in the HR strategic plan, we need to accomplish the following:

1. align the HR strategic plan goals with the university plan
2. develop metrics to evaluate each goal
3. identify barriers to achieving each goal

Align HR Strategic Plan with University Plan #4 Must Do

Back to Case Study 17.1

> *With the prioritization of the initial draft goals completed by the HR Advisory Team, Lisa, William, and James prepared to present the draft HR strategic plan to the cabinet. However, they knew the president expected that the goals in the HR strategic plan align with the university's strategic plan. In reviewing the university's strategic plan, which includes the components of university mission, vision, core values, and strategic directions, the HR Advisory Team felt the areas outlined in Exhibit 17.9 were those with which the HR strategic plan aligns.*

Develop Metrics to Evaluate Plan #5 Must Do

How can we measure the value of the strategic contribution of the HR strategic plan goals to senior managers, supervisors, middle managers, faculty, and staff? Metrics, standard measures to assess performance in a particular area, focus on an organization's ability to meet stakeholder needs and strategic objectives. In our case with the HR strategic plan goals, another term for metrics is "strategic HR deliverables," or those outcomes that accomplish the university's strategy.

STEPS TO MEASURE PROGRESS

- Step 1: Develop goals
- Step 2: Define the metrics for each goal
- Step 3: Assess current status of the metric
- Step 4: Develop a monitoring system for the metrics
- Step 5: Communicate metrics
- Step 6: Review metrics

Exhibit 17.9 HR strategic plan alignment with university strategic plan

Abridged Select Mission: "*Fostering the scholarly activities of faculty, students, and staff related to teaching, research, intellectual activities, creative expression, and service.*"

Vision: "*Enrichment and Leadership that emphasizes intellectual, civic, ethical, and personal development for students, faculty and staff.*"

Core Values:
- *Knowledge and continuous learning*
- *Quality and achievement*
- *Diversity and inclusivity*
- *Freedom and responsibility*

Strategic Directions:
1. *Promote representative leadership, responsive shared governance, and flexible resource stewardship*
2. *Develop a diverse, engaged community of lifelong learners and collaborative scholars*
3. *Foster research, intellectual activity, and creative expression*

Back to Case Study 17.1

    Step 1: *Develop goals. The HR Advisory Team completed the process of prioritizing the HR strategic goals, with the result of two major goals and ten sub-goals. In order to work through the process of measuring the success of a goal, we use the staffing goal "to develop leading practices in the recruitment and retention of outstanding faculty, staff, and administrators."*

    Step 2: *Define the metrics for each goal. Metrics need to help us track our progress to success. Examples of potential metrics or strategic HR deliverables for the staffing goal in our case study include the following:*

1. *attract and retain key faculty, staff and administrators*
2. *performance of newly hired applicants*
3. *extent to which required employee competencies are reflected in recruiting, staffing and performance management*
4. *percentage of high-performing key employees retained in the first three years*
5. *offer acceptance rate*
6. *amount of time to recruit and hire*
7. *success rates of external hires*
8. *number of workers' compensation claims*

How do we choose metrics, how many, and how do we know they are the right ones? Metrics should tell a story and relate to weaknesses or gaps. We chose the staffing goal as an HR strategic goal primarily due to the following weaknesses, gaps, or opportunities identified in the data gathering process:

- *lack of effective onboarding program for new faculty and staff*
- *weak position descriptions*
- *weak performance evaluation processes*
- *supervisors need training to deal with performance issues of staff reporting to them*
- *lengthy and confusing recruitment processes*
- *poor knowledge of candidate evaluation and selection processes*
- *lack of university employee core competencies*
- *high workers' compensation claims*
- *lack of career progression opportunities*
- *future faculty and staff retirements*

It is best to choose only a few metrics for each goal, as this helps to focus employees' actions and increases the opportunity for success. The HR Advisory Team chose the following metrics for the staffing goal:

1. *percentage of high-performing key employees retained in the first three years*
2. *extent to which required employee competencies are reflected in recruiting, staffing and performance management*
3. *amount of time to recruit and hire*
4. *number of workers' compensation claims*

> It is best to choose only a few metrics for each goal, as this helps to focus employees' actions and increases the opportunity for success.

Step 3: *Assess the current status of the metric. The data for metrics #1, #3, and #4 were available for the past five years. For metric #2, although the HR department determined employee core competencies for the HR staff, this process had not been developed at the university level.*

Step 4: *Develop a monitoring system for the metrics. The data for metrics #1, #3, and #4 were available through the HRS. Lisa determined that the HR managers would be responsible for accessing this data twice each year, in January and July. For metric #2, the HR managers would be responsible for gathering this data from recruitment and performance evaluation paperwork through the HRS after an integrated core competency framework has been implemented university-wide.*

Step 5: *Communicate metrics. Lisa, James, and William communicated the metrics to all HR staff by telling the "story" of weaknesses or gaps in services discovered during their research, the development of the HR strategic goals, and choosing relevant metrics to measure the success of these goals. The metrics would be communicated to the university community through the vetting of the HR strategic plan.*

Step 6: *Review metrics. Lisa, James, and William decided to review the metrics twice each year, and modify them for potential improvement. During the evaluation process, if the goal priorities changed, they planned to modify the metrics accordingly.*

Identify Barriers to Achieving Each Goal

It was determined that each strategic goal in the HR strategic plan aligned with the strategic goals of the university, and a plan was in place to measure progress toward the goal. It is extremely beneficial to determine, in advance of implementation of the strategic plan, any potential barriers to achieving the goals. Lisa, William, and James took this topic to the HR Advisory Team for their input. Exhibit 17.10 identifies several potential barriers for the staffing goal. Each potential barrier needs an action plan to address it proactively in advance.

Each potential barrier needs an action plan to address it proactively in advance.

Exhibit 17.10 Potential barriers to achieving the staffing goal in the HR strategic plan

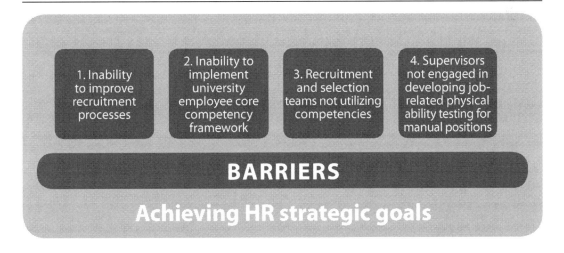

1. Inability to improve recruitment processes

2. Inability to implement university employee core competency framework

3. Recruitment and selection teams not utilizing competencies

4. Supervisors not engaged in developing job-related physical ability testing for manual positions

BARRIERS

Achieving HR strategic goals

The same process outlined for the staffing goal was utilized to measure the progress of the development goal.

Lisa, William and James believed that the plan was ready to present to their supervisors—the provost and vice president for academic affairs and the vice president for administration—and then to the entire president's cabinet for their review prior to obtaining additional input from the campus community.

To review Case Study 17.1 HR strategic plan go to **www.HR-higher-ed.com**

Case Study Questions

1. Other than asking the institutional research person to obtain demographic data for the HR strategic plan, Lisa, James, and William did not involve other HR staff members in developing the draft plan. What are the advantages and disadvantages of this decision?

2. What are the advantages of involving an HR Advisory Team at this point in the process?

3. What are potential metrics for the development strategic goal? Identify barriers to accomplishing the metric(s).

4. How can the efficiency and effectiveness of the process used in this chapter be improved?

To review discussion of recommendations for Case Study 17.1 questions go to **www.HR-higher-ed.com**

Summary

A model to complete the initial draft of the HR strategic plan includes the following components: review HR function, assess external environment, create an advisory team, develop a draft strategic plan, prioritize the goals, and generate measures of success.

Although the culture of each institution and its HR function may have differences, seven steps in the process of completing the HR strategic plan are essential. Those discussed in this chapter encompass reviewing the HR function; assessing the external environment; developing a draft strategic plan to include strengths, weaknesses, opportunities and threats; aligning the HR strategic plan with the university plan; and developing metrics to evaluate the plan.

Goals are implemented all the time with successful outcomes. However, determining "in advance" of implementation how we plan to measure the outcome of a goal definitely contributes toward improving the credibility of the HR function by stakeholders. In addition, having a sound measurement system improves decision-making by helping to focus on aspects of the HR function that create value, provide for the ability to make proactive rather than reactive decisions, and provide a valid and systematic justification for allocating scarce university resources. For each strategic goal in the HR strategic plan, we need to accomplish the following: Align the HR strategic plan goals with the university plan; Develop metrics to evaluate each goal; and Identify barriers to achieving each goal.

Evaluation of "Your" HR Department's Chapter 17 Outcome

Outcome Desired: Completion of initial draft of HR strategic plan

Change: Sustain action in the HR paradigm shift (change step 7)

Key Indicators of Success: (check if *"yes"*)

- [ ] Key components of the HR function are reviewed and relevant data collected
- [ ] Factors in the external environment are assessed
- [ ] HR staff are willing and able to tackle substantial campus-wide changes
- [ ] The process to develop the HR strategic plan reinvigorates the HR staff members
- [ ] HR staff feel a sense of accomplishment and excitement about the HR plan
- [ ] Key campus constituents provide advice and input to the HR plan
- [ ] A SWOT analysis is part of the draft HR strategic plan
- [ ] HR strategic goals are aligned with those of the university
- [ ] At least one metric is chosen to evaluate the successful outcome of each goal
- [ ] Potential barriers to accomplishing the strategic goals are identified
- [ ] An HR Advisory Team provides feedback and input to the draft HR strategic plan prior to it being vetted by all stakeholders

Potential Barriers to Change: (check if *"needs attention"*)

- [ ] Difficulty in obtaining advice and input to the HR plan from key campus constituents
- [ ] Not involving the HR staff in gathering and analyzing data
- [ ] Not including the equity and affirmative action or provost HR functions in the process of developing the plan
- [ ] Not doing a thorough and objective analysis of the HR functional areas
- [ ] Not doing a thorough and objective analysis of the external environment
- [ ] Not doing a thorough and objective analysis of the strengths, weaknesses, threats and opportunities facing the HR function and the university
- [ ] The HR strategic plan goals are not aligned with those of the university
- [ ] Metrics are not identified to determine the successful outcome of each goal

Engage the University in the Human Resources Strategic Plan

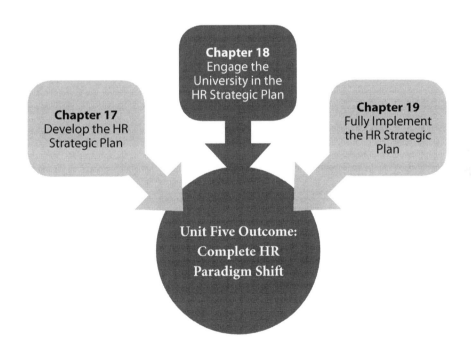

Chapter 18 Engage the university in the HR strategic plan

Unit Four involved the HR staff beginning to work externally with campus constituents on transformational work; Unit Five expands that work to a broader and more strategic level. Key constituents are immersed in analyzing the HR function and the external environment. They are involved in determining key strengths and weaknesses of the HR function, and threats and opportunities facing both the university and the HR function.

As a result, they begin to perceive the HR function, and its staff, differently. They are inspired to consider a changed university culture, one where individuals can work collaboratively to address and resolve issues and problems. To accomplish the outcome desired in this chapter, we MUST engage the support and input of the broad university community. Therefore, that is the outcome of this chapter.

The three chapters in this unit comprise the process that is necessary for the HR function to become a strategic partner. However, knowing there are varying university cultures, these are steps that MUST be included in order for the HR paradigm shift to integrate with the HR department culture. As a reference, Figure 18.1 repeats these steps.

"Must Do Steps" to Complete HR Paradigm Shift

1. Review HR function
2. Assess external environment
3. Develop draft HR strategic plan to include SWOT
4. Align HR strategic plan with university plan
5. Develop metrics to evaluate plan
6. Obtain input from campus stakeholders
7. Involve stakeholders in action plan

Figure 18.1 Steps that must be included to complete the HR paradigm shift

As summarized in Figure 18.2, the outcome of chapter 18 is the engagement of the university community in the HR strategic plan.

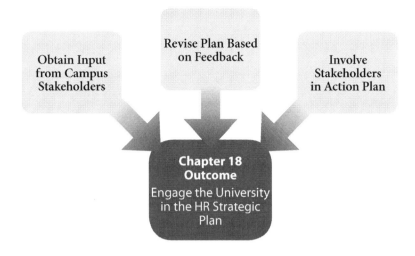

Figure 18.2 Model to engage the university community in the HR strategic plan

Obtain Input from Campus Stakeholders #6 Must Do

Although you may not feel it is necessary to bring together an HR Advisory Team to provide input to the draft HR strategic plan as outlined in chapter 17, there must be other methods to involve your campus constituents. In our case study, Lisa was fortunate that her university president called for the development of seven key operational plans, of which the HR strategic plan was one. This allowed for the vetting of all plans by faculty and staff simultaneously and through the same processes, and could include:

1. offering focus group sessions led by the president, vice presidents or leaders of each plan
2. presenting to governance groups, academic colleges or university-wide committees
3. placing the draft plans on a campus-wide bulletin board where they are accessible and feedback can be given easily
4. utilizing the transition monitoring team approach as discussed earlier in this book
5. holding one-on-one interviews with key constituents

Lisa felt that having seven university key operational plans available for the university community to review implied receiving more feedback on the HR strategic plan. However, with seven plans to read and evaluate, fewer people may choose to read the HR plan instead of another plan. In this case, perhaps the availability of the plans could be staggered over several months to allow more people to review the HR plan.

> The campus needs to see that top administration has determined that the HR strategic plan is a priority.

Regardless of the presence of other key operational strategic plans, the methods used to obtain feedback from stakeholders can include all those identified above. It is vitally important that the vice president of the HR function and the university president be involved in any or all of these communication methods. The campus needs to see that top administration has determined that the HR strategic plan is a priority.

Stakeholder Input on Current HR Programs

Obtaining the input of stakeholders regarding current HR deliverables—especially in an environment of scarce resources—is crucial. Whether or not this is an outcome of the work in chapter 7, the timing depends on your specific situation.

> Obtaining the input of stakeholders regarding current HR deliverables—especially in an environment of scarce resources—is crucial.

In their article, "Doing Less With Less," Vaillancourt and Brantley (2009) present a model to engage stakeholders in conversations to help evaluate the value and long-term impact of HR deliverables. The value of this process includes reducing the need for transactional HR work and freeing time for HR professionals to focus on transformational work.

Although you may consider making changes to this model based on your institution's culture and situation, following are the critical steps to use as part of engaging the university community to determine stakeholder value for the HR function (chapter 7) or the HR strategic plan (chapter 18).

STEPS TO OBTAIN THE INPUT OF STAKEHOLDERS REGARDING CURRENT HR DELIVERABLES

Step1: Review the institution's strategy, goals, performance measures and values that define its direction. Include what you have learned from conversations with stakeholders.

Step 2: With stakeholders and members of the HR Advisory Team, review existing HR deliverables with their ability to contribute toward accomplishing the institution's strategy and goals.

Step 3: As recommended by Vaillancourt and Brantley (2009), with stakeholder input place each deliverable into one of several "buckets." Their "four buckets" included the following: (1) strategic—can we grow a deliverable; (2) core—can we protect a deliverable; (3) requisite—can we out-

source or minimize a deliverable; and (4) non-core—can we discontinue a deliverable.

Step 4: **As the HR leader, recommend to your vice president to: (1) eliminate specific programs and deliverables with little or no stakeholder value and/or contribution toward university strategy; (2) change specific current services to align with stakeholder value and university strategy.**

Throughout this chapter, we continue to follow the case study of Lisa, the HR director at National University, a medium-sized Ph.D. granting institution with approximately 15,000 students.

Case Study 18.1

We left Lisa, William and James at the point where they had submitted their draft HR strategic plan to the provost and vice president of academic affairs and the vice president of administration for their review. Both were highly satisfied with the team's work, and asked Lisa, William and James to present key points to the cabinet during their next weekly meeting. Lisa had never attended a cabinet meeting, and she was excited about discussing the process they had used and the input of the HR Advisory Team.

The cabinet members were very impressed that an advisory team was involved in the process of improving the plan and agreeing on its goals. They decided to take three key operational plans—the information technology plan, the advancement and relationship development plan, and the HR support and development plan—to the campus for their input.

They planned to utilize a campus-wide bulletin board as the method to access the plans, to include the ability for faculty and staff to easily provide recommendations for improvements to each plan. Because the president had developed regular communication meetings with the governance groups, this topic was placed on those next agendas.

Focus group sessions over two weeks allowed faculty and staff to attend in person to provide input. All focus groups and presentations were planned no earlier than two weeks after the plans were available on the bulletin board site. Lisa, William and James participated in all presentations and focus groups. Lisa communicated with all HR Advisory Team members, who agreed to urge their constituents to become involved.

Lisa, William and James determined that one method to obtain feedback on the HR strategic plan goals was to meet with key constituents throughout the university for 30-minute interviews. This entailed a large personal time commitment, but they felt potential outcomes included higher quality feedback and increased engagement with stakeholders. They developed the 11 questions summarized in Exhibit 18.1, and chose 50 key constituents to include faculty, staff and administrators that represented all units throughout the university.

Shortly after the president notified the university community about the vetting process for the three key operational plans, Lisa sent an email to the 50 people identified for one-on-one interviews, giving the rationale for meeting, the list of questions, and the times available to meet. Subsequently, all 50 individuals agreed to meet.

Exhibit 18.1 One-on-one interview questions:

1. *What are the most critical current workforce issues in your department, college, or division?*
2. *Which HR strategic plan goals strike you as particularly important for your department, college or division? What about that goal or those goals make it/them most important for you?*
3. *Do you feel the key goals and objectives of your department, division, or college align with the goals listed? Are there additional goals you would like to see included that better serve you?*
4. *What barriers exist for you and/or other staff in your department/college/division in achieving your goals?*
5. *Do you have any suggestions for reducing these barriers?*
6. *What are the required knowledge, skills and abilities needed from the faculty, administrative staff, and support staff in your department/college/division in order to achieve your goals?*
7. *When you consider issues of staffing in your department, college or division in the next 5-10 years, what issues concern you the most? Are they issues of staff turnover, leadership development, skill attainment and/or refinement, some combination of these, or something else?*
8. *What skills or positions will no longer be needed in 3-5 years in your department, college or division?*
9. *Are there any changes that need to be made to recruitment policies to make processes more efficient and effective?*
10. *Training offered in _____ likely would prompt you to participate or to encourage faculty and/or staff in your area to participate.*
11. *Training offered in _____ likely would prompt you to encourage department chairs or potential department chairs in your area to participate.*

Due to offering multiple methods for providing input to any or all of the three plans, increased numbers of faculty and staff responded with recommendations to improve the HR Strategic Plan. Lisa, James and William found that their one-on-one interviews provided the most relevant and detailed feedback. Input from the campus community contained four major themes regarding the HR Strategic Plan:

1. *Coordination between the provost and vice president for academic affairs'*
   office and the HR department is critical, especially in collaborating in the
   development and provision of staff development and training activities, and in
   enhancing employee relations.
2. *The HR department and the provost's office must become more proactive and*
   developmentally oriented—leadership development must be a priority.
3. *Several HR functions remain at the departmental level, e.g., recruitment and*
   selection, etc., and the HR department serves as a resource or "consultant."
   Supervisors and department chairs need to understand HR management and
   see themselves as HR managers.
4. *The university needs to recruit and retain a more diverse faculty and staff.*

Revise Plan Based on Feedback

After we obtain input from the campus community on the HR strategic plan, the next step comprises revision of the plan based on that feedback. Kotter's eight-step process for leading successful change comes into play in two ways at this point. First, the HR department and its staff are in the seventh and eighth steps of the change process—implementing and sustaining change at the HR department level.

Second, the university is experiencing change in how it perceives the HR function as transformational in addition to transactional. University constituents work on teams brought together by HR staff to improve policies and procedures, confront and resolve issues important to faculty and staff, and work with supervisors and managers to restructure their department or unit. Faculty and staff engage as members of an HR Advisory Team, providing input to the HR strategic plan. HR staff reach out to the entire campus in multiple ways to engage stakeholders in the HR strategic plan.

> The first four steps in the change process create a climate for change and enable the entire university to participate in the change…

The first four steps in the change process create a climate for change and enable the entire university to participate in the change, as outlined in Exhibit 18.2.

Therefore, the next step in the university change process is to enable action by providing the opportunity to create short-term wins—to revise the goals in the plan according to stakeholder feedback, and to determine which goals to implement in the short-term based on those with the most attention and engagement by stakeholders.

Change Step 1—Increase urgency: The data in the HR strategic plan provide the rationale and urgency for change.

Change Step 2—Build guiding teams: The HR Advisory Team is the first team to engage with change. Others will be designed around goals in the final HR strategic plan.

Change Step 3—Get the vision right: Develop a draft HR strategic plan for stakeholders to review

Change Step 4—Communicate for buy-in: Vet the draft plan to the university using methods to obtain clear feedback, and engage as many stakeholders as possible.

Back to Case Study 18.1

Because the charge to the HR Advisory Team included providing advice on implementing goals in the HR strategic plan, Lisa brought the results of the campus-wide feedback to them for discussion.

The majority of the feedback confirmed the work of the HR Advisory Team in determining the two main goals and sub-goals. However, based on recommendations by university stakeholders, the HR Advisory Team members made the following changes to the HR strategic goals:

- *Move the sub-goal to reduce spending due to workers' compensation claims to the long-term perspective because this was not considered a priority by key constituents.*
- *Move the sub-goal to support the acclimation of new employees to their professional and social environment to the long-term perspective as stakeholders felt other sub-goals must first build a foundation for this important project.*
- *Add a sub-goal to the staffing goal to increase the diversity of faculty, administrative and support staff because constituents named this a priority.*
- *Add a sub-goal to the staffing goal to develop an institution-wide staffing plan as this is a priority of the vice president for administration.*

HR Advisory Team members confirmed that making these changes to the goals continued to align with the university strategic plan. In addition, the cabinet members supported these changes. As a result of these changes, the metric, "number of workers' compensation claims" was replaced by "increased percentage of diverse faculty and staff." Exhibit 18.3 outlines the HR strategic plan goals and sub-goals after stakeholder input.

Exhibit 18.3 Final HR strategic plan goals and sub-goals

Goal #1: Staffing: to develop leading practices in the recruitment and retention of outstanding faculty, staff and administrators
1. *Develop an institution-wide staffing plan.*
2. *Create greater transparency and speed in the hiring process for support staff.*
3. *Increase efficiency in the recruitment process for administrative staff and faculty.*
4. *Improve selection processes to optimize performance and commitment outcomes.*
5. *Increase the diversity of faculty, administrative staff and support staff.*

Goal #2: Development: to develop leading practices in the development of faculty, staff and administrators to allow for employee mobility and succession planning
1. *Improve supervisors', department chairs', and "line" managers' ability to create conditions that motivate employees, set goals for themselves and their employees, and complete performance evaluation of the employees they manage or supervise.*
2. *Support the creation of development plans for all employees, recognizing that faculty and ad-hoc instructional staff members have different responsibilities than administrative and support staff.*
3. *Offer leadership development training for individuals currently in leadership positions or seeking to enter leadership positions.*
4. *Offer continuous skill attainment, development and knowledge training for administrators, department chairs, team leaders, and supervisors.*
5. *Ensure that flexibility in career tracks meets the needs of each employee group.*

Involve Stakeholders in Action Plan #7 Must Do

In developing an action plan to implement the goals in the HR strategic plan, Lisa, William and James understood they must consider which to implement with "quick wins" in order to continue to engage university constituents. They prepared the action plan summarized in Table 18.1.

Explanation of Action Items from Table 18.1

Action Item A: Develop university-wide employee core competency framework: These core competencies serve as the foundation for accomplishing the staffing and development goals, and therefore must be one of the priority projects in the HR plan. In Unit Two we introduced a process to develop employee core competencies for the HR department. As a reminder, employee core competencies are clusters of universally expected, observable behaviors, necessary for successful perfor-

Table 18.1 Action plan to implement HR strategic plan goals

Action Item	HR Plan Goal/ Sub-goal Addressed	Team/ Timeline	Metric
A. Develop university-wide employee core competency framework	Staffing sub-goals 2, 3, 4 Development sub-goal 1	Team #1/ 1st semester	• employee competencies reflected in recruiting, staffing, performance management
B. Improve recruitment processes for faculty and administrative staff	Staffing sub-goals 2,3,4	Team #2/ 1st semester	• % retention • time to hire
C. Develop "Recruitment 101" workshops	Staffing sub-goals 2,3,4	Team #2/ 2nd semester; offer 3rd semester	• % retention • time to hire
D. Develop plan to increase diversity of faculty and staff	Staffing sub-goal 5	Team #3/ 1st and 2nd semester	• % diverse workforce • % diverse candidate pool
E. Improve administrative and support staff performance evaluation forms and processes	Development sub-goals 1,2	Team #4/ 1st semester	• increased employee skills and competencies
F. Offer "Performance Evaluation 101" workshops	Development sub-goals 1,2	Team #4/ 3rd semester	• increased employee skills and competencies
G. Develop plan for supervisory leadership training	Development sub-goals 3,4	Team #4/ 2nd semester; offer 3rd semester	• increased managerial competency at all levels
H. Develop plan for department chair training	Development sub-goals 3,4	Team #5/ 2nd semester; offer 3rd semester	• increased managerial competency at all levels
I. Develop template for a campus-wide staffing plan	Staffing sub-goal 1	HR Team/ 1st semester; take to HR Advisory Team and cabinet 2nd semester	• managers use available data to determine objectives and make key recruitment decisions
J. Develop plan to ensure flexibility in career tracks to meet needs of each employee group	Development sub-goal 5	Team #6/ 3rd semester	• % retention • employee satisfaction

mance in the position and in the university. These employee core competencies reflect the core values of faculty and staff, and define the skills, knowledge, learning and behaviors critical to achieving the university's strategic plan.

Employee core competencies serve as an "enabler" to accomplish the staffing and development goals. An "enabler" is an HR deliverable that reinforces or "enables" the accomplishment of a goal. For example, with our staffing goal to develop leading practices in the recruitment and retention of outstanding faculty, staff and administrators, employee core competencies contribute toward an improved candidate selection process, one that involves hiring faculty, staff and administrators that "fit" the core competencies of the university.

Chapter 16 includes a comprehensive case study outlining one model for developing university core competencies. The process utilized must involve discussions among the entire university community. What works well is to have several core competencies for "all" employee groups, e.g., collaboration, effective communication, leadership, inclusivity, innovation, etc. Then, each department or unit can determine additional competencies that are important to them, e.g., engagement, service orientation, growth/development, strategic responsibility. Finally, the university employee core competencies must be aligned with the overall strategic plan.

Action Items B, C: These sub-goals are designed to accomplish the overall staffing goal: to develop leading practices in the recruitment and retention of outstanding faculty, staff and administrators. The same team can work on both action items. First, they improve the recruitment and hiring processes, and then they can develop training for the university community. An alternative is that after improving the processes, the HR staff can develop a training program to take to the team for their feedback.

Training programs often target specific employee segments. For example, in developing training for the recruitment process, separate sessions may be scheduled for faculty, administrative staff and support staff. An optimal method is to schedule sessions on specific topics, e.g., developing a position description, screening candidates, behavior-based interviewing, evaluating candidates, paperwork process, etc., and offer them to all employees. Our experience indicates that these types of workshops are valued by all employees.

Action Item D: Develop a plan to increase the diversity of faculty and staff. Although this sub-goal contributes toward accomplishing the overall staffing goal, it is specific enough that it needs a separate team. Team membership includes an academic dean and representatives of faculty, administrative and support staff. Although it is a long-term goal to increase the diversity of university employees, a draft plan can be developed in one semester, or at the most, a summer and a semester. The plan will involve researching the best-practices of other universities, and collaborating with others in the higher education community.

Action Items E, F: One of the major needs of supervisory training is improving the skills of supervisors to evaluate the performance of those reporting to them. This comprises the ability to confront and resolve conflict in proactive ways. For many universities, the first step involves improving the performance evaluation forms for administrative and support staff. Politically, it is best to include members of governance groups representing administrative and/or support staff in revising the forms.

As with developing training for the recruitment function, the HR staff can develop the training and obtain input from the team. A crucial component of the training program is to offer sessions for supervisors as well as for administrative and support staff. Each will have a slightly different focus. Both groups will be interested in the purpose and outcomes of evaluating performance, the revised forms and processes used to evaluate performance.

Action Items G, H: Both these action items contribute toward the accomplishment of the development goal: to develop leading practices in the development of faculty, staff and administrators to allow for employee mobility and succession planning. Note that one action item targets managers within the administrative and support staff, and the other targets department chairs. For many universities, each group works within somewhat different environments and cultures. Therefore, develop separate training for each group.

Action Item I: Although listed under the staffing goal, the action item of developing a template for a campus-wide staffing plan can contribute toward the accomplishment of the development goal. During the first semester in implementing the HR strategic plan, the HR staff can research and draft a plan template. Doing so will increase the credibility of the HR function with top-level administrators. Next, the draft plan is brought to the HR Advisory Team and the focus groups of managers for feedback. Implementation of the plan involves participants of key administrators and managers.

Action Item J: Develop a plan to ensure flexibility in career tracks to meet the needs of each employee group. Due to work-life balance issues, there are times in a person's life cycle when he/she desires movement to another position of responsibility. An example is the option to move from a tenure-track faculty position to an instructional ad-hoc position. Another example is a person in a current support staff role who, because of obtaining a bachelor's degree and/or additional skills or experience, wishes to obtain an administrative staff role or work in a different area of the institution. One method for providing this flexibility is the "Leadership Fellow Program" described in Case Study 16.1.

Membership of Teams

Six teams are noted in our sample action plan outlined in Table 18.1. It is the responsibility of the HR staff, including those in the provost and vice-president for academic affairs' office, to bring faculty and staff together to implement the action items. In most cases, those university constituents involved in vetting the HR strategic plan will find that at least one of the topics is engaging and choose to participate in a team—especially if they view the HR staff and the strategic plan credible and action-oriented.

This is where all the hard work of the HR staff to move to a transformative culture pays huge dividends. The majority of the HR staff will possess the skills to lead and/or participate in one of the teams described in the action plan.

What happens to the HR Advisory Team? Exhibit 18.4 is the charge to the HR Advisory Team from our case study. Note that points four and five refer to implementation of the goals in the plan. Therefore, the team can continue in this role. In addition, members of the HR Advisory Team may decide to join other action teams.

Exhibit 18.4 HR Advisory Team charge

1. Oversee the development and implementation of the goals in the HR Strategic Plan
2. Involve the campus community in the improvement and implementation of the goals in the plan
3. Assist with the development of metrics to evaluate the outcomes of the goals in the plan
4. Provide advice and feedback on implementation of the goals in the plan
5. Evaluate the effectiveness of the implementation of the goals in the plan

Case Study Questions

1. In addition to those discussed in the chapter, what are other methods to engage university stakeholders in the HR strategic plan?
2. One of the barriers to achieving the staffing goal identified in chapter 17 is recruitment and selection teams not utilizing the employee core competencies. What are the reasons they are not using the core competencies? What are potential ways to address each reason identified above?
3. In our case study, Lisa, the HR director, did not have a collaborative or trusting relationship with the current chair of the administrative staff governance committee due to a past political situation. Lisa wanted the support and participation of the committee in reviewing the administrative staff performance evaluation form. What are ways for her to rebuild trust with the chair and obtain the support of the committee?

To review discussion of recommendations for Case Study 18.1 questions, go to **www.HR-higher-ed.com**

Summary

The model to engage the university community in the HR strategic plan includes the following three steps: obtain input from the university community, revise the plan based on feedback, and involve stakeholders in developing an action plan.

Kotter's eight-step process for leading successful change comes into play in two ways at this point. First, the HR department and its staff are in the seventh and eighth steps of the change process—implementing and sustaining change at the HR department level. Second, the university is experiencing change in how it perceives the HR function as transformational in addition to transactional.

University constituents work on teams brought together by HR staff to improve policies and procedures, confront and resolve issues important to faculty and staff, and work with supervisors and managers to restructure their department or unit. Faculty and staff engage as members of an HR Advisory Team, providing input to the HR strategic plan. HR staff reach out to the entire campus in multiple ways to engage stakeholders in the HR strategic plan. These changes enable action by providing the opportunity to create short-term wins—to revise the goals in the plan according to stakeholder feedback, and to determine which goals can be accomplished in the short-term with the most attention and engagement by stakeholders.

Major Themes

Leadership of Change was a major thread in this chapter, not only outlining change within the HR function, but also indicating how these changes impact the overall university culture.

Evaluation of "Your" HR Department's Chapter 18 Outcome

Outcome Desired: Engagement of the university community in the implementation of the HR strategic plan

Change: Engage broad university community in culture change (change step 7)
 Culture change is rooted in the HR paradigm (change step 8)

Key Indicators of Success: (check if *"yes"*)

☐ HR staff are willing and able to tackle substantial campus-wide changes

☐ The process to develop the HR strategic plan reinvigorates the HR staff

☐ HR staff feel a sense of accomplishment and excitement about the HR plan

☐ Key campus constituents provide advice and input to the HR plan

Potential Barriers to Change: (check if *"needs attention"*)

☐ Difficulty in obtaining advice and input to the HR plan from key campus constituents

☐ Not including the equity and affirmative action or provost HR functions in the process of implementing the plan

☐ Difficulty in engaging faculty and staff on action plan teams

Chapter 19

Fully Implement the Human Resources Strategic Plan

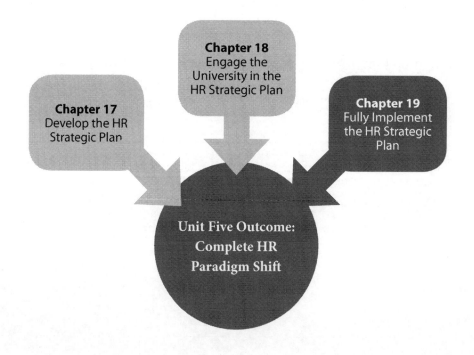

Completing the HR paradigm shift causes ripples of change throughout the university community. The outcome of chapter 19 is a fully implemented HR strategic plan, aligned with the university strategic plan. This alignment, along with increased engagement of constituents, augments the accomplishment of the university strategic plan.

Resulting from persistence and hard work, the HR staff possess highly developed and enhanced transformative skills. This change shifts the culture of the HR department to a strategic level. Outcomes include accomplishment of the necessary transactional work more efficiently, with stakeholder value consistently in mind. University constituents consider the HR department partners and collaborators, sought for advice and input, and as facilitators for strategic and difficult discussions. Rituals and symbols in the HR department signify a changed paradigm. Stories and examples about "how it used to be," signify why it is better now. People who recognize they no longer fit within the new HR department culture choose to leave.

The HR strategic plan is finalized, with the university community engaged in strengthening its goals and action plans. Teams of active participants passionately work to accomplish their charge. New leaders are hired, or evolve from current employees. Others exhibit new leadership behaviors and reinforce the university mission and vision. University constituents, including HR staff members, see top administration support the accomplishment of the HR strategic plan. The components needed to fully implement the HR strategic plan are outlined in Figure 19.1.

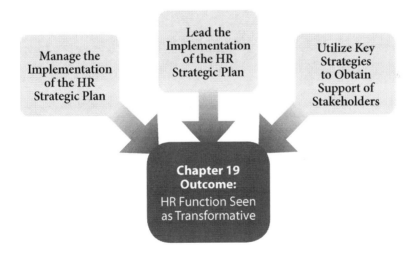

Figure 19.1 Model to fully implement the HR strategic plan

Manage the Implementation of the HR Strategic Plan

Normally, the HR director or vice president assumes the responsibility for leading the implementation of the HR strategic plan. The HR strategic plan implementation cycle consists of five phases that interrelate and continually rotate in a similar pattern. Shown in Figure 19.2, these phases serve as a method for further integration of the HR paradigm change into the culture of the HR department and the university.

Figure 19.2 Strategic plan implementation cycle

Implementing the HR strategic plan includes choosing and charging teams to put into operation specific goals and objectives of the action plan. Building effective teams comprises the process outlined in chapter 9, and includes:

- urgency of the team goal
- metrics and expected outcomes
- characteristics of an effective team
- meeting guidelines
- trust among team members
- roles of team members
- methods for dealing with conflict

Who charges the teams, leads the initial discussions, and is responsible for effectively managing the implementation of the HR strategic plan? Although all teams will have an HR staff member as a participant or leader, either the HR director or the vice president in charge of the HR function assumes this role and responsibility.

The work of each team comprises the following:

- evaluate outcomes, prepare time lines for the completion of expected outcomes
- provide progress reports of activities and accomplishments, tied to the metrics, to the HR director and vice president
- communicate barriers, issues or a need for additional resources promptly

The HR director and vice president evaluate the effectiveness of the team in accomplishing its charge. Options include team surveys, talking with team members one-on-one, and an analysis of the progress of their work. Potential questions to answer include:

- Are team members working together effectively?
- Are people with the necessary and complementary skills on the team?
- Are team members taking on leadership roles as needed?
- Does anyone need to be added to the team?
- Is anyone not participating?
- Does the team have the necessary resources to accomplish its charge?

The HR director and/or vice president revise the plan goals and action plan according to the outcome of the evaluation, communicate accomplishments of the teams to cabinet members and to all university constituents, and develop symbols or rituals to strengthen teams and celebrate major successes.

How do we make the strategic plan a living entity that continually is revisited and revised? Since one of the charges to the HR Advisory Team is to "evaluate the effectiveness of the implementation of the goals in the plan," they can serve in the role of a strategic planning team that consistently focuses on the effectiveness and outcomes of the plan, and recommends revisions to the plan.

Lead the Implementation of the HR Strategic Plan

At this point, the roles of the leader encompasses those functions outlined in Figure 19.3.

Enable "Quick Wins"

This role comprises the sixth step in Kotter's eight-step change process. Regarding change at the institution level, we facilitate further action by continually measuring the progress of the teams in creating short-term wins. In the HR strategic plan outlined in the chapter 18 case study, two high priority and valued sub-goals are scheduled to be worked on immediately by teams: improve faculty and admin-

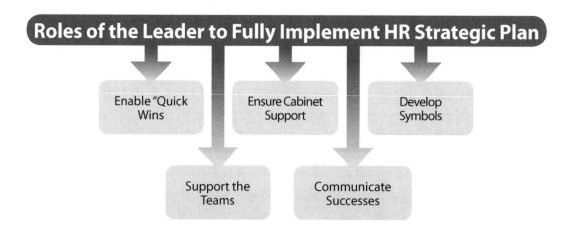

Figure 19.3 Roles of the leader in fully implementing the HR strategic plan

istrative staff recruitment processes; improve administrative and support staff performance evaluation forms and processes. Because these sub-goals incorporate stakeholder value, accomplishing them early in the implementation of the strategic plan provides synergy and increases the engagement of constituents.

Support the Teams

This role is to support the work of the teams—to ensure they possess the necessary resources to accomplish their charge. It may involve training in business process improvement, team dynamics, conflict resolution, giving time to work on team goals, or providing a facilitator to assist in the progress of the team. This includes the process of engaging faculty and staff to become team members.

Ensure Cabinet Support/Communicate Successes

Discussed in detail in chapter 15 are methods for the leader to ensure that top administrators support the change efforts and work of the teams, and to communicate to stakeholders valued accomplishments and successes of the teams.

Develop Symbols

Symbols form the foundation of a team, department, or organization's culture. Symbols can be utilized by leaders to interpret, explain and reinterpret experiences in order to provide a basis for understanding meaning and purpose. Symbols are powerful because they permeate every fiber of life within the organization. Leaders who comprehend the power of symbols can better understand and influence the vision of the institution. According to the book, *Reframing Organizations* (Bolman and Deal, 2003), the following core assumptions are valid around symbols:

- What is important is not what happens, but what it means.
- Events have multiple meanings because people interpret them through their individual experiences.
- Symbols are created during times of uncertainty to resolve confusion, find direction, and provide hope.
- Many activities and processes are more important for their symbolic value than their outcome.
- Culture unites people around shared values and beliefs.

The following symbolic forms can play a distinctive cultural role within the organization, especially during a period of transition and change (Bolman and Deal, 2003):

1. **Myths, vision and values** give an organization a strong sense of purpose, with myths serving as the "story behind the story." A story behind an event that expresses the "urgency for change," for example the case study in chapter 8 where HR staff filled flip charts with notes containing changes they experienced in the department, becomes a myth passed along from one employee to another. Perhaps there was discussion among the HR staff after the meeting where Dennis apologized to them, their comments expressing increased respect and trust in him. Providing an experience where individuals can "feel" and "see" the urgency for change and engage emotionally provides a strong sense of purpose and an opportunity for myths to develop.

2. **Heroes and heroines** are cultural icons, whose words and deeds exemplify and reinforce important core values. In chapter 9, we discussed the story of Betty, who served as a "water-carrier" in her role as an HR staff member. Cultural heroes and heroines are not concentrated at the top level of the organization, but are ordinary people who exist everywhere and at all levels. These individuals must be celebrated regularly.

3. **Stories** convey information, values, and myths vividly and convincingly. They disseminate values and keep the historical endeavors of heroes and heroines alive. Leaders can use stories as part of strengthening the work of teams, a department, a college, or an entire university. Stories can pass along traditions, train employees, empower individuals, and recognize accomplishments. The story of using "boas" in chapter 9 to build teams and engage those in other departments with the HR department is an example.

4. **Rituals** are day-to-day routines that help give structure and meaning to work life within an organization. Rituals include initiations of new faculty and staff onto teams or into departments. They also express the institution's values. Universities and their departments that do not have formal orientation programs for faculty, ad hoc teaching staff, or administrative and support staff make it difficult for newcomers to quickly feel part of the culture or learn the values of the university. An example is new directors of the HR function who enter higher

education from the private sector. Without formal onboarding rituals, many leave higher education within a short time—not being provided the ability to understand and work with the different culture of academia.

5. **Ceremonies** are elaborate, less frequent occasions than rituals, and contribute toward socializing, stabilizing, reassuring and conveying messages to constituents. Examples are installing a new chancellor, president or provost to the institution, an annual convocation beginning a new academic year, and an awards ceremony for recognizing faculty, administrative and support staff. Ceremonies also can be held on a smaller scale within a department, unit or college.

6. **Metaphor, humor and play** are indirect ways to struggle with issues that are complex or threatening, such as those around transition and change. An example used in chapter 8 to describe the neutral zone was the acronym *NEON*. This fun metaphor stood for "Not Employing Outdated Notions," and referred to thinking and working in new and innovative ways.

> **Assignment 19.1** *An extremely important role of the change leader is symbolic leadership. This role includes leading by example, using symbols to capture attention, framing experience, communicating the vision, telling stories, and respecting and using history (Bolman and Deal, 2003). As a leader of change in moving the HR function to the strategic level of the university, how will you utilize symbols?*

Utilize Key Strategies to Obtain Support of Stakeholders

Throughout this book, we addressed the issue of internal conflict and resistance to an HR paradigm shift within the HR function. However, we have not directly discussed the topic of conflict external to HR. What strategies do we pursue if one or more institution leaders or cabinet members do not accept HR as a strategic partner? Our process for HR transformational change emphasizes the following key strategies:

1. Know stakeholder value early in the change process (refer to chapter 7).
2. Build relationships of trust with key constituents, incorporating activities that provide that value (refer to chapter 8).
3. Communicate with stakeholders continually throughout the change process, listen and incorporate their feedback in transformational activities (refer to chapters 7, 10, 11, 15,18).
4. Address and resolve conflict or resistance promptly (refer to chapter 6).

5. Create an HR Collaboration Team to include the administrative leaders of the HR function (refer to chapters 15, 16).

Following are several examples that convey these key strategies:

Example 1: Stakeholder Value

Members of the HR Collaboration Team develop a process to build trusting relationships with cabinet members. In meeting individually with each cabinet member, an HR Collaboration Team member learns of his/her perspective of HR, what is important to his/her work, any current issues that demand attention, and how HR can assist in resolving these issues effectively. They learn that the vice president of student affairs feels several departments in her division need re-structuring. The vice president of administrative services and finance wants supervisory training for custodial and grounds supervisors. The provost and vice president feels faculty recruitment paperwork is too time-consuming. The president wants an institution-wide staffing plan. The vice president of the foundation feels several long-term staff members are incorrectly titled. Although some of these priorities are transactional work, most are transformational work. Some can be included as sub-goals or goals in an HR strategic plan. Others can be accomplished in the short-term.

Example 2: Build Relationships

Shared governance has a strong presence in your institution's culture and environment, with an active faculty senate and administrative staff senate. In meeting with their leadership, a member of the HR Collaboration Team learns that many senate members and other constituents do not value current policies for salary equity and promotion. You volunteer to present workshops on current processes and policies to interested senate members, and to participate in a task force to revise the policies. In addition, the HR Collaboration Team members decide to create a "Shared Governance" Team that meets monthly with the HR Collaboration Team to discuss and resolve potential issues.

Example 3: HR Collaboration Team

In meeting with the academic deans, an HR Collaboration Team member learns several recently hired deans have questions on HR legal issues, e.g., FMLA, ADA, etc. In addition, their feedback includes frustration among department chairs that the recruitment and appointment processes for ad-hoc instructional staff are lengthy and inconsistently followed. The HR Collaboration Team offers to provide legal training to the academic deans, including assistant and associate deans, and then to department chairs and academic program directors. One of the deans then volunteers to participate in a task force to evaluate the current recruitment processes.

Example 4: Communicate with Stakeholders

Consider Case Study 16.3 in chapter 16, where an academic dean, several department chairs and support staff resisted an HR transformational change activity. Note that leaders of this initiative failed to incorporate several key strategies from our listing.

Stakeholders often do not have a clear picture of those methods and activities that constitute transformational HR work. However, they value a relationship that addresses and resolves their priority issues. Through our own experiences, we have found that the approach of integrating these key strategies creates strong relationships among the HR function and stakeholders. Through developing these relationships, we learn of resistance early and can address it directly, utilizing the conflict resolution model expressed in chapter 6. Not incorporating these strategies can stall or force the HR paradigm shift process to return to earlier steps, as it did in Case Study 16.3. This can negatively impact stakeholder trust in the HR function.

Which comes first, the HR function perceived as transformational, strategic and a valued partner, or the HR function receiving the support of the cabinet and other campus leaders? Our experience indicates that in many cases HR first must accomplish several "quick-wins" along the HR paradigm change process before receiving the support needed. For example, HR staff members improve their skills and work differently to provide stakeholder value. These HR staff members proactively make improvements to internal and external HR processes valued by constituents, who begin to perceive HR differently. These constituents then approach HR with issues to resolve collaboratively and strategically.

In conclusion, at times the person or team leading the HR paradigm shift may have to "prove" to the cabinet and other institutional leaders that the HR function "can" work strategically with positive outcomes to the university. Then the support and commitment to the HR paradigm shift follows.

Summary

Responsibility for managing the implementation of the HR strategic plan lies with the HR director or vice president. This includes choosing and charging teams to put into operation specific goals and objectives of the plan, evaluating team outcomes and team effectiveness, revising the plan when necessary, and communicating team accomplishments to cabinet members and university constituents.

The process for HR transformational change emphasizes utilizing the following key strategies to obtain the support of stakeholders:

1. Know stakeholder value early in the change process.
2. Build relationships of trust, incorporating activities that provide that value.
3. Communicate with stakeholders continually throughout the change process; listen and incorporate their feedback in transformational activities.
4. Address and resolve conflict or resistance promptly.

Major Themes

Leadership of Change was a major thread in this chapter, with the roles of the leader comprised of enabling "quick wins," supporting the teams, ensuring cabinet support, communicating successes, and developing symbols for culture change.

Symbols form the foundation of a team, department, or organization's culture, and can be utilized by leaders to interpret, explain and reinterpret experiences in order to provide a basis for understanding meaning and purpose. Symbols are powerful because they permeate every fiber of life within the organization. Leaders who understand the power of symbols can better influence the vision of the department and institution.

Symbolic forms that can play a distinctive cultural role within the institution, especially during a period of transition and change, include:

- myths, vision, and values
- heroes and heroics
- stories that convey information, values and myths
- rituals that help give structure and meaning to work life
- ceremonies
- metaphor, humor, and play

Evaluation of "Your" HR Department's Chapter 19 Outcome

Outcome Desired: The HR function is seen as transformative by the university community

Change: Engage broad university community in culture change (change step 7)
Culture change is rooted in the HR paradigm (change step 8)

Key Indicators of Success: (check if "yes")

- ☐ Leaders model and encourage desired behaviors
- ☐ Change efforts are managed effectively throughout the university
- ☐ Desired behaviors are rewarded and recognized
- ☐ Faculty and staff are motivated and engaged toward achieving strategic goals
- ☐ The infrastructure and culture supports the new HR paradigm
- ☐ Faculty and staff model the core values of the institution
- ☐ New symbols and rituals appear that support the new culture

Potential Barriers to Change: (check if *"needs attention"*)

- ☐ Faculty and staff do not model the new competencies, but stick with the old, established norms of behavior and values
- ☐ New behaviors and values are not rewarded and recognized
- ☐ Change leaders are criticized
- ☐ Benefits of the change are challenged
- ☐ Newly hired faculty and staff leave the institution because they do not fit in

Unit Five Summary

In chapter 3 we outlined the model for accomplishing the HR paradigm shift, depicted in the graphic below.

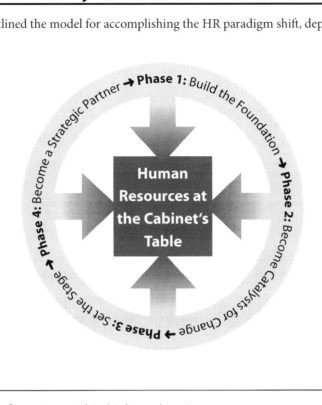

Model for HR transformation within higher education

With becoming a strategic partner in Unit Five, our HR paradigm shift is complete. We have moved from vision to action. Our HR function is valued, innovative, trusted, considered an advocate and influencer, works with a unified focus, and promotes synergy within the institution.

However, we cannot rest on this newly earned perspective, but must continue to enhance our strategic partnership with stakeholders and the institution. The human resources function at the cabinet's table must continually strive to:

- build a strong foundation
- serve as a catalyst for change
- broaden stakeholder value
- align strategically to strengthen institutional distinctiveness

"Tradition is a powerful force. Leaps into the future can slide back into the past. We keep a change in place by helping to create a new, supportive, and sufficiently strong organizational culture. A supportive culture provides roots for the new ways of operating. It keeps the revolutionary technology, the globalized organization, the innovative strategy, or the more efficient processes working to make you a winner" (Kotter and Cohen, 2002, p 189).

Unit Five Outcome Desired: Complete the HR Paradigm Shift

Chapter 17 Outcome: *Complete initial draft of HR strategic plan*

Key Indicators of Success: Check (x) if "yes"

- [ ] Key components of the HR function are reviewed and relevant data collected
- [ ] Factors in the external environment are assessed
- [ ] HR staff are willing and able to tackle substantial campus-wide changes
- [ ] The process to develop the HR strategic plan reinvigorates the HR staff members
- [ ] HR staff feel a sense of accomplishment and excitement about the HR plan
- [ ] Key campus constituents provide advice and input to the HR plan
- [ ] A SWOT analysis is part of the draft HR strategic plan
- [ ] HR strategic goals are aligned with those of the university
- [ ] At least one metric is chosen to evaluate the successful outcome of each goal
- [ ] Potential barriers to accomplishing the strategic goals are identified
- [ ] An HR Advisory Team provides feedback and input to the draft HR strategic plan prior to it being vetted by all stakeholders

Chapter 18 Outcome: *Engage the university in the HR strategic plan*

Key Indicators of Success: Check (x) if "yes"

- [ ] Key components of the HR function are reviewed, and relevant data collected
- [ ] Factors in the external environment are assessed
- [ ] HR staff are willing and able to tackle substantial campus-wide changes
- [ ] The process to develop the HR strategic plan reinvigorates the HR staff
- [ ] HR staff feel a sense of accomplishment and excitement about the HR plan
- [ ] Key campus constituents provide advice and input to the HR plan
- [ ] A SWOT analysis is part of the draft HR strategic plan

Chapter 19 Outcome: HR function seen as transformative

Key Indicators of Success: Check (x) if "yes"

☐ Leaders model and encourage desired behaviors

☐ Change efforts are managed effectively throughout the university

☐ Desired behaviors are rewarded and recognized

☐ Faculty and staff are motivated and engaged toward achieving strategic goals

☐ The infrastructure and culture supports the new HR paradigm

☐ Faculty and staff model the core values of the institution

☐ New symbols and rituals appear that support the new culture

Conclusion

Figure 1 Model of the HR function at the strategic level of the institution

We have accomplished a great deal in our HR paradigm shift. Transforming HR has resulted in stakeholders who:

- value the deliverables of the HR function
- perceive HR as adding value through innovation and broader thinking
- trust their relationship with HR and collaborate to resolve issues effectively
- discover they can influence organizational change
- consider the HR function to be credible, ethical, approachable and knowledgeable, with a unified strategic focus

As equal partners, together the HR function and stakeholders implement short- and long-term strategy. As outlined in chapter 2 and captured in the inner circle in Figure 1 above, a definite synergy develops within the institution as stakeholder engagement strengthens.

The outer circle of Figure 1 portrays that the strategic outcomes to the institution include an integrated strategy that influences the identity, culture, and image of the university. Through the HR paradigm shift, the capabilities of the institution are created, developed or enhanced. Short-term and highly valued wins usually create momentum for stakeholders to move on to bigger and deeper challenges. Transforming the HR function builds the foundation for institution change. This foundation then creates "waves of change" that ripple throughout the university and eventually change the culture of the institution.

Methods to Strengthen the Institution's Distinctiveness and Competitive Advantage

However, have we done all we can to tie the HR strategic plan to institution performance? Can more be done to contribute towards accomplishing the university's mission and vision and strengthening distinctiveness? With the human resources function at the strategic level of the university, the foundation is in place to accomplish the following three critical programs:

1. tie the HR strategic plan to institution performance
2. develop and implement a university-wide recruitment brand
3. develop and implement a university-wide leadership brand

Tie the HR Strategic Plan to Institution Performance

Although the goals in the HR strategic plan are evaluated in chapter 17 to ensure alignment with the university's goals and strategic plan, an organization's performance management plan details a process exemplifying greater alignment. Closely tied to the institution's strategic plan, the performance management plan is designed to provide transparency and accountability regarding the institution's overall performance. It allows faculty, staff and administrators at all levels and in all units of the institution to develop specific and measureable activities that contribute toward the accomplishment of the institution's vision, mission, and strategic goals.

Recall that example 7 in chapter 2 describes how President Gary Forsee of the University of Missouri System instituted 80 accountability measures—derived from the System's strategy, vision and core values—designed to provide constituents with the ability to customize their unit or department metrics to fit their specific missions and goals. (80 Ways to Measure Success 26).

Many of these accountability measures pertain to the HR function. For example, using the measure of "attract, develop and retain talented faculty and staff," the HR function can develop goals and metrics that contribute toward accomplishing this measure, and therefore tie the HR strategic plan very closely with university performance.

Develop and Implement a University-wide Recruitment Brand

The staffing goal and its sub-goals discussed in the chapter 18 case study are part of an overall university recruitment brand. Our job as an HR professional is to create an organization that constantly builds its capacity through building the capacity of the people we employ. In this regard, we ensure our higher education institution can attract, hire, retain and develop faculty and staff needed to accomplish the mission and vision in times of competitive change.

Recruitment brands, utilized in the private sector, are an example of a strategic tool that can be modified and implemented in higher education to play a critical role in both attracting and retaining talented individuals. Although it is optimal for the overall university to have a deliberate recruitment brand, in reality most do not.

In chapter 10, we focused on developing a recruitment brand for the HR function. Now, as part of the HR strategic plan implementation, developing a recruitment brand for the overall institution is imperative.

The main goal of creating a strong recruitment brand is to attract and retain faculty, staff and administrators having a strong "fit" with the relevant hiring department and university. In essence, the purpose of a recruitment brand for the university is to become an "employer of choice." Developing and continually improving our recruitment brand is a long-term effort that encompasses each step of the employee life cycle described in chapter 5: recruitment, hire, orientation, development, promotion, retention and engagement.

To be competitive in today's recruitment marketplace and to prepare for future growth, we must sell our university while attracting the right candidates. Therefore, the recruitment brand needs to convey the benefits of committing to work in the university, connecting both rationally and emotionally with potential and current employees. To maximize the recruitment brand, this process must be included during the first steps of the recruitment.

The university recruitment brand captures and expresses what it is like to work in our university, especially what is good about being a part of the faculty or staff. Although "word of mouth reputation" is always present— important in its own right—it may not be complete or even accurate. Developing a recruitment brand is a more sophisticated and integrated effort to create and deliver a credible and honest message about being a faculty or staff member at our institution. It is not just a vision or a promise; it needs to be consistent with reality, so honesty is the key component.

The benefits of an effective recruitment brand for the university are described in Figure 2. A crucial step in the process for the university-wide team charged with developing a recruitment brand is offering focus groups to generate discussions throughout the institution. The focus group process serves to explain the concept and advantages of a recruitment brand, and to gather the distinctive characteristics that will form the basis of the brand.

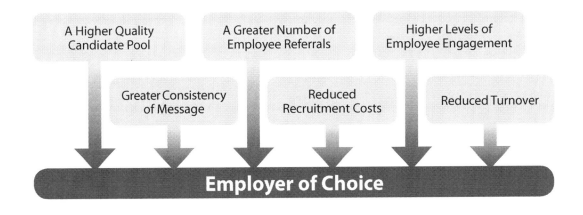

Figure 2 Key benefits of an effective university-wide recruitment brand

STEPS TO BUILD AN EFFECTIVE UNIVERSITY RECRUITMENT BRAND

Step 1: Define objectives and project scope

Step 2: Conduct an assessment process

Step 3: Develop employer distinctiveness characteristics

Refer to the process described in chapter 10 to develop an effective recruitment brand at the university level.

Develop and Implement a University-wide Leadership Brand

As with a recruitment brand, few universities develop and implement a successful leadership brand. We contend that both brands provide a competitive advantage for those institutions where the brands permeate the culture at every level.

In their book, *Leadership Brand*, Dave Ulrich and Norm Smallwood define a leadership brand as the "identity of the leaders throughout an organization that bridges customer expectations and employee and organizational behavior" (Ulrich and Smallwood, 2007, page 18). They indicate that an organization's unique leadership brand incorporates those elements of leadership that all leaders must demonstrate in order to be effective in accomplishing their responsibilities. In addition, stakeholders value these elements of leadership.

Although many organizations tend to focus on building individuals as leaders, an example being comprehensive Case Study 16.1, developing an institution leadership brand builds leadership as a distinctive advantage. Faculty and staff in institutions of higher education with recruitment and leadership brands know what work is expected of them, and are engaged at a higher level. Their work is aligned with the institution's strategy, core capabilities and values. Students, donors, alumni, and the public—as well as faculty, staff and the institution itself—benefit in the long-term.

Most importantly, both the recruitment and leadership brands must be preceded by developing the institution's core and leadership competencies. The strategic framework of an organization is composed of its core values, core competencies, vision and mission. From this foundation, the brands provide direction to create and communicate synergy and to produce more significant and consistent results.

For a more detailed discussion and process to build a leadership brand, refer to the book, *Leadership Brand*, by Ulrich and Smallwood.

Next Steps

The human resources function, in collaboration with the institution's stakeholders and cabinet, has the opportunity to accomplish the vision of reinventing our institutions of higher education. In this regard, the following efforts are crucial:

1. With the support of the cabinet, the HR function leads the effort to develop university-wide employee core competencies and a recruitment brand.
2. The president, in working with other cabinet members, develops a university-wide leadership brand that includes succession planning. HR leadership can assist by facilitating an institution-wide discussion to develop the leadership brand.
3. While it is the responsibility of the president and cabinet to develop and implement an institution-wide process to develop performance or accountability measures, a transformative HR function can serve as a strategic university partner in the following ways:
   a. Bring to the vice president of HR and cabinet the idea of institution-wide performance measures, how they contribute towards performance, successful examples of institutions utilizing them, and a potential process for implementation.
   b. Assist the president and cabinet by functioning as a facilitator to develop an institution-wide performance or accountability measurement system.
   c. Develop goals and metrics as part of the HR strategic plan that align with one or more institution performance measure.
   d. Serve as a facilitator to work with other university departments and units to develop their specific goals and metrics that tie into one or more of the accountability measures.

As we "reinvent" ourselves as higher education institutions and develop new strategies for self-sufficiency, having the HR function at the cabinet's table serves as a key tool to facilitate discussions and engage the innovative skills and expertise of the entire community for transformational change.

"The single biggest argument offered against the need for transformation is that organizations can succeed with incremental change. A 2 percent improvement here, a 5 percent cost reduction there, and you win. In the short run, in certain industries, this can be true. ... How long do you think it will take to move incrementally from the twentieth-century model to the twenty-first? And what do you think will be the consequences if you don't get there fast enough?" (Kotter, 1996, p 173).

References

80 Ways to Measure Success, *The Higher Education Workplace*. Fall 2010: 26.

Academic Freedom and Educational Responsibility. *AAC and U Board of Directors' Statement.* January 6, 2006.

American Association of State Colleges and Universities. Faculty Trends and Issues. *Policy Matters.* April 2006, Volume 3, Number 4, p 1-4.

American Council on Education Center for Policy analysis. *National and International Projects on Accountability and Higher Education Outcomes.* www.acenet.edu/Content/NavigationMenu/ OnlineResources/Accountability/index.htm

Autry, James A. *The Servant Leader.* New York, NY: Crown Publishing Group, 2001.

Basso, Susan McGarry. Transforming HR Through Technology. *The Higher Education Workplace.* Winter 2009: 20.

Bolman, Lee G., and Terrence E. Deal. *Reframing Organizations.* San Francisco, CA: Jossey-Bass Inc., 2003.

Bridges, William. *Managing Transitions: Making the Most of Change.* Cambridge, MA: Perseus Publishing, 2003.

Building Bridges Across Maryland. *The Higher Education Workplace.* Winter 2009: 27.

Cheldelin, Sandra I., and Ann F. Lucas. *Academic Administrator's Guide to Conflict Resolution.* San Francisco, CA: John Wiley and Sons, 2004.

Cohen, Dan S. *The Heart of Change Field Guide: Tools and Tactics for Leading Change in Your Organization.* Boston, MA: Harvard Business School Press, 2005.

The Collaborative on Academic Careers in Higher Education. *The Experience of Tenure-Track Faculty at Research Universities: Analysis of COACHE Survey Results by Academic Area and Gender.* Harvard Graduate School of Education, July 2010: 1-72.

The Commission Appointed by Secretary of Education Margaret Spellings. *A Test of Leadership: Charting the Future of U.S. Higher Education.* 2006: 14-15, 21.

Costantino, Cathy A., and Christina Sickles Merchant. *Designing Conflict Management Systems.* San Francisco, CA: Jossey-Bass Inc., 1996

DePree, Max. *Leadership Jazz: The Essential Elements of a Great Leader*. New York, NY: Random House, Inc., 2008.

Eckel, Peter D., and Jacqueline E. King. *An Overview of Higher Education in the United States*. American Council on Education: 2004: 1-18.

Feldman, Daniel A. *The Handbook of Emotionally Intelligent Leadership: Inspiring Others to Achieve Results*. Leadership Performance Solutions Press, 1999.

The First-Year Employee Experience: A Unique Onboarding Program. *The Higher Education Workplace*. Winter 2009: 7.

Fisher, Roger, and William Ury. *Getting to Yes: Negotiating Agreement Without Giving In*. New York: Penguin Books, 1983.

Fletcher, Adam. *FireStarter Youth Power Curriculum: Participant Guidebook*. Olympia, WA: Freechild Project. 2002.

Franke, Ann H. *Faculty in Times of Financial Distress*. American Council on Education. 2009: 1-2.

Goleman, Daniel. *Working with Emotional Intelligence*. New York, NY: Bantam Books, 1998.

Green, Kenneth C. with Doug Lederman and Scott Jaschik. Presidential Perspectives: The 2011 Inside Higher Ed Survey of College and University Presidents. *Inside Higher Ed*, 2011.

Grote, Dick. *The Performance Appraisal Question and Answer Book: A Survival Guide for Managers*. New York, NY: American Management Association, 2002.

Helgesen, S. *Web of Inclusion: A New Architecture for Building Great Organizations*. New York, NY: Currency/Doubleday, 1995.

Helms, Robin Matross. *New Challenges, New Priorities: The Experience of Generation X Faculty. A Study for the Collaborative on Academic Careers in Higher Education*. Harvard Graduate School of Education, 2010: 1-22.

Hoevemeyer, Victoria A. *High-Impact Interview Questions: 701 Behavior-Based Questions*. New York: American Management Association. 2006.

Intagliata, Jim, Ulrich, Dave, and Norm Smallwood. Leveraging Leadership Competencies to Produce Leadership Brand: Creating Distinctiveness by Focusing on Strategy and Results. *HR Planning*, 2000, Volume 23.4: 12-23.

Kline, Missy. Shared Services: A New Incarnation of HR. *The Higher Education Workplace*. Winter 2009: 16.

Kotter, John P. *Leading Change*. Boston, MA: Harvard Business School Press, 1996.

Kotter, John P., and Dan s. Cohen. *The Heart of Change: Real-life Stories of How People Change Their Organizations*. Boston: Harvard Business School Publishing, 2002.

Lazer, Robert L., and Karen Robilotta. Shifting Gears Through Process Change. *The Higher Education Workplace*. Winter 2010-11: 26.

Lederman, Doug. Perspectives on the Downturn: A Survey of Presidents, *Inside Higher Ed*. March 4, 2011, p 1-6.

Lilly, Catherine, Sabrina Garrett Owens, and Kelle Parsons. Better Together: University of Michigan's Labor-Management Partnership. *The Higher Education Workplace*. Winter 2010-11: 19.

Lyall, Katharine. *Seeking Sustainable Public Universities: The Legacy of the Great Recession*. Center for Studies in Higher Educational Research & Occasional Paper Series: CSHE.10.11. June 2011: 1-4.

McGarry Basso, Susan. Transforming HR Through Technology. *The Higher Education Workplace*. Winter 2009: 20.

Nelson, Cary. From the President: The Last Chance. *Academe Online*. January-February 2011.

Orem, Sara L., Jacqueline Binkert, and Ann L. Clancy. *Appreciative Coaching*. San Francisco, CA: Jossey-Bass Inc., 2007.

Survey: HR Departments Working to Expand Level of Responsibility in Key Areas. *The Higher Education Workplace*. Winter 2009: 6.

Ulrich, Dave, and Wayne Brockbank. *The HR Value Proposition*. Boston, MA: Harvard Business School Press, 2005.

Ulrich, Dave, Justin Allen, Wayne Brockbank, Jon Younger, and Mark Nyman. *HR Transformation: Building Human Resources from the Outside In*. New York, NY: McGraw Hill, 2009.

Ulrich, Dave, and Norm Smallwood. *Leadership Brand: Developing Customer-Focused Leaders to Drive Performance and Build Lasting Value*. Boston, MA: Harvard Business School Press, 2007.

Vaillancourt, Allison M., and Andy Brantley. Doing Less With Less. *The Higher Education Workplace*. Winter 2009: 23.

Whitney, Diana, Amanda Trosten-Bloom, Jay Cherney, and Ron Fry. *Appreciative Team Building*. Lincoln, NE: iUniverse, Inc., 2004.

Additional Reading

Anderson, Dean, and Linda Ackerman Anderson. *Beyond Change Management: How to Achieve Breakthrough Results Through Conscious Change Leadership*. San Francisco, CA: Pfeiffer, 2010.

Anderson, Linda Ackerman, and Dean Anderson. *The Change Leader's Road map: How to Navigate Your Organization's Transformation*. San Francisco, CA: Pfeiffer, 2010.

Bolman, Lee G., and Terrence E. Deal. *Leading with Soul: An Uncommon Journey of Spirit*. San Francisco, CA: Jossey-Bass Inc., 1995.

Bradberry, Travis, and Jean Greaves. *The Emotional Intelligence Quick Book: Everything You Need to Know to Put Your EQ to Work*. New York, NY: Simon & Schuster, 2003.

Fitz-enz, Jac. *How to Measure HR Management*. New York, NY: McGraw Hill, 2001.

Fitz-enz, Jac. *The New HR Analytics: Predicting the Economic Value of Your Company's Human Capital Investments*. New York, NY: AMACOM, 2010.

Lewis, Sarah, Jonathan Passmore, and Stefan Cantore. *Appreciative Inquiry for Change Management*. Philadelphia, PA: 2011.

Ulrich, Dave, Huselid, Mark, and Becker, Brian. *The HR Scorecard: Linking People, Strategy, and Performance*. Boston, MA: Harvard Business School Press, 2001.

Index

Made in the USA
Middletown, DE
25 March 2018